Nyerere

Nyerere
The Early Years

THOMAS MOLONY
Lecturer in African Studies
at the University of Edinburgh

JAMES CURREY

James Currey
is an imprint of Boydell & Brewer Ltd
PO Box 9, Woodbridge, Suffolk IP12 3DF (GB)
www.jamescurrey.com

and of

Boydell & Brewer Inc.
668 Mt Hope Avenue, Rochester, NY 14620-2731 (US)
www.boydellandbrewer.com

© Thomas Molony 2014
First published 2014

1 2 3 4 5 18 17 16 15 14

All Rights Reserved. Except as permitted under current legislation
no part of this work may be photocopied, stored in a retrieval system,
published, performed in public, adapted, broadcast,
transmitted, recorded or reproduced in any form or by any means,
without the prior permission of the copyright owner

The right of Thomas Molony to be identified as
the author of this work has been asserted in accordance with
sections 77 and 78 of the Copyright, Designs and Patents Act 1988

British Library Cataloguing in Publication Data
A catalogue record for this book is available from the British Library

ISBN 978-1-84701-090-2 (James Currey cloth)

The publisher has no responsibility for the continued existence or accuracy
of URLs for external or third-party internet websites referred to in this book,
and does not guarantee that any content on such websites is, or will remain,
accurate or appropriate.

This publication is printed on acid-free paper.

Typeset in 11.5/12.5 Monotype Garamond
by Avocet Typeset, Somerton, Somerset

To my parents, in appreciation of the many sacrifices they made for our schooling

Contents

List of Photographs, Figures & Maps	ix
Acknowledgements	xi
List of Abbreviations	xiii
Glossary	xiv
A Note on Nomenclature	xvi

Introduction — 1

1
Butiama: The Abandoned Place — 11

2
Musoma & Tabora: Kambarage, Spirit of the Rain — 37

3
Makerere: Becoming Julius — 62

4
Return to Tabora: African Associations — 78

5
Scotland: Great Conceptions — 100

6
Edinburgh & Uhuru: Politics, Philosophy & Economics — 132

7
Edinburgh & Ujamaa: History & Anthropology — 163

Contents

8
London & Pugu: Teaching & Politics   180

9
The Early Years: Legacy & Reappraisal   199

Select Biographies, Bibliography & Sources   208
Notes   225
Index   279

List of Photographs, Figures & Maps

Photographs

A.	Chief Nyerere Burito with his first wife, Magori Masubugu and his bodyguard, Kitira Buhoro, Mwitongo, Butiama, c.1940–41	14
B.	Aerial view of Mwitongo	15
C.	Julius Nyerere's mother, Mugaya Nyang'ombe, Butiama, 1966	35
D.	Chief Edward Wanzagi Nyerere at the opening of a school and hospital in Mgeta, Ikizu, January 1953	45
E.	Julius Nyerere and other Tabora pupils, c.1942	58
F.	The Tabora Boys prize shield won by Nyerere as 'Hardworking, 1937–1942'	60
G.	Magori Watiha. May 2010	85
H.	Julius Nyerere, passport photo, c. 1946	95
I.	Maria Nyerere, Musoma, Tanzania, early 1950s	99
J.	John Keto with African students, George Square, University of Edinburgh, c.1953	140
K.	Father Richard Walsh	177
L.	Julius Nyerere and fellow students after their graduation, University of Edinburgh, 4 July 1952	182
M.	Family record in Julius Nyerere's personal Bible	190
N.	Julius Nyerere and guests after the Honorary Degree of Doctor of Laws ceremony, University of Edinburgh, 5 July 1962	195

List of Photographs, Figures & Maps

O. Julius Nyerere giving the Lothian European Lecture, 'Africa: The Third Liberation', at the University of Edinburgh, 9 October 1997   198

P. Jack Nyamwaga and Jackton Nyambereka Nyerere, Butiama, July 2011   221

Figures

1. Nyerere kinship chart   31
2. Magige kinship chart   92

Map

1. Tanganyika, c. 1948   10

Acknowledgements

This book was written in Edinburgh and Butiama. It would not have been possible without the support and good will of members of the Nyerere family. I thank in particular Mama Maria and Rose for their faith in my lengthy endeavours, and Madaraka for all the time that he has given to the research. My spritely assistant in Butiama has been Mwalimu Jack Nyamwaga, my mentor in all things Zanaki, and whose contribution is evident by his name appearing throughout the text.

H.E. Mwanaidi Sinare Maajar and then H.E. Peter Kallaghe were instrumental in seeing that requisite funds were provided by the Office of the Prime Minister. The support of both was crucial, as was the courteous assistance provided by Celestine Mushy and Frank Ngoiya. I am also grateful for finances from The Carnegie Trust, the University of Edinburgh's Hayter Fund, the School of Social and Political Science Strategic Research Support Fund, and from the University's Moray Endowment Award.

Space constraints prevent me from detailing the individual contributions of the following, whom I list in alphabetical order: Gallus Abedi, Edgar Atubonekisye, Alan Barnard, Paul Bjerk, Patricia Boyd, Joseph Butiku, Ismaila Ceesay, Tom Cunningham, Owen Dudley Edwards, Tom Fisher, Nicholas Flavin, Joost Fontein, Denis and Katio Galava, Jonathan Hargreaves, Julie Hartley, Emma Hunter, John Iliffe, Nick Jewitt, Clare Kamanzi, Steve Kerr, Isaria Kimambo, Kenneth King, Jerome Kiria, James Mugabu Kisige, Demere Kitunga, Shem Koren, Yusuf Lawi, Mosses Lukuba, John McCracken, Audax Mabulla, Rob Macdonald, Derek MacLeod, Giacomo Macola, Asha Maji, Narenda and Hemal Majithia, Adam Marwa, Iddi Selemani Masenga, Ross Methven, Theophilus Mlaki, Mwanahamisi Mmtengula, Anna Mulungu, José-María Muñoz, Victor Amani Mushi, Wence Mushi, Fausta Musokwa, Andrew Mussell, Pamphil Mwaimu, Hamadi Mwange, Juma Mwapachu, Nesse, Raphael Nombo, Marwa Nsabi, Paul Nugent, Zawadi Nyakiriga, Magige Nyerere, Nuru Nyerere-Inyangete, Geoffrey Owens, the late John Rajabu, John Masalu Rubale, Abdi Kigeso Rubugu,

Acknowledgements

Shaun Ruysenaar, Ethan Sanders, David Sawe, George Shepperson, Jan Bender Shetler, Paul Swanepoel, Baba T, Apollo Temu, Richard Tibandebage, Moh and Farida Versi, Carol Vickers, Martin Walsh, Clarice Mumbua Wambua, Sylvestar Emmanuel Wambura, Gaude Waziri, Iain Whyte, Arnott Wilson, and Wolfgang Zeller. In Dar es Salaam I am always happy to spend my time in the company of Anton and Veronica Msinjili, whose kindness to me knows no bounds. Fred and Hassan also deserve mention, not least for their thorough attempts to broaden my exposure to some of Bongo's lesser-known blistering chairs.

I thank Ian Duffield, who spent many long hours moderating the first draft of this book, and who went to great lengths to improve its content and my use of English. His attention to detail is first class, and I have benefited much from his attempts to help me understand the various African and European contexts of the issues that I deal with. The comments of Jaqueline Mitchell and an anonymous reviewer were also invaluable. Last word goes to James Brennan, whose painstaking reflections generously helped to avert another tiresome and factually questionable hagiography. Any mistakes are mine alone.

List of Abbreviations

ASMA	*Archives de la Société des Missionnaires d'Afrique* ('*Pères Blancs*', 'White Fathers'), Rome
CAF	Central African Federation
CCM	*Chama cha Mapinduzi*; Party of the Revolution
CDWS	Colonial Development and Welfare Scheme
CID	Criminal Investigation Department
DC	District Commissioner
EUL	Edinburgh University (Main) Library
FCB	Fabian Colonial Bureau
LSE	London School of Economics
MDB	*Musoma District Book*
NA	National Archives, London
TAA	Tanganyika African Association
TANU	Tanganyika African National Union
TAWA	Tanganyika African Welfare Association
TNA	Tanzania National Archives, Dar es Salaam
UTP	United Tanganyika Party
WASU	West African Students' Union

Glossary

Unless indicated otherwise, terms are Swahili and/or are used regionally by various tribes. Only terms used more than once are listed here.

abhakuru (sing. *omukuru*) (Zanaki)	important ancestors; old grandfathers who are still alive
abhanyikura (sing. *omunyikura*) (Zanaki)	(members of) the active generation class
abharwazi (sing. *omurwazi*) (Zanaki)	those who hold influence and who persuade, acting as 'whips'
akida	Swahili-speaking, and usually Muslim, African or Arab administrator(s) under German and early British direct rule
askari	(African) soldier
Baba wa Taifa	Father of the Nation; in Tanzania, Julius Nyerere
bao	complex mancala game played with seeds or balls
bhakisero (Zanaki)	those circumcised at the same time (on the same cattle skin)
ebhitara (sing. *ekitara*) (Zanaki)	cylindrical granaries
ekyaaro (pl. *ebhyaaro*) (Zanaki)	territory; country of a clan, tribe or nation
eriikura (pl. *amakura*) (Zanaki)	warrior age-grade
eriisaga (pl. *amasaga*) (Zanaki)	co-operative labour system
erisaambwa (pl. *amasaambwa*) (Zanaki)	spirit(s) believed to dwell in rocks, big trees, and along river beds
eryoobha (Zanaki)	unique, supreme god associated with the sun
ezinyaangi (sing. *enyaangi*) (Zanaki)	(some specific) rites of passage within the Zanaki social scale; lit., 'ritual'

Glossary

ikulu	state house, presidential lodge
ikuru (Zanaki)	big
mahari	bridewealth/brideprice
mganga (pl. *waganga*)	herbalist; witchdoctor; diviner, soothsayer rainmaker
mwami	rainmaker
mwanangwa (pl. *wanangwa*)	headman; sometimes also used for a head boy at school
mzee (pl. *wazee*)	respected old man
okung'atuka (Zanaki)	retire, relinquish, progress
omugabhu (pl. *abhagabhu*) (Zanaki)	diviner
orukobha (pl. *ezikobha*) (Zanaki)	belt made of skin; ceremony where territory is metaphorically bound to treat its wounds
orusoro (pl. *ezisoro*) (Zanaki)	mancala game, known as *bao* in Swahili
shamba (pl. *mashamba*)	cultivation plot, farm, smallholding; plantation
taifa	nation; race
uhuru	freedom; independence
ujamaa	brotherhood, familyhood; (African/Tanzanian) Socialism
wananchi	ordinary citizens

A Note on Nomenclature

As the text progresses through Nyerere's early life, I tend to use the names that he was given until they were formally changed. Thus I begin with the name 'Kambarage' until the point that he was baptised 'Julius'. I proceed to 'Mwalimu' (teacher, Swahili) when he became a teacher. I am aware that he embraced the 'Mwalimu' political moniker more formally later.[1] At times I adopt the term where others have used it even when they are referring to the days before he became a teacher. I also use '*Baba wa Taifa*' (the Father of the Nation), especially for the post-independence period. The spelling of the names of less well-known individuals tends to vary depending on the source. For some names it has been difficult to get the 'official' spelling – if there is one – and in these cases I have favoured the version adopted by the closest friends or relatives of the person concerned. Julius Nyerere's mother's name, for example, I have given not as 'Mgaya' Nyang'ombe, but 'Mugaya', which is the spelling that Nyerere himself wrote in the family history section of his personal Bible. If there are two versions of the same name, I eschew foreigners' spelling. In some cases – especially with Judith Listowel – they are confusing bastardisations. Informants sometimes give women's full names with the inclusion of '*wa*' ('of'), as in Magori wa Masubugu: Magori (born) of Masubugu. For women's names I have dropped the *wa*, since it is used inconsistently. However, I do not change the spelling of any names where I quote verbatim from written text. When in the main text I refer to terms that also feature in quotations that I use, I have added the English, Swahili or Zanaki translation. For ease of reading the main text, I tend not to indicate whether the word is Swahili or Zanaki – although this will be obvious to those reasonably familiar with either language. Zanaki is chiefly a spoken language. The spelling of the Zanaki words presented here often differs slightly from that given in a number of other texts. For Zanaki spelling I defer to the knowledge of Shem Koren, one of a tiny number of professional Zanaki-speaking translators. I quote verbatim in Swahili, but when using English I generally omit Bantu prefixes to proper names. A member of

A Note on Nomenclature

a tribe, the tribe itself, and its language are all described by the Bantu stem alone (e.g., Haya, Luguru, Zanaki). The locational prefix is used when describing the area in which a tribe lives (e.g., Buhaya, Uluguru, Uzanaki).[2] I use the term 'ethnic group' purely for variation.

Notes

1. See Brennan, J. 'Julius Rex: Nyerere through the eyes of his critics, 1953–2013', paper presented at the Centre of African Studies seminar series, University of Edinburgh, 27 February 2013, pp.11–12.
2. The colonial administration often used 'Buzanaki' to refer to the land of the Zanaki. Here 'Uzanaki' is used, which was Nyerere's preference. (See, for example, his Introduction to *Freedom and Socialism*, p.3.)

Introduction

Nyerere called on the people of Tanzania to have great confidence in themselves and to safe-guard the nation's hard-won freedom. Mwalimu warned that the people should not allow their freedom to be pawned as most of their leaders were purchasable. He warned further that in running the affairs of the nation the people should not look on their leaders as saints and prophets.

Report of a 1967 speech given by Julius Nyerere, from *The Nationalist* newspaper at the time[1]

This book is a study of the first thirty years of the life of Julius Kambarage Nyerere – or 'JUKANYE', as he signed off in a newspaper piece on African socialism about six months into his studies at Makerere College in Uganda. The time period covered is mainly from his birth in Mwitongo in 1922 until his graduation from the University of Edinburgh in 1952. It was after his return to Tanganyika from Edinburgh that Nyerere formally entered politics. He went on to lead the efforts of many others in delivering Tanganyika Territory to independence, and then served as President of Tanzania until his retirement in 1985. The book aims to deliver an original portrait of Nyerere's early life and to provide a fresh insight into his character. This helps to see his later political life in a new light.

To date, much of the biographical work on Nyerere tends to lack depth, frequently relies on familiar sources, and can sometimes be described as 'hagiographic'. The term hagiography is often now used pejoratively, to mean an account which only describes the good and positive aspects of a life, and which neglects criticism. This is an accurate description of some of the works claiming to cover Nyerere's entire life. But it would be a harsh label to attach to any study that details the young, first third of any person's life – during which, in Nyerere's case, he was still receiving a formal education. The much rarer contemporary use of the term hagiography is its *sensu stricto*: in the Christian sense, the attention to the lives of those canonised by, among others, the Roman

Catholic church.[2] In the literal hagiographic sense, the beatification process of 'Servant of God Julius Nyerere' is now underway. This is explained in a piece by Pascal Durand, who aims 'to start some kind of conversation among us and anyone interested, especially in view of the decision by the Catholic Church of Tanzania of starting the – usually long – process of finally declaring him a saint, technically known also as *canonization*' (original emphasis).[3] Durand's short piece clearly contributes to the case for the sainthood of the Father of the Nation but, motivation aside, it does provide something of a new (in this case, overtly Christian) perspective that differs from the usual panegyrical narrative. Quite repetitive accounts of Nyerere's life have been published, especially during the early post-Arusha Declaration period. The work from that time seems now to reflect something of a personality cult created by Tanganyika African National Union (TANU) bureaucrats. Nyerere was not particularly keen on these encomia. Furthermore, as Donald Denoon (then at Makerere College) and Adam Kuper (an ex-Makerere lecturer) wrote around that time, 'African history is too important to be left to politicians'.[4]

The motivations for this book are threefold. In the first place, still 'there is no adequate biography' on Nyerere's life, even thirty-five years after the comment was first made by John Iliffe in his seminal *Modern History of Tanganyika*.[5] The lack of interest in Nyerere is in contrast to the academic treatment of the lives of other celebrated African leaders such as Jomo Kenyatta, Kwame Nkrumah and Nelson Mandela.[6] There is a case for arguing that we are close to exhaustion with biographies of the late Nelson Mandela, and these nearly always cover his formative years to some degree.[7] Nor is there any shortage of biographies on Kwame Nkrumah, including one dedicated to his years abroad when he was studying in the United States and later in the United Kingdom, supposedly also studying.[8] The same can also be said for Jomo Kenyatta, for whom one biography in particular devotes significant space to his time in London and the early experiences in Africa and Europe that influenced his later political life.[9] There has been no such study of Nyerere.

This is not a biography providing a commentary to Nyerere's entire life. The detail is on Nyerere's first thirty years, although reference is necessarily made to his years as a statesman. Attention is given to *ujamaa* (Nyerere's version of 'African socialism') and major declarations where they relate to his formative experiences, but the focus is on the influences of Nyerere's earlier life. There is no room to provide further in-depth critique of his policies, and doing so would detract from what is being attempted here. This is a roughly chronological account of Nyerere's formative years, foregrounded by the historical context of the territory in which he was born.

This book builds, inevitably, on the work of others. I have not altered the words of informants, but I have of course been selective in my choice of what is presented from many conversations. Here it is worth noting a comment made by the late John Keto, who studied at Edinburgh with Nyerere and was particularly forthcoming about the limits of his memory in informing this account. On more than one occasion he said that he would not pretend to remember more than the little he could recall about his university days with Nyerere in case, as he put it, 'we begin to create a new history that never took place'.[10] Or as David James Smith has expressed in his biography of Nelson Mandela's formative years: 'Memory can be an unreliable, inconvenient and sometimes contradictory witness to history.'[11] This is especially the case for the public memory of '*Baba wa Taifa*' which, particularly in Tanzania, continues to play a role in stifling any criticism of Nyerere.[12]

Smith's study of Mandela's early years raises an important point on the craft of writing about any substantial period of a life, and not least a high-profile figure such as Nyerere. Mark Gevisser notes that in Smith's attempt to counter those who 'won't hear a word against' Mandela, the biographer sets himself the task of finding all the 'words against' South Africa's former premier. In so doing Smith 'sometimes loses sight of the primary reason for biography, which is to make sense of a life within its times, and to bring us closer to understanding its subject'.[13] In general I would agree with Gevisser that understanding a life within its times is a good reason for biography. Similarly, John Iliffe states in his recent biography of Olusegun Obasanjo that his chief task as biographer was to try to understand the General.[14] I have aimed at much the same here by adding a good deal of flesh to the skeletal biographies of Nyerere's early life that have been available until now. In so doing, I have avoided the small town gossip that pervades Smith's biography of Mandela. I have relied instead on verifiable sources who – with one exception – are happy to be named. Smith's method and product does indeed offer different opinions that may bring us closer to a description (if not an understanding) of Mandela during his early life. For Nyerere, I espouse a more holistic approach to the study of his early years that seeks to illustrate a richer and more complex form of biographical narrative, fulfilling both the objectives of the biographer and the historian.[15] Esperanza Brizuela-Garcia argues that this calls for a combination of the methods applied to this study – life description, literary account and historical analysis – to achieve the historical reconstruction of the life.[16] This should not ignore the importance of historical context, however, which Giacomo Macola observes to be one of the key ingredients of scholarly biography – a literary genre that holds out the promise of 'illuminating the interplay between individual agency, on the one hand, and more profound structural historical dynamics, on the other'.[17] It is scholarly biography's detailed focus on individuals that allows us to fill in some of the potholes – and sometimes to bridge the gaps – in the ongoing building of Tanzania's national history, and to better inform those of the present generation who, in Vedastus Kyaruzi's view, 'prefer to jump from the "Vita ya Majimaji" [1905–07 rebellion in German Tanganyika] to TANU as if nothing happened in between.'[18]

The *Modern Tanzanians* volume of biographies covers this period between Kinjikitile Ngwale and Julius Nyerere, avoiding the narrow focus on the 'winners' of the various inter-African nationalist contests.[19] Yet, as the editor acknowledged at the time, there are no Muslim religious leaders among the thirteen figures covered in the collection, no Roman Catholics, and not a single woman.[20] And as the late Susan Geiger observed in her history of the women who used TANU to shape, inform and spread a nationalist consciousness, biographies written in aid of the dominant nationalist narrative depict nationalism in Tanganyika as primarily the work of a 'few good men'.[21] Some still contend that the dominant nationalist narrative also seems to be one of a 'few good *Christian* men' – with an overbearing focus on Nyerere. I point here to a number of contributions covering the lives of Muslims in the nationalist movement.[22]

In keeping with my desire to accurately represent the views of individuals who have informed this research, I have not altered the words they report Nyerere to have spoken. Nevertheless, I have decided only to quote from Judith Listowel's *The Making of Tanganyika* where I can be reasonably sure of its accuracy. Suffice to say I understand that her quite readable account was apparently not held in great esteem by the President. This was conveyed in a letter to me from the late Joan Wicken – Nyerere's personal assistant from the time he became leader of Tanganyika until his retirement – who emphatically remarked that 'you should NOT depend upon that book at all' (original emphasis).[23] Reading between the lines, this terse ad hominem remark points to a disagreement that Nyerere and/or his trusted confidante Wicken seem to have had with Listowel over interview transcripts and drafts of her *Making of Tanganyika*.[24] Close family, if not Nyerere himself, provided Listowel with information on Butiama and Zanaki culture, but a number of glaring factual inaccuracies (the misspelling of Nyerere's pre-baptismal name, the burial place of his father, and so on) still made it into print – either because Nyerere did not have the time to review all the drafts, Wicken was not au fait with local issues, or Listowel did not listen closely enough.[25] The minor details are not so important, but they do provide an early example of the bigger issue of the control over the production of the story of the birth of the Tanzanian nation. Listowel, one of the 'midwives of Tanzania's decolonization',[26] was, in a sense, *making* Tanganyika with her 1965 account, bringing into existence a chronicle of the new nation over which its President – and his gatekeeper – had little control. Both Nyerere and Wicken would have been aware of the potential reach of a book that at the time had few serious rivals as an authoritative history of the nation. Yet while Nyerere and Wicken could stall biographies on the President himself, neither could halt the publication overseas of a book that relied on scores of relatively high-profile informants, including former colonial officials whose personal (and at times myopic) accounts of the struggle for independence Listowel was happy to include.

Listowel is clearly sympathetic to TANU, and in particular its leader (whose photograph opens her book). In it she is at pains to point out the names of the black racialists in Tanganyika, and Nyerere's opposition to them. Her social circle was one of high-ranking colonial officials,[27] and Nyerere's moderate position on race suited her own view of a future Tanzania that gave more room for Europeans than many other African politicians were prepared to entertain. Nyerere needed to be painted in a favourable light, and Listowel's African nationalist informants obliged. But the accounts of her European friends also had to feature in the nation's history. Any voices of opposition towards Nyerere the non-racialist were left on the cutting room floor.

John Iliffe lists a section of Listowel's *Making of Tanganyika* as one of two sources on the young nationalist leader. He correctly points to Listowel's heavy reliance on the dominant position of Tanganyikan history that was traditional among liberal Europeans of the time. He also notes her disregard for the economic, social and political influences on nationalist political developments.[28] Iliffe's other source is William Edgett Smith's *Nyerere of Tanzania*.[29] Wicken mentions both books, remarking that while Nyerere had granted Listowel interviews, the journalist frequently reported his accounts inaccurately. *Nyerere of Tanzania*, by contrast, was 'the opposite – almost without inaccuracy insofar as it goes. That is my opinion – and was Mwalimu's.'[30] Edgett Smith has created a hard act to follow, but I do feel that I have introduced a large number of new sources hitherto overlooked in all accounts of Nyerere's early life. In doing so I have sought to create a balance between the pure but dry presentation of the contemporary evidence and, where applicable, a confident conjecture that introduces a more human image of the young Nyerere. We do not know for sure that he arrived in Edinburgh full of hope and more than a little apprehension, for example, as I have suggested in the opening of Chapter 5. But these instances of conjecture help to create a more engaging and flowing narrative that is informed by my impression of the development of Nyerere's character after many years studying his early life.

The second motivation for this study concerns the oral primary sources that it draws upon. To put it crudely, those venerable men and women who knew Nyerere in his early life are either in their advanced years or, in most cases, have passed away. Those who are still with us are our only interactive sources of information on Nyerere's early years. This has heightened the urgency to capture their accounts before they are lost forever. A number of individuals who were interviewed for this study have since departed. Among them are the likes of John Nyambeho, a childhood friend of Nyerere's alongside whom who he was circumcised; another is John Keto. Neither feature prominently in accounts of Nyerere's life, but they both deserve such mention. The same can be said of other less celebrated figures who are not captured in any accounts of Nyerere's life. For example, few people outside of moral philosophy circles will have heard of the Scotsman William Macmurray – although he came to the attention of the media a few years ago for apparently being a great influence on former British Prime Minister Tony Blair.[31] Even fewer people will have heard of the Australian social anthropologist Ralph Piddington. While not hitherto recognised, both Macmurray and Piddington had an enormous impact on Nyerere's formative years. Both, by extension, made a significant contribution to the history of Tanzania.

The third stimulus relates to my first motivation concerning the need for a biography. The opportunity is presented for a study of Nyerere's early life, and there is a case for an account of this to be given by an Edinburgh academic. One ought to be sceptical of those who hold positions of high status and seem to believe that the titles bestowed upon them mean that they are the authority on all things Nyerere. It is down to everyone interested in the history of a nation to enrich it, whether farmer, bureaucrat or Professor. The history of no subject is the preserve of an individual on account of his title, nor for that matter, his longevity or nationality. As Nyerere himself put it at a conference on history at the University of Dar es Salaam:

> The fact that people from all over the world, and many different institutions, are involved in the work of re-discovering our history, means that there is a wide variety of experience and techniques which can be used in the investigations. We do not become defined by the traditional study methods of any one University or country.[32]

The historian George Shepperson wrote to Nyerere in 1964, asking the President if he might undertake some research to provide an account of his career to date. Shepperson was a lecturer at Edinburgh when Nyerere studied there, and by the early 1960s had realised that his friend the former student was destined for a celebrated life in politics. Wicken handled the correspondence, consulted Nyerere, and she wrote to Rex Collings at the Oxford University Press, informing him that 'The President says that if he was willing to have a biography written there is no one he would rather have do it than Professor Shepperson … I think that the President will continue to refuse everyone but will finally agree to your request.'[33] Shepperson never undertook the considerable task of the biography. A year later Wicken was still insisting that, while Shepperson could collect information, 'the clear and important condition' was 'that publication will not take place for a *long* time and not without prior consultation with the President!' (original emphasis).[34] Despite the more forthcoming exchanges between Shepperson and State House up until this final reply, Wicken's firm declaration is revealing. It indicates Nyerere's apparent reluctance to entertain a biography at the time. More significantly, it is revealing of Wicken's role as a significant controller of Nyerere's life story and, by association, a controller over accounts of the history of the nation.

Yet while Nyerere himself was famously shy about personality cult developments, and would not have liked much of the TANU and government hagiographies, from the 1970s he did grant considerable access to biographers of whom he approved. Edgett Smith is one, and another is John Hatch, a former Member of Parliament and Labour Party Commonwealth Officer who was hardly detached from Nyerere having debated alongside him in Edinburgh in opposition to the Central African Federation. He was also a staunch TANU supporter.[35] These biographers clearly suited Nyerere, who was astute enough to know what to emphasise in interviews, for example, by explaining to his friend Hatch that as a young man he would dutifully listen to the elders[36] – thereby helping Nyerere to affirm the 'tradition' that applied to the contemporary leadership he was trying to sustain at the time of the interview. Journalists such as Peter Enahoro, Ad'Obe Obe and Ikaweba Bunting were also granted long interviews much later. Given the restraints put on Shepperson – influenced, undoubtedly, by a feeling that Listowel's account was inaccurate – then it would be fair to assume that to some extent those writers who were later given access to the President were closely vetted, and their drafts subject to approval.[37] This is one of the ambiguities of Nyerere, in that while he was a modest man, he also had sufficient ego to lead. It also points to his awareness of the need to sustain his own image as the humble and approachable leader of the people – the same leader who saw to it that his writings and speeches were published in three weighty (and carefully abridged) volumes for all to read.[38] With Nyerere's passing, and that of his gatekeeper(s), so the issue of prior consultation has also passed. Now is the ideal time for serious study of his life, beginning with his earliest years. As Alan Feinstein reminds us in his biography of the Nigerian politician Aminu Kano: 'In dealing with a birth and then a life, the further back in history one goes, the more fully the mantle of the legend and myth casts its protective shadow over the life. All sorts of magical qualities can be attributed to a noted man.'[39]

An advantage that I hold in having never met Nyerere is that I have not been seduced by his charm, nor exposed to any other force of his personality. As a non-Tanzanian, my outsider status also allows me to be more objective. Whilst I attempt in this book to present a fresh and detailed account of his early life, completely eradicating bias in such a venture is almost impossible. Nevertheless, I can declare with confidence that no member of the Nyerere family – nor, for that matter, any member of the Government of Tanzania – told me what should be included or omitted from the book. I did not press the Nyerere family on the awkward issue of an 'authorised' biography.[40] Yet their willingness to host me for long periods in their family home, and to engage in frequent discussion with me in full knowledge of my research aims, would suggest that those family members who I know personally are supportive of this project at some level. Indeed, the final manuscript upon completion of my longest stay in Butiama was read, and commented on, by Rose and Madaraka Nyerere, and they then discussed it together with me and Mama Maria. This is not in any sense an authorised biography, and the decisions over the use of material are mine throughout.

I can, however, sympathise with those who argue for 'unsanitised' biographical accounts that include their subject's imperfections. Omitting these flaws, so the argument goes, is to dilute a person's later achievements.[41] Thus the writer is faced with decisions over inclusion and exclusion of material. The politics extend to the realm in which individuals are given voice in informing, and in writing, biographical accounts.[42] In focusing on Nyerere's pre-political years, this study has been fortunate in not having to rely solely on the accounts of overtly political actors. But the reach of 'Nyerere nostalgia', to use Susan Geiger's phrase, still pervades in many of the accounts that this study has drawn on.[43] Many of the interviewees who inform this study still seem unconsciously to engage in self-censorship, and this extends to Nyerere's pre-presidential life.[44] His imperfections are probably not as evident here as they would have been if the research was undertaken by an Edinburgh academic in the 1950s.

The chapters of this book represent stages of Nyerere's early life. Each chapter begins with a summary. The opening chapter begins in Butiama, Nyerere's ancestral home. It outlines the social and political structures of the Zanaki, and considers the extent to which these influenced Nyerere's later life. Chapter 2 looks at Kambarage Nyerere's first years in an apparently egalitarian rural society, his primary and secondary education at Mwisenge Native Administration School and Tabora Boys, and his transition from an environment of traditionally-held beliefs to Catholicism. The third chapter looks at Nyerere's adoption of the name 'Julius', the context and influences of Makerere College, and his activities concerned with the socio-political interests of his countrymen in Uganda and Tanganyika. Chapter 4 follows Nyerere back to Tabora, details the background to his marital relationships, and considers his political activities while teaching at the Catholic St Mary's school. Chapter 5 proceeds with Nyerere to Edinburgh, outlining what and why he studied at the University, and his relationships in the city. It is set within the context of national and international events, with particular reference to race, democracy and liberation. This is followed by a chapter that reveals Nyerere's political contact with fellow Tanganyikans in the United Kingdom, and his interest in the proposed Central African Federation. It examines the development of Nyerere's understanding of religion, traditional society, freedom and democracy in the context of his studies in political economy and moral philosophy. Chapter 7 remains with Nyerere in Edinburgh, analyses his university instruction on collectivity and political systems in Africa, and relates this to his later writings on *ujamaa*. It also considers how the Christian environment in the city impacted on his religious views and his thoughts concerning a vocation in the Church. Chapter 8 covers Nyerere's move to London and the political environment among African nationalists in the metropole. It then follows him back to Uzanaki, and looks at the development of his relationship with political activists who held territorial-level ambitions. The chapter ends with Nyerere's resignation from St Francis College, Pugu and his entry into full-time politics. The concluding chapter summarises the inaccuracies and silences revealed by the new sources unearthed in this study, and assesses them as a symptom of the unexplored history of the father of the Tanzanian nation. The discussion is foregrounded by an acknowledgement that many portrayals of the man have been made in retrospect, shaped by the knowledge of what he became. It argues for the need to explore beyond the virtues and admirable principles of his early life that so frequently prejudice accounts of his later political career. The chapter suggests that some depictions of the more positive aspects of Nyerere's character in his formative years are indeed accurate, but it balances this with a more candid character reference that highlights the critical traits of his personality as it developed prior to his formal entry into politics. The chapter also brings together the influences that he was exposed to from the early 1920s until the early 1950s, allowing for the creation of a more complicated and human portrait of Nyerere during his early years.

Thomas Molony
Butiama

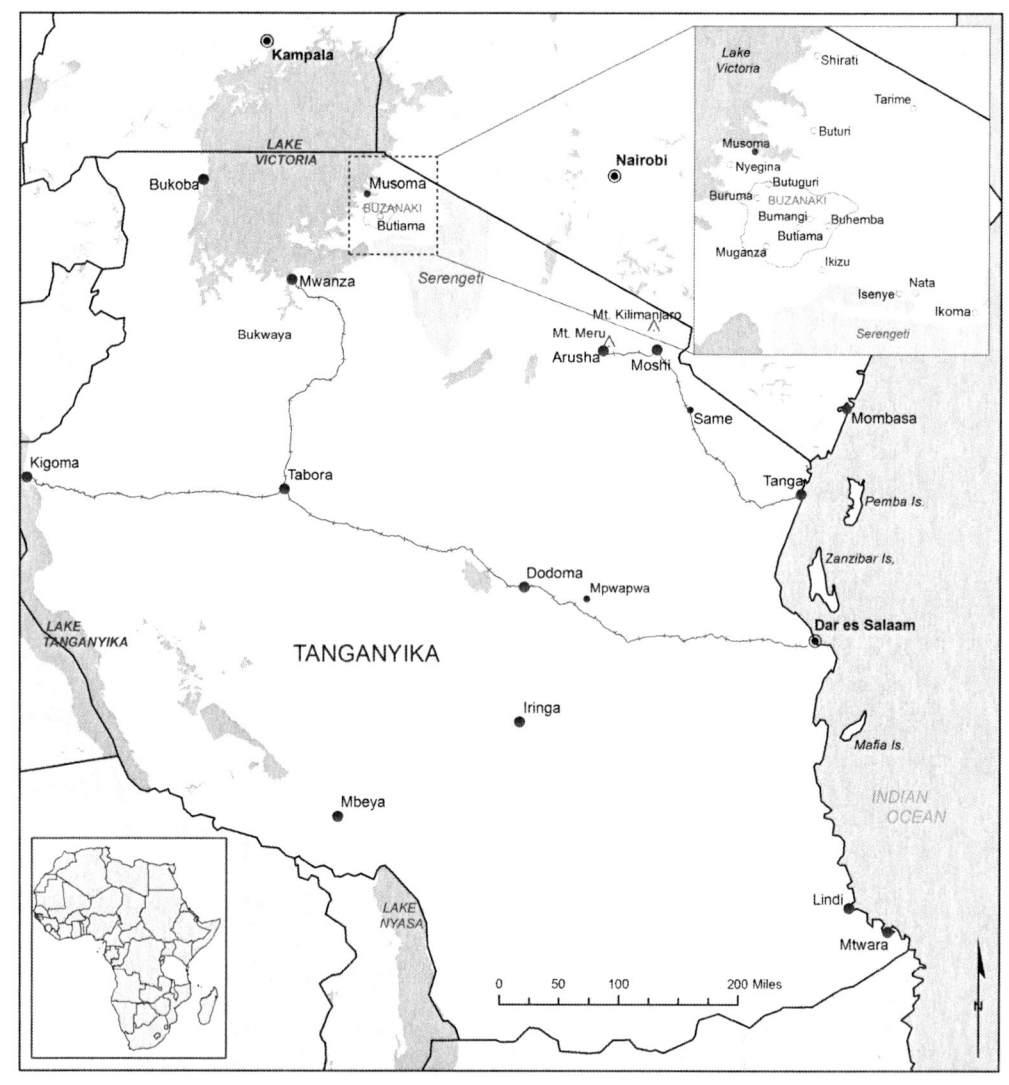

Map 1. Tanganyika, with inset of Uzanaki and surrounding area, c. 1948

1
Butiama

The Abandoned Place

> *The past and the present are one. ... Different as are the lives of modern Africans from those of our grandparents, still we and our ancestors are linked together indissolubly.*
>
> Julius Nyerere, opening speech at the International Congress on African History, University of Dar es Salaam, 26 September 1965[1]

Julius Kambarage Nyerere was to travel far from home during his early life. This was unusual for most young men born in Tanganyika Territory. But if at one level Nyerere was an unusual young man – thanks largely to the privileges that came with his father's chiefly status – then at another level his early life was fairly ordinary. Butiama, the village of Nyerere's birth, was little different from any other rural settlement in north-western Tanganyika. The Zanaki tribe into which he was born was so small and unremarkable that most inhabitants of Tanganyika Territory did not even know of its existence. Yet it was Butiama village and the wider lands of Uzanaki where some of the young Kambarage's beliefs were instilled; and it was to Butiama – and often further afield – where President Nyerere's mind constantly returned when he thought of the idyllic 'traditional' Africa towards which he encouraged all modern Tanzanians to aspire.

This opening chapter engages with the physical and mental geography of the place that first created Nyerere. It is essential background in understanding his formative years, and sets the stage for the subsequent chapters that cover his life before he formally entered politics. It begins by locating the Nyerere ancestral home geographically, outlines the social relations of the Zanaki, and situates these within the traditional spiritual environment of supranatural beings and ancestor worship. It then considers understandings of 'traditional' governance structures in Uzanaki, and the impact of colonialism on local political leadership. The necessary interrogation of some academic sources (principally in the

'Lives of the Living' section) is then followed by a more narrative charting of the rise of the favoured chiefs in Butiama: Nyerere Burito (Julius Nyerere's father), who was succeeded by the formally-educated Edward Wanzagi Nyerere (Julius's half-brother). The chapter draws on new information provided in a correspondence from Joan Wicken, as well as on perspectives offered in interviews with some of Julius Nyerere's childhood friends, and with Maria Nyerere.

Mwitongo

Julius Kambarage Nyerere was of the Abhakibhweege clan,[2] one of five clans in the village of Butiama near the east coast of Lake Victoria. The clan is within the Zanaki tribe, a small ethnic group that currently numbers less than 50,000 people.[3] Today the Nyerere family is partially dispersed, with some members in Tanzania, others overseas. The nucleus remains in Butiama, where some 15,000 people reside. Butiama's trading centre is known as Stendi, where the bus stand is located at the end of the bitumen-surfaced road that leads to the main Mwanza to Musoma highway. The eleven kilometre stretch of road from the highway to Butiama was built five years after Nyerere died because, as with some other projects that planners proposed the President should approve for his home region, he overruled their decisions as he did not want his village to receive special favours.[4] At Stendi, a petrol station and collection of shops selling household goods can be found. Nearby is a government primary school, one of three in the village from which some students progress on to the local secondary school. Near Stendi is a large mosque built by funds gifted by the late Muammar Gaddafi after the local sheikh in Butiama approached President Nyerere for assistance, who then mentioned this to the former leader on a visit to Libya.[5] Seven Christian denominations have places of worship in the village including, *inter alia*, the Roman Catholics, the Lutherans and the Mennonites.[6] The administrative centre is at Ukumbi, the hall, which is the location of the offices of the government and the ruling Chama cha Mapinduzi (CCM, which formally replaced the Tanganyika African National Union – TANU – in 1977). The 14th October is a national holiday marking the death of Julius Nyerere across Tanzania.

The Nyerere ancestral home is located in an area of Butiama known as Mwitongo, a Zanaki word which means 'the abandoned place'. This name was given relatively recently, but there is evidence to suggest that the area was frequented as early as the Late Stone Age period. Evidence comes in the form of art located on the face of a rock overhang-cum-shelter in the centre of the Mwitongo settlement. The art is thought to date back from between 5,000 to 20,000 years before present. Executed in red, the designs appear to include three circles (one with externally radiating lines), a stylised human figure, and at least two antelope. These are thought to fall within the Red Geometric Tradition that forms the predominant rock art in Mara Region.[7] More recently, Mwitongo was the home of Julius Nyerere's father, Chief Nyerere Burito. Upon the chief's death in 1942, and following Zanaki custom, Nyerere Burito's wives were inherited by his brothers and nephews. The mothers of Chief Wanzagi and Julius Nyerere were not inherited, and with the departure of Burito's wives the place was left to ruin.[8]

Western Serengeti peoples followed the distinctive house style of their Great Lakes Bantu-speaking predecessors, favouring round buildings with thatched roofs, surrounded by a tall fence with a main gate.[9] Traditionally the number of houses depended on the number of wives the owner married, and on the number of his married but not yet independent sons.[10] Although people living together in a homestead were usually biologically related, households also incorporated strangers and dependents, all of whom contributed to the domestic economy.[11]

The homestead of Nyerere Burito in Mwitongo fitted this description before it was abandoned upon his death. His dilapidated house was demolished some years ago. Around 1974 Joseph Kizurira, a son of the chief, oversaw the construction of a round stone building, now used as a hall, marking the location of the chief's residence, the front door facing south as it did before. In those days the compound was surrounded by a thorn and cactus fence, and this perimeter delineated the four acres that is now known as Mwitongo.

The chief's original house, a circular one-storey building constructed using wattle and daub, had a bedroom at the rear and a sitting room at the front to receive guests. In front of the house was a cattle corral holding some fifty or so cows. Surrounding the corral were the houses of the chief's wives. The Zanaki custom was for the odd numbered wives (the first, third, fifth, and so on) to reside consecutively to the left as he exits his own house, and the even numbered wives (his second, fourth, and so on) to the right.[12] Thus the chief's first wife, Magori Masubugu, lived to the left as he looked towards his cattle, and his second wife, Muse Tanangibo, to the right. The compound could not accommodate dwellings for each of the chief's many wives, so those who he married later shared with earlier wives. The total number of wives' houses was eleven: seven odd numbered wives, six even. Facing the corral, Chief Nyerere Burito could see the house of his fifth wife to the front and slightly to the left. This was the house of Mugaya Nyang'ombe, (Julius) Kambarage Nyerere's mother. Its location – Julius Nyerere's birthplace – is today marked by a bust of her son, facing his mausoleum and beyond that to the entrance to the Mwitongo compound. When the chief was alive, the house of Magori Masubugu,

Nyerere

Photo A. Chief Nyerere Burito with his first wife, Magori Masubugu, and his bodyguard, Kitira Buhoro; Mwitongo, Butiama, c.1940–41.
(*Reproduced by kind permission of Godfrey Madaraka Nyerere*)

the senior wife, was easily identified by visitors as it then faced the gate to the compound, across the corral. Visitors were to report first to the senior wife – whose status was indicated by the belt (*kisaho*) that she wore. Magori Masubugu had control over who was allowed to stay and where they could visit. Women and small children were permitted to enter the houses of the other wives, but the movements of men who visited were closely scrutinised. Immediate male relatives could usually freely enter the women's houses, but their sons and nephews slept in separate detachments within the compound. The chief's two assistants (sing., *tarishi*; pl., *matarishi*, literally 'messengers') acted as bodyguards and general factotums. Today the graves of some ten of Julius Nyerere's relatives are situated close to the houses of the fourth wife, Magori Wanzagi. There lie Julius Nyerere's sisters Adelaide Nyangeta (second daughter to Nyerere Burito and Mugaya Nyang'ombe) and Nyabikwabi Nyakigi (the couple's fifth child), along with Magembe, a brother of Chief Nyerere Burito. Julius Nyerere ensured that his father and mother's resting places were renovated and they are still maintained. The graves of the chief and his fifth wife are now among the most prominent features of the Mwitongo residence.

The first building that is now most visible upon entering the compound of Mwitongo is a large modern house that was gifted to President Nyerere upon his retirement. The army contributed towards its construction with

Butiama: The Abandoned Place

Photo B. Aerial view of Mwitongo. Nyerere's house is to the right. The Muhunda forest (not shown) lies further to the right.
(*Photograph by author, with thanks to Coastal Aviation*)

money drawn from all the soldiers' and officers' salaries. The government later worked on the building until its completion in 1999. Despite being a presidential residence, it bears few signs of the ostentation of many African palaces. The contents are largely those that have an everyday practical purpose. The resident matriarch is Mama Maria Nyerere, who receives local visitors and the occasional government delegation. In the early morning she attends Vespers, followed by Mass, and then spends much of the day studying or engaging in softly-spoken conversations with padres and sisters from the local church. Nyerere himself lived in the house, but only for two weeks shortly before his death.

Less visible to the eye of the new visitor entering from the main gate is Julius Nyerere and Mama Maria's earlier house. It is still regarded as Nyerere's home. Built in 1972 in immediate proximity to Chief Nyerere Burito's former residence, Nyerere insisted that the building was constructed from rocks and other material found in the area. Surrounding the south side of the house are two groups of four cylindrical granaries (*ebhitara*) which in Nyerere's time were still used for storing millet. One group of *ebhitara* is next to a covered seating area where Nyerere would receive guests and where he had a table for playing what is known locally as *orusoro* (*bao* in Swahili), a complex mancala game played with seeds or balls, in which one needs to plan many moves ahead and remember the sequence in order to win. Located at the northern

15

edge of the compound, the three-storey house is something of an eagle's nest, perched on the highest point of one of Mwitongo's large boulder outcrops and watched over by scores of black kites and the occasional grey kestrel. On the top floor, Nyerere's bedroom and his personal office overlook a valley sprinkled with small farms and houses. The Gabizuryo Hills are to the east, the Mtuzu Hills lie to the north, and Lake Victoria shines bright on the north-western horizon.

Lives of the Spirits

While Kambarage Nyerere 'greatly respected his Father's beliefs',[13] it is very likely that by the time he turned to Catholicism he did not subscribe to the attitudes surrounding supranatural beings and ancestor worship. It could be argued however, that Nyerere's exposure to, and tolerance of, those who showed their respect to the ancestors may in turn have heightened his respect towards traditions within his immediate community. As it was put in a textbook that Nyerere read when he was studying in Edinburgh:

> anyone familiar with primitive culture knows that an institution such as ancestor worship, itself inconsistent with Christian teaching, produces a respect for the authority of chiefs and parents, an observance of the rules of property, sexual codes and the like, and the sense of tribal community and continuity which is threatened by the disintegrating effect of European civilization.[14]

At one side of Mwitongo lies a dense forest known as 'Muhunda', after an ancestor who some still believe inhabits the forest. To this day it is forbidden for women to enter the woodland during menstruation, for couples to engage in sexual intercourse there, or for anybody to collect firewood unless it has fallen from a tree. Apparently in acknowledgement of the local respect for Muhunda, Nyerere had the forest on the edge of Mwitongo fenced, and insisted that it remain untouched. This position also served to continue his quest for the preservation of the natural environment surrounding Mwitongo, which can also be seen in his planting of four hectares in the area around his house. Some argue that environmental preservation was the real motivation for Nyerere's support for the safeguarding of Muhunda's dwelling in the first place.[15]

In Zanaki, Nyerere's mother-tongue spoken by the tribe into which he was born, such spirits that reside in a particular area are known as *amasaambwa* (sing. *erisaambwa*). *Amasaambwa* are one of three categories of supranatural beings that play an important part in the religious life of polytheist Zanaki. One is *eryoobha*, a unique, supreme god associated with the sun who was formerly worshiped – or at least 'paid respect to', as Wicken tells was the case for Chief Nyerere Burito: '[Mwalimu] told me that his

Father used to go every morning to the top of a particular large rock near his compound, and there formally welcome the Sun as it rose. Mwalimu denied that his Father was "worshiping" the Sun; he was "paying respect to it".[16] Preferring to put their faith in the reliable and visible over the inconsistent and intangible, a tiny minority of illiterate elders in Butiama are said to still pray to the sun for their daily protection.[17]

The second category of supranatural being is *abhakuru*, the name given to old living men who are grandfathers, and the important ancestors.[18] Today many living elders in Butiama, including some Christians and Muslims, are said to have faith in the power of *abhakuru*. Some adherents wake early in the morning to secretly leave small gifts such as milk, snuff or millet at the resting place of the *abhakuru*. Others still believe that an ancestor can make his will known through the diviner (*omugabhu*; pl. *abhagabhu*) if he wants a child to be given his name, and that the ancestors live on through those who bear their names.

Amasaambwa, the third category of supranatural beings, are the spirits that are believed to dwell in rocks, big trees, and along river beds. Each clan had their own spirits who some believe still live in their area. Many people have been given names of *amasaambwa*, such as Wambura, Kahazi, and Kambarage.[19] There were thought to be at least seven *amasaambwa* in Butiama. Those in the area close to Mwitongo include 'Maji Moto'(literally, 'hot water') – which to the Western mind would be considered a geyser – and another similar hot spring known as 'Kibiriri' that appeared later than Maji Moto and then disappeared. While considered by some elders to be an *erisaambwa*, in its day Kibiriri appeared to be less respected by children, who used it to cook goats.

The extinction of Kibiriri was believed to be caused by Muhunda, who it is said chased the spirit away because of its rival's proximity to his residence in the forest next to Mwitongo. Muhunda normally takes the form of a great male baboon, but some believe that he can also appear as a large white goat or an enormous snake. While the baboon seldom appears, to a number of Butiama residents he is still very much present. Muhunda is not forgotten. Muhunda is considered potentially dangerous and malevolent, but is also perceived to be beneficent, bringing to the people of Butiama messages that can either be good news or bad news. As Jan Bender Shetler explains, people in this area of western Serengeti have combined the idea of spirits of particular *abhakuru* with the *amasaambwa* spirits (of particular places) to the point where they are now indistinguishable as *amasaambwa*. For this reason, it is argued, believers perceive *amasaambwa* as beneficent – because they are known ancestors, not forgotten and lost spirits.[20] Muhunda of Mwitongo is not worshipped however, nor is he considered to be one ancestor in particular. He is neither thought to be Chief Nyerere Burito, the former resident of Mwitongo, nor is he Nyerere Burito's son, Chief Edward

Wanzagi Nyerere. Rather, he is regarded to be a spirit of the former chiefdom as a whole.

On the now rare sightings of Muhunda – usually in baboon form – he is said to sit at his 'seat', a large rock towering over his forest, from where it is reported that he faces eastwards (towards Mwitongo) and barks with a commanding voice. Word spreads across the village of his appearance, speculation begins as to whether his message is good or bad, and some residents look for any accompanying signs that might give a clue. If the matter is thought to concern an area rather than an individual family, those few men of particular clans of the active generation class (*abhanyikura*) are said to still consult an *omugabhu* to interpret the meaning.

Traditionally, the *omugabhu* to be consulted must be based far from the chiefdom so that he is less likely to know of particular local conditions such as a flood or a famine. In the past neighbouring *abhagabhu* were avoided to prevent prior knowledge influencing any advice given, which may in turn have been influenced by personal relations or interests. Diviners as far away as Tarime were therefore sought for cases arising in Butiama. When the advice was given to the *abhanyikura* they then reported to their leaders and the retired men, who then ordered that the advice of the diviner is carried out.[21] Jack Nyamwaga was told by his elders that, before colonial times, the recommendation of the *omugabhu* was sometimes to have a baby sacrificed and buried in another chiefdom.

More recently, other signs have been interpreted locally without consulting a diviner. During the six-month war in 1978–79 between Tanzania and Uganda (known in Tanzania as the *Vita vya Kagera*, after the area that Idi Amin's forces invaded), a Tanzanian fighter airplane heading to Mwanza overshot the runway, ran out of fuel and crashed during a blackout. Of all places in the vast area of north-western Tanzania to crash, the site was on the boundary of Muhunda's small forest. The pilot was thrown into the woodland and found dead. Immediately afterwards at the crash site locals spotted a leopard – an animal that was thought for many years to have been extinct from the area – and it is said to have fiercely guarded the pilot's body. These unusual occurrences, happening in quick succession, were seen as a sign that the war Nyerere declared on Idi Amin would soon be won.[22] The war was won.

The Swiss cultural anthropologist Otto Bischofberger records that in the 1960s the advice of the diviner was still sought whenever something unusual happened, such as when big rocks fell down from a hill.[23] Rational explanations aside, such an event in Butiama would still be considered out of the ordinary today, as would the presence of a large solitary baboon in an area far from where these creatures normally reside. Jack Nyamwaga offered an unprompted recollection of a sighting of Muhunda sometime in 1999 when the baboon appeared in Mwitongo and called out loudly for a number of days. Locals believed that this was a sign of an impending catastrophe. Muhunda then disappeared and, shortly afterwards, a large section of the uppermost boulder that the baboon had sat on then fell away from the rock face. Julius Nyerere, who was then aged 77 years, was informed of the incident next to his house and responded: 'There is an end to every creature.' Nyerere's reply was interpreted locally as an acknowledgement that he knew his own end was near. He passed away that same year.[24]

Lives of the Living

When Kambarage grew up in the village he was surrounded by those who held traditional religious beliefs. Individuals and particular groups – both the living and the dead – held positions of spiritual influence. Political authority was similarly stratified, and Kambarage was socialised to think in terms of age-grades within the Zanaki governance framework.[25] This section considers the social and political structures of Nyerere's homeland. It offers a critique of the sources on which the existing knowledge of Zanaki structures is based. This serves to highlight the weaknesses of the dominant view that *ujamaa* – Nyerere's own version of 'African socialism',[26] and one of the defining aspects of his leadership of an independent Tanzania – was influenced almost exclusively by his Zanaki upbringing in Butiama and the surrounding area. This issue is raised here while we are dealing with the physical and mental space of Uzanaki. In later chapters we discuss the secondary academic sources that Nyerere studied in Edinburgh, which offer more compelling evidence to suggest that his African socialism was influenced much more by his studies abroad – and, while there, his memories and understandings of social and political life back home.

The most detailed analysis of the age-grade system in Uzanaki has come from Bischofberger's fieldwork over nine months in 1965 and 1968, which was published in 1972 as *The Generation Classes of the Zanaki*. It is tempting to use the study as a pointer to the influence that generation classes may have had on young men of Nyerere's generation. Its main weakness, however, is that Bischofberger closely follows the post-Malinowskian Africanist anthropologist genre that favours closed description of '"the way it probably was" before the colonial period, as if native life could be conceived as a self-contained system uncontaminated by outside contacts'.[27] While Bischofberger's study gives the impression that the age-grade system was still in existence during his 1965 and 1968 fieldwork, his timeless and abstract description gives no indication of the extent to which the age-grade system was adhered to in the 1960s, nor any earlier. The title of his book also suggests that his fieldwork covers Uzanaki as a country, yet he goes on to blend his depiction of the part of the small territory that he covers with unhelpful generalisations about the continent as a whole: 'A common characteristic of age group systems in Africa', he expresses, 'includes relations between age mates that are bound by permanent obligations of cooperation, solidarity and mutual help.'[28]

Viktoria Stöger-Eising has used Bischofberger's study as a launch pad to assert her belief in the importance of *eriisaga*, which she sees as a form of traditional Zanaki 'social security' association that later influenced Nyerere's *ujamaa*.[29] She proposes that Nyerere had the 'traditional' Zanaki generation class system in mind when establishing TANU institutions such as the ten house cell system, or '*nyumba kumi*', which then formed the basis of his larger political nation-building project. The generation class system, so Stöger-Eising's argument goes, forges a kind of 'horizontal integration' that cuts across lineage and clan lines making for egalitarianism, cohesion and loyalty between different lineages and clans, and even creates bonds between ethnic groups.[30]

As with Bischofberger, Stöger-Eising's account also lapses into a strange timelessness that again gives little indication of Nyerere's exposure to the generation class system and to *eriisaga*. The young Nyerere would have been a member of an age-grade by default. Had he not taken part in *eriisaga* (more accurately, a form of co-operative labour system), he would certainly have known of its existence – not least because his half-brother Chief Edward Wanzagi, with whom he was close, used it to provide manual workers for construction projects.[31] What is less certain is the degree to which Stöger-Eising's understanding of the institutions as published in the twenty-first century are compatible with Nyerere's exposure to these apparently timeless and static practices from the 1930s onwards. Stöger-Eising takes the 'acephalous', 'democratic' and 'egalitarian' Zanaki society as her historical starting point, but seems to derive this solely from the accounts of 'early European travellers'.[32] This appears only to be the Austrian explorer Oscar Baumann, who spent precious little time in Uzanaki and who gives negligible coverage to its institutions of governance.[33] Stöger-Eising also bases much of her understanding of the generation system on the information revealed in Bischofberger's study. Bischofberger is clear from the beginning of *The Generation Classes of the Zanaki* that his fieldwork dealt only with the minority Turi blacksmith society, not in fact the entire Zanaki that his book title implies. Bischofberger was located in Bumangi-Busegwe, did not conduct research in Butiama province, and pays no attention to the larger Biru society from which Nyerere descends. With little other detailed research to inform our knowledge of generation classes elsewhere in Uzanaki, it is a leap of faith for Stöger-Eising to then assume that Bischofberger's findings can be simply lifted to apply to Nyerere's understanding of institutions such as age-grades and *eriisaga*.

Benjamin Mkirya, Stöger-Eising's other major source, is equally problematic. Not only did Mkirya also closely follow Bischofberger's *Generation Classes*, but the publication in which Mkirya presented his account is none other than his own edited *Historia, Mila na Desturi za Wazanaki*. The publication lets off more than a whiff of the 'history, customs and traditions' approach that typified colonial-tribal knowledge. Stöger-Eising rightly notes that Mkirya attributes great importance to *eriisaga*, but she fails to appreciate that Mkirya's account (like her own) is tainted by the all too seductive desire to provide evidence that suggest *ujamaa*'s Zanaki roots.[34] Eliud Maluki attempted to show the proof of a link between *ujamaa* and Nyerere's upbringing in Butiama – using psycho-cultural theory, as far as one can – but he based his argument on the assumption that the political structures of his analysis (the Sukuma, Sonjo and Masai) can be applied to the Zanaki.[35] Kemal Mustafa's study of *ujamaa* also suggests a convenient link between Zanaki institutions and Nyerere's African Socialism, but the evidence is strongly influenced by his Musoma-based sources.[36] What is important to remember with such studies is that African Socialism was the order of the day – almost literally – when the likes of Maluki, Mustafa and Mkirya conducted their fieldwork. There may well have been some Zanaki influence in Nyerere's creation of *ujamaa*, but there was also considerable Zanaki influence to some East African researchers' writings about its roots. The ambitious Mkirya, for example, was a Zanaki himself and a Nyerere loyalist with local political interests. Mustafa relied for a primary informant on Joseph Kizurira – also a Zanaki, the TANU Youth Leader for Dar es Salaam, and the President's brother.

Stöger-Eising was also informed by Julius Nyerere himself, whom she interviewed during his retirement. However, her account suggests that Nyerere refused to be drawn into making an explicit link between *eriisaga* and *ujamaa*. Instead, with Stöger-Eising and at other times, Nyerere always chose to refer to the influences of 'African society', or 'traditional society' on *ujamaa*.[37] This was in part because, ever since he launched *ujamaa* in the 1960s, Nyerere was always at pains to play down any specific tribe's influence in the origins of his 'African'-inspired policy. Later, by the time of Stöger-Eising's interview, Nyerere also knew not to romanticise the past (too much) – perhaps because by that stage he was aware of the inaccuracies in his earlier depiction of pre-colonial African society, which had been questioned by popular Tanzania-based scholars such as Cranford Pratt, whose works he closely followed.[38] Nyerere may also have been aware of the thin boundary between the communal self-help of Butiama's past (*eriisaga*), and the forced labour in lieu of taxes that his father's native authority was required to raise for the colonial state. We return in Chapters 6 and 7 to an analysis of the academic literature that informed Nyerere's understanding of traditional institutions.

Nyerere

As with Nyerere's knowledge of the Zanaki generation-grades that he was born into, he would have known of the *orukobha* ritual, in which the chosen few from the Sai and Zuma cycles would walk around the chiefdom with their secret medicine: 'These men do it to treat the country', describes Jack Nyamwaga, using the present tense for practices that he acknowledges are now of the past: '"*Orukobha*" is Zanaki for "belt" [made of skin], and by passing the belt they are binding the country. They are treating the country [with medicine]. You must have a purpose to round the country. They are treating the *ekyaaro* [territory].'[39] It is most likely that Nyerere would have known of *orukobha*, if not its secrets, since it is claimed that his father introduced the now obsolete ritual, as the late John Nyambeho explains:

> It was Nyerere Burito who started it to prevent enemies. He did it to prevent misfortune. They [the chosen] passed on foot through eight chiefdoms of the Zanaki. The men were the *abhanyikura*, and they would cover all the boundaries of the territory. … If there was something bad in the country, Nyerere [Burito] would choose men to go in different directions [including] up to Sukumaland and Tarime. … It is a treatment of the country, and then *unakona* – you have treated the land. Nyerere Burito was the founder [of *orukobha*].[40]

Whether Nyerere Burito was the originator of *orukobha*, or whether he is remembered by those who lived during his chieftaincy to be its instigator in the territory, it was appropriated by his son Kambarage. As Jan Bender Shetler notes, Nyerere later instituted what was the most important symbol of Tanzanian national unity, the annual ritual 'walk' around the nation carrying the *mwenge* torch from the top of Mount Kilimanjaro.[41] Indeed, as Shetler details elsewhere, elders she interviewed explicitly compared the ritual walk of a new generation-set (*rikora*) to the running of the national torch around the country.[42] This is an observation that John Nyambeho offered – completely unprompted, when discussing *orukobha*, explaining: 'It is like the *Uhuru* [independence/freedom] torch that is walked around the whole of Tanzania. We thought that Mwalimu himself learnt from his father this *orukobha* issue.'[43]

Orukobha, which Bischofberger also describes as performed to keep misfortune away from the *ekyaaro*,[44] was similar to – if not the same as – a ritual detailed by Shetler in which the retiring generation-set performs a ceremony (*kukerera*) to encircle the boundaries of the *ekyaaro* territory with a ring of protection. *Kukerera* is described by Shetler as having involved the retiring generation-set, which was apparently not an explicit requirement for *orukobha* as presented by informants in the immediate vicinity of Butiama. (Although it is possible that the *abhanyikura* were instructed to perform the ritual by, or were accompanied by, the retiring or retired generation class.[45]) The word that unites these two ceremonies is the Zanaki term *ekyaaro*, which literally means 'country', but was also used by the Zanaki to refer to a clan territory.

Equally, however, as in the English word 'country', *ekyaaro* can refer to the whole tribe, and even to the nation.[46]

Another word from local vocabulary close to one used at the national governing level is *ikuru*, which in Zanaki means 'big', and across Tanzania now refers to a/the 'state house' (*ikulu*). The best-known 'big house' is the President's official residence in Dar es Salaam. Other buildings also known as *ikulu* are smaller presidential lodges in various regions across the country, along with Nyerere's home in Butiama, where locally *ikuru* refers to Mwitongo – the location of the big house. It has been suggested that *ikulu* is a variation of Zanaki word '*neikulu*':

> It was not a council. *Neikulu* was young men. You go until you reach a certain stage, then you progress (*kung'atuka*). Now these become elders. And here elders of another kind, senior elders. You will find there are *wenyekura, wenyebireti*. … Those *wenyekura* didn't just disappear, they didn't just end, youth move on. When they reach their age they step back. Now those who were herded behind them come forward. Those others [behind them] continue in same way.[47]

As with western Serengeti interpretations of the annual ritual walk around the nation, and along with the supposed appropriation of *neikulu* to regional and state administration, Nyerere himself also explicitly adapted a local term to the national level. When announcing his decision to step down as President, Nyerere used the Zanaki word for retirement of the generation-set, '*okung'atuka*'.[48] It is Mwitongo where Nyerere was based during his (highly active) retirement, and where he now rests.

Zanaki Origins

The name 'Zanaki' is thought to come from the question of an old man from the Jita tribe when an immigrant family wanted to settle in his area: 'What did they come with?' ('*Baja na ki?*') he asked.[49] The family had no property, so the Jita man drove them away and they moved to what is now Uzanaki.[50] The Zanaki live about 30 miles south-east of the shore of Lake Victoria, in a land area of around 440 square miles, north-west of the Serengeti plains. The land is at an altitude of some 1,300 metres above sea-level. It is not particularly fertile, although the soils are fairly resistant to erosion, and deciduous broad-leaved trees abound. As is the case throughout most of present-day Tanzania, agriculture in Uzanaki is the backbone of the local household economy. Finger millet is the traditional staple crop and is important in many rituals. Corn, groundnuts and, more recently, cassava are also cultivated. Cotton is a local cash-crop, cattle and goats are common livestock.

Uzanaki is susceptible to drought, and a great famine known as 'the Hunger of the Feet' hit western Serengeti in 1894.[51] Père Maillot, writing in 1909, observed that the houses of the Zanaki were well hidden among the rocks, trees and bushes.[52] This would have offered some protection against Masai raids that were reported by 'White Fathers' missionaries (officially known as Missionaries of Africa) who had established themselves on Ukerewe Island in Lake Victoria by 1893.[53] By 1916 the Zanaki were thought to number some 20,000 (about 4,000 of whom were 'men fit for bearing arms'), and a census five years later recorded them at just over 35,000.[54]

To the north of the Zanaki lie the Kwaya tribe, to the east are the Kuria, to the south the Ikizu, and to the west are the Jita and Shashi.[55] Hans Cory vaguely puts forward that the Zanaki and their neighbours 'have a dash of Hamitic or Nilotic blood in them'.[56] Indeed in his earlier 'Report on the pre-European tribal organizations in Musoma (South Mara) District', his account opens by the remark: 'About 16 generations ago all Buzanaki were under one powerful chief called Kakwaya who was defeated by Kamara … whose ancestress was Muse, a skilled rainmaker from inKiziba in Bukoba District. Kamara became the ruler of Buzanaki and called himself '*Mwami*' (rainmaker).'[57]

Shetler provides more detail from long before this period, arguing that people speaking East Nyanza Bantu languages, and living among people speaking other languages, diversified over time as they separated. About 1,500 years ago those staying near the lakeshore came to speak Suguti languages (Jita, Kwaya, Regi and Ruri) and those who went inland came to speak the Mara languages. Those who crossed the Mara River formed the language communities of North Mara (Gusii and Kuria), while those in South Mara (Musoma) broke into distinct groups some 500 to 3,000 years ago: Ngorome, eastern South Mara (Ikoma, Ishenyi and Nata) and western South Mara (Ikizu, Shashi, Sizaki and Zanaki). Although local convention recognises each of the western Serengeti languages as a separate language today, Shetler argues they are all closely related and thus, linguistically, represent one group of people with a common heritage in the past.[58] A common local version of the origin of the Zanaki is provided in a short history by Chief Edward Wanzagi Nyerere. According to Wanzagi, a group came from Egypt, through Sudan, and when they arrived in what became known as Tanganyika they divided, one group going to Ukerewe, another to Urange (after which they migrated to Busegwe), and a third group went to Sukuma. The Sukuma group left and came to occupy Uzanaki.[59]

Uzanaki comprises some forty different clans.[60] The oral tradition of even a limited number of clans points to the Zanaki being composed of groups that came from different directions: the Kirongo of Busegwe 'from the other side of the Lake', the Turi (blacksmiths) of Bumangi-Busegwe from Uzinza, the Kyora of Buturu from the island of Isese (Majita), the Kirunga of Buturu from the Kuria country, and the

Mwanza of Butuguri from Usimbiti (North Mara).[61] The Musoma district officer E.C. Baker, writing in 1929 and exemplifying a knowledge and epistemology that is recognisably colonial, suggests that the Waturu may have been the original inhabitants of Uzanaki, 'with an admixture of Kuria blood from the North and a heavy strain of Sukuma from the South'.[62] The archaeologist John Sutton has since argued that these Tatoga groups were probably 'Bantuized' by the Zanaki.[63]

Baker's view is of course from a time long before DNA analysis could possibly be applied to show such conclusions to have little scientific foundation. It is typical of the understanding of many colonial officers, few of whom even after the 1930s received anything more than the most superficial of anthropological training. Oxford, Cambridge, and University College London anthropological teaching at the time was 'largely mistaken and misguided – not only by modern standards, but by the standards of the day at the London School of Economics (LSE) and in America. It was full of diffusionist and evolutionist assumptions, and confused by doses of physical anthropology, still racialist in orientation'.[64] C.G. Seligman's 'Hamitic Hypothesis', which put forward that there were cultural links between Ancient Egypt and Black Africa, informed colonial officers' understanding of migration and culture contact[65] – hence Baker's idea that the original inhabitants of Uzanaki had 'admixture of Kuria blood … and a heavy strain of Sukuma', and Cory's insistence that the Zanaki have 'a dash of Hamitic or Nilotic blood'. The official view, notes Sally Falk Moore, was that it was usually easier and more efficient to teach a British political officer some anthropology rather than to try to tolerate the peculiar ways of anthropologists whose interests did not always fit well with those of the colonial administration.[66] At the time this position was naturally regarded with disdain by the International Institute of African Languages and Cultures. Its offer to provide specialised research was rejected by Donald Cameron, the Governor of Tanganyika at the time, because he feared it would interfere with his administration.[67]

In Musoma District, within which Uzanaki fell, the British headquarters' preference for political officers saw the likes of E.C. Baker (in the 1920s), J.L. Fairclough (in the early 1930s), then A.C. Davey and H.C. Baxter (from the late 1930s into the 1940s) produce the essential records of governance. They set out to capture not only land use and settlement, trade and census data – creating something of a Musoma District Doomsday Book of their time – but, crucially, they also sought to chronicle and describe tribal history and legends, and the existing systems of government that fell under their overall control.[68]

The administration sought a more thorough type of researcher when, in 1943, a detailed study was required to investigate whether Nyamwezi and the Sukuma secret societies might be potentially subversive organisations. They turned to the son of a Viennese musical family, the Austrian-born Hans Koritschoner, a fifty-five-year old who had been wounded while fighting under von Lettow-Vorbeck. Koritschoner managed sisal estates after the First World War (Ernest Hemmingway based the planter Kandinsky in *Green Hills of Africa* on him), and he then became a temporary District Officer under the British administration. By the time he was hired as sociologist to the Government of Tanganyika, he had anglicised his name to Hans Cory.[69]

As Government Sociologist, Cory advised the administration on a myriad of social problems.[70] He was one of a small handful of professional researchers who presented the British administration with a significant body of commissioned material to suit their needs.[71] With a brief that covered the entire Tanganyika Territory, the largely self-taught Cory acted as trouble-shooter where an 'authoritative' (Austrian) understanding of (African) 'tribal matters' required credence.[72] Yet while Cory would not always agree with his patrons, his judgement was certainly central to the appointment of chiefs to many tribes in Tanganyika. Towards the end of his life he admitted that – if not as a direct result of his pronouncements – 'find the chief' was indeed played during his watch in Tanganyika.[73] Subsequent studies have concluded that Cory's analysis was sometimes fundamentally flawed. As Thomas Spear has shown of Cory's actions in the creation of the Arusha constitution of 1948, for example, the Government Sociologist ended up fabricating an entirely new 'traditional' social entity for the 'modern' world. In doing so he provided a stellar example of the ways in which 'colonial authorities sought to legitimate their rule in terms of tradition, while fabricating and perverting those terms to "make customary law"'.[74]

Incompetence is no excuse for the complicity in the manufacture of convenient findings that Cory all but admits to. Kanyama Chiume offers the benefit of the doubt to those many colonial officers who failed to master anthropological inquiry. Chiume generously argues that, even if colonial officers were gifted with the necessary qualities of mind and character that enabled them to train themselves, they were shifted around too much to get anywhere close to mastering local history and belief systems.[75] Cory's job certainly made his travels extensive, and they took him to Musoma to investigate the political organisation of tribes in pre-European times, especially in regard to the authority of the traditional leaders, and to make recommendations to the Government concerning 'legitimate' chiefs. Again Cory's findings were off the mark, if not this time so obviously to suit the more favourable choice of those 'traditional' leaders who could best work with the British but, as Bischofberger argues, they were certainly based on inaccuracies. The Government Sociologist speaks of the 'exclusive role of the clan system' in Uzanaki. This contrasts with Bischofberger's own finding that decisions in affairs concerning the whole province were made by all men of the retired generation class, not by the clan-heads alone.[76]

Cory's work in Uzanaki also comes in for criticism from Mustafa, who argues that while together the Government Sociologist and E.C. Baker provide the most information on early Zanaki history, their accounts conflict. Baker, notes Mustafa, saw traditional political organisation in terms of age-grades and the council of elders, while Cory made the mistake of ignoring these pre-colonial structures in the mistaken hunt for a central 'ruler' – the *mwami* being the nearest he could find.[77] It is on this dubious foundation of historical record, often hastily compiled by colonial officers with a smattering of research training at best, and a keen interest to find the most pliant (and competent) 'traditional' rulers, that the account of the social, economic and political history of Uzanaki is based.

Although western Serengeti peoples now understand clans as subsets of ethnic groups, Shetler's analysis of oral tradition from South Mara suggests that clans in this area seem to have preceded ethnic groups.[78] What the anthropologist Evans-Pritchard says of the Nandi-speaking peoples of neighbouring Kenya is also true of the Zanaki: The country of each tribe 'was divided into a number of territorial segments, which we may call provinces, and these segments were not only geographical divisions of the country but also political units'.[79] Uzanaki is divided into nine provinces whose boundaries (usually distinct physical features such as rivers and hills) are clear-cut and well-known locally: Buhemba, Bumangi, Butuguri, Busegwe, Butiama, Buturu, Buzahya, Muganza and Buruma.[80] These territories are often named by using the prefix for place designation, *bu-*, with the clan name, as in Busegwe, the place of the Segwe clan.[81] Each clan territory (*ekyaaro*) controlled the land within its extensive boundaries.[82] The nine Uzanaki provinces, of which Butiama was one, were individual political units.[83] Into at least the 1960s, clans were reported as not integrating members into a territorial and political unit, and decisions in affairs which concerned the whole province were not made by the clan-heads, but by all men of the retired generation class.[84] *Ezinyaangi* rites of passage were individual, whereas the handing-over ceremonies – such as *okung'atuka* – performed by the generation class, were communal.[85]

Joseph Kizurira Burito Nyerere has offered a summary of the Zanaki traditional political organisation. He begins with the *abhanyikura*, who were members of the *eriikura* age-grade that consisted of warriors. The *abhanyikura* were the ruling generation that formed the government of the Zanaki and made laws. The *abhanyikura* elected eight advisers (*abhazaama*; sing. *omuzaama*) from the next ascending age-grade of elders. The *abhagaambi* (sing. *omugaambi*) were 'spokesmen' in the *eriikura* warrior age-grade, but it is not clear whether they were the same as or distinct from the informal leaders known as *abharwazi* (sing. *omurwazi*), the influencers or 'persuaders' who act as 'whips'.[86] The *abharwazi* were also elected by the *abhanyikura*, but had no political power and were responsible for coordinating the members of their villages in communal activities.[87] Adherence to such customs as *ezinyaangi* rites of passage and handing-over ceremonies is today defunct in Uzanaki, and the traditional political organisation is now of the past.[88] It was in Julius Nyerere's time that these structures were first challenged by new powers seeking to impose their own foreign systems of control.

Colonial Rule in Uzanaki

The use of multiple words for 'chiefs', such as *machifu*, *mutemi*, and *mukama*, suggests that in pre-colonial times the Zanaki had no clear conception of chiefship.[89] In the absence of hereditary 'chiefs' ruling over well-defined 'tribes', the colonial powers sought to enforce their rule through appointed 'traditional' authorities who, in different situations, were a prophet, an age-grade leader or a titled elder.[90] The Germans were the first European power to attempt this in what they called Deutsch-Ostafrika (German East Africa), and in 1891 established a military post in Mwanza, at the southern end of Lake Victoria, some 190 kilometres from Uzanaki.[91] Only after 1900 did they attempt to administer the area to the north, through posts at Shirati and (Nyabange) Musoma along Lake Victoria. It took some years for a more direct German impact to be felt with the construction from 1905 of Fort Ikoma, a permanent station on the western edge of the Serengeti plain.[92] Musoma town was founded in 1912 and soon became the administrative capital of the district. Indians, who by this time had secured control of the retail trade in much of the interior of German East Africa, owned a number of the small shops in Musoma and helped establish the town as a centre of commerce.[93]

The Zanaki long resisted the sultans or *akida* intermediaries whom the Germans installed to supervise taxation inland.[94] At times they used their feared poisoned arrows to harass foreign expeditions that ventured into the hinterland. Such was the danger of these weapons that the British declared that in Uzanaki: 'No person shall carry bows and arrows by day or night.'[95] On a visit in 1910 to the 'Sultans' of Bumangi and Buhema, Maillot described the Zanaki as 'the terror of the small neighbouring tribes'. Probably expressing the opinion of his local informants concerning the Zanaki, Maillot writes:

> The blacks never lack for stories, each more terrible than the others, about them [the Zanaki] … it is clear that they are a warlike people who have established a reputation of superiority throughout the land. They are a rough and energetic mountain people, hard-

ened against fatigue. They are not very hospitable towards strangers, and the other blacks do not willingly stop in the middle of their mountains.[96]

An unattributed extract in the Cory Papers, printed in German, refers to the Zanaki as '*ein übles Schweinezeug*', or 'notoriously bad pig-matter' – an extremely rude and harsh term, even by the racist standards of the time.[97]

Colonial authority weakened during the First World War, after which the British military ruled from 1917 to 1920. This first period of European rule in Tanganyika was a topic that Julius Nyerere had studied, having read *German Colonization, Past and Future: The truth about the German colonies* by Heinrich Schnee, the last governor of German East Africa. 'What the natives really want', argued Schnee, '[is] the continuance of German dominion.'[98] Nyerere was gifted the book by his Edinburgh friend the historian George Shepperson, to whom he apparently commented that the German occupation of his country was, perhaps, not as bad as it was sometimes made out to be[99] – a curious comment from the future leader of Tanganyika's independence struggle, given that Schnee's bitter book was an attempt to vindicate German colonialism. Nyerere's personal copy of the book is full of his hand-written exasperation, including a furious exclamation mark at the claim that 'Germany's colonies were no man's land before she occupied them'.[100]

In the brief time between the German withdrawal from Shirati and Ikoma and when the new British administration took its grip, following the First World War, many German-appointed chiefs were ousted. As one British official noted, they 'had no tradition to support them and …, moreover, they were chosen often without consultation of the wishes of the people.'[101] However, The British quickly reinstalled those chiefs whom the Germans had selected, or held limited elections to choose between the chiefs' relatives. In one case during the 1918 transfer of power from the German administration to the British, the newly instated Provincial Commissioner was forced to rush from Mwanza to clear up an incident that was later communicated by Joseph Kizurira Burito Nyerere. Chief Nyerere Burito's clerk took action on behalf of Zanaki dissatisfaction with the District Officer he worked for, along with a Ganda *akida* called Jaberi, and another Zanaki who was said to be responsible for murder. This clerk was Wandiba Nyang'ombe, 'a short, very serious type of man'.[102] Wandiba wrote a letter to Jaberi, ostensibly written by the District Officer, ordering the *akida* to kill this 'murdering' Zanaki.[103] Jaberi slipped the letter into a pile of papers which he took to the District Officer to sign when the colonial official was in one of his customary drunken states. The District Officer signed the letter unknowingly, and the *akida* quickly carried out the execution. The Zanaki rose up against this 'officially' sanctioned killing and asked: 'How can we have a man in charge of us who goes around murdering people?' The District Officer was transferred and Jaberi the *akida* – whose actions demonstrate that the dismissal of unpopular chiefs was a two-way process – was deposed.[104]

Tanganyika Territory became a British mandate under the League of Nations, and civilian rule began in September 1920. Rule was based on the Tanganyika Order in Council which created the offices of governor and executive council.[105] From the perspective of those subjected to both German and British administrations, the transfer is described in a wholly believable summary by Cameron and Dodd, who assess that 'as far as the African inhabitants were concerned, one set of foreign rulers had merely been replaced by another who, even if more tolerant and lenient, were certainly no more popular and no more easy to understand'.[106] Governance under the British changed several times, from a centralised form with one chief, to decentralised rule with provincial chiefs.[107] It was around this period, according to one Musoma District Officer, that: 'So died the last vestige of the indigenous administration, and the direct rule of Agents, Akidas, Sultans, and *Wanangwa* replaced it. It died not altogether unmourned, though it is doubtful if the mourners knew exactly what they mourned. Few records are traceable, and those that remain are largely of European origin.'[108]

The arrival of Sir Donald Cameron as Governor in 1925 ushered in not only more efficient record-keeping – the Germans had done a thorough job at removing or destroying most of their official documents – but also a fundamental overhaul to the political-administrative system.[109] Among the innovations that Cameron introduced were a revamping of provincial administration, the formation of a (at this time unelected and unrepresentative) Legislative Council, and the establishment of a system of indirect rule. 'Indirect administration', to use Cameron's preferred term, allowed for a variety of 'traditional authority' patterns from paramount chiefs, a federation of chiefs, a tribal council comprising of petty chiefs or headmen, and a small chief or village headman.[110] The government retained its veto to refuse to accept a chief though and, with the assistance of local colonial officers such as E.C. Baker in Musoma, they often applied their rudimentary anthropological techniques in the search for 'traditional' authorities who best matched their needs. In theory, the ruling structure mirrored pre-colonial forms of governance, legitimising the colonial presence through (subordinate) 'traditional' chiefs, in geographical areas that suited the local British administration. Since all Europeans belonged to nations, the theory went, so all Africans belonged to tribes that could be packaged into discrete, governable territories. As in the earlier times of German rule, however, there is reason to believe that in some cases the British simply created chiefs where none existed before.[111] But one of the incongruities of indirect rule is

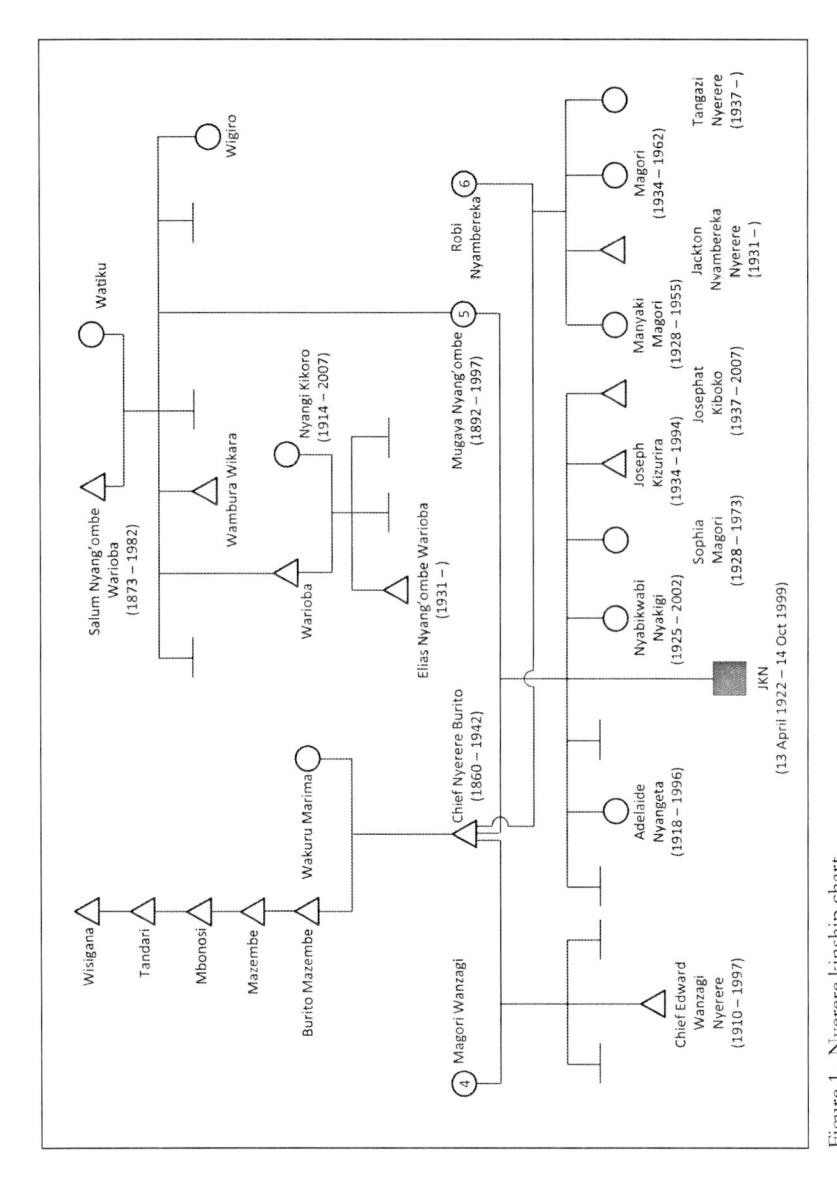

Figure 1. Nyerere kinship chart.
(*Some wives and children have been excluded due to space constraints; only known dates are given.*)

that many African groups had not before been ruled by chiefs. Of the Zanaki, for example, none other than Cory – a senior architect in the fabrication of past political entities to fit the modern world – was even prepared to acknowledge that the British administration had made a mistake by imposing a form of hereditary chiefdomship.[112] Individuals were given powers that had never before been wielded in their communities. But if a chief then did not comply with the administration's wishes, for example by expressing open opposition to unpopular policies, they could dismiss him for insubordination. 'A withdrawal into apathy and alcoholism was a not uncommon reaction to the contradictions of their position on the part of many chiefs', notes Bruce Berman of indirect rule in neighbouring Kenya.[113] The same applied south of the border, where a number of South Mara chiefs were replaced for their persistent absence when the authorities were seeking their co-operation. Once given official sanction by the colonial administration however, most chiefs then tended to jealously guard their authority and to resist any attempt aimed at evolving democratic systems of representation.[114]

The Chiefs:
Nyerere Burito and Edward Wanzagi Nyerere

The first Chief of Butiama was said to be Buhoro, the *omurwazi*, whose position combined leadership in war with administrative and religious functions. He was appointed by the Germans sometime in the late nineteenth or early twentieth century.[115] Buhoro feared the colonisers, and when they sought him he would go hunting in areas where he could not be found.[116] His lack of co-operation led to his removal as chief in 1915. The Germans then appointed his more compliant cousin, 'Nyerere of the Butiama sultanate' – Chief Nyerere Burito.[117] The chief, Julius Nyerere's father, was born in 1860 to Burito Mazembe and Wakuru Malima,[118] and was given the name 'Nyerere', meaning 'caterpillar' in Zanaki, after a plague of army worm caterpillars that attacked the countryside at the time of his birth.[119] He was an 'assessor' to Ihunyo, the senior chief of the Zanaki Federation.[120] According to one Zanaki account, Nyerere Burito was originally a 'seer' who, long before the arrival of the colonial powers, had envisaged the coming of 'another strange-looking people'. The first German to reach Butiama was taken to Nyerere Burito, who was asked: 'Is this the person you envisaged?' He answered that it was. Captain Gaston Schlobach, the commander of a German expeditionary force that toured the region east of Lake Victoria in 1898,[121] was suitably impressed by Nyerere Burito, and regarded him to be a leader of the Zanaki. Schlobach 'appointed Nyerere Burito "chief of Butiama'".[122] Upon the dismissal of Jaberi in 1918, Nyerere Burito briefly served as the chief of all Zanaki. As chief of Butiama, Nyerere Burito was described thus:

> A gentleman of the old school; he is one of the oldest Chiefs of the district. If he is shewn [sic] the respect due to his years and experience, he responds very well to the treatment. In the Council, he is represented by his son Wanzagi who is his probable successor. In his own village, he is apt to nurse old grievances about his boundaries and he will continue to nurse the same until he dies. He is always glad to see an Administrative Officer in his village and dearly loves a chat about old times.[123]

Makongoro of Ikizu was regarded by the British as 'the most responsible chief in South Mara' (if 'a little tiring'); 'Sultan Nyerere' came in second. Shining in comparison to other Zanaki chiefs, the contrast between the two friends and their counterparts could hardly have been more stark.[124] The administration's antipathy towards the majority of the chiefs was reflected in the annual reports of the Lake Provincial Commissioners, one of whom reported in this same year:

> With a few honourable exceptions, which may be counted on the fingers of one hand, the dominant characteristics of the Musoma chiefs are those of apathy, venality, conspicuous lack of dignity and a standard of general intelligence so low that it is often difficult to believe that the underlying motive is not one of deliberate obstructiveness. It is, in fact, a measure of the lack of respect which these chiefs command that the district is not in a state of revolt. For the most part the people go their own way and have as few dealings as possible with their leaders.[125]

The British administration's 'Character Studies' ('Native Administration in Practice') demonstrate their disdain for the majority of the South Mara chiefs. Mageye of Munguru, who 'became too mad to carry on … has no authority and is an expert at connivance in minor lawlessness (at a profit to himself)', while Magero of Magana 'hides himself away in his village which is conveniently distant from a road so that surprise visits are impossible'. Surveillance on Manyori of Muganza proved equally tricky for the British, since 'he only works when we are watching and we cannot watch all the time'. Other chiefs were described as drunkards, not least Manyama of Majita, who 'at the early age of 20 had developed a taste for moshi beer', and was reserved for the most contempt by the authorities – and apparently also those he purportedly lead. The chief is described as 'inefficient and is suspected of dishonesty … [and] his inevitable collapse is awaited with eagerness.'[126] Nyerere Burito, on the other hand, was 'courteous in character'. His main weakness, it seems, was his relationship with women: the 'gentlemanly ancient' was 'much worried by his wives who run away whenever he comes to Musoma'.[127]

We know of one of Chief Nyerere Burito's errant wives, Nyanjiga Samba (his third wife, a Jita), who absconded to Mombasa. But it appears that the chief himself was no stranger to the occasional wander, for he spent so much time in Ikizu that he is known for speaking better Ikizu than Zanaki. On one journey away from home he was caught in a compromising position with a local woman and was tied up by a group of angry locals who prepared to lynch him. The mother of the woman saved the chief's bacon, however, insisting that if the man was to be tied up, then so too should her daughter. Knowing that her tribesmen were much less likely to kill one of their own, she defused the situation by showing them that they should not discriminate against the foreigner – the implication, apparently, being that many Ikizu men could also have transgressed with the woman, but they would not have been dealt with as severely. On another occasion the chief was falsely accused of murder and arrested, but once again an old woman came to the rescue. Somewhat surprisingly, these events are said to have solidified relations between the Ikizu and the Zanaki of Butiama for the better. Evidence for this includes Chief Wanzagi's marriage (albeit later dissolved) to Nyambata of Ikizu, Julius Nyerere's close friendship with Chief Makongoro (after whom he named his fifth son), and the already existing friendship between many of the men's children.[128]

The number of wives Nyerere Burito had – errant or not – was twenty-two. While Joan Wicken puts the figure at twenty-three, and Ovchinnikov comes in with a mere eighteen,[129] Julius Nyerere consistently put the number at twenty-two.[130] In an interview with Edgett Smith, for example, Nyerere said: 'The only thing the British had against [my father] was his twenty-two wives.'[131] He was consistent with this figure later in life. In an interview shortly before his death he spoke of his studies at Makerere College on the subjugation of women and maintained: 'My father had 22 wives and I knew how hard they had to work and what they went through as women',[132] – suggesting that his father treated his wives harshly; this, in part, is probably a reason that they were frequently running away, and also perhaps a reason that Nyerere opposed polygamy. (It is surely his father whom he refers to when, in the Makerere essay that he wrote shortly after the chief died, he writes: 'I know an elderly man who had twenty-two wives, but the sum of his children did not reach thirty.'[133]) Local sources also point to this number of wives, some of whom are listed by name in Figure 1 above. Local sources are also clear on where Nyerere's mother, Mugaya Nyang'ombe, was placed in Nyerere Burito's nuptial chronology.[134] Maria Nyerere, who later married Julius Nyerere, the second child of the eight that Mugaya bore to Burito,[135] recalls that her mother-in-law was the fifth of twenty-two wives, and adds that Burito had twenty-seven children.[136] Mugaya was born in 1892 and was married to the chief in 1907 at the age of fifteen. The marriage came about when Wandiba, the 'very serious' clerk who Nyerere Burito had hired (and who successfully orchestrated

Butiama: The Abandoned Place

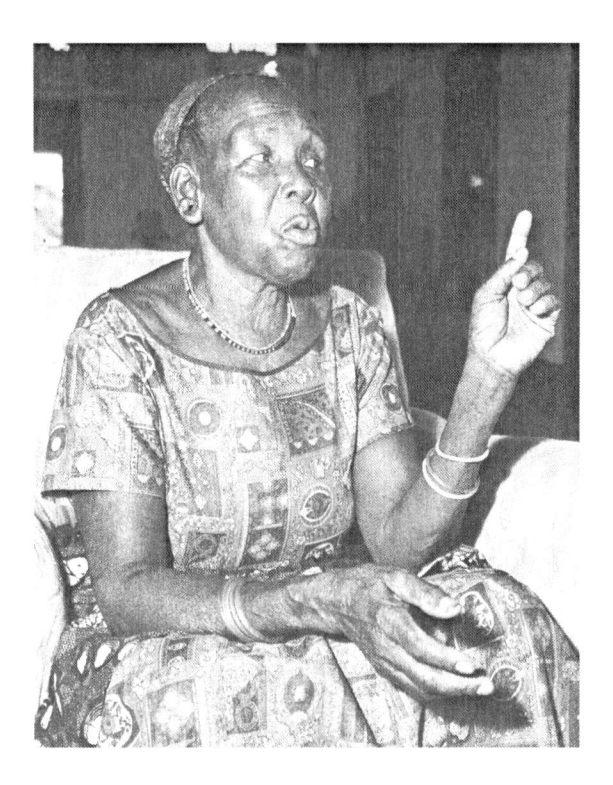

Photo C. Julius Nyerere's mother, Mugaya Nyang'ombe, Butiama, 1966. (*Reproduced by kind permission of A24 Media/Camerapix/ Mohamed Amin Collection.*)

the deposition of Jaberi, the Ganda *akida*), told the chief that 'our sister Mugaya is well-mannered: marry her' – and Burito married the girl.[137] She was baptised Christina Mugaya when in her mid-seventies.[138]

To Governor Cameron, education policy was one of the most important embodiments of the British system of indirect rule.[139] His Director of Education summarised in a report the government's combined educational and administrative aims, listing at the top: 'The education of the sons of chiefs'.[140] This, Cameron reasoned, was so that the position of chiefs would be guarded 'against assaults which may be made against it by Europeanised natives seeking to obtain political control of the country.'[141] The education of chiefs' sons came in the form of the Native Administration school. There the chiefs-to-be were instructed in how to rule the British way, as a 1928 education report put it:

> The principles of native administration are taught both by formal lecture and through the organization of the school itself. A school court with a local chief as president tries offences against conduct and discipline once a week. The procedure adopted is an exact replica of that which is in force in the Native Courts of the District.[142]

In one school during the 1920s the teaching of the principles of native administration was taken to the extent that,

> The 154 boys of the school are divided up into 'villages' according to their classes. Each village consists of six huts and is named after the clan which resides in it. It is supervised by a teacher, assisted by a head boy or *M[w]anangwa*, who is responsible to the *Mtemi* or captain of the school for the welfare and discipline of the 'village'. Each hut is under the charge of the *baba* whose duty it is to see that the school rules and standing orders as regards cleanliness in the hut, &c, are properly maintained.[143]

In 1924, just one year before Cameron's arrival in Tanganyika, Chief Nyerere Burito sent his son Edward Wanzagi Nyerere, born in 1910 to his fourth wife Magori Wanzagi, to the newly-opened Native Administration School in Musoma.[144] Managed by the Native Authority, but basically a government primary school built from local treasury funds,[145] 'the school started in 1924 as a mud-brick affair in a corner of the present Musoma air-field.'[146] At the time this was the only school in the district and a day-school at that so, as a pupil hailing from Butiama village some twenty-five or so miles away, Wanzagi lodged in Irengo Minor Settlement.[147]

In September 1934, some few years after Wanzagi had left school and gained valuable skills in government administration, Chief Nyerere Burito approached the District Officer and stated that he wished it to be placed on record that he desired his son Wanzagi to succeed him as chief. He was informed that 'no guarantee that his desire would be carried out could be given as the appointment of a Chief did not necessarily depend on nomination by his predecessor but also on the will of the people and the candidate's acceptability to Government.'[148] He was, however, promised that his desire would be recorded.

Eight years later, in March 1942, Chief Burito lay in hospital and called a family meeting that one of his sons remembers. Speaking in Zanaki and pointing at Edward Wanzagi Nyerere, the ailing chief told those present, 'I can see that I am dying. When I die you [Edward Wanzagi] will be chief.' The clarification, apparently, was to confirm his choice that his successor as chief would be Wanzagi and not Warioba, another of his sons. Burito asked Edward Wanzagi to look after the family and pay for Kambarage's school fees. Still speaking in Zanaki, Chief Nyerere Burito apparently also added that he had a dream that Kambarage would do something significant in what he called the '*ekyaaro*'. The ambiguity of *ekyaaro*, however, meant that those present did not know whether he was referring to Butiama, or further afield – the clan territory, the whole tribe, or the nation.[149]

2
Musoma & Tabora

Kambarage, Spirit of the Rain

> *When government was mentioned, the African thought of the chief – a person, not a building. Unlike the Briton, he did not picture a grand building in which a debate was taking place.*
>
> Julius Nyerere, Symposium on Africa,
Wellesley College, 17 February 1960[1]

This chapter looks first at Kambarage Nyerere's earliest years in the village. It identifies his age-mates, among them John Nyambeho who recalls the circumcision right that he undertook with Kambarage, and their years herding livestock. It considers the influences of Nyerere's early home life in an apparently egalitarian society, and discusses how the chief's son later dealt with accusations of elitism and privilege. This is then related to Nyerere's first exposure to formal education and to a new religion. His performance and reputation at Mwisenge Native Administration School is discussed, along with the influence of teachers and local missionaries. An account is then given of Nyerere's new religious instruction and his transition from traditional beliefs to Catholicism. The chapter charts his progression to Tabora Boys, and compares the elite institution with other secondary schools in East Africa. It looks at Kambarage's social life alongside the other pupils, the death of his father, and his close relationship with his brother. Sources include Nyerere's correspondence with Shepperson in which they discussed this period, interviews with Butiama residents who knew Nyerere at this time, and the recollections of some individuals who were well-placed to provide accounts of his early instruction.

Mugendi

Kambarage Nyerere, as Julius Nyerere was called before he was baptised into the Catholic Church, was born in Mwitongo, Butiama on 13 April

1922. For decades Nyerere did not know his actual date of birth, and he used February 1921 for at least the first twenty-five years of his life. He indicated this date in his 1948 application to the Colonial Scholarship Scheme for funds to study in the United Kingdom.[2] Nyerere was still not sure of the real date of birth in 1960.[3] The matter was finally put to rest in the late 1960s when, on a rest visit to Butiama, some elders visited the President with an exercise book belonging to an old man called Mtokambali Bukiri.[4] Mtokambali was born in Mtuzu sometime before the First World War and practised as an *omugabhu* in and around Butiama. A product of the school in Shirati established in the German era, Mtokambali is described as 'a researcher of his day' who, unusually for both the time and his profession, wrote detailed notes about his medicines and their cures. He was one of only two local 'highly literate men' who recorded events in the community and, it is thought in Butiama, Mtokambali was the chronicler who confirmed Kambarage's birth date.[5]

In Butiama, Nyerere also learned that his given name at birth was initially Mugendi, meaning 'Walker' in the Zanaki language.[6] He was then taken to an *omugabhu* because he cried so much. The crying stopped when he was named Kambarage.[7] It was raining hard on the day that the diviner was consulted, and the diviner chose this name in honour of the *amasambwa* called Kambarage, a spirit of the rain. While not associated with Mwitongo specifically, the spirit was believed to move freely around Butiama.[8] Kambarage is a female *erisaambwa*, and until that point the name was apparently reserved for women. Kambarage Nyerere is thought to be the earliest male to be given this first name. It has since become a popular name for Zanaki men.[9]

Kambarage's very earliest years were spent in and around his mother's house. From infancy he was used to doing small jobs on the *shamba* (smallholding), helping in the farming of the millet, maize and cassava. He was barefoot and he often ate only one meal a day.[10] In these respects, he was very much like other children in the village. Sometime before he reached the age of twelve Kambarage was circumcised in a ritual that Bischofberger describes as 'the door into adult life'. Performed then on both boys and girls, Bischofberger explains that in earlier times the boys were usually older (about eighteen), and there was no seclusion period, and no extensive instructions were given: 'The operation is performed near a granary on a cattle skin … [and] apart from the burying of the foreskin … at the foot of the granary, no important rituals are connected with circumcision.'[11] Those who underwent the operation in the same cohort were known as *bhakisero*, 'those circumcised on the same cattle skin'. Accompanying Kambarage in the ceremony was his age-mate John Nyambeho, who recalled the day: 'The place was called Gabizuryo, about two kilometres from Butiama. The circumciser (*omusari*) was called Sange. … If you made wrinkles in the eyes then it was regarded that you had cried. ... You have to suffer pain, you should experience it. We did not cry. You could not.'[12]

In his spare time Kambarage liked to be with his age-mates, including John Nyambeho and, among others, Karumbete from Mtuzu, John Nyamazanzare, Nyakiriga Mukija, and Nyamura Risyatogoro. As with other young boys, they would herd goats together and, later, cattle.[13] Looking after livestock is what young boys did, developing toughness whatever their physical stature. Some three-quarters of the post-independence elite interviewed by Raymond Hopkins had engaged in herding cattle and goats during their youth. In this respect Kambarage was no different from many of his other peers.[14] Herding gave them the opportunity to learn to fight, to learn wrestling, high jumping and running, and as they grew older they would travel further from home.[15] They slowly learned how to take responsibility for themselves. The plains of Butiama were well-known for their rich game,[16] and they hunted for birds together and brought them to Kambarage's father.[17] In an interview shortly before independence, Nyerere used his experience from these days to explain his difficult position as Prime Minister: 'After raising goats and sheep and hunting I realized that there is a certain pattern. When hunting there is no problem. ... Problems start when the animal has died, that's when fighting starts, because this one wants that piece and another cuts another piece, and that's when people start to get their fingers cut.'[18]

When recalling his childhood Nyerere said: 'I was a peasant. I grew up in a peasant area.'[19] He was the son of a chief though, but he was keen to point out that the economic benefits of this social status were not great. He recalled that one of his earliest memories was trying to sleep under a leaky roof at home, and that there was not always adequate food for what was often the family's single daily meal.[20] These early life experiences, argues Hopkins, were among those that seemed to influence Nyerere's attitudes and actions in later life. Deference and respect for elders, expectations of docility and obedience from youth, and an abiding concern for the poverty-level living conditions of the vast majority of Tanzanians, Hopkins believes, were important characteristics of Nyerere's later leadership.[21] As the son of a chief with some twenty-two wives who lived in close proximity within the same compound, the young Nyerere would also have been used to communal living and the co-operative that he later espoused in the self-reliance of *ujamaa*. Arguably, however, the influences of communal living were little different from those to which any other child living in a Zanaki village would have been exposed. Certainly attitudes of submissiveness, humility and compliance towards older generations were not unique to the young Nyerere when compared to his contemporaries growing up in rural parts anywhere else in Tanganyika.

When asked in an interview why he had not acquired the 'son-of-a-chief' mentality, Nyerere continued to play down the role:

> Although it is true that I am the son of a chief, if you study the sociology of the population in the Lake Victoria region, the tribes of the south and the west have chiefs, but the tribes to the east traditionally have no chiefs. But the Germans came and they had the fixed idea that every African tribe has a chief. Then they came to my little tribe, we fought them, we lost and my father's cousin, clever and intelligent fellow that he was, said: 'Let's face it, we have lost this war.' So he went to the Germans and said: 'I am the leader of the group.' He was no leader of the group at all, but they decided to make him chief. He was chief for three years. Everybody called him chief, the poor fellow. He used to get drunk, and my father took over. My father, appointed by the Germans, was beginning to build the mentality of a chief, but the whole thing was quite ridiculous.[22]

William Macmillan's *Africa Emergent*, one of the more progressive books to which Nyerere was exposed during his later studies in Edinburgh, strongly denounced chiefly administration. Nyerere shared Macmillan's criticism towards those the author called the 'pawns of the colonial state'.[23] But at no time did he ever go so far as to directly disparage his father's chiefly position. To all intents and purposes, Chief Nyerere Burito was an intermediary who implemented the directives of a foreign government – to which the colonial authorities saw that he 'responds very well'.[24] In this respect the chief can be seen as a collaborator; at times perhaps even a 'yes-man'. (But presumably not, in his political son's eyes, a quisling, for '[a] Tanganyikan who helped the imperialists was regarded as a traitor.'[25]) By playing the white man's game and accepting the hegemony of the imperial power, Chief Nyerere Burito secured his own status – and, so long as his sons were also compliant, he secured the position of any of those among them who might wish to continue to reap the benefits of chiefly power.

Kambarage and his brothers were well aware as young men of the mechanisms of their father's governance. In time they were also conscious of how it fitted within the overall structure of colonial domination. Women and young men crouched when interacting with the chief, whose power was held most visibly in Mwitongo where his many *ebhitara* (granaries) stored the millet that villagers presented to him for feeding his household. The full *ebhitara* were symbols of Nyerere Burito's authority and, to some poorer subjects in times of famine, the bulging food reserves were also a representation of his chiefly oppression: while 'Chief Nyerere was on good terms with the elders and had no trouble in obtaining tribal dues, consisting of so many head of cattle, sheep, goats and fowls,' notes one commentator, 'the Zanaki were not supposed to taste any of their harvest without giving him a share of the sacrifice.'[26] The chief dispensed native customary law, and by the Second World War he and other chiefs were expected to provide manpower for the military and for plantations.[27] Chiefs also controlled the physical enforcers of power. Nyerere Burito, much like his counterparts throughout Tanganyika, ran a prison – the ultimate symbol of his ability to check dissent. It was in such an environment that Kambarage Nyerere was exposed to African-administered power, control and authority, at least within the parameters permitted by the colonial state that he later challenged. His father was a small but essential, and locally very significant, part of the apparatus – 'a government chief', as John Iliffe has described him.[28]

Chiefs were so 'ridiculous', as Nyerere had put it, that in 1963 he dissolved their powers. The nationalists' reasoning at the time was that, despite the progress made with elected or representative tribal councils, chiefs were still largely autocratic, almost feudal, and they slowed down modernisation. Nyerere and TANU wanted to make a fresh start. The chiefs, it seemed to them, and often with good reason, embodied the past and had to go.[29] It is notable that later, in the mid-1990s, Nyerere regretted having abolished chiefs. It is also worth bearing in mind that chiefs were certainly not ridiculous to others in Tanganyika, nor to all TANU supporters.[30]

Nyerere preferred instead to refer to his father as a kind of 'Speaker' who led the people in democratic decisions about their welfare.[31] This attitude, expressed retrospectively, fits neatly with Nyerere's argument that in traditional African democracy 'elders sit under the big tree, and talk until they agree'.[32] Stöger-Eising describes Chief Burito as slow and careful before acting, and believes that he always insisted on giving his people their rights. She attributes the Zanaki culture as acting as the foundation on which Nyerere's moral and political sensibilities were built, long before the later influences of his formal education.[33] Another foreign scholar, John Hatch, points out that during boyhood Nyerere was introduced by his mother and other female relatives into the lore of the community and the spirituality of the society in which he lived. This, Hatch concludes, 'was perhaps the deepest educational experience … [that] can form a permanent foundation for those with the initiative to build a richer, wider life'.[34] Again, this was not particular to Nyerere's childhood.

When Nyerere was asked what he felt were the greatest influences in the early stages of his life, he agreed that his mother and father played a key role. Still, the chiefly title that his father had acquired from the British essentially made him local administrator to the colonial power. Much of Nyerere Burito's energies were taken up in raising manpower, dealing with the running of the local court and in the collection of taxes for the native treasury.[35] Together with the constant worry about his fleeing wives – and his preoccupation with extra-marital activities that may have pushed them to head elsewhere in the first place – the chief would have had little time to spend with his children. Kambarage was just one of his many offspring. The sense is not necessarily one of a big happy household, but rather a couple of armed male assistants and a collection of women who ensured that the chief got what he wanted. Kambarage was closest to his mother. As one of a number of younger wives, Mugaya Nyang'ombe and the others waited on the first wife hand-and-foot, and treated her as their own (rather fearsome) mother. Just like any other young boy at the time in Tanganyika, Kambarage was used to authority, orders and strict discipline.

Nyerere also acknowledged, almost implicitly, the autochthonous roots grown from the seeds planted by home life in the community. What he did not acknowledge directly in his answers about his parents is that as the son of a chief he was inevitably surrounded from birth by the structures of power – however local and limited that power may have been. Just as G. Andrew Maguire notes in his micro-political historical study of Sukumaland, so also in Uzanaki the chiefs were the territory's very first politicians.[36] As much as Nyerere played this down later in life, there is no denying that – leaky roof and empty stomach notwithstanding – his upbringing was relatively privileged, and at home he was brought up in the midst of a deeply political milieu where those around him were in a stronger position than most to quarrel and bargain with European administrators. Nyerere's conclusion on the question of the greatest influences in the early stages of his life was characteristically philosophical, but in an interview in 1983 he still dismissed the significance of his father's chiefly position:

> I think parental influence was the greatest. I was born in a rural area, very poor, in spite of the fact that I am the son of a chief. In spite of this nonsense about being a chief's son, I put on my first clothes the day I was taken to school. I was 12. When you grow up in a rural area like that – in a poor area – but a poor area where all others are poor, there is not this comparative wealth which makes you feel rather bitter. So the atmosphere in which I was brought up was one of basic rural equality.[37]

Nyerere's description of his upbringing in an egalitarian society should be put into perspective. If he were to have compared structures of governance in Uzanaki to those of the more hierarchical and stratified society of the Nyamwezi or Chagga, for example, then this is a plausible synopsis. Yet his comparison is not with different forms of governance across Tanganyika, but with wealth in his local area; and as we have seen, he grew up in a chief's household. Despite his best efforts to play down the relative wealth of Nyerere Burito, his father was not poor. Here there is an element of Nyerere as President seeking to show himself as having been at the level of *wananchi* (ordinary citizens), as a man who has lived the travails of poverty and is comfortable with a spartan existence.[38] But it can also be seen as the statement of a man who at the time of the interview above, in 1983, *was* being relative (albeit unconsciously, perhaps) by putting his experience into ever wider perspectives of, for example, the education, to which he himself was privileged enough to be exposed. While young boys in Tanganyika who went to primary school in the mid-1930s were privileged locally, they were not unusual at Tabora Government School. By the same token, Makerere students' social origins were sophisticated when compared with those of East Africa generally, yet humble compared with students in the western world.[39] So in the perspective of the wider world that Nyerere was fortunate enough to experience, he grew up in a poor family. But in the eyes of a poor woman in Butiama's village of 'basic rural equality', the chief's son was privileged beyond belief.

Kambarage: A Completely Tribal Boy

'Then there was school. Basically one had to learn to read and write, but I cannot say I read some book which influenced me at that stage. Our teachers had influence on us, but the influence of education is very gradual.'[40] This was Nyerere's summary of the beginnings of his formal education, which started when in February 1934 he first attended the Native Administration School at Mwisenge, Musoma.[41] By this time the school had moved from the 'mud-brick affair' where his half-brother Edward had studied, to its present site where a more permanent style of building was erected and boarding houses established.[42] Accounts vary on how Kambarage ended up attending school, but it is clear from them all that his father made the final decision. More than one source suggests that initially Chief Burito felt that one educated son, Edward Wanzagi, was sufficient. He was reluctant to send Kambarage away 'because there were things to do at home, caring for goats and cows'.[43] Later Nyerere had said, 'my father had thought two sons at school were enough' – presumably in reference to Edward Wanzagi and himself.[44]

One account, recalled by Joan Wicken and similar to Hatch's version,[45] was that sometime in early 1934,

> [a] 'District Officer' (British of course) was passing through the vicinity, stopped near a group of boys all of whom except one ran away; the D.O. talked briefly to that boy and at request was taken to his father. He told the Father [sic] that the boy was bright and should go to school, whereupon the Father went to see Chief Burito for advice. The Chief talked about this to his eldest son, Wanzagi. Between them they agreed that it was not politic to ignore what the D.O. said, but the boy should not go to Musoma school alone; Wanzagi said that Kambarage was always wanting to learn to read and write, so why did they not send the two boys – the one originally approached and Kambarage. That is what happened.[46]

In this account the instigation came first from the District Officer. This seems quite plausible in the eyes of Charles Meek, a colonial officer who later got to know Nyerere well.[47] Meek notes that at this time Kambarage, as a herder of goats, would have been contributing usefully to the family economy, and that parents usually resisted in every way the loss of their children's contribution. From the British side, however, 'every administrative officer had experience of the struggle to ensure that school places were fully taken up, and we all preached and cajoled and cozened and bullied to that end. I should be surprised if Chief Nyerere was not pushed by arguments of duty into sacrificing Kambarage.'[48]

Father Arthur Wille, a Maryknoll missionary who spent much of his life in Zanaki country, gives a different version as to why Kambarage was sent to school. Wille introduces Chief Mohamed Makongoro of the neighbouring Ikizu tribe. Makongoro was a frequent visitor to Chief Nyerere Burito, and on some occasions when he came to visit and Burito was busy with his responsibilities as a chief, Kambarage would engage their visitor in *orusoro* (a mancala game, also known as *bao*). Kambarage began to defeat the visiting Makongoro at the game, and one day the visiting chief told Burito that he should send Kambarage to school. It was because of the urging of Makongoro, believes Wille, that Burito sent his son to primary school.[49]

In a similar story, but with a different protagonist, Listowel is of the belief that Kambarage constantly beat Chief Ihunyo of Busegwe at *orusoro*, and that it was Chief Ihunyo who insisted to Burito that his son should be schooled.[50] Chief Ihunyo also features in Hamza Mwenegoha's version, in which Kambarage would plead to his father to send him to Musoma after seeing that his friend Marwa, son of Ihunyo, was attending school there. Chief Ihunyo, along with Chief Marwa Omari Isasia Mang'ombe of Butuguri, would drop by for discussions at the house of their friend Chief Burito, and when Kambarage begged his father to send him to school, he could not refuse.[51]

While these accounts vary in their characters, together we can draw from them that Kambarage was eager to go to school, and that elders were impressed by Kambarage's sharp mind such that they urged Chief Burito – who may initially have been reluctant – to see that his son acquired a formal education. Edward Wanzagi, whose opinion his father respected, very likely played a key role in the chief's final decision. Indeed, at Wanzagi's funeral in 1997, Nyerere acknowledged that his half-brother was responsible for him attending school at all.[52] The idea that Kambarage be sent to school worked for both parties: the British had bagged a future possible administrator for their government; Burito and Wanzagi had secured a future possible heir for their chiefdom. Either way, the decision to educate the young man was a significant milestone in his life. But it may not have occurred in the first place had Nyerere not been the son of a compliant chief.

Musoma & Tabora: Kambarage, Spirit of the Rain

Photo D. Left to right: Oswald Mang'ombe Marwa, Chief Simeon of Ngoreme, Chief Edward Wanzagi Nyerere, (Arthur) Brian Hodgson, Chief Mohammed Makongoro of Ikizu, unknown, Mzee Mato; at the opening of a school and hospital in Mgeta, Ikizu, January 1953. (*Reproduced by kind permission of Samson Wanzagi*)

Kambarage was again more privileged than many of his Butiama contemporaries for whom primary school – if it were desired by their parents, that is – was an unobtainable luxury. Yet in select pockets of Tanganyika basic education was beginning to thrive for the chosen few. By 1934 the White Fathers in their Lake Victoria Nyanza and Tabora vicariates, along with the Holy Ghost Fathers in Bagamoyo and Kilimanjaro, ran the mission schools with by far the highest intake of boys in Tanganyika Territory.[53] Indeed, as early as 1927 the Vicariate of Victoria Nyanza (which at the time included the region south of Lake Victoria) had 210 schools, many of which were native schools, staffed by native teachers.[54] The concentration of pupils attending mission schools was focused in Southern and Iringa Provinces, the latter of which in 1934 had twice as many pupils as Lake Province.[55] What is striking about the distribution of Government and Native Authority schools, however, is that across the eight provinces from 1934 – the year Kambarage first enrolled – more than one-third of the Native Authority schools were in Lake Province, where Native Authority School Musoma was located. The province had the most schools of any type, and also the highest number of boys attending school. (There was no single government girls' school in the province at the time.) Kambarage was located in the area of Tanganyika where the highest proportion of boys studied.[56] Regionally, this made him but one pupil in a proportionally very large elite of young men. The stakes were high, and primary schools pupils were subjected to rigorous assessment among stiff competition.

As Kanyama Chiume put it: 'If one failed to secure one of the few places available in Standard V, one felt condemned to being classed as poorly educated for life.'[57]

In mid-April 1934, Kambarage journeyed the twenty-five or so miles from Butiama to Musoma. He was accompanied by Kitira Buhoro, one of his father's bodyguards, and the two proceeded on foot. Few vehicles took the route, but after some time a lorry passed, Kitira flagged it down, and Kambarage apparently took his first ride in a motor vehicle.[58] At that time the maintenance of pupils was a charge against the native treasuries concerned,[59] so Kambarage's school fees were paid by his father (likely with money raised from local taxes), while Wanzagi contributed his brother's living expenses.[60] On 20 April, a week after his twelfth birthday, Kambarage enrolled in Standard I at Native Authority School Mwisenge and was given the registration number 308.[61] A boy who met him for the first time that day was Selemani Kitundu, who recalls that the son of Chief Burito 'was wearing *rubega* [a robe passing under one arm and slung over the opposite shoulder] and a rag-tag pair of shorts. He was slim, had piercing eyes and was jovial.'[62] Kambarage's closest friend at school was another Zanaki boy called Mang'ombe Marwa, who he knew prior to Mwisenge because his father was Chief Marwa Mang'ombe of Butuguri, Chief Nyerere Burito's friend. Other close companions were John Nyambeho (who he had been circumcised with), and Marwa Ihunyo from Busegwe.[63] Marwa Ihunyo recalls how on weekends he and Kambarage would go hunting, and one day they both aimed at the same bird and killed it together: 'So because of that we called ourselves cousins. … And if we had money we could go to town for tea and buns.'[64]

A month after enrolment the boys were provided with their first school uniforms, consisting of collarless white shirts and khaki shorts. Kitundu was struck by Kambarage's command of arithmetic: 'He was very quick in giving correct answers to sums which he calculated at an incredibly high speed. He also excelled in other subjects, at which he was the best pupil.'[65] After six months the pupils sat an examination in which Kambarage, along with Kitundu, apparently performed so well that they were allowed to skip Standard II and were transferred straight to Standard III. There they were taught by Joshua Gunza, James Irenge and Daniel Kirigini – the former cook of Kambarage's older brother when he attended Mwisenge, and who graduated from Mpwapwa Teacher Training College to become a teacher.

Kirigini, who died in 2002 at the age of 104 years, was similarly responsible for another enrolment at Mpwapwa; that of his colleague James Irenge.[66] Irenge began teaching at Mwisenge the same year as Kambarage started his schooling, and recalled that in those days his pupil was, 'just an ordinary child, but he had an unquenchable thirst for knowledge and a great interest in working in cooperation with others. … It was obvious since his childhood that he was born with certain qualities and had an innate ability to be a role model for others.'[67] Kitundu tells that Kambarage was not arrogant, as other children of chiefs could be, and that he was respectful towards his fellow pupils and the teachers.[68] In one almost Dickensian incident however, Kambarage is said to have stood up to the head teacher, a Herman Abdallah from Lindi. The likes of Abdallah were the African employees of the colonial administration – those 'cultural commuters' whom Andreas Eckert describes as 'at the center of British attempts to impose discipline in school and administration, to regulate time, space, clothing and food – of 'character training', as the British called it.'[69] Abdallah was apparently something of a bully and on one occasion had relieved Kambarage of two shillings, a considerable sum in the mid-1930s. On a later date Abdallah was carrying out an inspection with Irenge, who on that day was Teacher on Duty. The head teacher asked the pupils if they had any complaint, at which point Kambarage asked for his money to be returned. The two shillings were returned, but not before Kambarage was whipped for his troubles.[70] The impression is one of a privileged and precocious young boy with a strong sense of fairness.

True to his subsequent academic life, Kambarage was no sportsman. He preferred his books to the football pitch, and spent most of his free time reading in the dormitory. But despite his best efforts to absorb himself in his studies while his contemporaries were playing, Kambarage's scholastic endeavours only drew him to his fellow pupils, who apparently regarded him as 'our centre of admiration and investigation'.[71] Many of the boys 'spied on his movements and actions, designed to establish the secret of his brilliance', says Kitundu, who recalls one incident where Nyamuhanga Mageta, the prefect in charge of all dormitories, intimidated Kambarage when he was reading: 'The rest of us were playing. Mageta teased Nyerere by telling him that '*Afya ndiyo mali*' ('Health is wealth'); a cynical reference to his slim physique. He did not react emotionally.'[72] In a bid to find an ideal hide-out for undisturbed reading away from provocative pupils, Kambarage explored the Mkinyerero Hill area a short distance away from the school. He acquired some medicine against mosquitoes from a pupil called Masingiri Makoba, and located a cave that he is said to have converted into a private study.[73] Recalling surely some period of his life as a student, Nyerere later gave a speech on the importance and pleasure of reading in which he said: 'Books can break down the isolation of our lives and provide us with a friend wherever we may be.'[74] The irony, of course, is in Nyerere's relative aloofness by becoming a solitary reader of books who was content to detach himself from the other more sports- and social-oriented students.

Kambarage became close to his purveyor of insect repellent, and their friendship developed when they attended Roman Catholic instruction. Along with his friend Mang'ombe Marwa, the boys trekked fourteen miles back and forth to the Nyegina Mission Centre for religious lessons. Kambarage apparently first attended instruction because he was driven by boredom, as Joan Wicken retells:

> Mwalimu once told me – when I specifically asked about it – that at the Musoma primary school he became friends with a boy from another area, and they often did things together. This boy used to go to a Priest every Sunday for 'instruction'; as there was nothing else for him to do, Kambarage took to going with him. After a while, the other boy stopped going to the Priest, but Kambarage continued.[75]

The beginning of Nyerere's exposure to Christianity was 'by accident', as he later explained to Father Wille. When the bell rang for religion class, Mang'ombe grabbed him and said, 'Come we go to study with the padres', and so they went. Marwa soon stopped attending the Roman Catholic instruction (although he was later baptised as Oswald Mang'ombe Marwa),[76] while Nyerere continued.[77] Yet while Nyerere later spoke of the ease in transition from traditional African society to modern secular life – 'I don't believe it is as hard as one might think. … In any case, I'm tolerant of the beliefs of my own people, and of science too' – his religious transition seems to have been more difficult:

> In a sense, if you have become satisfied with one form of life, the question is, How do you make the jump? Almost by what the Christian calls revelation. If you have lived one life and have matured in that life, it is very difficult to make such a leap from Hinduism to Christianity – even, I think from Protestantism to Catholicism. My confirmation in tribal life was never wiped out. As a boy of twelve, I already had beliefs I had accepted, I had to be convinced before I could accept a different kind of faith, a faith in a defined God.[78]

When Nyerere later explained his transition from traditional beliefs to Christianity, he used as an analogy an early experience from his youth when a relative used 'magic' to succeed in getting a balking goat to become more docile and to follow him: 'All I know is, the goat followed. The maximum I can say is: I don't know [what influence the 'magic' had on the unwilling being].'[79] This slightly enigmatic statement has been interpreted to mean that when Nyerere was confronted at an early age with the choice between 'tribalism' and Christianity, he decided to become a Christian, but that he was unable to give an exact reason as to why he made the change.[80] The inference is that the young Nyerere was drawn to this new faith by some unseen power; the work of God, as many believers would proclaim. From the theological perspective, as Brian Stanley explains, one 'cannot rest content with any understanding of conversion to Christ as purely a matter of human agency, whether on the part of the evangelist or the convert…. [C]onversion to Christ requires the agency of the Spirit.'[81]

Kambarage's spiritual influences had hitherto been similar to that of many other young boys and girls in colonial Tanganyika. From 'old-fashioned and ignorant' parents, as he later announced with undoubted reference to his own upbringing, he believed that the young child 'absorbs beliefs about witchcraft before he goes to school'.[82] Yet the new monotheist religion with its foreign God was difficult for his animist father to comprehend. While the chief had conceded to the wishes of those who insisted that his son receive an education, he still, like Thompson Samkange's father, 'scorned both church and school'.[83] To Nyerere Burito of Uzanaki, as to his counterparts in Ukimbu, 'the ancestors are the real wielders of power in the chiefdom, and the reigning chief is merely their representative who is granted a limited share in their power'.[84] From the chief's perspective, the obscure God of the Europeans posed a threat to power which, while endorsed by the colonial administration at their territorial level, for him was a power that lay with the ancestors at the local level. Worship of the *amasaambwa* (see Chapter 1) was crucial to Nyerere Burito in maintaining authority across his chiefdom. Respect to the white man's God, on the other hand, risked the chief losing control over the people and their land; and, by extension, he then risked losing control over his wealth and authority. It also put his educated son at danger because Kambarage's interaction with missionaries and assimilation to their alien identity made Kambarage susceptible to the loss of his spiritual agency.[85] Worse still, as Frederick Cooper summarises, Christianity was 'focused on the individual, shunting aside kinship groups, councils of elders, age groups, and other collectivities basic to African social life'.[86] These were institutions that the young Nyerere was familiar with from Uzanaki, but his increasing distance from them meant that any future plans Burito may have had for his son to come back to a governing role in village life would have to be put on hold. There was also the risk of losing Kambarage to become the white man's proselytiser, for in the Roman Catholic church that his son had engaged with during his education, 'vocations to the priesthood were detected among primary-school pupils'.[87] Unlike the government schools, which were interested in creating administrators and clerks for local and central government, the conscious aim of the missions was to prepare Africans for ordination.[88] Catholic and Protestant missionaries alike looked forward to the time when their educated young men, fully instructed in the Word of God, would spread out into the villages and preach it with the full wealth of African metaphor and simile.[89] The missionaries were generally suspicious of chiefs such as Burito, who presented old ways. In time the missionaries made the claim that the chiefs did not truly reflect African public opinion. As Cameron and Dodd have observed, 'this suspicion planted some of the seeds of the attitude towards traditional authority which was adopted by the

African politicians who came into power a generation later'.[90]

As Kambarage's father soon realised, the decision that he attend European school first exposed his son to influences beyond the localised beliefs of Butiama. In the village, Kambarage was insulated from the wider world, contained by the local spirits and the associated moral rules within the microcosm of the immediate community.[91] When he travelled to school and stayed there for months on end, the boundaries of the microcosm ceased to confine him; he became aware of the missionaries' supreme being of the macrocosm, rationalised by a fascinating narrative offered by the white man. The new narrative provided an intellectual challenge to the young Nyerere. As it won him over, so it also challenged his own father's directive to adhere to the local beliefs of his village. Kambarage attended instruction nonetheless, well aware that doing so would incur his father's wrath. The situation was similar to that of the Tanganyikan Jeremiah Kissula – later a Bishop – whose parents were strongly entrenched in the traditional beliefs and practices. 'When his father heard of the conversion he roared with fury,' documents D.N.M. Ng'hosha, 'for the new faith was anathema to him. Kissula was ordered to abandon the "white man's faith".'[92] The young Nyerere took no such action, and ignored his father by turning to the coloniser's God.

We simply do not know whether Kambarage actively engaged in any traditional religion before he attended Catholic instruction. It therefore cannot be said for sure whether he actually substituted one religion for another. But we do know that Nyerere's exposure to Christianity occurred as he was entering his teenage years, a time when the adolescent mind is prone to first exploring new experiences in the wider world – be it, in Kambarage's case, by either simply accompanying Mang'ombe Marwa on walks to religious instruction well beyond the confines of the school compound, or perhaps in a conscious bid to question the beliefs that had been ascribed to him in the village.

The compelling Christian narrative that Kambarage received in Musoma was delivered by the White Fathers, European priests who were more compassionate and reasonable than the colonial officials he had experienced in Butiama. They were instructed by a constitution that urged them to 'adopt all the exterior customs of the natives, speak their language, wear the same kind of clothes, and eat the same food'.[93] Urged on by the philosophy of deep Africanisation adopted by their founder Cardinal Lavigerie, many White Fathers 'were outstanding linguists and highly knowledgeable about local customs and history. They lived a good deal closer to village life than did most other missionaries.'[94] The White Fathers were in missions, with a medical dispensary and well-kept farms that provided Nyerere with a memorable image of order and harmony. It remained with him when he later encouraged Tanzanians to build self-reliant settlements. Although the White Fathers dressed in distinctive white cassocks – 'a habit modelled on the *djellaba* and *burnous* [cloaks] of the North African desert'[95] – in the main these disciplined men were gentle Europeans who tolerated the questioning African mind. Compared with the colonialists who barked orders and distanced themselves from Africans in their impenetrable enclaves of segregation, the simple White Fathers of Musoma were approachable and far more relatable. The young Nyerere may have had little choice as to which denomination to follow, but the effect on him of being under the wing of the Catholic White Fathers is that he spent time with Europeans who, in contrast to the Anglicans, were sufficiently differentiated from the British rulers.[96] As foreigners themselves, Kambarage's new acquaintances were distant from the regime, and were keen to maintain a separation from the rulers.[97]

A more significant pull factor towards Christianity however, was that – irrespective of the denomination – it offered education to the ambitious. 'By joining with the missionaries,' believed Leonard Mwaisumo, 'I will have the opportunity to learn very quickly at school.' As Sekibakiba Lekgoathi, Timo Mwakasekele and Andrew Bank have concluded,

> It was a decision Mwaisumo took for practical reasons 'to advantage his educational ambitions.' As he saw things then, 'it was more difficult for those people or children who were not Christians to get a better education than those who had already registered with missionaries.' Leonard's view of Christianity was therefore pragmatic. He saw the religion as a vehicle for accessing education and securing a place within the tiny but influential new African elite.[98]

Whether or not at some point Kambarage's gravitation to the white man's religion was also purposefully instrumentalist, there is no doubt that it provided openings. Christianity offered educational opportunity, helping to satisfy a sharp and engaging mind. The alternative was poor schooling, or none at all, as Nyerere later wrote, perhaps with his own situation in mind: 'The days when our people chose between accepting the Christian religion or remaining uneducated have now gone.'[99] Of course Christianity also provided spiritual motivation – the hope of heaven and the fear of hell. As Monica (Wilson) Hunter noted of Nyakyusa: Life after death is the usual reason for conversion.[100]

Summarising his introduction to Christianity, Nyerere later began with another example where he sought to emphasise his relatively humble roots:

> I was a completely tribal boy. But … I was the friend of a neighbouring chief's son, who said, 'Why don't you come with me to my [religious instruction] class?' So I went. But I used to protest to him about this peculiar teaching. I told him I couldn't believe in this bearded man, and I felt we should only worship the gods we knew.[101]

Nyerere

What may well have given away Kambarage's 'tribal' background was his filed teeth, the result of a procedure that he underwent with his *bhakisero* age-mate, John Nyambeho: 'It was a fashion … Mwalimu did it voluntarily. He had to confirm to the society that he was wanting to be accepted by them. … It was very painful. But if you did not do it, you could not get a girlfriend!'[102] Whether Nyerere decided to have his upper-front teeth filed into a triangular shape because he wanted to entice girls is irrelevant. Teeth filing, and the associated desire for young men to demonstrate to their community that they wanted to be accepted by it, brings to mind the motivations of typical adolescent boys with a full life ahead of them. John Nyambeho, Kambarage Nyerere and their Zanaki contemporaries had no choice over their circumcision, but they could make a statement in accepting a potentially more painful dare that exhibited their stoicism as long as they lived, and forever identified them as Zanaki. It may have been around this time that Kambarage also took up smoking, a habit that he embraced with gusto for a number of decades.[103] 'The bearded man' introducing the young Kambarage to a new religion had much work to do.

Competing with Christianity for Kambarage's interest and time was further study. This took place under the instruction of James Irenge, who had first taught Kambarage formally in Standard III. Under the pretext of learning what they did not understand in class, Irenge would apparently invite some of his more inquisitive students to his home in the evenings. Kambarage would sometimes attend, and they discussed history, geography and arithmetic. The conversation also got on to politics, which the colonial authorities forbade in the classroom. As Irenge put it much later in an interview:

> Kambarage would come with his friends and they would sit at the table, and I would sit on the bed … I was teaching them a certain 'special' subject of politics, of history, of things of the past and how they were, and how we would be able to govern for ourselves … I was telling them we should remove the foreigners … 'Guns by themselves, and cannon, we can't use. We are not experts with them … We'll use another way, of just the lips.' … If I had taught these things in class I would have been fired, or hung, by the colonialists.[104]

Irenge believed he planted the seed of independence in the mind of the young Kambarage. He claimed to have demonstrated how 'militarism of the tongue' might work, telling the fifteen year-old stories of the small birds who defend their nests against crows by flocking and dive bombing the invaders. When his young charges protested at his proposition that 'the way of the lips' could defeat colonial military force, Bjerk recounts how Irenge continued with his fairy tales, picturing African people as a blind mass to be united when they learned to see for themselves.[105]

In Bjerk's analysis of the establishment of sovereignty in Tanganyika he suggests that – to the extent that Irenge's memories represent an accurate portrait of his influence on the future Father of the Nation – we can take these ideas to be ingredients of Nyerere's early political thought.[106] There is of course an obvious case for scepticism here, since there were incentives – not least the prestige – for a man to claim to be the one to have taught Nyerere his politics. One should therefore be wary of taking all of Irenge's word at face value. Yet his claim is not entirely unbelievable when set aside similar accounts from elsewhere in Africa around this time. For example, Aminu Kano was a teacher in his earlier life and his 'students flocked to [his] house after hours, where they would discuss extracurricular matters well beyond the daily curriculum'.[107] Closer to home, Kanyama Chiume records that his mathematics and science teacher at Dar es Salaam Central School was also in on the game. As he puts it, Mwalimu Joseph Matovu – who was later in United Kingdom at same time as Nyerere – 'used to take us home and give us some political lessons'.[108] These accounts suggest that teachers would whisper 'the secret of politics'[109] with their students, and that Irenge's story was not entirely fabricated.

Kambarage completed his studies at Mwisenge in 1936.[110] In his concluding exams at the end of his primary schooling he came first among all the pupils in the then Lake Province and Western Province.[111] Commenting on Kambarage's school days, his mother later said that she noticed a change in her child after he started school: 'He was still considerate and helped me during the holidays, but he seemed always deep in thought.'[112] This was also expressed by his friend Selemani Kitundu who remarked that despite Kambarage's joviality, 'quite often, he was in a pensive mood, reflecting deep thoughts'.[113] His friends at home said that despite his new love of reading, he would still herd goats and cattle with them as before he left for Musoma. But he would stop every so often and teach them to read and write by using the sand on the ground in place of a blackboard.[114] Aged fourteen, the signs pointed to Nyerere as a teacher in the making.

Tabora Boys: Town and Gown

Kambarage was apparently bored by the lack of learning and challenge at primary school.[115] In 1936 he came top in the highly selective territorial examination. The following year he received a government scholarship – a terrific achievement in itself – and then passed through the incredibly competitive admission of the elite Tabora Government School.[116] A student who was accepted at Tabora found himself in a special environment, as one former pupil explained: 'Life was better here than before; we had food, blankets, and even a bed and sheets.'[117] This was in contrast to earlier school, which another erstwhile student recalled in none-too flattering terms: 'We slept on the floor and had to cook our food and do manual work. ... I liked secondary school because there was more respect for students than primary school where beating as a method of making a pupil understand was used.'[118] Professor Julian Huxley – a celebrated evolutionary biologist who visited East Africa in 1929 to advise the Colonial Office on education, whose lectures Nyerere later studied in Edinburgh,[119] and himself an Old Etonian – described the government secondary school at Tabora as 'the Eton of Tanganyika'.[120] Nyerere drew the same parallel, describing 'Tabora Boys', as Tabora Government School was often called, as being 'as close to Eton as it could have been in Africa – fagging, sportsmanship, fair play, all that. If you went through it for six years, and succeeded, that was really something.'[121] As one British staff member described Tabora Boys: 'It had great status and reputation. The buildings were large and imposing. The older Italianate Lower school dated from 1926 being a double storey structure set round an open quadrangle; the Upper school, completed during the war, single storey in quadrangle form. Wide playing field[s] surrounded the school.'[122]

To all intents and purposes, Tabora Boys was an English public school in Africa. This was the result of the efforts of Stanley Rivers-Smith, the territory's long-serving Director of Education who willingly supported the missions' idea of importing the English public school spirit to Tanganyika. He saw it as a contribution to Governor Cameron's system of indirect rule, and stated that in the schools for the sons of chiefs (such as Tabora Boys), 'the Prefect System made possible the full realization of the British ideal to delegate authority to those who by heredity ought to possess and exercise it.'[123] To these ends, among the trappings of the English public school that Huxley mentions were, 'the standard educational grounding, as well as a taste for football, a good deal of discipline, and a real esprit de corps. In addition, special attention is given to what may be useful to [pupils] later. For instance, they are taught the use of ploughs.'[124]

Huxley was writing a little before Nyerere's arrival at Tabora Boys, although the basic curriculum seems to have changed little over the next decades. Almost twenty years later, it was officially stated that African secondary education 'prepares pupils for the Cambridge School Certificate examination as a qualification for higher educational studies'.[125] This included the staples of Mathematics, Science and English classes, during which Nyerere was first introduced to the writings of Booker T. Washington.[126] Sporting excellence was alongside the British elitist school tradition of privilege that these young men were exposed to, but sport was still not one of Kambarage's interests.[127] In the Boy Scouts he became a Patrol Leader and a Rover Scout,[128] but a fellow student commented how later at Makerere College Nyerere 'did not play games and he did not go to dances. … The usual pursuits of young people held no attractions to him'.[129] At Tabora Boys football was obligatory, but Nyerere was unlikely then to have taken up with much enthusiasm some of the other typical English public school sports that were on offer, among them hockey, boxing and the highly idiosyncratic game of Eton fives.[130] His preferred pastime of *bao* was played by the pupils, but only in between the typical chores of sweeping, cutting the grass and collecting water.[131] All movements were closely monitored by frequent roll calls, and the boys were kept on their toes by regular military-style inspection parades below the 'Union Jack', flag of the colonial masters.[132]

From 1935 gifted commoners could also sit for Tabora's entrance examination, meaning that some of the most promising young Africans from all parts of Tanganyika went there.[133] Whatever their background, all of the pupils knew what a great achievement it was to be at Tabora Boys. From 1947–48 select pupils at Tabora Government School, along with those at St Mary's Tabora and St Andrew's Minaki, began to take the prestigious Cambridge School Certificate.[134] The attainment again emphasises the status of Tabora Boys, but this also needs to be put into the regional perspective. Schools in Kenya and Uganda had begun offering the Cambridge School Certificate almost a decade earlier.[135] Tabora Boys was excellent – as everyone kept on saying – but it was certainly not the equivalent of Kenya's Alliance High School, which at independence accounted for ten of the seventeen ministers in the Kenyan cabinet, nine of the fourteen permanent secretaries and the posts of Attorney-General, Chief Justice and Commissioner for Police and Prisons.[136] Tabora did provide cabinet ministers and permanent secretaries in the immediate post-independence period, but a significant number of former pupils who reached these positions of authority had attended Malangali, Tanga, Minaki, Ikuzu, Likoma, and St Joseph's schools, while others had four years of schooling at Ilboru, Alliance High School (Tanganyika) and Dodoma schools before proceeding to Tabora for two years. Tabora was important to Tanganyika but, compared with Kenya, the territory had a more varied background than a single school.[137] Tabora was certainly an elite school for Tanganyika but, as Tom Cadogan rightly stresses, it must be viewed in relation to its institutional counterparts, not set apart.[138]

Nevertheless, the sense of elitism that the grandeur of Tabora Boys generated throughout Tanganyika must surely have affected the pupils. Certainly it happened elsewhere in Africa, where the hubris and arrogance of the English public school appears to have made its way to the continent unencumbered.[139] It cannot be known for sure whether

Kambarage also felt a certain pride at being one of the chosen few, nor whether he showed it at times. There is nothing from the scant evidence to suggest that he joined in with the snobbery, although his contemporaries' later accounts of the Father of the Nation's schooldays are too adulatory to deal with such embarrassments to the official record. That said, there is nothing about Kambarage's character at this time to suggest that he thought he was any better than other pupils, or superior to those less fortunate than him in receiving an elite education. Rather, through long periods of voracious reading alone, it appears that the young Nyerere turned his back on any opportunity to waste his time engaging in the baser pursuits of pretention or disdain. This in itself could indicate a certain arrogance towards his contemporaries – a desire to deal with more important matters in splendid isolation – and mark him out as a loner who shunned batting for the team. Instead the picture that emerges is one of a studious pupil who was comfortable in his own company. Diminutive in stature even in his teenage years, he simply had no appetite for being bashed around on the sports ground. But Kambarage did throw himself wholeheartedly into Boy Scouting which, according to Leander Stirling, he took the lead (with Emmanuel Kibira) in introducing to Tabora Boys. True to form, he managed this only after reading a manual (*Scouting for Boys*, alone). With his bookish knowledge and – undoubtedly, a carefully prepared pitch – he is said to have convinced the headmaster to assign a number of teachers to serve as scoutmasters.[140] Unlike many contact sports, the Boy Scouts was a voluntary pursuit over which, as its joint-initiator, Kambarage had a measure of control. For his new venture to succeed however, he needed to convince his fellow pupils to get involved – which, like *ujamaa* later, he managed to a degree.

Lacking the physique required for more brutal pastimes such as boxing, the young Nyerere stirred the schoolboy masses and generated a self-sustaining esprit de corps in scouting; a proto-National Service (of sorts). His love was always reading – and, a little later, debating – and he spent some of his happiest hours eagerly devouring literature. He knew that through assiduous study he could excel academically, and simply found it most productive to study alone. This attitude points to Nyerere's personal independence and self-belief, and to a strong conviction that if he was going to succeed, he should best go it alone.

From the late 1920s into the 1930s Tabora Boys educated the likes of Adam Sapi Mkwawa, Abdallah Said Fundikira, Humi Ziota, Haroun Lugusha, David Kidaha Makwaia, Thomas Lenana Marealle, Patrick Kunambi and John Ndaskoi Maruma.[141] Among Nyerere's contemporaries were Joseph Adolf Sawe and Dunstan Omari, both of whom he was to meet later when they were studying in the United Kingdom. Adam Marwa recalls how at Tabora Boys, 'Omari was very brilliant, but he used to be sick after exams and worry about his progress, and Nyerere would console him.'[142] It was at this time that Kambarage also met for the first time another future political figure, Vedastus Kyaruzi, who was attending St Mary's School, also in Tabora.[143]

Kambarage's father was among a group of chiefs who were taken on a tour of Tabora Boys in 1938. The purpose of the visit is not clear, but the combination of a delegation of chiefs at the leading school where many of their sons were being educated was weighty enough to warrant the presence of the Governor.[144] A district officer, writing at the time when Kambarage was studying there, described the elite institution as, 'an aristocratic school, confined to the sons of Government and Native Authority employees and of a few rich men … with the result that a far greater disparity is growing up between them and the rest of the community than existed under primitive tribal conditions'.[145] Tabora town had been an important trading station since the early nineteenth century and its material and social inequality of fabulous wealth alongside grinding poverty was new to Kambarage, at least at this scale.[146] Among Kambarage's school duties was cleaning the faculty room, to which he had access. Apparently in a bid to learn English to a very high standard, he used this access as an opportunity to 'borrow' books from the faculty library. The budding scholar was soon caught red-handed, and when apprehended explained to the master that he was trying to improve his English by reading as much as possible. Recognising the truth, it is said, the teacher told Kambarage that his own library was superior for these purposes, and thereafter allowed him to borrow his personal books.[147] Another master – or perhaps the same one, in a books-for-tuition deal – assigned Kambarage 'to give voluntary evening tuition to his dull son who was Mwalimu's class-mate.'[148]

In another incident passed on to Father Wille by Nyerere, Kambarage came across a student whose hands had been tied by a prefect. He protested to the headmaster, who sided with the prefect and ordered Kambarage himself to administer four strokes of the cane. Kambarage obeyed his orders, but apparently with little enthusiasm. He was prefect of 'Kifaru' (later 'Blumer') house, having been given the job of Junior House Prefect already within a year of beginning at Tabora Boys.[149] He was later recommended by the teachers to be head prefect, but the promotion was vetoed by the headmaster who 'felt he was too kind for the job'.[150] Wille also explains how on another occasion Kambarage protested to the headmaster against the custom for prefects to receive twice as much food as the other students. By Julius' intervention, Wille gushes, 'once again his sense of justice came to the fore'.[151] If the accounts of these incidents are accepted at face value, then they are yet further cumulative evidence of Nyerere's exemplary character as a youth through his defence of the less privileged. But what these morality tales

Nyerere

Photo E. Julius Nyerere and other senior pupils, Tabora Boys, c.1942. Nyerere is sitting third from right, beside E.S. Williams, the headmaster.
(*Reproduced by kind permission of the Acting Director General, National Museum of Tanzania*)

also emphasise is the need for scepticism over what informants deem important to pass on – in this case, both what the 'blue-eyed boy' wanted to share about his early life, and what Wille felt necessary to preserve.

Between fagging, cleaning the faculty room, avidly reading and occasionally punishing wayward scholars, Kambarage set aside time for debating. The beginnings of the 'English Debating Society', to use its correct name, are not well documented. On the face of it, Ramadhani Kilongola's 'Historia ya Mwalimu Julius Kambarage Nyerere' provides much tempting detail on Kambarage's involvement in debating when studying at Tabora Boys. It apparently covers his years as a pupil, although it is exceptionally anachronistic in nature. (Its content in fact discusses a later period when Nyerere was a teacher at Tabora St. Mary's, and not when he was a student.) Without access to the original sources, one cannot be so certain about the veracity of all of Kilongola's verbatim quotations. Equally dubious is Smith's statement that Kambarage actually founded the debating club himself.[152] This is improbable. It is one thing for a young man to press for scouting to be taken up at school, but quite something else for a lone junior pupil in a tightly controlled public school environment to have established such an important institution as the school debating society – not least since

Nyerere's profile was so low at the time that Andrew Tibandebage did not remember him being at Tabora at all.[153]

Whether or not Kambarage actually founded the English Debating Society, there is no doubt that he heavily involved himself in it. This was a time when debating clubs were beginning to gather pace across East Africa. Alliance High School's inaugural debate ('Should Germany's colonial claims be accepted by Britain?') took place in 1939.[154] Formal debates were first allowed in 1942 at Dar es Salaam Central School. As Kanyama Chiume recalls of his time there, the bitterness towards Europeans 'was reflected in the school debates…. [and] within the limits imposed by school discipline, we were able to air our views.'[155]

Debating allowed pupils to develop their thoughts about issues of the day, and to present them in a cogent argument. Yet as Isabel Hofmeyr reminds us of the Lovedale Mission in South Africa, 'debating always has a potentially radical edge to it…. [It] draws together those in similar circumstances and allows them a chance to share and analyse their problems, refine their discourses, and sharpen their grievances.'[156] The British were well aware of this but, from the perspective of some educators, debating also acted as an escape valve for aggrieved young men to let off steam – the floor serving as the academic equivalent of the sports field. When Kambarage took the floor he is said to have come across as clear, intelligent and persuasive.[157] As with other young African men who later entered politics (among them Kwame Nkrumah and Tom Mboya), for Nyerere school debates first provided the opportunity to discover his aptitude for oration – a skill that he honed in subsequent years debating in Uganda, Scotland and then back in Tanganyika.[158]

During Kambarage's final year at Tabora, in March 1942, his father Nyerere Burito died. He had been ill for some time, so it is probable that the chief's health was discussed with Kambarage six months earlier when some guests from Butiama visited him at school on behalf of the chief.[159] In a decision that would surely have embittered the young scholar in at least the short term, Nyerere was refused permission to travel from Tabora to Butiama to attend his father's burial. Barely out of his teenage years and prevented from saying goodbye to his father in person, Kambarage had to rely on second-hand accounts of the days surrounding the ceremony at Mwitongo. As some of those who attended the events have passed down, drums were beaten to indicate the death of the chief, and almost the entire village of Butiama attended the funeral. All the Zanaki chiefs were in attendance. As is customary for Zanaki chiefs, Nyerere Burito was buried sitting down. Jack Nyamwaga, aged five years old at the time, did not understand that the chief had died and recalls creeping into Mwitongo to investigate the fuss. Hoping while he was there to greet the elderly chief who used to give him milk, he tracked his friend down to the burial plot. Preparing to ask the seated corpse for

Nyerere

Photo F. The Tabora Boys prize shield won by Nyerere inscribed, in Swahili: 'Hardworking student, 1937–1942, Kambarage Nyerere'. 'Julius', in brackets, appears to have been added later.
(*Reproduced by kind permission of the Acting Director General, National Museum of Tanzania*)

a cup of his favourite drink, he was spotted by some angry mourners and chased away from Chief Nyerere Burito's final resting place.[160]

The 'gentlemanly ancient' was eighty-two years of age when he died, and was apparently well-respected in Uzanaki. He had accomplished much for those under his chiefship – not least by agreeing to the schooling of his son Edward Wanzagi Nyerere, whose progressive approach to the chiefship that he took after his father's death had a tremendous impact on Butiama and the schooling of his younger half-brother Kambarage, whose academic future was now looking brighter than ever. Wanzagi the '*akili*',[161] or chief's deputy or counsel, dealt in the more complicated administrative matters of the day. In his capacity as adviser under the late chief, he was neither the 'traditional' ruler that his father was, nor was he an African official on the payroll of the foreign regime – one of 'the hidden linchpins of colonial rule', as it has been put.[162] Kambarage was close to Wanzagi, and over time he witnessed his older half-brother's interactions with the British. He slowly became aware that Africans could operate within a more modern administration than that of their father. The educated brothers – Wanzagi the more worldly, experienced and sophisticated of the two and Kambarage his inquisitive protégé – were able to discuss school life and their hopes for the future. In many ways their affinity was similar to that of Léopold Sédar Senghor – the most prominent Francophone African intellectual of his generation, and the primary spokesman for *négritude* – and his half-brother René Senghor. In this respect Janet Vaillant's description of the relationship between the two Senegalese brothers bears an uncanny resemblance to that of Wanzagi and Kambarage around the same time of rapid change on the continent, in British and in French Africa alike. In both cases the older half-brother (René and Wanzagi) realised the shortcomings of their father (Diogoye and Burito) in the modern world, and mentored his younger sibling. The welfare of Sédar, writes Vaillant, was increasingly taken responsibility of by René: 'It was he who visited Sédar's teachers, inquired into his progress, and puzzled about the future of this studious half-brother. In several ways he was better placed for this task than his father. Not only was he younger … but he knew the French world far better than [their father] Diogoye did.'[163]

Some seven months after Nyerere Burito's funeral in Mwitongo, in September 1942, staff from Makerere College came to Tabora Boys and are said to have told Kambarage that he should apply to continue with his studies at their institution. The following month he completed his secondary studies in Tabora and boarded a Mwanza-bound train for his journey home.[164]

3
Makerere
Becoming Julius

In societies lacking centralized government,
social values cannot be symbolized by a single person.

From an introductory text on African political systems,
listed in Nyerere's Social Anthropology reading list at Edinburgh[1]

This chapter opens with Nyerere's baptism in the Catholic church, his adoption of the name 'Julius', and his entry to Makerere College in Uganda. It considers Makerere's academic environment, Nyerere's exposure to a wider student body from Eastern and Southern Africa, and his enthusiasm for debating. An analysis is then given of Nyerere's first known published work of a political nature. The chapter considers his activities as a Catholic in Uganda, as well as his early interaction with a number of Tanganyikans with whom he maintained political ties. It closes with an analysis of Nyerere's activities in a Makerere-based student organisation concerned with the socio-political interests of Tanganyikans. The evidence is drawn from contemporary sources, including a document on African socialism, authored by Nyerere, that has hitherto not been examined in any detail.

Back to Nyegina

Sometime shortly after his return home to Butiama, Kambarage travelled to Nyegina Mission, eight miles from Musoma. Founded by the White Fathers who established themselves on Ukerewe Island in Lake Victoria in 1893, Nyegina Mission was built in 1911 after the missionaries made journeys to maintain contact with those converts who had returned to their inland homes as the great Hunger of the Feet famine of 1894 abated.[2] The further purpose of the Nyegina venture was to reach Christians in Ikizu, Ngoreme, Zanaki, Majita and Ruri.[3] By 1936, the (French) White Fathers Roman Catholic Mission had a nine-acre plot with a brick church, a boys' school and medical centre.[4] Kambarage spoke with the Missionaries of Africa pastor Father Matthias Könen, and asked him for baptism.[5] Father Könen refused, explaining to his visitor that baptism was sacred and required special preparation in order to receive it. Despite Kambarage's reply that he had already been a catechumen for ten years and knew it well, Father Könen insisted that he be prepared for baptism by a catechist.[6] It is feasible that Könen was wary of the stranger, a chief's son and his father's possible successor, at a time when it was a common assumption that chiefs were all polygamous and could therefore not be Christian. Petro Maswe Marwa, a catechist who was formally uneducated, taught the young scholar.[7]

In November 1942 Nyerere took the entrance examination for Uganda's Makerere College, one of the continent's most prestigious higher education institutions.[8] With the backing of his former Headmaster at Tabora Boys, E.S. Williams,[9] Nyerere then obtained a bursary to study a teacher training course the following year.[10]

With his father's demise Kambarage was free to be accepted in the Catholic Church. This was something that the late Chief Nyerere Burito, a polytheist, had disapproved of, as Joan Wicken explains: 'Mwalimu did not say much about visiting a Priest or Priests in Tabora, but he did say that he decided to become a Catholic while he was at Tabora Secondary School, but would not 'enter' while his Father was alive, because it would upset his father.'[11] On 23 December 1943 Father Aloysius Junker, also a White Father, baptised Kambarage in the chapel of the Nyegina Catholic Mission.[12] At this point Kambarage became the first person in Butiama to be baptised a Roman Catholic. Indeed, he was one of the first Zanaki to be baptised a Roman Catholic[13] – although it is thought that Mwalimu's friend Oswald Mang'ombe Marwa, who became a teacher before him, may also have been baptised earlier.[14]

The lack of local Catholic men, however, meant that Nyerere had to find a godfather from outside Uzanaki. He chose Petro Maswe Marwa, his catechist from the Ngoreme tribe. Kambarage Nyerere was now Julius Kambarage Nyerere, an enforced change of name that apparently irritated him but by which he wished to be known thereafter.[15] This contrasts with the opinion of a much closer informant, one of Nyerere's sons, who recalls that his father was proud to have a Catholic Christian name: 'If he had doubts over the name, then it may have been a later reflection, after studying Julius Caesar.'[16] Jack Nyamwaga, another educated local source, is of a similar opinion. Nyamwaga recalls that in a conversation he had with Nyerere about his name: 'Mwalimu said, "I became Julius – but Julius [Caesar] wasn't a Christian!" But he wasn't sorry about it. ... Mwalimu was old enough to choose his name by then – he had completed Class Ten at Tabora and was over twenty years old, so it was his decision. He wasn't sorry about being called Julius. He was very proud of the name.'[17] There is of course absolutely no question that a Catholic would be named after the wicked heathen Gaius Julius Caesar. He is more likely to have been named after one of the four martyred saints called Julius (the better-known being Julius of Caerleon and Julius the Veteran), or named after Julius I ('Iulius'), pontiff from 337–352 and, of the three popes called Julius, the only saint.[18]

Though filled with pride at being accepted into the Roman Catholic Church and knowing that he was soon heading to another country to undertake studies at tertiary level, the recent passing of his father also marks the early 1940s as a time of loss for Julius Nyerere. Of all his siblings to turn to at this time, Julius was said to be particularly close to one brother, also called Burito.[19] Thought to be the first son of Chief Nyerere Burito and his third wife Nyanjiga Samba, little is known about this Burito Nyerere other than that he had a serious character, he was rumoured to be *persona non grata* in Butiama after allegedly fornicating with one of his father's wives and – like a great number of men from Musoma District – he served in the King's African Rifles.[20] Burito died towards the end of the war in inglorious circumstances, apparently after falling from a train while on his way to Butiama. Still less is known about the discussions between Julius and this closest brother, although Burito would have certainly shared his stories of adventures in foreign lands – and perhaps reflections on homeland, travel and identity that in other African soldiers (*askari*s) is said to have inspired a wider vision of anti-colonial nationalism.[21] Julius would also have been well aware that his brother was only on the train that he fell from because he had been fighting the white man's battles. He was soon to publicly denounce the 'abominable war'.

Julius was also leaving his country for the first time. In January 1943 he took a ship from Bukoba in north-western Tanganyika to Port Bell in Uganda where, en route to Makerere College, he had his first encounter with Andrew Tibandebage.[22] The two sat next to each other on the train to Kampala, but Tibandebage recalls how the conversation on this first meeting was halting:

> At St Mary's I had neither seen him nor heard about him; for he was not an outstanding footballer or an athlete, nor even a member of Tabora School's brass band. … Handsome and given to smiling faintly, he talked but little and appeared to be that sort of imitator who cannot exchange a word before the English formal introduction. Slightly turning left, I said to him: 'I think you are Kambarage'. 'Yes', he said, smiling a little. That day we talked no more.[23]

JUKANYE

Nyerere was aged twenty-two when he arrived at Makerere College. Godfrey Kayamba had been the first Tanganyikan to attend.[24] Founded in 1922, the initial purpose of the institution was to instruct Ugandan students in Medicine, Agriculture, Veterinary Science, Elementary Engineering and Survey, and Teacher Training. By 1929 'it was accepted that higher education for Africans of the Eastern African territories should be centred at Makerere'.[25] Another reason for developing the institution was to prevent East Africans absorbing subversive ideas at foreign universities.[26] This, it could be argued, Makerere failed to do. The academic environment was apparently one that encouraged staff and students to forge intellectual relationships across the racial divide, allowing for the crafting of individual identities appropriate to a liberal Oxbridge-type environment.[27] It was a new concept for colonial East Africa, and it undoubtedly took some time for the racialised legacy of 'native' education to subside.[28]

Makerere's relatively more progressive pedagogic attitude introduced Nyerere to a new world inhabited by the very best young men – and later, women – from the entire region. The institution attracted the strongest students from a cross-section of the best secondary schools in East Africa, among them Alliance High School, Kakamega and Maseno (Kenya); King's College Budo and Namilyango (Uganda); and Tanganyika's St Mary's (Tabora, which served Catholics) and Minaki (Kisarawe, formerly St Andrew's College Kiungani, which served Anglicans).[29] The academic competition between the many gifted and ambitious young Africans was fierce,[30] such that for one medical student the pressure to succeed was so great that, after failing to make the grade, he committed suicide.[31] The student-lecturer ratio was particularly favourable when Nyerere joined in 1943, the enrolment of 141 new students down from well above 200 in 1939. The overall number of new entrants had not been this low since 1928, although the number of new students from beyond Kenya and Uganda was healthy. In Nyerere's first year, five new students from Tanganyika attended, along with five from Zanzibar. The following year then saw the first Makerere students from Northern Rhodesia and Nyasaland. This introduced the young Nyerere to an even wider perspective of experiences beyond East Africa.[32] Despite attracting the best students however, there were misgivings about their quality.[33] This appears not to have bothered the students though, and even as late as the mid-1960s one commentator still referred to the products of Makerere as the 'presumptive elite'.[34]

At Makerere, Julius rubbed shoulders with the sons of Tanganyika's nobility. They were the likes of Abdallah Fundikira, son of the Nyamwezi chief, and the Sukuma David Kidaha Makwaia who, like Nyerere, was a Catholic (having converted from Islam) and a chief's son.[35] Another was Vedastus Kyaruzi who, like Andrew Tibandebage, had also entered Makerere a year before Nyerere and was in his second year.[36] Despite mixing with the sons of relatively wealthy chiefs, however, Nyerere's finances were tight at Makerere and he was forced to remove one of his dependants from school until he completed his studies.[37]

For young men far away from home, Makerere was a prime opportunity to further their education at a prestigious academy and, as many did, to build the solid foundations of an illustrious career. As with many students entering tertiary education for the first time, Makerere also provided the perfect chance to really explore what the world had to offer away from the confines of familial constraint. As one student at the time recalls, the young undergraduates had established 'the Alcohol Testing Club, which tried very much to promote itself and recruit members. [But] Mwalimu did not join this group, nor did he waste his time joining purely social groups, just to socialise and draw attention to himself.'[38] In many situations Nyerere kept a low profile. As Abdallah Fundikira later put it: 'If you want the truth, one did not particularly notice Nyerere.'[39] That said, there was certainly an aura about Julius, such that 'at Makerere ex-Tabora School students talked about him; that he was of a superior intellect and a bookworm, but he was also "wild". He did not look so wild.'[40] As at Mwisenge, 'his main preoccupation was books', remembers Vedastus Kyaruzi, but Andrew Tibandebage notes that this was, 'not to pass exams but just to know things, and everything. He did not read or study in order to compete with anybody, and he never failed in his studies.'[41] Vedastus Kyaruzi continues, 'I don't remember seeing him participating in any kinds of sports. But in those days he was a conversationalist, and people liked very much talking to him.'[42]

The students seem also to have liked listening to Nyerere, who started giving talks when he first arrived at the college, as Andrew Tibandebage recalls: 'He started talking about Mahatma Gandhi, Dr. James (Kwegyir) Aggrey who was the first African from [the Gold Coast] to earn a doctorate in the United States, and other subjects. He knew a lot of things.'[43] Tibandebage also added that his first impressions of Nyerere were incorrect, for 'He was not ... as I saw soon, the imitator of English manners I had imagined him to be. He was very friendly, generous, wise, and very voluble while discussing a subject; he would go deeper into the subject than most of us were used to seeing among ourselves.'[44] Julius soon gained a reputation as star debater in the Makerere Debating Society,[45] the report for which contains the delightfully optimistic raison d'être: 'We are a living society of energetic and anxious speakers whose sole motive is to solve the problems of all existence.'[46] Among the debates during this time of Kyaruzi was the irresistible motion that 'The white man has brought good things to Africa'. Vedastus Kyaruzi recalls how he proposed the motion with a colleague, while two others opposed it:

> We had a full house [comprised of] both students and tutors, both black and white. … The discussion was lively and it looked as if the house was equally divided. Then one Kenya student calmly asked for the floor and serenely posed a question: 'When you refer to the white man do you still include the Kenya settler?' When assured that the motion made no distinction, he stood still for some moments, looked around the house, and solemnly declared, 'Ladies and Gentlemen, I am sure you don't know what you are talking about'. Saying this, and tears running down his cheeks, he walked out, followed by [a] number of Kenyan students.[47]

Kyaruzi then adds that in 1942, the year before Nyerere entered Makerere, there were signs in many shops in Kampala which indicated service for Europeans only – and some shops that would serve Africans did so 'through small windows on a take-it-or-leave-it basis. The African had to take whatever was offered, be it stale bread or go without it. As most shops were Asian-owned, discrimination against us were [sic] carried out by them.'[48] Swimming was also segregated when Nyerere joined Makerere, as indicated by a signboard at a bathing area which read that it was out of bounds for 'Africans and dogs'.[49] The sign was only removed after a particularly vile incident that occurred during Nyerere's first year at Makerere, which Kyaruzi attributes to having 'awakened the students' interest in politics':

> The British Provincial Commissioner in Kampala … made an official visit to Makerere. During the course of his tour, he entered the Biology lab and found us at work with impressive appliances. … For [an] unknown reason he asked the tutor whether we knew English. Since our textbooks, lectures, tutorials and examinations were in English the tutor must have thought the question was silly. He only replied, 'I suppose so'. The Resident turned round and surprised one student by asking him the meaning of 'All your geese are not swans'. Before the student could reply, the Resident went out of the room laughing and apparently satisfied with himself. The effect of this action on the students was dramatic. Although 'hate' would be too strong a word, we certainly disliked him and his like. The essays that week were so bitter that the College authorities made enquiries as to what happened.[50]

Nyerere was unlikely to have been in the same class as Kyaruzi and probably did not witness the incident first-hand. He was at Makerere at the time though, and would quickly have heard of what happened. We can be fairly sure of Nyerere's stance on overt racism at the time, which was in part influenced by his cordial relations with genial European missionaries in Musoma. In his notes for a long presentation he was preparing to give at Makerere, we can see that Nyerere was very aware of the strength that could be gained through treating people as individuals, and not grouping all Europeans as one:

> In reading his [Booker T. Washington's] three volumes at the College I have managed to find out one thing that he hated ... and that was hatred. ... He was mistreated by ignorant whites, but he knew very well that there were thousands of Whites not only in the North but in the South too who had the welfare of the Negro at heart. When the ignorant Whites treated him discourteously he used to take them as individuals and not as representative of the character of the whole white population.[51]

This conciliatory position is one that Nyerere developed from towards the end of his time at Makerere, but it is not one that he always held. A glimpse at Nyerere's political stance when he first started at the college can be seen in an article published in the *Tanganyika Standard* only six months into his time at Makerere. In a letter written on 10 July 1943, authored in Kampala and cryptically signed off by a 'JUKANYE' – presumably JUlius KAmbarage NYErere – he makes the argument that capitalism is alien to African society. The piece is entitled 'African Socialism', a phrase that has yet to be attributed to Nyerere's credo at this early point in his life. Indeed, in the East Africa context it is usually associated with the *ujamaa* of post-independence Tanzanian politics.[52] Where Nyerere had picked up the term 'African socialism' by 1943 at the latest is unclear. In their 1964 anatomy of African socialism, the political scientists William Friedland and Carl Rosberg suggest that the 'new doctrine [was] largely unknown only five years ago' – the late 1950s.[53] Ruth Schachter Morgenthau, also writing in the early 1960s and shortly after a gathering of African nations in Dakar to discuss the (Pan-African) character of African socialism, was of the belief that the phrase was used first in French, as *socialisme africain*. She argues that its antecedent can be traced back to Leopold Senghor, who coined the phrase when he, and Mamadou Dia with others representing the rural areas of Senegal, broke from what was then the only Senegalese party, a branch of the French Socialist Party, *Section Française de l'Internationale Ouvrière*.[54] This was the late 1940s – around five years after 'JUKANYE' penned the phrase 'African Socialism' in Kampala. There can be little doubt that this was indeed Julius Kambarage Nyerere, for it surely stretches far beyond the bounds of mere coincidence that three factors point to the author as being the same person who was to become the leader of an independent Tanganyika: at the time the letter was sent from Kampala (the post town for Makerere), Nyerere was in the same location; Nyerere went on to champion the phrase 'African Socialism' in his homeland; and, to seal the argument, the initialism draws on the first letters of Nyerere's full and unique name. If there is still any doubt however, a brief analysis of his comment as published in the correspondence section of the newspaper leaves the matter to rest, and also provides a scintillating insight into his political maturation. The letter as it appears in the *Tanganyika Standard* is presented here in its entirety, punctuated with brief discussion. No text has been removed, and (with one exception, in square brackets) the mistakes are as they appear in the newspaper.[55]

Writing while undertaking his studies in Kampala, Nyerere opens with a global view of contemporary events, framed around the ongoing Second World War that was soon to take his brother Burito Nyerere. He attributes the chief causes of war to economic factors, and shows an awareness of economics in determining past world events, the present conflict and in shaping the future of Africa. He quickly states his key belief that Africans are inherently socialistic, but the young student perhaps gives too much credit to the assumption that his white audience might care whether the future of his fellow Africans is taken into consideration. The question this raises though – and one that is worth bearing in mind when reading Nyerere's early letter – is which audience he had in mind: European readers (mostly comprising colonial administrators and settlers) or Africans and Asians throughout Tanganyika, and perhaps also East Africa?

> Sir,–We are now living in a world which is changing very rapidly. Now that the world is at war and at war mainly because of economic reasons it is almost certain that economic changes will be inevitable in future. What we ask is that while these changes are taking place it must always be borne in mind that the African is by nature a socialistic being and all those changes which affect him must be regulated with this view in mind. European countries, most of them at least, are divided among themselves between capitalists and socialists and before the outbreak of this war Russia's communist policies were threatening all the rest of Europe, capitalists there being far more than socialists. The sense of capitalism is so much rooted in some European countries that although they acknowledge the natural righteousness of a socialistic policy, they are still very reluctant to accept it.

With the benefit of hindsight a reader today could be tempted to think that at this time Nyerere was already contemplating an independent Tanganyika. There is some sense from this letter that this may have been the case. If not, then would he really have thought that a British-governed Tanganyika could be socialist? More likely, Nyerere was thinking beyond a time when foreigners ruled his native land. He is writing in Uganda, to a newspaper readership that was chiefly based in Dar es Salaam and the Tanganyikan coastal (and predominantly Muslim) settlements of Tanga, Lindi, Mikindani, Mtwara, and in Zanzibar.[56] His motive at this stage may have been to stir up his African brothers and sisters – via the educated Africans who he refers to more than once, those who would have had the ability to read his message in English and would then have passed on the sentiment in local tongues. A good number of those who read the European-owned newspaper, however, were Europeans. In addressing his readers Nyerere uses the collective 'we', apparently as a spokesman for 'the educated African' and 'the indigenous native'. There is also more than a hint that already at this stage Nyerere was thinking about '*Ujamaa* – The Basis of African Socialism', a pamphlet in which he later expressed his aversion to the untrammelled individualism of Western capitalist society, and argued for an extension of a communitarian ethic: 'We, in Africa, have no more need of being "converted" to socialism than we have of being "taught" democracy. Both are rooted in our past – in the traditional society which produced us.'[57] That was 1962, but very similar to his 1943 newspaper article, where Nyerere continued with a misty-eyed view of an Africa familiar to those who have read any of his romanticised accounts of idyllic village life in 'traditional society':

> Wi[th] Europe, however, whether socialism is accepted now or later on, it does not matter very much because the capitalists are the 'most important' people there.[58] But with us here it is different. Our population is mainly African and the African being naturally socialistic, economics in East Africa should be based on socialistic principles. The indigenous native knows no other way of living. He is very socialistic (not by any means a communist in the strictest sense of the word, except on a small scale in the use of land). He will always help his neighbour in any difficulties. If his neighbour thinks he won't be able to harvest his maize alone, the Native is willing to send his wives and children to help him. If he has many cattle and gets more milk than his family needs, his neighbours are always welcome to it without accepting anything in return.
>
> The educated African is often blamed by foreigners because of his hospitality to his relatives, and the foreigners think that unless he stops this kind of unselfishness he won't make enough money to meet modern needs and make enough progress. The European tendency is to be as individualistic as possible. But it is not African.

Nyerere then guides his discussion onto issues of land use and economics in Tanganyika, where he was undoubtedly aware of the British administration's efforts during the inter-war period to push African peasants into growing cash crops for export to their home market. Cotton was one such example where, in a highly *dirigiste* and intrusive manner, the administration sought to implement their policy that Africans must plant the crop.[59] The policy had the interests of British cotton threads textiles manufacturers chiefly in mind, and Nyerere would have been aware of resistance to the crop in Uzanaki, where elders devised a plan to cook the plant's seeds in boiling water, thereby successfully ensuring that the Agricultural Officer struck the district off his list of areas suitable for cultivation.[60] Nyerere also shows an awareness of land tenure in Kenya, a situation that he is keen for Tanganyika to avoid:

> No African worth the name, be he educated or uneducated will suffer to see his people, who form the strength of the clan, and the tribe, to starve when he can help. If the African is to be educated 'along his own lines' then economically he must be educated along socialistic lines because he is naturally so. The peasant has to be encouraged to

lead that sort of life on modern lines. In most parts of Tanganyika land is still held completely by Natives, but if the time comes when it must be held individually, as we hope, it will be wise not to commit the folly which has been committed by our neighbours, of putting it into a few hands leaving the majority with out any means of earning a living except by being squatters on some landlord's piece of land. I don't mean to say that land is going to be distributed in the near future, but if it were to, fairness would have to be used, and very strict fairness too. Unless the peasants feel that there is a good deal of fairness in their land tenure, all attempts to make them lead a socialistic life will be futile, which will be a great blow to our society.

Here the tone becomes a touch more confrontational towards capitalists in Europe, 'the "most important" people there' – and the young Nyerere may well have been tempted to write 'the "most important" people here' instead. Indeed it is worth noting that, as with any letter to a newspaper, the final published text could have been altered for ease of reading or any other reason that the (European) editor is at liberty to omit. The sentiment of the letter certainly comes across though, and Nyerere refers again to the collective 'us here' in East Africa, the majority (black) African whose outlook is naturally socialistic – something he returns to in letters from Edinburgh when he discusses his desire to help out his family in times of need. As later in his life, Nyerere is also at pains to stress that while the African is socialistic, he is not communist. On the issue of hospitality we see in the writing of Erasto Mang'enya that when travelling to a meeting of a sub-committee of the Department of Education not long after Nyerere returned from Edinburgh the two were discouraged from residing with whites.[61] In this letter Nyerere uses the opportunity to state how unpalatable he finds what he sees as the European tendency towards individualism: 'it is not African'. On this note he then turns to the necessity of sharing of land and his opposition to its distribution to individual proprietors in a future Tanganyika. This, of course, became a key feature to the policy of the *ujamaa* that he was to introduce over twenty years after this early letter. In this respect the document could be as Nyerere testing the political temperature on the audience, something that he later did with a longer manuscript, also written when he was still a student, 'to discover to myself what ideas I had on the subject'.[62]

In the final section Nyerere makes a clarion call for educated Africans to take the lead in guiding their 'indigenous brothers'. Again with the benefit of hindsight the letter now reads as if Nyerere was also drafting his own plan of action, in Biblical language reminding his readers – or perhaps reminding himself – 'to feel that he is the light', and 'the leader'. These educated Africans were indeed British government employees or, in Nyerere's own case, an employee of the Missionaries of Africa. He then draws to a close by pointing to socialistic role models elsewhere on the continent, stimulating his fellow educated Africans into believing that a positive future for Tanganyika is possible if together they are to take control:

> The educated African should take the lead. He should show his indigenous brothers that he is much interested in the well-being of the community and is working for its promotions. He, generally, being an employee of the state or somebody else, can play his part best by showing a strong sense of society welfare with his fellow-employees. He has to feel that he is the light, the prototype and the leader of a large population. His socialistic life with his fellow workers, in societies formed for the promotion of the good of the community will be admired and emulated. It is only through such bodies of workers that actual success can be obtained in economic and social affairs. Anybody doubting the importance of such unions can only learn something about the Industrial and Commercial Workers' Union in South Africa, the cocoa-growing in Gold Coast and the progressive Kilimanjaro Native Growers' Union to see what good they have done to the Natives. Such unions should be the whole ideal of the African, at least for the time being, for it's no good talking about socialistic life if we haven't the unity and the money necessary for its achievement. On the whole success must be aimed at, for unless it is achieved the wealth of this country is going to be in the hands of a few people and all of us shall have to be forced to live a dependent sort of life on those selfish capitalists who have mainly caused this abominable war.– JUKANYE.

Kampala, July 10 [1943]

Nyerere's letter is a testimony to his independent intellectual growth, certainly when compared with that of some of his Makerere contemporaries whose academic ability was questioned by staff members. The notes of Kenneth Prewitt, a visiting lecturer at Makerere, show something of the College's prevailing academic culture of the time. Prewitt complained in no uncertain terms that the students lacked any risk of toying with ideas, but were satisfied with simply playing it safe and passing exams: 'Consume, and maybe learn, but take no risks,'[63] he griped. That was the mid-1960s, for students who Prewitt described as the 'presumptive elite'. When viewed in this context, Nyerere's 'African Socialism' from more than twenty years earlier was the product of a young man who was not afraid to take risks.

The letter also serves to mark the beginnings of Nyerere's political maturation, chiefly in absorbing and developing the views of leading black thinkers of the time. Indeed, it preceded the 'Towards Colonial Freedom' pamphlet of 1945 in which Nkrumah, relying heavily on the writings of Marcus Garvey, C.L.R. James and George Padmore, outlined the philosophy he had developed from his London days until his return to the Gold Coast. Like Nyerere, Nkrumah spoke of the exploitative nature of foreign rule in the colonies, which Europeans were interested in for little more than their raw materials.[64] Yet while Nkrumah argued that the colonies must stand together to achieve political independence, at this earlier date Nyerere was concentrating on 'the wealth of this country'. The country he referred to was Tanganyika Territory, for although Nyerere was in Uganda at the time, the letter was sent to the

Tanganyika Standard. From as early as 1930 the newspaper was a popular vehicle through which African Association leaders voiced their opinion, but it was at the time that Nyerere was writing – the final stages of the Second World War – that the African Association's correspondence showed an increased interest in territorially-specific issues.[65]

That Nyerere signs off with 'JUKANYE' suggests that he was writing as an individual and not on behalf of the African Association. Still, those members in Tanganyika who knew the Makerere branch leadership would easily have been able to identify the Kampala-based scholar as the author. Yet it must be understood that the vibrancy of the African Association was not solely down to the intellectuals of Nyerere's calibre, for the nationalist movement was far from an educated elite affair.[66] Nyerere was well aware of his status and, in a bid to avoid alienating himself and the small number of other intellectuals in Makerere, he sought to embrace as many of the 'educated African' category as possible by indicating that it stretched beyond scholars but to state employees and others. Away from home, Nyerere was aware of the need to build political bridges with his 'indigenous brothers' in Tanganyika, not to destroy them.

Continuing to write for an audience beyond Makerere, Nyerere twice won first prize in an East African literary competition. In 1941 he had already won the Tanganyika African Authorship Competition with an article on 'The Wa-zanaki Country and Customs of the Wa-zanaki'. This time he won with an essay on the subjugation of women, and applied Mill's perspective to his native Zanaki society.[67] 'John Stuart Mill's essays on representative government and on the subjection of women – these had a terrific influence on me', he said.[68] Nyerere later offered the recollection that, 'I was instantaneously reminded of my Zanaki society and of the situation of my mother. She had to toil a lot!'[69] Describing the inspiration for his 1944 'Uhuru wa Wanawake' essay, he adds: 'My father had 22 wives and I knew how hard they had to work and what they went through as women.'[70] Nyerere's views on the freedom of women were unusual for a man in East Africa at this time, and it was out of the ordinary for a twenty-two-year old to write what is essentially a treatise on the subject. Yet while Pascal Durand is correct in pointing out that this was several years before the 1948 Universal Declaration of Human Rights of the United Nations Organization, his claim that Nyerere's 1944 essay 'was long before any serious movement towards women's liberation was born anywhere in the world, even in the western world,' is well off the mark.[71] Mary Wollstonecraft's *A Vindication of the Rights of Woman*, published in 1792, defied assumptions about male supremacy and championed educational equality for women. By the later nineteenth century, though still a minority movement, what was mainly a middle-class feminism was established in many English-speaking countries. By the pre-First World War era there was much talk among progressive intellectuals about 'the New Woman'. Be that as it may, Nyerere continued to fight for gender equality when, many years later, he wrote that 'it is essential that our women live on terms of full equality with their fellow citizens who are men'.[72]

Gender was certainly a topical issue in Makerere at the time, with the admission in the mid-1940s of the first women – initially six – all but one of whom were already experienced teachers.[73] With their arrival, observes David Mills, racial hierarchies began to be expressed in concerns over student sexuality.[74] Erasto Mang'enya describes how prior to this period 'Makerere was a man's institution. This was so well known in Uganda and Kampala in particular that even the wives of the members of the staff never walked across the paddocks of the College. As for the daughters, they avoided coming near the boundary of the College.'[75] The new intake of women resided in three on-campus residences solely for female students, one of which was variously known as 'Complex' or 'CCE', where 'the girls here proudly go by the name "Crocodiles".' CCE was previously the residence for Nyerere, one of the young men who were phased out of the hall with the growth of the female population on campus.[76] He appears to have had no animosity towards the female students however, and notes that they proved their academic ability in examinations.[77] Yet worries about men and women being too close to each other at Makerere persisted and, shortly after Nyerere had left the College, Mills remarks that,

> the personal files of Makerere's Dean reveal a long-running and anxious correspondence about the first student College Dance held in 1947. After much disagreement amongst staff … the students were encouraged to police the dances themselves, and an elaborate set of rules ('Ladies invited should know how to dance') was drawn up; it ended with the admonition that no person might stay in the refreshment room for more than 15 minutes.[78]

For earlier students at Makerere, there was a light system of 'fagging' – something the young Kambarage was familiar with from his days at Tabora Boys. It was apparently new to some of the other Tanganyikan students. The fagging was 'light', Mang'enya explains, because first year students did not clean prefects' shoes or plates, but, 'all the same, first year students at Makerere who, say joined cricket, had to carry all the cricket kit from the College to the cricket pitch and from the pitch to the College. There were quite a number of other things too that were left to be done by the two first-year students.'[79]

In the year that Nyerere entered Makerere close to half the students attending the College enrolled in teacher training.[80] Besides teaching, the other local opportunities open to Africans beyond school levels of education were chiefly in the technical and theological fields.[81] Apparently with no vocation to join the Church at this stage, Nyerere's obvious choice was to train to become a teacher. He also took elementary Chemistry and a full course of Biology.[82] Of his other studies we know that Nyerere was especially good in English.[83] He also studied Greek and Latin. Father Wille explains how when Nyerere was helping him with some translations much later, the young teacher found the older version of English in the text difficult to handle when he was translating the Sunday epistles and gospels. Nyerere asked Father Wille for his Latin Missal and, when Wille enquired if he knew Latin, Nyerere replied that he had studied a year of it at university – presumably at Makerere – and he translated from Latin. On another occasion when Nyerere found some of St Paul's epistles difficult to understand, he asked for a Greek New Testament, to which Father Wille then asked if he could understand Greek. Nyerere replied again that he had studied a year of it at university.[84] This was presumably at Makerere College since – despite the very best efforts of some administrators later in the United Kingdom – Nyerere seems to have managed to avoid both ancient languages during the remainder of his formal education.[85]

On religious matters Father Wille informs us that Nyerere told him that at Makerere he wanted to understand his faith well, so he not only read all the Papal Encyclicals but studied them.[86] He also read the Catholic philosophers such as Jacques Maritain and others whose writings were available in the College library.[87] The image is one of a devoted neophyte Christian with an enormous thirst for the knowledge underpinning his growing faith – at least as reported much later by Nyerere's Catholic missionary friend, who knew what his saint-like protégé went on to achieve. Either way, Nyerere had known some form of clerical authority since childhood. But his actions now had the effect of showing some Catholic Europeans that he really was serious about his faith in God. Given the right opportunities, the young man could go far.

Andrew Tibandebage tells that Nyerere founded a branch of 'Catholic Action', defined by Pope Pius XI as 'the participation of the laity in the Hierarchic apostolate, for the defence of religious and moral principles, for the development of a wholesome and beneficent social action, under the guidance of the ecclesiastical Hierarchy, *outside and above political parties*, with the intention of restoring Catholic life in the family and in society' (emphasis added).[88] Tibandebage adds that Julius's best friend at Makerere, Hamza Mwapachu (with whom Nyerere shared a dormitory), 'used to call it "mass action" because we organised such religious activities as annual retreats and pilgrimages to Namugongo, the place where Charles Wanga, Mathias Mulumba and other Christians had been murdered'.[89] Tibandebage added that the friends 'also got a choir going, which had its ups and downs both vocally and organisationally'.[90] Nyerere had his own focus though, and on 30 May 1944 he received the sacrament of Confirmation at Rubaga Mission.[91] In doing so he affirmed his Christian belief and was admitted as a full member of the Catholic Church.

Since Hamza Kibwana Bakari Mwapachu's birth in Tanga in 1913, he had been raised by a strict Islamic family. He was schooled in his hometown until the completion of his secondary education in 1931, when he gained a place to study medicine in Dar es Salaam.[92] The Ocean Road Hospital was designated for Europeans, and Mwapachu was based at Gerezani Street's Sewa Haji Hospital that catered for civil servants, troops, Africans, Arabs and Indians.[93] In the city he stayed with the family of an age-mate of his father and a member of his Digo tribe, Mzee Aziz Ali, who introduced Mwapachu to fellow Muslims. These men formed a core of early political activists based in Dar es Salaam. It was through Aziz Ali that the promising medical student then met with Kleist Sykes, a founder of Dar es Salaam's African Association, an organisation with origins that can be traced back to at least the early 1920s.[94] During his time studying in Dar es Salaam Mwapachu also first met with Kleist Sykes' sons Abdulwahid, Ally and Abbas, with Thomas Plantan, and Aziz Ali's eldest son, Dossa Aziz. When in 1934 Mwapachu qualified as a Medical Assistant he then practiced in Iringa and Same districts, before being posted for further training in Mwanza, and then in 1942 on to take a Diploma in Medicine at Makerere College. It was while at Makerere that Mwapachu met the younger Nyerere and – despite nearly a decade in age between the two Tanganyikans – the first-year students quickly became close friends.

The following year Nyerere then suggested to Mwapachu and Andrew Tibandebage, his classmate in education and fellow Catholic, that they form the Tanganyika African Welfare Association (TAWA) – which elsewhere is referred to as the Tanganyika Student Welfare Association (TASWA) or the Tanganyika Students Association (TSA). The Association aimed to assist the small number of Tanganyikan students at the University College.[95] In his memoirs, Tibandebage recalls Nyerere's key role:

> Soon he organized us, that is, a number of ex-Tabora School senior students and three or four others, to form the nucleus of TAWA, the Tanganyika African Welfare Association. ... We elected him Secretary. The following year he was re-elected, with me as Chairman.... We held the same positions in the Debating Society and the Catholic Action. Let it be confessed that he alone bore the onus of running the three organisations, and did so very well.[96]

Discussing TAWA, Nyerere put it that 'its main purpose was not political or anti-colonial. We wanted to improve the lives of Africans. But inside us something was happening.'[97] Nyerere later told that, having drafted the TAWA constitution, he sent it to a number of friends and to people who he thought might sympathise and join: 'One of them wrote back saying that there existed an organisation in Tanganyika which would be excellent for my purposes, the Tanganyika [*sic*] African Association.'[98] ... Unfortunately TAA [Tanganyika African Association] had sunken to a tea-party organisation, and my friend suggested that we bring it to life again.'[99] In 1946 the Makerere-based Association was dropped in favour of reinvigorating the campus chapter of the African Association that had been established earlier in the 1940s.[100] It was this group of young Tanganyikans who in mid-1946 first referred to themselves in passing as members of the *Tanganyika* African Association, even though officially going by 'African Association, Makerere Branch, Kampala, Uganda'.[101] As Ethan Sanders notes, however, there is no evidence that it was Nyerere's idea to start using the African Association in Makerere as a political group for Tanganyikans.[102] The Makerere branch was short-lived, and it ceased to exist after 1947.[103]

In a letter to a lifelong friend, Nyerere later described the Makerere branch of the African Association as, 'a sort of socio-political organization ... [which in July 1954] we transformed into the Tanganyika African National Union, a fully fledged political organization which pledged itself to work for self-government'.[104] Among the Kampala-based members were David Makwaia, Andrew Tibandebage, Abdullah Fundikira, Hamza Mwapachu and, as Secretary, Vedastus Kyaruzi.[105] Later, when Kyaruzi left Makerere and forged stronger ties with headquarters, he investigated why the branch file of the Makerere-based African Association was so thin and the communication so poor with Dar es Salaam: 'Because the educated young were employed by the colonial government, the government made sure that anyone who was involved in politics and was an activist was transferred from Dar es Salaam ... to the regions.'[106] Despite this, for Nyerere and his colleagues the Makerere branch of the African Association provided them with an initial experience of direct political organisation. This came around the same time as the first stirrings of a national concept of politics in Tanganyika.[107]

4
Return to Tabora
African Associations

There was never a time in my youth, no matter how dark and discouraging the days might be, when one resolve did not continually remain with me, and that was a determination to secure an education at any cost.

Booker T. Washington, quoted by Nyerere in undated personal notes for a presentation at Makerere College[1]

This chapter begins with Nyerere's career as a teacher in Tabora. It outlines the circumstances leading to his favouring St Mary's, a Catholic school, over his alma mater, a government institution. It tracks the intensification of his political activity with the African Association, and the recognition at the territorial level of his potential in politics. The chapter analyses explanations for the Zanaki custom of child marriage, and introduces Nyerere's first wife, a figure who is almost entirely side-lined in accounts of his early life. It discusses his article on education that was published in a Makerere College magazine, continues to follow his debating in Tabora, and reveals his communication concerning social and political developments in Dar es Salaam. These documents discuss trusteeship, and the recurring issue of colonialism. The chapter then turns to Nyerere's first meeting with Maria Waningu, and the slow progress of their relationship. It closes with Nyerere's desire to continue his education, the apparent pull of local politics, his attraction towards studying overseas, and his engagement with Maria shortly before he left for the United Kingdom. The new sources in this chapter include a letter to Nyerere written by the political activist Hamza Mwapachu, analysis of a piece Nyerere authored on women's freedom, and findings arising from a rare interview with Magori Watiha, his child bride.

Magori Watiha

On completion of his three-year teacher training course, the chief's son

Julius Nyerere graduated from Makerere with a Teachers' Diploma.[2] In the same year, 1945, a territorial conference of Provincial Commissioners back home in Tanganyika noted that

> there can be but little doubt that during the years immediately preceding the war a number of factors, amongst which may be included the growth of a semi-educated class and the illiteracy of many Native Authorities, has fostered in the minds of some members of the younger African generation a belief that they were at least the mental equals of some of the chiefs who ruled them and that they themselves were becoming entitled to a share in the general administration of their chiefdoms.[3]

The young graduate spent the summer at home building a house for his widowed mother.[4] Otherwise he was studious – as he was now in most of his breaks in Butiama – and would lock himself in his room to study for long periods. Jack Nyamwaga recalls how, 'at this time [Mwalimu] walked around the village, visiting relatives. … He would mix freely with people. … With all his education, he still knew more of the Zanaki vernacular than all of the other Zanaki. … And he would cultivate like an ordinary man, using a hoe.'[5]

At some point during his time in Butiama, between reading and farming, Nyerere received an offer to return to Tabora Boys to teach. This would not have been the first time that he revisited his alma mater since finishing his studies there in 1942 for, as part of his final year at Makerere, he had undertaken teaching practice at his old school. Andrew Tibandebage, who being a year ahead of Nyerere at Makerere had already graduated and begun teaching at the Catholic St Mary's School in Tabora, took this opportunity to showcase the school to his friend.[6] Tibandebage recalls that, 'For his [Nyerere's] official teaching practice he came to his old school, Tabora School. … I asked him what he thought of our joining hands at St Mary's the following year. To my pleasant surprise, his ready answer was the short question, "Why not?" This I duly reported to the Headmaster.'[7]

Tibandebage first approached the Director and White Father missionary, an Irishman from Kerry called Father Richard Walsh. Tibandebage persuaded Walsh that he should take Nyerere after he completed his Teachers' Diploma.[8] This took some doing – not, it seems, because of any doubts over the young trainee's ability, but because,

> Walsh did not believe that Mwalimu Nyerere would agree to accept that position because he was promised to be paid 6.5 (British) pounds per month when an African teacher at a government secondary school was being paid more than twice that amount. By contrast, a (white) teacher from Britain … was paid 38 pounds per month.[9]

Father Walsh objected to boys who had studied at the town's rival school, as Tibandebage tells:

> [Walsh] said that Tabora School boys were big-headed and likely to give trouble, so he would have none of them at St Mary's. Seeing that his remark had puzzled me, he asked if there was anything to be said in his favour. Of course there was, and he heard a few bits. Then he wrote to an acquaintance of his who was teaching at Makerere; he soon received such an encouraging reply that he apologized, to me, for having been so hasty.[10]

Tibandebage then fully convinced his friend Julius that St Mary's was the place to come to for his first teaching job.[11] The best schools in East Africa in the mid-1940s were King's College Budo in Uganda, Alliance High in Kenya, and Tabora Boys in Tanganyika. The headmasters at the elite institutions had much leeway in choosing the best teachers.[12] When still at Makerere, Nyerere had received an offer to teach at Tabora Boys. He also now received an offer from Father Walsh to teach at St Mary's.[13] Apparently already convinced by Tibandebage that he should head to the new Catholic school, to Nyerere the prospect of returning to the prestigious Tabora Boys, now as a fully-qualified teacher, must have been tempting nonetheless. Erasto Mang'enya, when faced earlier with a similar decision as to whether he should join mission service or government schools, wrote that 'to me the joining of Government service was crossing the Rubicon. It meant going away from home, while joining the Mission services meant very meagre material remuneration, which meant that there would be no room for improving my lot.'[14]

Joining Tabora Boys, rather than St Mary's, also meant being a government employee. The advantage of this situation to the colonial government, as one official wrote of Harry Nkumbula in Northern Rhodesia, was that as 'an African Civil servant it would be very much easier to control his views'.[15] While mulling over which offer to accept, Nyerere was unaware that two Europeans, one of them a priest, were placing bets on his decision. According to Father Wille, 'the headmaster of the government Tabora Boys placed a bet with Father Richard Walsh of St Mary's that Julius would choose the government school.'[16] Julius chose St Mary's and the priest won the wager, after which the government – at this time paying the salaries of all the teachers, both government and mission – wrote to Nyerere to say that at a mission school he would not get the same salary. Also, they added, if later he transferred to a government school, he would not be able to count towards his pension the years spent teaching in a mission school. 'Julius was furious at this', recalls Father Wille, 'and replied in a letter: "If I ever hesitated, your letter has settled the matter. The mission teachers are doing as much as the government teachers are."'[17]

Beginning at St Mary's in January 1946,[18] Julius Nyerere was initially given a small office in which he put his bed. There was no room for his younger brother, so Joseph Kizurira Burito Nyerere stayed with his colleague Andrew Tibandebage.[19] Nyerere taught Biology and History.[20] He is remembered by his students for the understanding he could communicate to them.[21] He also gave free tuition outside the school, as Tibandebage remembered: 'When the literate young and middle-aged members of the Combined Club asked to be taught English, Nyerere and I took turns, each three evenings a week, at this important duty, a duty that Nyerere considered noble enough to call for voluntary, unpaid service to the community.'[22] In formal tuition, Father Walsh described Nyerere as

> an excellent teacher. He had a real gift for funnelling knowledge into the heads of his pupils. He first showed his metal by his prompt defence of a fellow teacher, Joseph Kasella [Bantu], who had been given a raw deal. Here was a potential leader, who would act with force whenever he believed the principle was at stake.[23]

Nyerere's intervention apparently resulted in Kasella Bantu being reinstated.[24] Bantu went on to become a founder member of TANU, but he soon broke ranks and joined the short-lived opposition and the two became the most intractable of enemies. Nyerere later acted with the same force he showed in Tabora, and Kasella Bantu was eventually arrested under the Preventative Detention Act.[25]

Vedastus Kyaruzi, by this time based at the African Association headquarters in Dar es Salaam, reports that, shortly after being employed at St Mary's, Nyerere joined the recently-opened African Association branch in Tabora. His political activities became much more intense.[26] Nyerere was elected branch Treasurer,[27] a post that Andrew Tibandebage is also said to have filled when Nyerere was Secretary and Hamza Mwapachu, their medical friend from Makerere who was working at the Government Hospital, was elected President of the Tabora branch – perhaps, it is suggested, because it was (and still is) largely a Muslim-populated town.[28]

A few months after settling in Tabora town, Nyerere travelled to the African Association's conference in Dar es Salaam. He joined delegates such as Chief Abdiel Shangali, George Masudi from Zanzibar, and Joseph Kimalando from Moshi.[29] The April 1946 meeting was hugely important for the future of Tanganyika because resolutions were passed that marked the African Association's first coherent demand that the colonial territory should become an independent nation state. This heralded 'a significant advance in political consciousness' in Tanganyika, as John Iliffe has put it.[30] The question of East African unity was discussed – a motion that 'every member seemed to be utterly opposed to'[31] – along with the issue of chieftaincy. Some delegates argued that Africans and not the colonial government should be able to choose their native authorities. A growing number of voices called for a reform of the system based on Europeans' perception of pre-colonial chieftaincy.[32] Nyerere's own stance on this matter at the time is not recorded, but it may have been the beginnings of his recognition that a large number of delegates eschewed the institution that had given his father authority to rule in Uzanaki – the same institution that he abolished as one of the independent government's first legislative acts.[33] The Association-wide conference was Nyerere's first chance to meet delegates from throughout Tanganyika. Here he got a feel for the most important issues that concerned the African political class across the territory. Nyerere used the opportunity of the meeting to present a memorandum that he and Tibandebage had together persuaded their branch to place on the agenda. It formed the basis of a conference resolution demanding constitutional advance through a pyramid of elected councils. With the Tabora resolution successfully passed, Nyerere left Dar es Salaam satisfied in the knowledge that he was able to make his high-pitched voice heard at the territorial level. Whether or not he was 'an inexperienced schoolteacher thrust into the role of political activist',[34] the 1946 conference 'marked Julius Nyerere's entry into territorial politics'.[35] A twenty-four year old novice he may have been, but the flyweight had now been noticed by the political heavyweights.

Back in Tabora, an African Association shop was opened that sold basic provisions such as sugar, flour and soap. Nyerere used the profits to cover his expenses.[36] He had gained some experience of retail in the same town having served for a short time as a government 'price inspector', the term Nyerere used in a later interview.[37] (He might not have been so forthcoming with the term 'tax collector', which suggests an even greater degree of complicity with the colonial state.) When money went missing in the African Association shop, Nyerere apparently required an assistant he felt he could trust, and invited his half-brother Joseph Muhunda Nyerere (whose mother, Mugara, was Chief Nyerere Burito's twelfth wife) to come from Butiama to help him. With Joseph Muhunda Nyerere came Warioba Kiasaga (another of Nyerere Burito's wives), and together they travelled by bus from Butiama to Musoma and then by ship across Lake Victoria to Mwanza.[38] They travelled by rail to Tabora, sharing a second class compartment. In those days the first class coaches were solely for Europeans and, very rarely, big chiefs. The second class coaches that the young party from Butiama were sat in were mainly for Asians and a few Africans, usually chiefs of lesser importance. 'Very senior African public servants and African businessmen also got this privilege sometimes,' recalls Erasto Mang'enya, 'but these of course were very few indeed. The third class was mainly for Africans.'[39] The three classes that fitted Tanganyika's stratified society so very neatly went beyond trains. A visiting British Railways trade unionist wrote that in Dar es Salaam 'practically everything was organised on a tri-racial basis.'[40]

Another passenger in the group travelling from Butiama to Tabora was a young girl called Magori Watiha. Julius' father betrothed her to him when she was around three or four years old. Julius was still at Tabora Boys at the time (or had just left), and resigned himself to accept the Zanaki tradition of a father giving his son a wife. This practice was not unusual for the time, nor exclusive to the Zanaki. Chilongola Jenga, a chief in Idibo near Kilosa, was also married to a 'strange girl', and both were taken by surprise when the ceremony took place at the behest of the young man's uncle.[41] When Magori was a few years older, Julius had to accept his relatives' decision that she undertake her primary school education in Tabora and that they live together.[42]

One explanation for the Zanaki custom of child marriage, given by James Irenge, is that a boy gets married to his first wife at the behest of his parents; that is, his first wife is his parents' responsibility to choose for him. Shortly before the chief died he expressed that his son deserved a wife.[43] But because Kambarage (as he was then still known) wanted further education and was not ready to get married, yet could not refuse to accept cows for bridewealth, it was felt that a young girl should be found for him and cattle should be paid as was traditionally done by the Zanaki. After the girl grew up and became old enough to be engaged, so the reasoning went, Kambarage would also have finished his studies. So a young girl was chosen for him.[44]

Another explanation is more functional. If a family is in financial difficulty, they can agree that a daughter who is still a child can be married to a man. This was not unusual for the time when Magori was betrothed to Kambarage, as he wrote a few years later in reference to another such union: 'In all honesty, I know a child aged nine years who was married to a man who could not have been less than fifty years.'[45] In the situation of pecuniary difficulties, cows are given to the girl's family in exchange, thereby alleviating their woes. When the girl reaches six or seven years old she is sent to the home of her future husband, although they are not permitted to have sexual relations. When the daughter becomes of age she is then returned to her own family and it is decided whether she is to be married to the man. If they do not marry, then her family returns the cows. Using this context, Wille adds that in Julius' case the girl was older than him, and so Burito knew that she would not wait for his son to be mature enough to marry her. Instead, so the reasoning apparently went, the girl would look for another man, and that man would then need to return the cow bridewealth to Nyerere's family in order to marry her. But if Magori Watiha is indeed the woman in question here (and there is no suggestion that there was any other child bride) then Wille is mistaken in this assertion. Magori is clearly younger than Nyerere – a fact that Magori herself agrees to, and which is also supported by the accounts of Jackton Nyambereka Nyerere and Joseph Muhunda Nyerere, the latter of whom was a youth when he took Magori to Tabora, with Joseph Kizurira Burito Nyerere and Julius Nyerere, when she was a child.[46] Nevertheless, Wille's analysis of the motive for this union still holds: Burito paid these cows for Magori so that his son would have them for bridewealth when the time came for him to get married. In the event of a divorce, the Zanaki custom is that the cows are returned to the person who gave them; meaning that the cows would belong to Kambarage,[47] and he could then use them as bridewealth for the bride of his own choice.[48]

Of the young men accompanying Julius, Joseph Muhunda Nyerere stayed with him in Tabora town and was taught by nuns at the mission church. Joseph Kizurira Burito Nyerere, who had by now apparently also received from his father permission to attend school, studied at Tabora Boys. Julius had his own bedroom, and the others shared the second room, with a cook called Nyambura – who, like Daniel Kirigini, later became a teacher, in Butiama. The young men remained in Tabora for three years, but the young Magori apparently 'did not enjoy primary school and was too young to carry out household tasks, and she cried too much'.[49] She was eventually accompanied by Joseph Muhunda Nyerere to return to Butiama.

At the time the young Magori believed that she was on a short visit back to Butiama. She soon understood that it was permanent, and was taken to Julius's mother's family at Busegwe and then stayed with Julius's mother at Elias Nyang'ombe Warioba's house. Apparently 'Kambarage preferred to have his fiancee [*sic*] ('wife') get some education. He felt that there was no place where he could trust to have her kept, except mine.'[50] This may have been the case, although there is no indication whatsoever that Nyerere wished for this union to last, so he may not have referred to Magori as his 'fiancée', let alone his 'wife' (to-be).[51] Only later did Magori realise that she was Julius' wife when, on trips back from Tabora during his holidays, Julius used the Zanaki language to address her with '*Nyakisaho*', the greeting to a first wife that acknowledges her as wearer of the *kisaho* belt. Until that point Magori was not aware that she was married to Julius. All she can recall of the ceremony was that a man called Nyaburi who was working at Burito's house carried her to the chief's compound, apparently to meet an uncle who was working there.[52] Much later, Father Wille recalls an incident when he was driving with Nyerere in Butiama and 'Julius … suddenly yelled at a woman, calling her name, "Boke Boke". Julius got out and talked with the woman for some time. When he returned he explained to me that this woman had been his wife.'[53]

In time, and now with one less person to accommodate, Julius Nyerere and Andrew Tibandebage shared a house together in the centre of town, paying the rent collectively. This was in the Gongoni area, where the two stayed even after Andrew married Catherine in July 1946.[54] Julius slept little, maintaining that the night was just too long,

Photo G. Magori Watiha, whom Chief Nyerere Burito betrothed to his son Kambarage when she was around three or four years old.
(*Photograph by author, May 2010, Butiama*)

and at breakfast they read poems in turns. Some mornings Nyerere had already written a long paper about various issues concerning the territory and, as he did at Makerere, he frequently wrote articles for newspapers and magazines.[55]

It was in Tabora that Nyerere wrote what is one of the earliest records of his strong feelings towards the value of education. This was a recurring theme throughout his later writing and speeches, and was a central motivating force of his public and private life. The article, published in the first issue of the *Makerere* magazine, comments on a speech given by Arthur Creech Jones, then Under-Secretary of State for the Colonies, who visited the college when Nyerere was studying there. The article also touches on remarks by Dr William Lamont, Principal of Makerere, who gave a speech at Tabora Boys when Nyerere was there.[56] Nyerere wrote:

> While I was at Makerere I understood that my government was spending annually something in the neighbourhood of £80 on my behalf ... today that £80 has grown to mean a very great deal to me. It is not only a precious gift but a debt that I can never repay. I wonder whether it has ever occurred to many of us that while that £80 was being spent on me (or for that matter on any other of the past or present students of Makerere) some village dispensary was not being built in my village or some other village. People may actually have died through lack of medicine merely because eighty pounds which could have been spent on a fine village dispensary were spent on me, a mere individual, instead. Because of my presence at the College (and I never did anything to deserve Makerere) many Aggreys or Booker Washingtons remained illiterate for lack of a school to which they could go because the money which could have gone towards building schools was spent on Nyerere, a rather foolish and irresponsible student at Makerere. ... The educated man is not important in himself; his importance lies in what he can do for the community of which he is a member.[57]

Nyerere makes clear in the article, published in November 1946, that when he was at Makerere he did not consider the responsibilities that came with the privilege of being able to study at tertiary level.[58] It is a warming message, and the canny Zanaki was doubtless aware that it would have been read by gentlemen on the territorial education boards that considered scholarships for grateful young students with a social conscience. The writing of this article may also be the first time that Nyerere's philosophy of education for self-reliance was actually formulated in his mind. He had been developing these ideas earlier in the year, however, as evidenced in a letter he wrote to Arthur Creech Jones in protest against the proposed East African Federation. In the letter he demanded that, 'we want all the chief resources of this country such as gold, coal, diamond and tin mines to be developed by the Government and the money obtained to be used for our education and general development'.[59] The St Mary's teacher's views on education, and on colonialism, were also aired publicly in Tabora in a debate between the town's two rival secondary schools. Nyerere and Tibandebage were frequently invited back to Tabora Boys to debate.[60] Armed with the skills of debating that he had further developed at Makerere, Nyerere's regular opponent was the disciplinarian headmaster James Blumer, with whom he deliberately raised political issues.[61] In one debate against Mr Blumer and the headmaster's assistant, Mr Armstrong, the two St Mary's teachers opposed the motion that 'The African has benefitted more than the European since the partition of Africa'. Nyerere's speech was against imperialism and the effects of the partition of Africa by the Europeans. When the motion was put to the vote only the English teacher, Miss Cowan, supported it. The next day Nyerere and Tibandebage were said to be declared 'prohibited visitors to the school, let alone participants in future debates'. Kanyama Chiume had attended the debate as a pupil, and recalled that 'rather than dismay us, this had the effect of making us sneak out on Saturdays and Sundays to Mwalimu's house at St Mary's where he gave us weekly lectures on Africa and the struggle for freedom…. Our hatred for colonialism became increasingly intense.'[62] Rashid Kawawa, who was later to become Nyerere's deputy in power, had recently started at Tabora Boys and recalls the occasion when he first heard Nyerere's strength of argument:

> He was so convincing that he converted us all – we all voted for his side. The subject was 'Wealth Is Better Than Education', and he was against that, of course. He said 'I chose the teaching profession in order to make people understand; and once you understand, then you are a happy man. Not because you are wealthy; you can be a wealthy man but not a happy man.'[63]

At night Nyerere would discuss political issues concerning Tanganyika.[64] Joseph Muhunda Nyerere recalls that on a number of occasions 'a Chief from Unyamwezi would visit and they would talk politics until very late…. Around that time it seemed [Mwalimu] was getting political ideas.'[65] By this time Hamza Mwapachu, now working for the Social Welfare Department, had already applied to study for a Diploma in Social Work in the United Kingdom. He secured a scholarship, and in 1947 was admitted to the University College of South Wales at Cardiff.[66] Nyerere and Tibandebage remained in Tabora and embarked upon the rewriting of the constitution for the African Association.[67] They later used the organisation to mobilise opinion in the district against Colonial Paper 210, which made provision for each territorial legislature in East Africa to elect one additional member.[68] Europeans were naturally favoured because they held majorities in all three legislatures, but there was at least an opportunity for African opposition to the paper to be voiced by the African members of the Legislative Council.[69] These were Chief Abdiel Shangali of Machame (whose son-in-law, Solomon Eliufoo, had been at Makerere with Nyerere) and Chief David Kidaha Makwaia (also at Makerere with Nyerere) – notably both native administrators rather than members of the modern elite.[70] Nyerere met with Makwaia when the chief's train stopped in Tabora en route to the meeting in Dar es Salaam. He urged Makwaia to use his speech to attack the proposal, and pointed out that Colonial Paper 210 was a gross betrayal of the democratic principles for which Britain had professed to fight the war and which had been used as the main recruiting appeal amongst Africans. After this meeting Nyerere was then incensed to read in the *Tanganyika Standard* that Shangali and Makwaia – who he was soon to come across again in this early stage of his political life – had abstained from voting.[71] Later Nyerere temporarily took the place of Makwaia on the Legislative Council, an exposure that would likely have redoubled his determination to create a larger political role for himself.[72]

All the while Nyerere remained active in local African Association politics. He was doing something of note because, when in 1947 the leadership of the African Association Tanganyikan headquarters was discussed, some of the Dodoma leaders hoped that the seat would go to the up-and-coming branch of Tabora that he led.[73] Nyerere was also keeping a keen eye on political developments elsewhere in the territory. With Hamza Mwapachu in Dar es Salaam he had a trusted informant on branch politics at the coast. An indication of this is in an undated and unaddressed letter, written by Mwapachu to Nyerere, which offers an insight into issues discussed during a meeting in Dar es Salaam.[74] The subject of Mwapachu's report to Nyerere is unclear. It is tempting to conclude that it addresses African Association meetings, but Mwapachu may instead be referring to the Hamsa u Ishirini club, a club for Africans and Europeans 'without constitution or financial contribution … the cardinal law [of which] was not to admit any senior government official' – nor any Asians, whose relationship with Africans 'was mainly cool'.[75] Nyerere was apparently not a member of Hamsa u Ishirini, since it seems to have been Dar es Salaam-based only, although the club's ethos does point to a racial tolerance – albeit among its small membership, and towards some of the European community – that accounts of this period often attribute to Nyerere alone. The instigator of the club was a friend of Hamza Mwapachu named Mr H.H. Thornton, at the time a young colonial administrative officer who suggested small informal gatherings, as Vedastus Kyaruzi recalls:

> The subscription was to be a bottle of beer each and we would meet in homes.[76] … As Africans had no cars our European friends provided transport. … One evening the club met at my house at Ilala near Msimbazi Mission – in a housing estate recently opened for Africans. At the time all the towns in Tanganyika were demarcated into racial locations. To see so many Europeans at my house that evening was something previously unknown and more surprising to see them down to earth and enjoying themselves. …
>
> The main thing was to get together, bridge the gap between whites and blacks, and get to know each other and enjoy ourselves. Very rapidly the racial tension, which had become apparent subsided. Although no one could pinpoint the 'Hamza [*sic*] u ishirini' as the sole cause of the improvement in racial harmony, the club certainly made a significant contribution in Dar es Salaam. The fact that Europeans spent an evening at an African home at Ilala in an African area, drank, sang and behaved like human beings was an eye-opener to our people and gradually influenced their views and behaviour for the better.[77]

Of the eighteen topics that Mwapachu informed Nyerere were discussed, most were of a political nature, or concerned the betterment of Africans. The first on Mwapachu's list of discussions that his group had engaged in was 'Trusteeship as compared to Protectorate + Mandate'. This became an issue with the collapse of the League of Nations and was not resolved until 1947. By that time Britain was bound to prepare the territory for independence, and the United Nations Trusteeship Council had been empowered to send a visiting mission every three years to receive written and oral petitions from inhabitants.[78] The visiting missions then reported to the international community on administrative and political development in the territory. In doing so, they inspected numerous schools. Tabora was visited: it was the only place in Tanganyika to find upper secondary schools. It is not known if Nyerere attended, but there is every chance that he took the short walk to his alma mater to attend the 1948 visit there by Dr Lin Mousheng, the mission's delegate from the Republic of China. Dr Mousheng lectured the boys on the United Nations and the aims of the Trusteeship System. Emphasis was laid on the fact 'that Tanganyika was a trust territory in which the inhabitants were being trained to govern themselves, and he expressed the hope that in five to ten years' time he might see some of his audience in China!'[79] Had Nyerere not attended this inspiring lecture, then there is little doubt that he would have done his utmost to hear

Mousheng when he presented to the Standard XII pupils at his own St Mary's. It is again unknown whether Nyerere attended this inspirational visit by an eminent guest. If he was in town at the time, however, it is unfathomable that he would have missed the lecture. The native of China 'informed his listeners that they were the men who must lead the country and be its great men', and he had also expressed his hope 'to see some of them in New York!' Seven years later Julius Nyerere visited New York to address the United Nations Trusteeship Council.

Trusteeship had been on the agenda at the April 1946 African Association meeting in Dar es Salaam. It was closely linked to the second issue on Mwapachu's list that he sent to Nyerere: 'White Paper 191', published as Colonial Paper 191 in December 1945. White Paper 191 proposed the appointment of an East African High Commission consisting of three Governors as the apex of constitutional authority, under the Chairmanship of Kenya.[80] Other discussion topics that the Hamsa u Ishirini club engaged with included the related issue of 'White settlement in Tanganyika' and 'Who treats the Africans better, the Europeans or Indians' – both topics that Nyerere later addressed in Edinburgh when writing on 'The Race Problem in East Africa'. Alongside 'Hobies' [*sic*] and 'What would, according to the present African Society, be better Polygamy or Monogamy?',[81] Mwapachu also mentioned in his letter to Nyerere that issues of education and of religion were discussed. The debates for these topics would certainly have been of interest to both Mwapachu and Nyerere: 'Is the Educated African more happier [*sic*] and more useful to a community than an uneducated Africa?' was one debate, as were 'State vs. Mission Education' and 'Is Christianity good for the African at present?'[82] Together the topics covered in Mwapachu's letter point to the fact that Nyerere was balancing many commitments. He spent long hours dealing with concerns voiced by African Association members in his local branch and further afield about the future of Tanganyika and its peoples. All the while Nyerere was on a full-time teaching contract at St Mary's, where he taught both Biology and History, and also offered English tuition to members of the Combined Clubs. It was while in the midst of all this that the busy young bachelor was made aware of a young woman with whom he could share his faith – and, as it turned out, a woman who was to remain with him for the rest of his life.

Maria Waningu

Maria Waningu Gabriel Magige was born in Kiabaibi, Baraki village, in Tarime/North Mara (now Rorya) District, in November or December 1930.[83] Her parents were Hannah Nyashiboha and Gabriel Magige – a staunch Catholic who in 1933 was one of the first five Simbiti men to be baptised in a new White Father's mission in Buturi, Tarime District.[84] In Baraki, Maria's eldest brother, Joseph Mwita Kitigwa, taught Maria to read under a *minyaa* tree (*Euphorbia tirucalli*, Milk Bush, Firestick Plant, etc.) that acted as the village school. Maria went in 1938 to the White Sisters' School for girls at Nyegina, and in 1941 then attended Ukerewe School until she finished Standard V in 1944. In 1945 she progressed to Standard VI as a boarding scholar at Sumve Teacher Training College in Mwanza where, in Maria's own words, she was taught by 'highly-professional teachers. They were White Sisters, one from the Netherlands, and another from Ottawa University who was called Sister Prisca.' Maria obtained a Teachers' Certificate from Sumve in 1947, and went on to become a teacher at Nyegina Primary School in Musoma.

Maria Waningu was regarded as a capable woman of integrity, so much so that when a local District Commissioner was in search of a young educated woman to sit on the Tarime District Council, he came to find her.[85] According to Father Wille, the colonial official was shocked when he found Maria hoeing in her father's field, and equally surprised when she turned down his invitation.[86] This was not to be the last time that she declined an offer. Perhaps because of the unsuitability of the young Magori, Irenge states that, 'we thought that we would find a... mature girl who was educated. This was a headache. But we finally heard good things about a girl, Maria Gabriel, who was a teacher at Nyegina Primary School, in Musoma.'[87]

A couple who were very eager to see Maria and Julius together was a teacher at Nyegina, named Nestori Nyabambe, and his wife Anastazia. Nestori had studied in Tosamaganga, near Iringa, and was transferred to Kigoma town on the shores of Lake Tanganyika. When switching trains on the journey to and from Kigoma, the couple would spend the night with Julius in Tabora. During one such stay, so Maria tells, Nestori said to Julius: 'You look like a good boy, but you do not have a girlfriend. There is another teacher called Maria who you should meet. Both of you are light skinned and have good behaviour, so you will have good children.'[88] Maria says Nestori Nyabambe and his wife Anastazia were the ones who first told her about a young man, Julius, who was still single.[89] Maria recalls that her attention was raised when the couple reported to her that, 'Julius goes to church each morning and he is of good behaviour and does not fool around.'[90]

The first meeting between the two is said to have been arranged by Nestori and Anastazia. They took the opportunity for an initial rendezvous between Julius and Maria when the Governor came to visit Musoma. The visit also brought out the local chiefs, and the occasion called for all government workers to be present. This prompted Maria and her fellow teachers to bring to Musoma the children from their nearby school in Nyegina in order to welcome the officials – at which point the matchmakers introduced Maria and Julius (who then was on vacation) to each other.[91] Having been introduced, Julius seems to have been keen to conduct a follow-up with his new sweetheart. Shortly afterwards he met again with Maria at Nestori and Anastazia Nyabambe's house.[92]

Maria had severe misgivings about 'the teacher from Makerere', as she referred to him then. Her concern was spiritual, she recalls, and she was worried that a relationship with a chief's son would be difficult because he could not possibly be a Christian. Maria set about trying to discourage Julius from showing interest in her, and asked him why he would not marry a Zanaki woman. His explanation was that educated Zanaki men knew not to marry their own women because the inheritance – usually cows, but in a notoriously factious process[93] – is not passed on to his children but to those of his sister. Julius used his school friend Oswald Mang'ombe Marwa as an example of an educated man who had married a woman from another tribe. He also cited the case of Daniel Kirigini, his teacher at Mwisenge.[94] Nyerere later said that, while he understood the logic, he did not like the tradition. Although inheritance between a Zanaki man and a Zanaki woman was matrilineal, he noted, it was patrilineal where the wife was not Zanaki – as was the case for his wife. Nyerere explained that he believed the tradition was motivated by the fact that while one can never be certain who a child's father is, one can always be sure that the children belong to their mother. He apparently repeated to his children that, because he did not want them to be cheated, the rule did not apply to his family.[95]

Another issue that was on Julius' mind, notes Father Wille, is the lack of Catholic women for him to have chosen from among the Zanaki. Since Julius apparently wished to marry a Catholic – and his reportedly strong faith at the time would suggest that this was the case – he would marry outside his tribe by default.[96] A similar explanation was also offered by Jack Nyamwaga: 'Maria was only [in] class four, but she was the only literate woman around. And Mwalimu was looking for a Catholic – only a Catholic would do. So it was Maria: a literate Catholic woman.'[97] Julius would also have been aware that time was not on his side, and that he would have rivals to compete against in winning the young woman's hand in marriage. At the same time as Maria was clarifying Julius's credentials, other young men were also showing interest in her. During the school holidays potential suitors would propose. For advice Maria would turn to Joseph Mwita, who had studied in neighbouring Kenya. The family depended on Joseph for his wisdom since – like Julius' brother Burito – Maria's brother had some worldly experience having fought for the British King's African Rifles during the Second World War. With one wooer Joseph recommended to Maria that she should tell him to return after six months; only later did she realise this was a polite refusal.

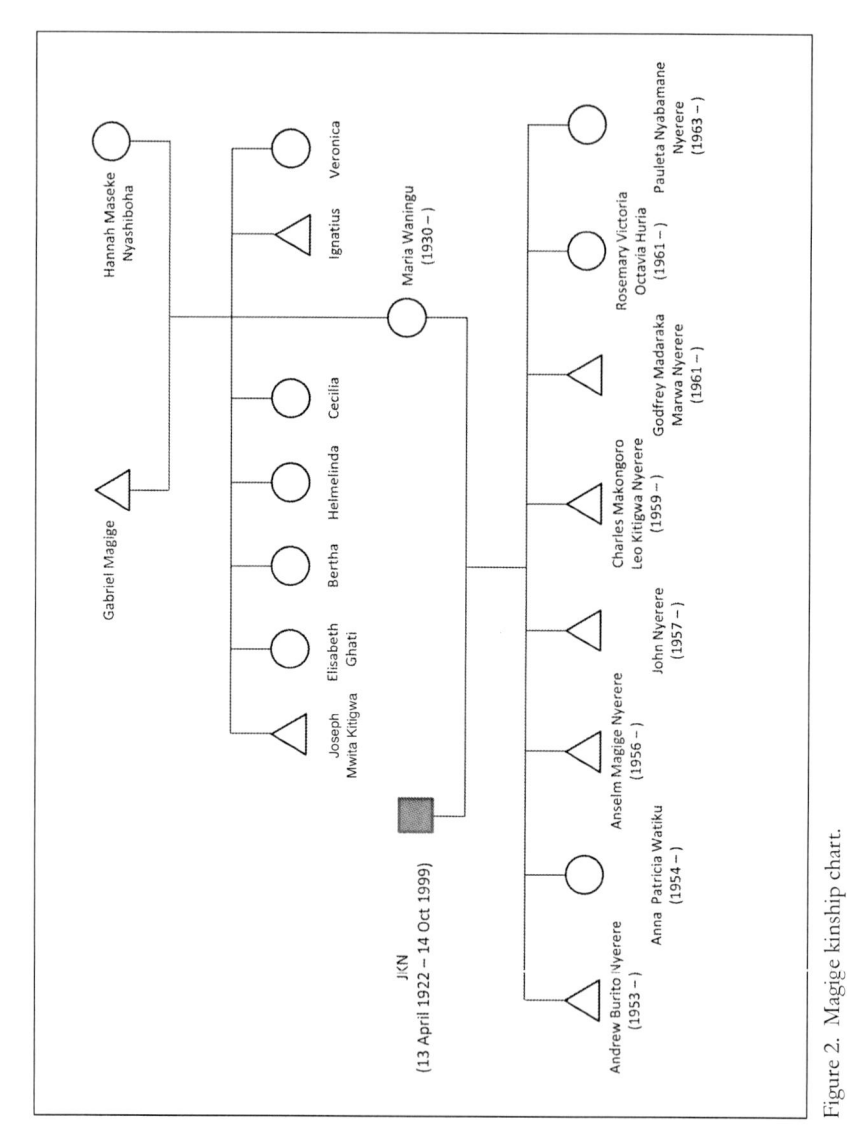

Figure 2. Magige kinship chart.
(*Some wives and children have been excluded due to space constraints; only known dates are given.*)

A Personal *Ekyaaro*

As well as marriage, at St Mary's Nyerere was also considering his education. Dissatisfied with it, he told Father Richard Walsh, the Director and his tutor, that he wished to continue his studies.[98] Walsh, along with various Catholic Maryknoll Fathers and Brothers of the Musoma area (particularly Father William J. Collins), is thought to have had considerable influence on Nyerere's life and thought.[99] At time the British had misgivings about the Irish priest's encouragement for his pupils to become the future leaders of Tanganyika.[100] Walsh entered Nyerere into the University of London Matriculation Examination. The examination was used to assess a student's suitability for certain universities in the United Kingdom. Nyerere sat the examination in Tabora and was tested on English, Swahili, Elementary Mathematics, Biology, and History of the British Empire.[101] He passed with Second Division in January 1948.[102]

Father Walsh wrote to friends in England to raise money to support Nyerere's higher education. He succeeded in getting funds, but Julius declined the offer on two different occasions. Reflecting on why Nyerere would turn down the opportunity to go abroad for further education, Father Wille surmises that it was 'because he was afraid that spending a few years abroad in Europe, he would return less African. He loved his culture. He loved his roots.'[103] This may have been the case, but it is unlikely to have been the central reason that Nyerere did not travel overseas at this time. Practical reasons probably played a part. Perhaps he had been given a teaching offer that appealed in the short term. It is also conceivable that he was seriously considering the priesthood; we simply do not know. It does seem that there was still an enduring political motive though, and that he was indeed bound to his roots and to the future of the Zanaki in rural Musoma, Lake Province – where the African Association (or the *Tanganyika* African Association from 1948) was now at its most active. The Association was so vigorous in the area that it was agreed at a 1948 Provincial conference that the National Headquarters be moved to Mwanza as the Dar es Salaam office seemed 'dormant'.[104] An elder in Butiama recollects how on one occasion when Julius returned from St Mary's, 'Mwalimu tried to hold meetings with elders and influence the eight Zanaki chiefs to come together. The chiefs seemed to support the idea of a single Zanaki chief.'[105] Nyerere is then said to have 'embarked on a journey in Zanaki country, akin to the ritual walk his elders called *kukerera*. He walked the land … building consensus among the notable citizens of Zanaki country as a personal *ekyaro* [territory].' Whether Nyerere made such a journey is hard to know for sure.

What is perhaps more important, it has been suggested, is the *memory* that he did, grounding his ascension to authority in a local idiom.[106]

Walsh continued to urge Julius to go abroad to study.[107] According to one of Nyerere's childhood friends, however, his continuing interest in politics almost prevented him from the next move in his career as a student. So the account goes, a local British official wrote to the Governor in the belief that Nyerere should be prevented from studying overseas because he was 'politically minded and might pose a threat when he returned'.[108] Nyerere was nevertheless allowed to apply for a scholarship under the Colonial Development and Welfare Scheme (CDWS). Funded by the Colonial Development and Welfare Act of 1940 which provided imperial finance for long-term colonial development plans, the scholarships were awarded 'to suitably qualified persons of all races who wish to obtain the necessary qualifications to fit them for higher posts in the public service'.[109] Nyerere applied for a scholarship to study Education, with Administration as his second choice. He received a reference from Father John Stanley, the headmaster of St Mary's, who wrote that Nyerere was 'an excellent young man: intelligent, enthusiastic, industrious and conscientious to a very high degree ... a fine type of character, open as a book'.[110] The Tanganyika Territory Scholarships Selection Committee then supported the application, considering Nyerere to be 'well suited to undergo a Teaching Course at the Colonial Department of the Institute of Education at London University'.[111] Despite this recommendation, he applied not for London University but for a Scottish university. His grades and references notwithstanding, Nyerere was unsuccessful in his first attempt. He did not 'completely satisfy the requirements of Scottish Universities Entrance Board for the award of a Certificate of Fitness, inasmuch as his Matriculation Certificate did not include a pass in English Literature, nor a language other than English approved by the Board'.[112]

Nyerere followed the recommendation to re-submit for consideration to study in the United Kingdom in 1949. Students of Nyerere's ilk were just what the home government now wanted. Some in Whitehall began to realise a trend away from imperialism and toward self-rule: changes were underway in British dependencies as a result of the war effort, and both the British and Dutch empires in South-East Asia had collapsed under the onslaught of the Japanese in 1941–42. Increasingly the Soviet Bloc, the new Communist regime in China, and the United States all looked askance at and undermined the old European colonial regimes. Britain now began to realise that it needed to rethink its obligations to its future leaders. If it failed to do so, she risked losing the colonial elites to the alternatives presented by the United States or to Communist foes.[113] Conservatives still maintained, however, that the system of indirect rule would have to be preserved. They viewed the

Photo 11. Passport-size portrait of Julius Nyerere, c. 1946, submitted with his application to study in the United Kingdom.
(*Reproduced by kind permission of The National Archives, United Kingdom*)

introduction of political change in terms of several generations. Those generally affiliated with the Labour Party, by contrast, were relatively more inclined towards an acceleration of the political systems within African dependencies. Some contended that only immediate and direct exposure to modern political processes would truly prepare Africans for self-rule. Others in Attlee's 1945 Government, however, were much less enthused by the idea of rapid decolonisation.

Daniel Smith's archive-based thesis argues that in the United Kingdom at this time the Fabian Colonial Bureau was the most influential and prestigious of the progressive activist groups geared towards these ends. The organisation was founded in October 1940 by Labour Member of Parliament Arthur Creech Jones and the British socialist leaders Marjorie Nicholson, James Betts, and the South African Rita Hinden, as an extension of the British Fabian Society.[114] The Bureau's purpose was to collect and coordinate information concerning activities in the dependencies and to encourage demands within the home government for the dissolution of the Empire. By 1945 the Fabian Colonial Bureau had taken a special interest in Tanganyika Territory and had begun to probe official parties which it suspected of not always serving the best interests of the African population. It later made contact with sympathetic figures such as Chief Kidaha Makwaia, Thomas Marealle, and a young Julius Nyerere.[115]

A more progressive official environment was evident in a July 1947 memorandum from the Colonial Office's new African Studies Branch. It emphasised the crucial importance of 'incorporating' African students, as future leaders, in 'the social, political and economic scheme'.

The plan was being developed by Andrew Cohen of the Colonial Office and Arthur Creech Jones. They aimed to modernise local government in the African colonies and employ western-educated Africans in it: 'It would scarcely be too much to say that the whole political future ... is bound up with these few men, whether as the heirs of government in West Africa or leaders of the principal race in the future partnership governments of East Africa.'[116] The future of British colonial Africa was to be placed in the hands of a tiny cadre of Africans who were to be educated as black facsimiles of (rather idealised) white colonial officials. This was merely an extension, some might argue, of the old policy of educating the sons of African chiefs for future roles in government. It is no surprise then, that between 1945 and 1951 the number of students sponsored by colonial governments in Britain rose from 396 to 1,313.[117]

The board for the CDWS scholarships met in March 1948 and considered candidates from Zanzibar, British Somaliland, Kenya, Tanganyika and The Gambia. Twenty-six applicants were shortlisted to study in the United Kingdom. Of those remaining, an applicant from Tanganyika who was not recommended on this occasion was 'considered a weak candidate [for whom] it would be extremely difficult to suggest a possible course'. Another was simply deemed to be too old. J.C.A. Mbelwa was denied because he had recently completed a teaching course, while Abdallah Fundikira and I.S. Ishingoma's proposed courses were too similar to their previous studies at Makerere.[118] The selection committee for the '£1,000,000 Colonial Development and Welfare Scheme' decided to recommend fifteen of the applicants. One was 'J.K. Nyerere'.[119]

Despite the rare opportunity to study abroad however, Nyerere was still pulled by a sense of obligation at home. His efforts among the chiefs had paid off, and many of them were supportive of the election of a Zanaki paramount chief. Some elders are said to have urged him to pursue a course in law so that he could be an advocate and defend his countrymen in various cases.[120] Among them was his brother Wanzagi,[121] with whom 'Mwalimu ... had a very good relationship when Wanzagi was chief. They would have meetings between themselves and discuss issues. Chief [Wanzagi] had nobody older to counsel him, and he went to Mwalimu for advice.'[122]

Torn between home and abroad, Julius looked for advice. He apparently turned to James Irenge, who summarised Nyerere's reasoning thus:

> If the problem is how to get an appropriate leader that all the chiefs can trust and accept to be the leader of all of Zanaki-land. If this is the question, and they can't find another but think that I (Kambarage) would please them as the chief they want to lead them, then I am ready to postpone the trip to England to study for the opportunity I was given there.[123]

Indeed, while there is no evidence of hereditary ascension to the Zanaki paramountcy, it does seem from Hans Cory's hand-written notes that – at least among the Zanaki of Butiama – Kambarage was considered after Wanzagi to be next-in-line to the chiefship.[124] Irenge, the self-proclaimed deal-breaker, told Julius to go for the studies in the United Kingdom. 'When he would return', thought Irenge, 'without doubt he would lead all of Musoma and not just Zanaki country which is but a small part of this district.'[125]

Julius decided against a course in law. He 'stuck to his ambition to specialise in teaching, arguing that as an advocate, one sometimes had to tell lies, and this would betray his conscience'.[126] While a star debater, 'he didn't like law because of the unfairness in manipulation by strength of argument'. This, of course, is one of the main attributes of the successful debater and of the politician that Nyerere became. As a teacher, on the other hand, Nyerere could 'help more people'.[127] He finally sided on his own teacher's advice and took up the offer 'for a four-year scholarship for a Science degree course'.[128] This was with the understanding, so thought the Secretary of State for the Colonies, that Nyerere would use his studies in the United Kingdom to become a qualified Science teacher.[129]

Engagement

Julius was aware of the customs that a young man had to follow if he was to ask for a woman's hand in marriage. He was familiar with the general procedure for a number of tribes, and he knew the particularities of the Zanaki custom in detail.[130] In love, and perhaps also mindful that his chances of finding a suitable African woman in the United Kingdom were slim, Nyerere proposed to Maria a few months before leaving. Maria agreed to the proposal, and the couple were informally engaged at Christmas 1948.[131] Julius wished for the marriage to occur before his departure, but the ceremony did not take place. Neither was there an exchange of bridewealth; strictly speaking, therefore, the agreement was not deemed formal. The bridewealth custom was something that Nyerere had strongly opposed for some years, and he devoted an entire chapter to it in his earlier 'Uhuru wa Wanawake'.[132] In the essay he points out that the English translation of *mahari* is 'bride-price', which makes explicit that the arrangement is an exchange of the bride for an agreed sum of money.[133] If the marriage union amounts to little more than transaction, Nyerere continued, then essentially the *mahari* custom allows for us to buy our women. This, he argued, is tantamount to the slavery that he so vehemently opposed.[134] Using his own tribe as an example – and perhaps with the experience of close friends or relatives in mind – Nyerere went on to further explain his opposition to the practice, arguing that

> bridewealth has meant that marriage is extremely burdensome for women. Husbands have no threat for their wives other than beatings, or to remind them that they are married as an exchange and that if they get up to mischief they will simply dismiss [i.e., divorce] them and reclaim their property. Many very poor women would like to leave their cruel husbands, but they do not dare to since they are unable to return the bridewealth [because they cannot afford to].[135]

Maria's father Gabriel opposed the exchange because he felt that if the bridewealth was received it would mean that his daughter would be left among the Zanaki people. Gabriel feared that the Zanaki would torment Maria with hard work and 'wear her out'.[136] Father Walsh supported this arrangement, as did the bishop – possibly because they both knew that their young convert would not be able to become a Roman Catholic priest if he married. Gabriel said that if Julius still wanted to marry his daughter when he returned from Britain, he would give it his blessing. If the couple did not still wish to marry, however, then Maria would still be young enough to find another bachelor.

The proposal that worked for Julius was that Maria study Domestic Science in Uganda. The idea came from Father Walsh, who suggested Maria proceed with her studies so that there was less difference in formal education between the two.[137] Or, as the Colonial Office's education policy put it, 'reasonably well-trained women' would ensure 'that clever boys, for whom higher education is expedient, [could] look forward to educated mates'.[138] Maria again turned for the advice of her brother Joseph Mwita Kitigwa. Joseph agreed that she study and, on the recommendation of Father Walsh, Maria attended Stella Maris College, a Catholic sisters' school in Nsube, Uganda. Despite the lack of a bridewealth payment, and therefore technically there being no formal agreement, the young couple had agreed between themselves to be faithful while they were abroad.[139] When Julius then received for his scholarship an advance payment to cover some of his expenses in Tanganyika, he gave some money to his fiancée, to his brother Edward Wanzagi, and to his mother.[140]

Around the time of his engagement, close to Christmas 1948, Julius cycled from Butiama to the house of Omar Marwa Mang'ombe and Mama Magori, in nearby Nyigina (Butuguri). He had travelled there to see his Mwisenge school friend Oswald Mang'ombe Marwa, who at the time was on leave from his teaching job at Bwiru Technical School and was staying with his parents. It may have been that, as Father Wille tells it, this was the occasion when Oswald helped Julius to make arrangements for his marriage.[141]

In March 1949 Nyerere said his goodbyes to acquaintances in Tabora,

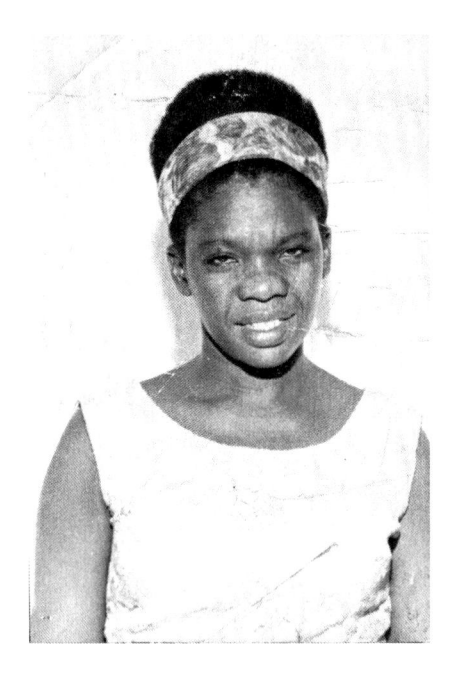

Photo I. Maria Nyerere (née Waningu Gabriel Magige), Julius Nyerere's wife; Musoma, Tanzania, early 1950s. (*Reproduced by kind permission of Joseph Muhunda Nyerere*)

and deposited his belongings there with his trusted friend Andrew Tibandebage.[142] The same month Nyerere revisited Oswald's house in Nyigina, wearing what for that time were his customary white shorts, white shirt, and long white stockings – the uniform of a teacher. Oswald's parents ran to greet him and Julius called out, 'I am going to Europe!' – telling them that he was saying his goodbyes to them but that he was in a hurry to leave in order to prepare himself for his travels. Mama Magori was having none of it, and insisted that since Julius was going so far he had to have a good meal as she did not want to be blamed if he was not well fed for his journey. When it came time for Julius to leave, Mama Magori said: 'Go there, and when you have finished, don't forget us: come back.'[143]

5
Scotland

Great Conceptions

> *The sense of being in the centre of things yet not in the eye of the storm ... my destiny was here; I knew it in my bones. I dug my heels in even deeper in Edinburgh. ... Strangely, in this remote bit of the continent, everything important felt within reach: the sky, the ocean, the past, the end of Europe and the beginning.*
>
> 'The Magic Place', Kapka Kassabova[1]

This is the first of three chapters that follow Nyerere to the United Kingdom. In this chapter we note Nyerere's Tanganyikan predecessors who had previously studied in England, and reveal his reason for deciding to take a degree at the University of Edinburgh. The chapter offers an overview of race relations in the United Kingdom at the time, and details the Communist Party's interest in African students. It then outlines the courses that Nyerere took over his three years in Edinburgh, introduces some of his main lecturers and the readings they prescribed, and considers the Tanganyikan student's performance alongside his British peers. An investigation is conducted into Nyerere's financial difficulties, leading to an assessment of what this tells us about his character at the time. New information is offered on Nyerere's friendships in and outside university. This is set within the context of national and international events, with particular reference to race, democracy and liberation. The chapter draws on the author's correspondence with White Fathers missionaries, and with various University of Edinburgh academic and chaplaincy staff who knew Nyerere in Edinburgh. It considers Fabian Colonial Bureau correspondence with Tanganyikans, Nyerere's correspondence with colonial officials in London and Dar es Salaam, and newspaper articles that he read. The chapter serves as one of three chapters that together contribute to a first comprehensive examination of the academic literature that Nyerere studied in Edinburgh. These are used to assess the influence that his choice of degree programme had on his future writing, speeches and policies.

Communists

On Saturday 9 April 1949 Julius Nyerere boarded the state-run British Overseas Airways Corporation's new Short Solent 2 flying boat 'Southampton' for his first flight in an airplane, complete with the luxury of 'four-course meals and Pullman-style upholstery'.[2] He boarded at the Customs House jetty in Dar es Salaam on a flight that had originated in Johannesburg and which took him through East Africa, and up the Nile. Taking off from the South Creek, the unpressurised plane flew during daylights hours and stopped overnight en route to the English southern coastal town of Southampton.

Nyerere's arrival in England is an opportunity to debunk the popular myth that he was the first Tanganyikan to ever venture into the metropole in pursuit of learning.[3] A number of Tanganyikans had of course visited the United Kingdom before him. Among them were Chief Makwaia of Usiha, who had travelled to London in 1931 to testify at hearings on the question of closer union for the East African territories. His son, David Kidaha Makwaia, 'a very good type of African', showed much promise as a student of Philosophy and Politics at Lincoln College, Oxford, but his responsibilities as chief only permitted him to study for one year.[4] Other Tanganyikans had also studied in the United Kingdom, further negating the perpetual assertion that Nyerere was the lone pioneer.[5] This is simply not correct. The Zanzibar-born Mathew Ramadhani was the first African Tanganyikan to hold a British degree, awarded by the University of Sheffield.[6] Thomas Marealle, 'senior African collaborator with Lord Twining' and later Paramount Chief of the Chagga, studied at Cambridge and in 1946 completed a course in social welfare at the London School of Economics (LSE).[7] The mission-educated Frederick Mchauru, later one of Nyerere's first Principal Secretaries, also took a two-year course at the same institution, returning to Tanganyika in 1946.[8] Godfrey Kayamba was at Southampton University College in the same year, Paulo Mwinyipembe was at Durham, and the following year Hamza Mwapachu was admitted to the University College of South Wales at Cardiff. While Godfrey Kayamba was sent back home because he studied so little, his grandfather, Hugh Peter Kayamba, was more successful during his two-and-a-half years at Bloxham school, Oxfordshire, which he attended as early as 1883.[9] At the English public school at the same time was Henry Nasibu, who by 1921 had become head of a school in Pemba.[10] Cecil Majaliwa, a Yao freedman who in 1890 became Tanganyika's first African priest, had earlier attended St Augustine's College, Canterbury.[11] If Nyerere is to be regarded as a Tanganyikan pioneer, it should be for what he did with his formal education.

Nyerere

Nyerere arrived in Southampton on 12 April 1949. This was only a few months after the *Empire Windrush* had docked in England as the start of a wave of immigration from the West Indies. Many white people in Britain were horrified at this development, and within two days of the ship's arrival a group of eleven Members of Parliament wrote to the Prime Minister calling for controls on black immigration.[12] The 'colonials', so it seemed to many white Britons, were getting above their station. From the black perspective, however, they were getting more organised, especially in the few short years since powerful contingents from West Africa and West Indies had attended the 1945 Pan-African Congress in Manchester. The meeting's impact remained in the capital where, not long before Nyerere first reached the city, George Padmore's flat was still the place for many West Indians and Africans to discuss politics. Post-war London was home to black radicals, among them Jomo Kenyatta, Ras Makonnen, Peter Koinange, Peter Abrahams, C.L.R. James, and Kwame Nkrumah.[13] Nyerere knew about some of these men from their coverage in the newspapers back home. But none of them had heard of the young Zanaki schoolteacher by the time his plane landed at Southampton. Nor, for that matter, did they hear of him until years later.[14] Nyerere's arrival was uneventful. He was met at the airways terminal and accompanied by train to London's Waterloo station.[15] His first full day in Britain was his twenty-seventh birthday, which he spent in London, lodging for a week at The Balmoral Hotel in Victoria. He had a series of meetings at the Colonial Office headquarters on Victoria Street to discuss his degree course studies.[16] On the morning of 20 April 1949 took the eight-and-a-half hour journey on *The Flying Scotsman* from Kings Cross to the Scottish capital. The train made only one stop, Newcastle, before reaching its destination, Edinburgh, 'The Athens of the North'.

Nyerere's train pulled into Edinburgh in the light early evening of Wednesday 20 April. His first prolonged residence in a city – Tabora and the outskirts of Kampala were the only settlements of any size that he had spent much time in – the young Tanganyikan was full of hope. Aware of the opportunities that an Edinburgh degree would bring, and confident of his academic abilities in the East African context, Nyerere was now in uncharted territory. He would have known that many Makerere students' social origins were sophisticated when likened to those of East Africa, yet humble compared with students elsewhere.[17] In Edinburgh the vast majority of students' parents were literate, and Nyerere surely wondered what qualities his classmates held in the competition for grades and the pressure to succeed.[18] Together with the excitement as he entered this grand city came more than a little apprehension about his future in it.

Nyerere was met at Edinburgh Waverley railway station by a member of the Colonial Office Welfare Department.[19] It was important for more than reasons of practicality and hospitality that new African arrivals were met in Edinburgh. Reverend Dr W.D. Cattanach, the Chaplain to Overseas Students, remembers that, 'people from the Communist Party cells were also at Waverley station meeting students, and the followers of Frank Buchman in the Moral Rearmament Movement were also keen to meet and influence possible Third World Leaders coming to the University.'[20]

Both Aminu Kano from Nigeria and Joe Appiah from the Gold Coast report of being courted by Communists during their time studying in the United Kingdom.[21] While Cattanach prefaced that this would 'sometimes' occur, a number of figures in the British establishment 'widely believed that the Communist Party contacts "all" colonial students on their arrival'.[22] Alexander Carey writes that the authorities put forward no evidence for this, although it does seem plausible that the Communist Party's limited resources prevented them effectively recruiting members from the African student population when they arrived. On the other side, Carey goes on, 'many colonial students are convinced that the Colonial Office keep an eye on students with extreme left-wing views, possibly with harmful effects on their careers'.[23] What constituted 'left-wing views' was open to interpretation though, as Hamza Mwapachu, studying at the University College of South Wales in Cardiff, wrote to Rita Hinden at the Fabian Colonial Bureau: 'Socialists and people with socialist connections tend to be labelled "Communists" here. In fact, it would appear that the greater bulk of Europeans, both officials and non-officials out here, to say the least, have no respect for liberal reformers.'[24]

There does appear to be some evidence that authorities in the United Kingdom did indeed observe potential Communists. British intelligence interest in the activities of some colonial students was sparked by riots in Accra a year before Nyerere arrived in Edinburgh. It was suspected that the disturbances had been planned in London.[25] Kwame Nkrumah had registered for a Ph.D. in Anthropology at the LSE.[26] British police then found among his personal effects a membership card from a London branch of the Communist Party. At this point the security services immediately intensified their surveillance on overseas students.[27] The authorities' worries also stretched to Nyerere's homeland, and during his time in the United Kingdom an Edinburgh newspaper ran a story with the title, 'Concerns in UK of risk of Communism in East Africa'.[28] The sentiment in Britain towards the communist threat became evident when, not long before the Nkrumah incident, Arthur Creech Jones visited a Fabian Colonial Bureau conference at Pasture Wood in Surrey in the south-east of England. The offending events of the meeting were described in

Wodehousian language by an official who was present. The Secretary of State, apparently,

> stopped a bucket of Bolshie stuff from some of the Colonials present. He was distinctly stirred up about it, and in a few sentences I had with him he was full of 'something must be done about it,' etc. Vickers and I both thought it was too good an opportunity to miss of capitalizing on the opportunity of ensuring that the S. of S.'s explosion should be exploded into the transmission.[29]

Segregation

Safely protecting his fresh-faced young charge from any Bolshevist would-be meddlers, the Welfare Officer accompanied Nyerere in a taxi from Waverley to his accommodation – during which time he would have caught a glimpse of the trams, which in those days still reigned supreme on the city's streets.[30] The officer delivered his fellow traveller to 2, Palmerston Road in the city's desirable suburb of The Grange, comprised at that time of little more than large late-Victorian stone-built villas. Then called Colonial House, 2, Palmerston Road was a residence for 'all sorts of colonial persons', and not only those of African descent.[31] The *Student's Handbook*, an introductory guide to the University that was issued to Nyerere, describes Colonial House as providing both club and temporary residential facilities for colonial students. It was also the location of both the Afro-Scottish Society and the Edinburgh African Association monthly meetings.[32] A short walk from the central teaching rooms and administrative offices of the University, an official in the Welfare Department of the Colonial Office described the communal life of such a residence as 'the ideal environment for the African student ... where he can associate with home students and share fully the amenities of University life.'[33]

A brief letter from a Brian Cross to the editor of the Edinburgh University students' magazine, *The Student*, written some months after Nyerere arrived at Colonial House, suggests that at Edinburgh all may not have been as rosy as Colonial Office officials might have hoped: 'Has the time come for all Edinburgh University Hostels to take a quota of coloured students? I appreciate there are many arguments against this policy but feel the possible gain far outweighs these. Are we not showing signs of prejudice and unreason in our own University?'[34] Cross's apparent support for residential intermingling between races is not outlined in any further detail. What is slightly alarming is that, despite the Welfare Department in London's promotion in 1946 of integration between African and home students in university hostels in Britain, still in 1950 there was a call for the introduction of non-white students into Edinburgh student accommodation.[35] Talk of 'a quota of coloured students' to resolve this issue might indicate that there was some resistance among students – presumably home students – who could offer the 'many arguments against this policy'. Possibly more conservative elements of the University Administration supported them at this time. Yet this is a far cry from the situation of many black students in America at the time, where, as a 1950 article in Edinburgh's *The Student* magazine bemoaned, 'increasing jimcrow and segregation' meant that in some cases 'the Negro is now admitted to a previously all-white institution separated from the white students behind a screen.'[36]

The other side of Edinburgh's de facto segregation was that during their spare time African and other colonial students could live together at Palmerston Road alongside fellows with more similar backgrounds. In this respect Colonial House may have been a welcome respite in evenings and over the weekends, when residents could write home undisturbed, and share news with their new African friends and those from elsewhere across 'the colonies'. As an author around this time put it, these hostels were not only cheaper than private accommodation, but offered security and relief from loneliness. Above all, the hostels eliminated that spectre of colonial student life: 'the intolerant or grasping landlady'.[37]

Nyerere was fortunate to receive University accommodation in Edinburgh. The city was one of the main centres for Africans, but still was said to be 'notoriously bad to find really suitable lodgings for African students'.[38] Accommodation difficulties were a recurrent theme in the conversation of colonial students at the time, as one East African law student in London explained: 'I wasted from four to six weeks looking for a room. There can be no doubt that coloured people find this much harder than others. Looking for accommodation means, not only a waste of time, but to invite constant humiliation.'[39]

Writing a couple of years before Nyerere moved into his accommodation, John Keith, the Director of Colonial Scholars and a left-leaning liberal,[40] reported: 'The African student has been, and still is being, denied free access to lodgings which may be available to other classes of students.'[41] Of 225 prospective landladies in London, for example, 90 declared that they would accept all nationalities but 'no coloured', and 23 of the more thorough-going type of xenophobe said that they would allow 'all except Negro types/Negroes/blacks' to stay with them. Similarly, 90 per cent of registered landladies would not allow 'negroes' to stay on their premises.[42] In addition to this, African students faced an unspoken 'colour-tax' that prevailed among many landladies. Some feared having to provide coloured students with extra services such as 'fancy foods'. Cooking for Africans, it seems, was a particular worry for landladies. Mary Trevelyan, the University of London's adviser to overseas students, reported of one landlady who 'actually asked a coloured man with an Honours degree whether he liked his meat cooked or raw'.[43] Carey quotes an East African student who, suspecting a 'colour tax', put two advertisements in a local paper: 'The wording was the same in both cases, but in one of them I didn't state my nationality. … The first advert brought many more replies than the second. I also had two answers offering the same room; but in the case of the second advertisement, the price charged was ten shillings more!'[44]

The British Council later intervened in such cases, and acted as an agent of the Colonial Office in all matters affecting the welfare of colonial students. This was deemed appropriate if Britain wished to regain its long-standing principle that hospitality should be 'unofficial'. The British Council stood 'at arm's length' from Government, with a constitution supported by a Royal Charter.[45] It apparently won widespread confidence by the manifest goodwill and good sense of its approach. As the British Council told a Cabinet committee, the organisation was

> opposed to regarding Colonial students as a 'separate category' and thus engendering and encouraging the attitude of the Colonials that they are 'problem children'. … Such success as the Council has achieved is believed to be partly due to the fact that Council officers are not Government officials, but partly also because all overseas persons, white or coloured, old or young, distinguished or humble, are treated as human beings towards whom the Council's responsibility is that of ensuring that their time in the UK is profitable, as pleasant as possible, and that they return to their own countries with at least some understanding of the life and thought of this land.[46]

It was not always the prejudices of intolerant landladies that explained some colonial students' 'attitude of bitterness', as 'the very irresponsible disposition' of one of Nyerere's fellow countrymen was described. Godfrey Kayamba reached the United Kingdom two years before Nyerere. Kayamba was one of two Africans from Tanganyika selected for a Colonial Science course to train as an Assistant Welfare Officer at Southampton University College, but his apparent dubious way of life would have done little to endear many hosts.[47] Kayamba quickly found himself in financial difficulties, failed to pay his rent, and described the solution that his rent be paid directly to his landlady as 'humiliating and niggardly'. Kayamba's landlady later refused to allow him to lodge, and no other landlords would take him in. Southampton University College found his work 'dilatory', and he is said to have left London when practical social work had been arranged for him. As a result the Director of Colonial Scholars recommended that Kayamba's scholarship be terminated, and the Tanganyikan government acted on this advice by forcing him to return home before he could complete his studies. Kayamba eventually made it back to Tanganyika, but not before he became engaged to a 'Dutch girl to whom he represented himself as a large landowner'. She found out that he was still married from a Christian wedding and had children, by which time he had become 'something of an anglophobe' and 'anti-British and anti-Government'. In the eyes of some of those who had experienced unfortunate dealings with Kayamba, other Africans – and in particular Tanganyikans, such as Nyerere – ran the risk of being tarred with the same brush.

An Ordinary M.A.

Nyerere first raised his wish to study an Arts degree at his opening meeting with Colonial Office officials in London. This appears anyway to have been the understanding of some officials in both Tanganyika and the United Kingdom. During the preceding year, in March 1948, the Director of Colonial Scholars had drafted a note to a colleague to ensure that she make a special effort to place Nyerere, a '£1 million scholar', for a general Arts degree.[48] Other officials were then talking about a Science degree so that Nyerere would indeed become a qualified Science teacher.[49] Despite his remonstrations against studying Science, Nyerere's scholarship was extended for coaching for a non-qualifying year in Science subjects. With reluctance Nyerere took Chemistry (a subject he had studied at Makerere) and Physics in Edinburgh. The short course was tutored by a Mr McNaughton as preparation for the London External Intermediate Science course at Robert Gordon's Technical College in Aberdeen. This was qualification for entry to a university Science degree course in October 1950.[50] One commentator is of the opinion that education officials at the time may have been sceptical towards the academic abilities of Africans. Many Edinburgh staff at the time thought that the likes of Nyerere were not quite capable of reaching the required standards on an Arts degree.[51]

To avoid Science and to pursue the Arts degree that he preferred, Nyerere had three options.[52] Scotland's ancient University of St Andrews, some distance north-east of Edinburgh, was mentioned at an early date. This was soon dropped, presumably because, as the correspondence points out, for a St Andrews Arts degree he would have had to take up Arabic from scratch. The first option that was presented was to move south to Durham University.[53] The second option was to stay in Scotland and replace his non-qualifying course in Science with one in the Arts. This meant continuing with Latin, and the tedium of a year of study without a certificate at the end. The third option, which Nyerere favoured and pursued, was for a Scottish Arts Degree that would commence in only a few months. This required him to pass English Literature or Higher English as an 'Attestation of Fitness' – and, yet again, to study Latin.[54] Nyerere quickly passed Higher English in the Scottish Universities Preliminary Examination. As a special concession the University of Edinburgh allowed him to take English as a foreign language so that 'he will no longer be troubled with Latin'.[55]

Nyerere left Edinburgh at least once during the summer of 1949. In August he spent some time near Coldharbour, outside Dorking in the south-east of England. There he stayed at Broome Hall, a former White Fathers novitiate where young men would seek to deepen their life of prayer and commitment to the Missionaries of Africa.[56] It is not known for sure why Nyerere made the trip at this time, although the White Fathers were his employer in Tanganyika[57] and it is possible that before he had left Tanganyika Father Richard Walsh had supplied him with contacts among White Fathers in the United Kingdom. The hope may have been that Nyerere might at some point have a vocation.[58] Whoever made the invitation to Broome Hall, it is likely that Nyerere, having been away from home for four months, regarded the White Fathers as friends in a foreign land, and saw their Surrey country house as the perfect place for a study break away from his coaching in Science subjects in Edinburgh. Alternatively, he may have visited the White Fathers for discussion over spiritual matters, or he may have gone for advice on his future course of study. Had this been the case, then when he arrived he would have found a Broome Hall that was no longer a novitiate, but a place that had recently become a centre for the study of Philosophy – including Aquinas, Aristotle and Plato – for those who were seeking to join the Missionaries of Africa.[59] This exposure may have had an influence on the choice of university courses that Nyerere, 'Africa's closest approximation to Plato's "philosopher-king"',[60] was soon to make. He went on to study Plato's *Republic* after opting to take Moral Philosophy at Edinburgh.[61]

In October 1949 Nyerere received the welcome news that he was accepted for entry at the University of Edinburgh's Faculty of Arts to study for a Master of Arts degree. He matriculated that same month.[62] The degree could either be completed as a Master of Arts with Honours (which took four years), or what was known as an Ordinary Degree of Master of Arts (which took three years). Here it is worth correcting another popular myth about Nyerere's education. He took an Ordinary Degree which, while given the title 'Masters of Arts' (abbreviated as 'M.A.') at Edinburgh and Scotland's other ancient universities – the University of Aberdeen, the University of Glasgow, and the University of St Andrews – would elsewhere be called a Bachelor of Arts degree in the humanities and social sciences.[63] A Scottish M.A. is not a postgraduate degree, as is often claimed nowadays in Tanzania. Nevertheless, in Nyerere's time Edinburgh's Ordinary M.A. was taken by a high proportion of students, including a fair number of the most able.[64] Nyerere's choice of degree subject was simple, as he put it at the time in a letter from Edinburgh: 'if I can be useful to my country after my studies here, I will be more useful if I take an arts rather than a science degree.'[65]

Nyerere's comment is evidence that already in 1949 he was thinking carefully about the future application of his Edinburgh studies, and that he was seriously considering his possible impact when he returned to Tanganyika. In Scotland he had not been alone as an African who recognised the potential use of his knowledge back home. Some fourteen years earlier Hastings Banda wrote to a friend expressing his similar aim, 'to obtain a liberal and professional education and return to Nyasaland in the service of my people'.[66] Banda's vocation was in medicine, but Nyerere's was less clear. If the young Tanganyikan's future was to lie in challenging colonial rule, then he needed to study the rules of the game as taught in the metropole. His interaction with the African Association would have brought to his attention the need for Africans to broaden their horizons. As early as 1944 the Dodoma chapter was writing on where they saw their weaknesses, requesting history books on more advanced nations and literature concerning social, economic, cultural and political progress on the continent.[67] This was not possible in East Africa, where there was no formal teaching in political science until its introduction at Makerere in the mid-1950s.[68] Edinburgh provided just the opportunity. Nyerere persisted in persuading the education officials of his choice of degree until they yielded to his wishes.

The Ordinary M.A. degree allowed freedom of choice of academic interests. It provided 'a general education from which a man proceeded to his chosen trade or profession, in a university or elsewhere … and with which he proceeded to meet the chances and demands of life as he came to them'.[69] This degree sat well with the architects of the Asquith Commission (1945), a vision for the new British colonial university colleges that was working under the assumption that a university is a nursery for leaders. A recommendation of the Commission (but one which was never incorporated into the Asquith doctrine) was the need for future leaders to receive, at university level, a broad education:

> Every student, whatever subject or subjects he is studying in his regular course, should be given an opportunity to become aware of certain great conceptions … he should have learnt something of what is meant by sociology, so that he is aware of the other elements and forms of civilization. He should be enabled to gain some apprehension of what is involved in philosophy in its widest meaning, and some sense of the past as expressed in great literature and in the record of history.[70]

These aspirations did not fit the pattern of a London degree, but they were consistent with the pattern of curriculum in a Scottish university.[71] This choice of degree was unusual for Africans studying in Edinburgh. Of those Africans who made an important contribution to nationalism, all except Nyerere took a medical course.[72] Among the Edinburgh-educated Africans who made a mark on early African nationalist movements were the Nigerian Bandele Omoniyi, who matriculated in the Faculty of Medicine in 1907 and had his 'A Defence of the Ethiopian Movement' and three articles criticising British rule in West Africa published in Edinburgh. Others were Moses da Rocha, whose correspondence with an African-American black nationalist shows his interest in *négritude*; H.R. Bankole Bright, a founder of the National Congress of British West Africa; and Hastings (later Kamuzu) Banda.[73] To this list of Africans who studied at Edinburgh should be added Sir Dawda Jawara, Prime Minister of Gambia from 1962 to 1970, and Samuel Manuwa, who became Chief Medical Adviser to the Federal Government of Nigeria and President of the World Federation of Mental Health. Chief Sir Samuel Manuwa graduated when Nyerere was studying as an undergraduate at Edinburgh, and had conferred on him the Honorary Degree of LL.D. the year after Nyerere was honoured by the University in the same way.[74]

The African pioneer in Scotland's capital is another student of medicine, James Africanus Beale Horton, the Sierra Leonean child of Igbo recaptives. Horton, the first African graduate of the University of Edinburgh, was one of the fathers of West African nationalism.[75] The African graduate of Edinburgh with the most direct influence on Nyerere, however, was the late Dr Vedastus Kyaruzi, who joined the University later than Nyerere, but who graduated in the same decade with a Diploma in Public Health.[76] There are few documents on Kyaruzi's activities in the Tanganyika independence movement during his time in Edinburgh, although it is known that as a student he managed to find the time to research and co-author a published journal article on attitudes to cigarette smoking among pupils in four Edinburgh schools.[77] Four years later he was then listed in the *British Medical Journal* as being admitted as a Member *qua* Physician of the Royal College of Physicians and Surgeons of Glasgow.[78]

Records from 1950 show that by the time Nyerere had reached Edinburgh there were 571 students from East and Central Africa studying in the United Kingdom. This was an immense increase from 23 in 1939. These students formed 15 per cent of the total number of colonial students at British universities.[79] The following year there were 272 students from East and Central Africa at universities in England's capital, and of these the largest number (107) were studying Law. 25 East and Central Africa students were taking Medicine, 23 were student nurses and 21 were studying Engineering. Only four were taking Arts, and none Social Science.[80] When beginning his degree in 1949, Nyerere was one of only two Africans from East African territories pursuing a degree course in Scotland.[81] The other student was Othman Shariff, a Zanzibari who was studying at Glasgow University in the late 1940s.[82] Little is known about Shariff at this time, other than that his degree was in agricultural economics and he found a great deal of interest in the politics of Kwame Nkrumah.[83] Shariff went on to become Tanzanian Ambassador to Washington. Dawda Jawara, the first leader of independent Gambia, was studying in Glasgow all the while that Nyerere was in Edinburgh and informs that his old friend mysteriously disappeared from Zanzibar in the 1960s when Nyerere was President of Tanzania.[84]

The available records in Edinburgh do not indicate whether Nyerere joined any clubs or societies.[85] A number of organisations were devoted to debating, but he may have been put off by the 'gentlemen's club' feel to the advertising of the culturally and intellectually conservative Diagnostic and Dialectic societies. The Catholic Students' Union was Nyerere's most likely choice. His name is not listed on the books of any clubs and societies though, but there is nothing to say that he did not attend meetings on an *ad hoc* basis. We can be more sure of his studies, which are far better documented. Conscious of the need to broaden his horizons, Nyerere seized the chance with his choice of courses.[86]

In his first year he opted to take Political Economy and Social Anthropology. The latter was tutored by the Australian Professor Ralph Piddington, a leading scholar in his field and one of the many of Nyerere's professors at Edinburgh with strong feelings about the need for social justice in the world.[87] Nyerere particularly engaged with some of the readings on this course. As we discuss later, they had a tremendous influence on his future policies. Piddington judged that Nyerere performed reasonably well, and his name was mentioned in the class merit-list at second-class certificate level.[88] Nyerere's other first-year subject was English Literature, for which he acquired a large number of books.[89] He signed and dated much of his personal literature, many of which are still held in his personal library in Butiama. The collection from Edinburgh demonstrates Nyerere's exposure to English literature classics, from John Milton's *Comus*, and *The Prologue and Three Tales* by the fourteenth-century poet Geoffrey Chaucer, to a selection of pieces by William Wordsworth, *Poetical Works* by Scotland's Robert Burns, and Emile Legouis' *A Short History of English Literature*. This was a literature the young student greatly enjoyed, as he expressed later to George Shepperson: 'I have no doubt that the English Literature which I studied [in Edinburgh] for my degree is the thing which really mattered to me. It is that course – and its tutors – to which I owe whatever knowledge and delight I have in English literature now.'[90]

The texts for his English examinations were Milton's sonnets and Shakespeare's *Julius Caesar* – which he later translated into Swahili as *Juliasi Kaizari* (1963 and 1969), along with *The Merchant of Venice*, which he called *Mabepari wa Venisi* (1972).[91] Nyerere was successful in all of his summer 1950 assessments, although his good marks in English could have been aided by the fact that Milton and Shakespeare had been on the curriculum at Makerere.[92] He passed his first year with a performance that David Carmichael (then responsible for colonial students in Scotland, the north of England, and Northern Ireland) described to the Colonial Office as 'well above average'. He was allowed to proceed towards completing the Ordinary Degree of Master of Arts.[93]

In Nyerere's second year he opted for Economic History, given by Arthur Birnie. Perhaps with the African Association's acknowledged weaknesses in mind, he took the course 'primarily, to get some knowledge of economic forces in history'.[94] The course clashed on the timetable with Imperial and American History, given by the then-Communist George Shepperson. Nyerere decided not to sit the class, nor did he take Shepperson's Development of East Africa, 1854–1904 course. His stated desire was to broaden his education.[95] Nyerere decided on the survey course in British History, under the tutelage of the eminent Professor Richard Pares. One of the youngest professors in the Faculty of Arts, the Chair of History was adored by Nyerere's classmates, one of whom described him as a

> 'bland and brilliant Oxford don [who] has no wish to go south again, and is content to remain in this beautiful city, which he definitely prefers to the dreaming spires and foggy mediocrity of his alma mater.' All who have heard him lecture and been infected with something of his enthusiasm for History, will sincerely and thankfully echo that wish.[96]

This was certainly the case for Nyerere, who described his British History professor to John Keto his Tanganyikan contemporary at Edinburgh. Richard Pares, Nyerere remarked, was as 'a wise man who taught me very much about what makes these British tick'.[97] Nyerere's knowledge about British history was later reflected in his 'Democracy and the Party System' pamphlet in which, as we discuss, he critiques the Westminster system of democracy and the influence of the (mainly English) political psyche.[98]

In his third year Nyerere chose Professor Lawrence Saunders' Constitutional Law, a class famed for the variety of students who attended it. When Nyerere took the course it mainly attracted students 'studying for the combined degrees of M.A., LL.B., or the single LL.B. or B.L. ... and quite a few represent important Edinburgh legal families'.[99] Both Arts and Social Science students were attracted to enrol in Saunders' Constitutional Law, and

> students from foreign lands are also made welcome to the class: occasionally French, German, and American students attend, but the greatest number are from Nigeria and West Africa. Such students are interested from the legal, political, and civil service points of view, as Nigeria and West Africa are rapidly developing their own local government and the students taught in this country are forming their legal background.[100]

Scotland: Great Conceptions

The Constitutional Law class was perhaps the foundation of Nyerere's dedication to the rule of law later in life. As Hopkins has argued: 'For Nyerere, law is not a tool for the political struggle but a basic set of rules within which all conflicts and grievances must be worked out.'[101] As was the case for so many other African students, Saunders' lectures were Nyerere's first exposure to the formal rules of the game – at least according to how the colonialists said the game was to be played.[102] Referring after independence to the case of some British farmers whose land leases had been revoked, Nyerere cited the rules, and his apparent wish that the game be played fairly: 'If you have a grievance, sue my Government. You must get justice.'[103]

In his third and final year Nyerere also chose to study Moral Philosophy.[104] Along with Law, he said he chose the course in order 'to get a fairly broad course of study without bothering too much about the details of a specialist'.[105] The report on Nyerere, sent by the Secretary of State for the Colonies to the Government of Tanganyika, stated that he was 'in every way a satisfactory student'.[106] Margaret Bell, his British History tutor, apparently commented frequently that the style of Nyerere's essays was the best in her group. They had a polish that was unusual not only in a foreigner but also in a British student.[107] The vast majority of his classmates were British. Most came from the east side of Scotland, the Borders, or from England, and they usually entered Edinburgh around the age of seventeen or eighteen.[108] In contrast to these callow youths, Nyerere was twenty-eight years old when Margaret Bell wrote her progress report on him. At Makerere he had already been exposed to tertiary education. From this position as a 'mature student' or 'adult learner', Nyerere was by the end of his first year well aware of the weaknesses and failings of many of his younger contemporaries. He studied alongside them and, in the main, was treated by his lecturers as an equal to the European students. This was certainly a contrast to the demeaning way that some teachers treated black students in East Africa. In both Tanganyika and Uganda, Nyerere had always been sure of his abilities alongside fellow Africans. After some time in Edinburgh he overcame his initial apprehension and now gained confidence alongside his non-African peers. As at Makerere, in Edinburgh the competition between students was great. Some were brilliant, but Nyerere would have been aware that there were a number of dullards. Some, undoubtedly, had hopes for careers in the colonial service.

Nyerere's grades certainly allowed him to pass his courses. In the main they were not outstanding. For his first examinations he was awarded 52 for English, 57 per cent for Political Economy, and 65 per cent for Social Anthropology. In his second year he was awarded 58 per cent for British History, and 62 per cent for Economic History. In his final year examinations he climbed to a more respectable 68 per cent for Constitutional Law, and 63 per cent for Moral Philosophy.[109] Nyerere's Moral Philosophy tutor Axel Stern, a radical lecturer and notable Christian Socialist,[110] recalls that he 'certainly was a bright and lively member of the class and of the parties'.[111] Nyerere 'made a good report on (a section of) Mill's *Utilitarianism*'. Stern ranked the young Tanganyikan's essay, 'Is Happiness the Thing to Aim at?' as first of all students in the class, and he came fourth overall out of a group of sixty.[112] It is quite possible that the essay did not count towards Nyerere's degree however, for during this time at Edinburgh students were assessed on unseen 'class examinations' at the end of the Autumn and Spring terms and – so long as they gained 'Duly Performed' certificates for each course – were then permitted to take 'degree examinations' at the close of the Summer Term.[113] Nyerere was always permitted to proceed to the degree examinations. In Moral Philosophy, for example, he was awarded a B– (60) in his first term essay, 52 for the first term exam, a B+ (58) for the second term essay, and a B+ (58) the third term essay with a class mark of 57.[114] Nyerere's work was satisfactory. His examination results show an overall steady improvement during the course of his studies at Edinburgh.

Fortunately for Nyerere, one of the set books in the degree examination in Moral Philosophy was John Stuart Mill's *Utilitarianism*.[115] It was clearly a text that he studied closely, for his personal copy of *Utilitarianism, Liberty, and Representative Government* has extensive underlining and noting in chapter two of *Utilitarianism*, including the section on the Greatest Happiness Principle that he gained top marks in.[116] Leading the Moral Philosophy course – offered by an academic department first instituted in 1583 – was Professor John Macmurray, a strong adherent of pacifism and of Christian socialism, opponent of apartheid, and author of *Freedom in the Modern World*.[117] Macmurray and Stern provided a stimulating course focused on the ethics of governance. Their influence, together with that of Nyerere's professor in Political Economy, Sir Alexander Gray – author of *The Socialist Tradition: Moses to Lenin* (1946) – reinforced the inspiring possibilities that socialist ideals represented in post-Second World War Scotland.[118]

This adds to the picture of Nyerere as more than just a political person, but also deeply philosophical. His course options allowed him to explore beyond his formal studies. Indeed, according to Shepperson, while at Edinburgh Nyerere managed to read the proofs of a pamphlet of poems by the great Swahili poet and his personal friend, Shaaban Robert.[119] Edinburgh was a place where Nyerere enjoyed new levels of intellectual freedom. It offered an environment where – horseplay and pranks aside – students read widely and were inclined to discuss among themselves, and at length, important issues of the day.[120] In Nyerere's own words: 'I found that I had ample time to read many other things outside my degree ... I evolved the whole of my political philosophy while I was there.'[121] This is discussed in Chapters 6 and 7 with reference to the philosophical and anthropological literature to which Nyerere was exposed in Edinburgh.

Certainly Nyerere's frequent reference to past events in his writings and speeches reflects the historical leaning of his degree. The Scottish education that formed his knowledge of American, English and Scottish constitutional affairs is evident in pamphlets such as his 'Democracy and the Party System' where he draws analogies with Jacobitism and Presbyterianism.[122] It is also possible that the Constitutional Law course he took, in which Hamilton, Madison and Jay's *The Federalist Papers* was discussed in the prescribed texts,[123] had some impression on Nyerere when he was grappling with the many complicated problems of the sharing of power within and between states in Africa. This began with his theoretical discussions in Edinburgh and London concerning both racial representation in Tanganyika and the proposed Central African Federation. It stretched to his later more-practical decision-making in the age of decolonisation and into the decades of post-independence Africa.[124] The Church of Scotland missionary, Reverend Kenneth MacKenzie, a close friend of Nyerere while he was in Scotland, felt that this period in Edinburgh 'had a very direct and powerful influence upon his development as a politician. He was slowly building up his life-view, his basic orientation, about things like the nature of government ... [and] the rights of the individual.'[125]

Return to the Charge

Nyerere had to work hard to make the most of the academic opportunities that Edinburgh offered. There is nothing to suggest that he did not apply himself fully. A constant worry, however, and probably a significant distraction, was in the news he was receiving in his regular correspondence with Edward Wanzagi. His half-brother was frequently informing him of the family's more difficult financial situation back home.[126] Nyerere's scholarship included a dependents' allowance which covered the school fees and expenses for his fiancée Maria, and for two of his brothers, along with a maintenance allowance for his mother and sister.[127]

Nyerere wrote to the Colonial Office submitting the facts of his family allowance for reconsideration. According to his letters, Nyerere was sending money home in addition to the dependents' allowance. Very little is known about the jobs that he undertook while studying in the United Kingdom, although the prevailing colour prejudice meant that such an option was not always open to colonial students.[128] On at least one occasion he left Scotland to spend a week or two on vacation with a 'crowd of other students' on a Welsh farm picking potatoes.[129] This was presumably at least one of the sources of income that his fiancée, Maria, refers to of her time studying at Nsube: 'When I was in Uganda, Kambarage [when he was a student] used to work temporarily in Britain and would now and then send me as well as his mother a little money, while we continued to correspond.'[130]

Whatever the source of the money Nyerere could send home, it was apparently insufficient. He pointed out to the Colonial Office that his current allowance did not take into account inflation. It was also fixed at a rate based on his own assumption that his mother would not have to buy food in order to maintain the family. Ordinarily the family would grow its own food, but famine gripped Uzanaki in 1949.[131] The result was that Nyerere's earlier cost analysis was 'now completely dissolved, as not only my mother, but thousands of other peasants are forced to buy their food.'[132] This was a particularly painful situation for a son who later claimed that in 'traditional African society.... nobody starved, either of food or of human dignity, because he lacked personal wealth'.[133] During Nyerere's first few months in Edinburgh he sent money from his personal resources in an attempt to alleviate matters. Realising that this was unsustainable, he asked the Director of Colonial Scholars at the Colonial Office in London, John Keith, to consider raising the allowance as, 'even if I were to continue at that rate I would not make my family's condition really secure'.[134] So began three years of tedious wrangling concerning Nyerere's family allowance. On the one side was the '£1 million scholar', and those who by and large supported his case – the Colonial Office Welfare Officer in Edinburgh and the colonial authorities in London. On the other side were reluctant and suspicious government officials in Dar es Salaam, Tabora and Musoma, who did their best to ensure that their coffers were not affected by their 'unreasonable and extortionate' subject.[135] This brief interlude into Nyerere's campaign of persuading the colonial administration to increase his family allowance demonstrates his tenacity and shrewdness at a young age in the long-drawn-out battle with the authorities. The numbing minutiae of the protracted and slow-moving case must be summarised here. Some aspects of the detailed correspondence (as recorded in the file that the Colonial Office kept on Nyerere) are offered to show why Nyerere acted as he did when faced with the uncompromising attitude of British officials in Tanganyika.[136]

Five months passed after Nyerere first raised the issue of his family allowance with the Director of Colonial Scholars. Still he had received no positive response. In all likelihood Keith had contacted the Government of Tanganyika, they had not replied, and the matter was eventually lost amid the interminable fog of colonial bureaucracy. Anxious,

Nyerere wrote again stating that he regarded the question still unsettled: 'It is a grave matter, and I am certain it would be grave irresponsibility on my part if I continued to pursue my education at the risk of my dependants' welfare.'[137] He eventually met in Edinburgh with the enigmatic Keith, to whom he 'made further verbal representations on this subject … and appeared to be perturbed about the position of his family'. Keith had previously authored an article attacking 'those who criticise us for spoiling the students by giving them excessive allowances'. Now, moved by Nyerere's concern for his family, Keith urged the Government of Tanganyika to clear up the matter, 'in order that Mr. Nyerere can concentrate on his studies'.[138]

With no positive response some three long months later, and now showing his derision for the authorities in Tanganyika, Nyerere again wrote to the Colonial Office in London: 'May I beg, Sir, that instead of my Government having to decide whether to waste any more money on my dependants they pay the allowance on loan. I am prepared to sign any necessary documents to make the loan possible.'[139] He then threatened that a cash advance was one of only two options: 'Unless I can get another means of paying an allowance to my people [, a loan], to my mind, is the only alternative to stopping my studies and going home. In any case my studies could not be anything but a source of pain to me when I think of what they have led to.'[140]

Some ten months after the colonial authorities had first looked into the case, it appeared that it could finally be closed. The Tanganyika administration apportioned the blame to the most unlikely culprits: disorganised missionaries.[141] Exasperated by this frustrating response, Nyerere asked for passage to Tanganyika, for good. Close to a year from graduating, he explained his decision thus: 'I feel that I am duty bound to discontinue my studies at once and return home to assume my proper responsibility in the service of family and my country in whatever capacity I am called upon to render my service.'[142] He finished by accounting for this drastic position as, 'the only decision I can conscientiously make. No amount of education can justify my inflicting unnecessary suffering to my people. I will therefore be most grateful, Sir, if you could convey my decision to my Government and arrange my departure home as soon as you find it convenient.'[143]

The battle-weary Lieutenant Colonel Crook – the Colonial Office's Liaison Officer for East African students – then wrote a private minute note to Keith describing Dar es Salaam's response as one that was likely to continue to be 'one of unimaginative obstinacy. We can not leave them [colonial students] to stew in their own juice. The bitterness shown in Nyerere's letter … will remain, and return with him to Tanganyika, when it is unlikely to form an asset to the Government'[144] – which is presumably what the Colonial Office hoped he was otherwise going to be. In response, the Acting Director of Education in Dar es Salaam, C. Hinchcliffe, invited Nyerere to write a fully-detailed reassessment for careful scrutiny.[145] The young Tanganyikan student did so, at some length, stating first his impossible position versus the colonial Government in his country 'that knows better than I do how much the cost of living in Tanganyika has gone up'. Nyerere then explained how before he left for Europe he had agreed with his mother that he would 'help her with the school fees of the girl in Uganda [Maria] whose school fees at Nsube had now increased, and for financial reasons had been forced to leave school'. 'Until she gets a job', he added, 'I must remain responsible for her maintenance.'[146]

Nyerere next took the bold step of appealing to his hostile audience in Dar es Salaam. He knew anyway that although he was addressing his letter to the sympathetic Crook, it would quickly reach Colonial Service personnel in Tanganyika.[147] It did, and the Government soon considered Nyerere's calculation of an increased allowance to be an unreasonable sum. The irascible Hinchcliffe, proceeding as ever with his diplomatic blunderbuss, forwarded to Crook the Musoma District Commissioner's comments. Predictably, the District Commissioner considered the existing allowances to still be perfectly adequate, and suggested to the Lieutenant Colonel that:

> it may be impressed on Mr. Julius Nyerere that he is, or should feel, indebted to the tax paying public in general and that he might be more discreet in his expectations of what is allowed to him. Many undergo marked privations in order to educate their children, at their own expense, and the family of Julius Nyerere could put up with some hardship, particularly as he is being educated at the expense of the public.[148]

Nyerere tried yet again, but Hinchcliffe made it clear that 'if the District Commissioner does not recommend a higher award, then a higher award is not justified'.[149] The District Commissioner did not recommend a higher award. It fell to the compassionate Crook to pass on to Nyerere the disappointing final decision that the Tanganyika Government were refusing to increase his dependants' allowance.[150] The Minute Paper entries of two Colonial Office administrators adequately sum up the manner in which Dar es Salaam and the officers in Musoma and Tabora handled the matter: 'The high moral tone of [Hinchcliffe] is out of place', wrote T. Rogers in London, before adding, 'I am not at all happy that Tanganyika are handling these matters in the best way.'[151] Keith was of the same opinion, suggesting:

> This case ... does show that action by the colonial authorities at their end can create a good deal of unhappiness and ill-feeling among students over here. This is really a miserable business of a very few shillings payable as an allowance to the relatives of a very good student, Mr. Nyerere of Tanganyika .... I do not propose to take the high moral line with Mr. Nyerere which Tanganyika appears to think should be done. I find that the

paragraph at X in [Hinchcliffe's letter to Crook] is particularly irritating and, if you agree, I propose to let the matter drop, unless, of course, Mr. Nyerere returns to the charge.[152]

Mr Nyerere did not return to the charge; at least not until he was back in Tanganyika. In the meantime, he had shown his true colours to the colonial authorities. Here was an impertinent and – in the eyes of some in the Tanganyika Government – an impudent and contemptuous African who did not know his place in the colonial hierarchy. Nyerere may have been writing to them as a scholar in Edinburgh, but the administration in his country of birth was still British and had its racial structure to maintain. His persistent demands for more money, and his blunt request to return home, only proved the ungratefulness of a young upstart who had been given an immense opportunity at the taxpayers' expense. From another perspective, this was a principled and dependable young man who was driven to 'assume… proper responsibility in the service of family and… country' in whatever capacity he might be called upon to render his service. This was a twenty-one year old who had clearly stated that he had to do all in his power to help his fellows when faced with starvation. This was a man who would undoubtedly have acted on his convictions when push came to shove. Lest the colonial authorities might think otherwise, these were not the words of a spoilt, self-serving aristocrat who sailed through an elite education with a sense of entitlement.

A contextualised and dispassionate view of this prolonged episode offers a more nuanced interpretation that lies somewhere between these opposing perspectives. There is no doubt that the colonial officials in Tanganyika were bloody-minded in their indifference to Nyerere and his family's plight. The scholar certainly endured an inconvenience that he could have done without, as did his family. But the fact of the matter is that Nyerere's situation was not unusual. In East Africa in particular, assessment problems and delays in payments for most student bursaries was a very common difficulty.[153] Nyerere's family were facing hardship, but so at the time were many other families in Uzanaki and far beyond. While the Government would not be swayed on the proposed increase in the family allowance, it would be inaccurate to portray the Tanganyika colonial officials in the role of villains. Their pejorative tone notwithstanding, the administration in Tanganyika supported both student and family, as agreed in terms of the scholarship they were funding, and the administration kept to their commitment. In addition to his tuition fees and the (undependable) dependants' allowance, Nyerere also received a personal stipend of £305 per annum.[154] At £25 per month, the maintenance was £5 less than the £30 that the British Council estimated a foreign student would need for simple necessities. Given that Nyerere's scholarship also covered his travel expenses however, his overall allowance was roughly the same as the £24 that the British Council's breakdown of estimated costs amounted to – the following year, taking into consideration inflation and including accommodation.[155] Life in Britain in the late 1940s and early 1950s may have had its uncomfortable moments, but Nyerere was by no means destitute. His grumbles should be put into perspective. Edinburgh was nowhere near as hard for an African as the United States when Nkrumah visited a decade before.[156] Nor was it anything close to Banda's experience in America, where he had the harrowing experience of witnessing a lynching.[157]

The Colonial Office files of Nyerere's contemporaries no longer exist. It is therefore impossible to know if the likes of Gosbert Rutabanzibwa, Paulo Mwinyipembe and Frank Mfundo faced the same circumstances as Nyerere.[158] Certainly the families of other United Kingdom-based scholarship-holders who lived in north-west Tanganyika would have been similarly affected by the devastating 1949 famine that afflicted Nyerere's family. It was a time of such desperation that the parents of Mugara Marasi allowed her to become Chief Nyerere Burito's seventeenth wife so that they could purchase food with the bridewealth.[159]

The lack of other files offering the same level of detail as Nyerere's do also make it difficult to know whether his 'unreasonable and extortionate' demands, and his 'obstinate' response when rebuffed, were unique or typical.[160] What we can appreciate from Nyerere's theatrical warning – not one, but twice – that he was prepared to discontinue his studies over the matter, is that his threats to quit at this time were but an early example of what was to become a much-used weapon in his political armoury. He continued to threaten to quit throughout his entire career, often (but not always, as in this case) with great success. There were other times when Nyerere carried out the threat. In December 1957, for example, he resigned as a Representative Member of the Legislative Council after less than six months in the position over what he regarded as the government's blocking of any efforts towards self-government.[161] He also threatened that Tanganyika African National Union (TANU) ministers would resign unless Britain announced in December 1959 that responsible government would come during 1960.[162] Months after becoming Prime Minister, in 1961, he threatened to resign to prevent a racially-prejudiced (against non-Africans) citizenship bill from being passed.[163] He made the same threat in a TANU meeting a few months later, and eventually resigned as Prime Minister in January of the following year to devote himself 'to the full time work of TANU'.[164] The early dispute over his family allowance shows that already by the beginning of the 1950s Nyerere was demonstrating that he had a very shrewd side to his character. While in this case his pleas fell on deaf ears, Nyerere worked on the sentiments of his audience, playing the betrayed righteous figure, employing melodrama and even extortion to get what he wanted. All the while wrapped in the pious language of the saint.

Not the Usual Type

Nyerere's own situation in Edinburgh was clearly more comfortable than that of his family at home. It was also better than that of many of the black students who preceded him. In the case of Moses da Rocha in Scotland's capital, this entailed 'various troubles with beastly landladies'.[165] We know of no incidents of racial prejudice against Nyerere in Edinburgh, although that is certainly not to say that they did not occur. This was the case for the Trinidad scholar William Besson, for example, who recalled some isolated incidents of racism during his medical studies at Edinburgh from 1921 to 1926. Besson's overall sentiment, however, is that he experienced kindness while he was in Scotland.[166] Later, in 1938, Hastings Banda wrote from the Edinburgh University Union to a friend in Nyasaland informing him that 'white people in Scotland and England are very kind and friendly to me. … This does not mean that are all Europeans are angels. … But speaking as a whole or on the whole, I have no complaints to make about the way in which I am treated in Britain.'[167]

The country was certainly not sheltered from racial tension, as witnessed in the riots that took place at Glasgow Harbour earlier in the century.[168] But the more pronounced conflict lasting until Nyerere's time in Edinburgh was not between townsfolk and the temporary and limited population of black overseas students, but between white Catholics and Protestants. If Nyerere did encounter incidents of racial prejudice, then the experiences of other colonial students at the time suggest that British students were less prejudiced than the population in general.[169] As noted, when Nyerere began his degree he was one of only two East African students in Scotland. This may have served him well. Carey supposes that small groups of non-white colonial students had a better chance of adapting to the social life of a college than in the case where they form a large proportion of the total student population.[170] Certainly among Nyerere's contemporaries with experience of both London and other British universities, the majority felt that adaptation to the social conditions of London was more difficult than elsewhere.[171] This can be demonstrated by the case of another Kenyan student who was studying medicine and had been in Britain for over two years: 'He is now studying at a Scottish University, where the question of accommodation does not arise. This is perhaps the major reason why he felt much happier there than in London, but he also thinks that Scottish people are friendlier ... He has not made any close friends among English people.'[172]

John Keto mentions more than once that, 'the Scots were more welcoming than the English'.[173] Despite Scottish human warmth, however, we have seen from Reverend MacKenzie that Nyerere was less than happy with the weather – *The Scotsman* proclaimed 1951 to be a 'notably wet year'. Keto recalls how his fellow Tanganyikan complained about 'the intolerable weather up there, far in the north',[174] which for many months of the year meant unbearably cold outdoor temperatures. Under the terms of his scholarship he was also entitled to £35 as an outfit allowance, but Keto recalls that the African students still suffered because of 'the constant rain and the sharp wind' from the North Sea.

Nyerere's Edinburgh accommodation was on Palmerston Road, from where all of his Edinburgh letters are addressed. He did not write its official name, 'Colonial House', but he since confirmed that he lived there from late 1949 to about mid-1952.[175] He may have shifted accommodation briefly however, since Shepperson states that at some point Nyerere also lived at the British Council Residence in Bruntsfield Place.[176] Other colonial students lived at the residence, and Kojo Botsio, then Minister of Education in the Gold Coast, had been a visiting speaker.[177] Keto recalls that Nyerere spent many evening and weekends with Walter Wilson, a friend whose mother, Mrs Jean Wilson, was widower to a Catholic missionary doctor in the Belgian Congo and Angola. She acted *in loco parentis* to Nyerere.[178] The University of Edinburgh had long-standing traditions in their dealings with Africans[179] – albeit in small numbers – and the initial meeting with the Wilsons was probably through one of the British Council placements of sponsored students to recommended addresses.[180] Such encounters were not always so successful as that which led to the enduring relationship between the Wilsons and Nyerere. As a young West African law student commented of his experience: 'It seems to me that many of the people who go to the British Council to meet colonial students are cranks, although well-intentioned.'[181]

There were only around 1,000 non-British students in Edinburgh when Nyerere was studying in the city. His broad social network comprising of townsfolk such as the Wilsons, and students and staff, certainly sets him apart from many of his foreign counterparts whom the University Chaplain lamented over in his 1951–52 report: 'The situation of our overseas students is in some ways distressing. They tend to keep to their national groups and have not been sufficiently absorbed into University life.'[182] Nyerere seems not to have lacked companionship when in the city, and long after leaving for home he still had many friends in Edinburgh.[183] There are no further details of one of his group of friends other than that they 'did various things together and this included several female students. On that [issue] Mwalimu said he had got engaged to his future wife before he left Tanganyika 'for safety sake'; for the same reason he always went around with a group of girls, not a particular one!'[184] Besides, notes Carey, 'the majority of Colonials find it difficult to meet English [*sic*] girls, particularly of a similar background to their own'.[185] As a Kenyan student of Law put it after about eighteen months in Britain, 'such friendships can only lead to trouble'.[186] The 'trouble' was the kind of outrage that surrounded the 1948 interracial marriage in London between the Oxford-educated Botswana chief (and later the country's first president), Seretse Khama, and a white English woman that Khama met while he was a barrister in the city and she a clerk at Lloyd's of London.[187] Undaunted by the likely hostile reaction of many, Hastings Banda also seems to have thought that a permanent relationship with a European was possible, for he asked for the hand in marriage of no less than three Scotswomen – one of whom was in Edinburgh.[188] Commenting on her lengthy separation with Julius in Edinburgh, Maria recalls that they kept in touch by writing letters 'like brother and sister'.[189]

As one of the 'few' colonial students who was 'fortunate to make friends with home students and their families',[190] Nyerere would head to Walter Wilson's house for tea and cakes. Still favouring indoor over outdoor recreation, Nyerere played Lexicon or Canasta with his adopted family.[191] Mrs Wilson recalled that 'he was a very humble person',[192] delighted in the crossword puzzles in *The Scotsman* newspaper, and commented that with the word games Nyerere played: 'English was only his third language … but he always seemed to win.'[193] The close relationship with the Wilson family seems to have flourished at 44, Calder Crescent in Edinburgh's Sighthill area. When Shepperson wrote his *Gazette* article in 1960, he said that Sighthill 'still calls [Nyerere] a "second son"'.[194]

The Scotsman and Democracy

Jean Wilson's comments about Nyerere's love of crosswords raises an interesting avenue of slightly speculative research on one of the young man's influences beyond his academic studies: the media. In later life Nyerere was very fond of listening to broadcasts of world news on the BBC, as was the case for many Anglophone African statesmen of his generation. It is quite possible that in his Edinburgh days Nyerere kept an ear to the crackly airwaves of the Home Service, the 'highbrow' 'Third Programme', and maybe BBC Scotland – then a painfully constipated version (for the most part) of Reithian formality and sheer dullness, punctuated by rampant 'Brigadoonism' in representing Scottish culture. Hazarding a guess on what Nyerere might have listened to would be nothing more than pure conjecture. We can approach what he read with a little more certainty. We know that he read the newspapers when he was in East Africa, especially the *Tanganyika Standard*, where he also had a letter published in the correspondence section. We also know that when he was in Edinburgh he obtained copies of the *East African Standard* newspaper and that he enjoyed the crossword in *The Scotsman*.[195] There is of course a possibility that Nyerere picked up the local newspaper for nothing more than its puzzles, but this is unlikely for a man who spent much time debating on world affairs as evidenced, for example, in his Edinburgh speech of February 1952 (discussed in the following chapter) in which he denounced the proposed Central African Federation. What is also unlikely is that Marjorie Nicholson needed to write the following advice to Nyerere, who was probably already doing what his Fabian mentor had suggested. In a section discussing the British constitution, she offered: 'I do think that you would find it worth while to read your local papers while you are in Edinburgh and, if possible, find out how the political Parties work locally.'[196] There are no records that show whether Nyerere did this, but had he done so he would have found little to match his own politics – or, for that matter, to match his own religious leaning: there were still one or two councillors on the city council who represented the anti-Catholic (and in the 1930s, pro-Fascist) party, Protestant Action. Further, from the 1940s and until the 1970s the city was perpetually dominated by the 'Progressive' party of local Tory businessmen allied to the Conservative Party, which held the majority of Edinburgh's parliamentary seats.

A brief survey of the pages of the Edinburgh-published *The Scotsman* gives an insight into the local and international events that were brought to Nyerere's attention had he indeed ventured beyond the puzzles and into the content of the national newspaper. Before doing so, however, some political context of late 1940s and early 1950s British society and its direct influences on Nyerere is necessary to background the content of *The Scotsman*'s news pages. This also serves to foreground the discussion in the next two chapters.

At the national level, the Britain that Nyerere lived in was one that was only just beginning to recover from a war that for six long years had wreaked havoc on the country and its economy. The government's principal economic concern after the war was to raise output as fast as possible, and labour recruitment drives were launched overseas. As mentioned, less than a year before Nyerere had stepped onto British soil the *Empire Windrush* had berthed at Tilbury Docks with the first large group of post-war West Indian immigrants, and many organisations ran recruiting campaigns in the Caribbean. Nyerere would also have witnessed at some level the two general elections that were held during his time in the United Kingdom. The first of these was held in February 1950, and was the first general election after a full term of a Labour government. It was won by the Labour Party, but with a slim majority of just five seats. King George VI was concerned about leaving the country for his Commonwealth tour with a government with such a slender lead, and the Prime Minister, Clement Attlee, called a second election that took place in October 1951 at the start of Nyerere's last academic year at Edinburgh University. During that year *The Student* magazine published a story entitled, 'Kwofe's Vote: A cynical parable of democracy', in which an African student (probably from the Gold Coast) is introduced to democracy. He is invited to the meetings of three political parties before the election, is impressed by all, and is so taken by this apparently new system that on polling day he insists on voting, despite suffering from malaria. The hapless African spoils his vote though: 'how was I to know which man to vote for – they didn't have the party on the paper, and I couldn't remember the party man's name'.[197]

Nyerere's clearest reference to his experience of British elections is in 'Democracy and the Party System' (1963); his explanation for replacing the Westminster constitutional model with one that he regarded as more organically 'African'.[198] He ridicules the aftermath of the political campaigns, observing that the losing party produces 'the most high-sounding arguments in praise of their failure'.[199] He follows this with mention of both the Conservative and Labour parties that stood in the 1950 and 1951 elections,[200] and questions the logic of 'Her Majesty's Loyal Opposition' – 'an affront to reason…. suggestive of at least a mild form of political schizophrenia'.[201] The Two-Party system found in the Westminster type of representative democracy, Nyerere argued, was not democratic. Yet 'where there is *one* party, and that party is identified with the *nation as a whole*, the foundations of democracy are firmer than they can ever be when you have two or more parties, each representing only a section of the community!' (original emphasis).[202]

Some five years before independence Nyerere had insisted that Tanganyika was to be governed 'as a Democratic State'.[203] Democratic elections took place in 1958, and TANU won comprehensively, beating the multi-racialist United Tanganyika Party (UTP) and Zuberi Mtemvu's overtly racist African National Congress, which advocated 'Africa for Africans only'.[204] 'In retrospect', as Iliffe puts it, 'it is clear that the election was the key to Tanganyika's independence'.[205] The 1958 election was also the foundation of Nyerere's 'original, hybrid constitutional order, the democratic one-party state'.[206] Where formerly he had written that freedom to organise an opposition party was essential to democracy,[207] within a year his standpoint was that 'not having an opposition makes for spontaneity, which is free democracy'.[208] 'In the two-party system', he argued, 'opposition is normally automatically opposed to the other party' – to Nyerere's mind this was not free democracy.[209] Here he questions the applicability of what John Stuart Mill refers to as 'the unwritten maxims of the Constitution', or its conventions.[210] Sir Ivor Jennings, who Nyerere studied under Professor Saunders, notes that 'only the conventions provide for the continuance of the present [multi-party] system'.[211] 'Democracy and the Party System' can be seen as an extension of this hypothetical argument, in which Nyerere challenged the conventions of the (British) constitution, which he saw as inappropriate to the African setting. He was happy to follow Jennings' defence of freedom of speech, the protection of minorities, government by opinion ('government by discussion', Nyerere called it), and the separation of powers within the architecture of the state.[212] But he challenged the presumed constitutional setting that all these were located in, which for Jennings was the United Kingdom. Saunders offered his students comparative texts on the United States, but there was no suitable blueprint for Nyerere's Africa. By way of comparison, his Edinburgh studies could only offer the evolution of constitutions and governments in the dominion states of Canada, Australia, New Zealand and South Africa.[213] All were white-dominated.

Realising the massive support that the African-led TANU held, Nyerere quickly argued that 'if a government is freely elected by the people, there can be nothing undemocratic about it'.[214] His party had won by a landslide, in a democratic election. The same party then reigned supreme for decades, but unopposed – because opposition, Nyerere soon pronounced, was not African. In its truest sense, he was prepared to concede, democracy was 'as familiar to the Africans as the tropical sun'.[215] But this was the 'traditional democracy' of the 'typical African village' – Nyerere's ever-convenient Africa of old, where 'elders sit under the big tree, and talk until they agree'.[216] As Nyerere's political philosophy developed, two things alone were essential for representative democracy: the freedom of the individual, and the regular opportunity to vote. (That is, so long as the freedom did not extend to opposing the party, and the only party on the ballot paper was TANU.[217]) Freedom of speech and free elections are the two liberties of discussion in an outline of (British) constitutional law Nyerere studied under Saunders.[218] Press freedom is also included, although Nyerere was not so keen on this aspect of liberty. He subsequently introduced the Newspaper Act of 1976, which still gives the Minister of Information powers to ban or close down newspapers 'in the public interest' or 'in the interest of peace and good order'.[219] Additional parties only meant 'Party Games', for which the busy philosopher had little time.[220] Two-party democracy was nothing more than what Nyerere frequently referred to as trivial 'football politics';[221] which is how the general elections of the early 1950s in sectarian Edinburgh may have seemed to a visitor. The Conservative

Party went on to form the next government, under Winston Churchill, and put a halt to Labour's struggles to set up a welfare state that was nascent during Nyerere's first years in Scotland.[222]

Unlike any government initiative that Nyerere would have witnessed in Tanganyika, in Scotland, England and Wales he saw the beginnings of a welfare state that sought to guarantee to everyone, under any circumstances, a decent standard of living. This included treating education and health as public services. The contrast with provision of such services for Africans in Tanganyika could not have been more sharp.[223] No wonder then that, in a letter to the Colonial Office's Liaison Officer for East African students, Nyerere expressed his anxiety about his mother's health and the education and health of her other children. He pointedly added that whatever money left over from what she received 'might be spent to provide free dentures and spectacles or on moral rearmament'.[224] These were also years of large infrastructure schemes. The New Towns Act of 1946 brought in its first wave the development of towns such as East Kilbride (1947) and Glenrothes (1948) that grew while Nyerere was in Scotland, along with many new developments that he would have seen during his travels south of the border. In England, and certainly during any travels in Scotland's industrial areas, and through radio broadcasts, Nyerere would also have been aware that he was witnessing a period of nationalisation of industries – something he later brought to Tanganyika with the Arusha Declaration, the most explicit codification of his vision of socialism.[225] Labour's declared aim, like that of TANU later, was to take control of 'the commanding heights of the economy'.[226]

At the international level, Nyerere's first year in Britain saw the establishment of NATO, the official proclamation of the People's Republic of China (fundamentally changing the governance of villages such as Hsiao-Tung Fei's Kaihsienkung, discussed later), and the publication of the novel *1984*, George Orwell's dystopic vision of a totalitarian future. The 1950s saw intensification of the Cold War, into a global struggle for supremacy between capitalism and communism. It also saw the beginning of decolonisation in Asia and Africa. John Iliffe's opinion that 'Nyerere had been in Britain when the great issues of race and liberation in Africa were first being defined', is an accurate description of African affairs that featured in *The Scotsman* during this period.[227]

The predominance of race issues featured most obviously in *The Scotsman* articles on South Africa, such as one entitled: '"Apartheid" wall completed: Dr Malan's new bill on political rights: Gold Coast contrast'.[228] Another article discusses 'Racial contrasts prominent in South Africa: Natives lose tribal simplicity'.[229] An earlier piece notes one aspect of the new social change among 'natives' to be 'the comparatively rapid disappearance of tribal markings. The filing or removal of teeth is disappearing'[230] – something that may have struck a chord with Nyerere, a recipient from his 'tribal' days of the teeth filing 'fashion of youth' that for him, as with his peers, would never disappear. An anonymous letter to the editor presented something of one man's criticism towards an appeal from a Mr MacGregory, apparently a supporter of the Scottish Nationalist Party, who sought funds to support *Die Vaderland*, the South African Nationalist newspaper. 'It does not strike him [MacGregory]', wrote 'D.D.C.', that 'the ideas of the South African Nationalists are offensive to most Scotsmen and are foreign to the ideals of freedom and justice to which Scotland has always held.' The Scottish Nationalist party, D.D.C. continues, 'insults the memory of David Livingstone and Mary Slessor by its dealings with those who are setting out to destroy civilisation in Africa by breaking the last threads of understanding between White and Black'.[231]

Scottish nationalism was at the apogee of that time during Nyerere's years in Scotland, and was very much a feature of university politics in Edinburgh.[232] There was discussion on Scottish home rule, and much coverage of the removal and subsequent search for the 'Stone of Destiny', an oblong block of red sandstone that had been used for centuries during the coronation of medieval monarchs of Scotland, and later the monarchs of England, Great Britain, and the United Kingdom. Also known as the 'Stone of Scone', this potent symbol of Scottish nationhood was removed from Westminster Abbey on Christmas Day 1950 by four maverick Scottish students, to be left on the altar of Arbroath Abbey sixteen months later after an unsuccessful search ordered by the British Government.[233] A more conventional approach to nationalism that Nyerere also had the opportunity to observe during his years in Edinburgh was the progress of the 'Scottish Covenant' campaign, a scheme which, by 1951, had secured the pledges of some 2,000,000 Scots (out of an electorate of over 3,500,000) to work towards the establishment of a Scottish Parliament.[234] Cultural nationalism was aired in *The Scotsman*'s correspondence columns. Some letters were written in 'Lallans' (i.e., Lowland) Scots, a cause favoured by many nationalist intellectuals and literati who felt English was an imposed and alien tongue. Other letters debated the vexed question of the uncertain future of Scots Gaelic. Nyerere may have borne some of this in mind when later considering the rival merits of indigenous languages, and of Swahili as the official national language of Tanzania. Likewise, debates on 'independence or the union' in Scottish newspapers possibly affected Nyerere's later thinking on constitutional relations between Zanzibar and mainland Tanzania. Nyerere thought carefully about these issues in the United Kingdom, and was motivated to write an essay contrasting Welsh and Scottish nationalism.[235]

Nyerere's early 1943 article in the *Tanganyika Standard* suggests that his own nationalist energies were focused on home. The region that he addressed at that time was then covered in an article in *The Scotsman* in August 1950. In an article entitled, 'Future of East Africa: Racial antagonism and political immaturity', Nyerere would have read how populations in East Africa 'have not yet begun seriously to question the presence of the British – but they will'. The article then calls for Colonial Office control, and warns against not decentralising any further in favour of the Legislative Councils. The anonymous journalist was of the opinion that East Africans were ready for nothing more: 'I do not believe it is yet possible to foresee a time when the East African population will master the techniques and acquire the unified social organisation necessary for successful self-government in this land. But long before they have acquired these techniques, they will be demanding political control.'[236]

Nyerere's 'Race Problem in East Africa' manuscript, written in Edinburgh sometime before September 1951, should be regarded as a considered response to the kind of racialist opinions as expressed in *The Scotsman* article from the previous year.[237] Nyerere took his time to reflect on the subject matter, and dealt with the issue of race in East Africa as a whole, not in Tanganyika alone. In part, this was in direct reply to the territories that the newspaper article addressed. It was also because ever since his Makerere days, and now in the United Kingdom, Nyerere was influenced by the experiences of not just his own countrymen, but also Kenyans and Ugandans who shared their stories of worse race relations. He was also aware of Tanganyika Territory's special international status which, by contrast to Kenya and Uganda, maintained certain pressures on the United Kingdom to prevent widespread alienation of land to European settlers, and (theoretically) mitigated racial discrimination.[238] But while the African Association in Tanganyika was increasingly interested in territorially-specific issues,[239] here Nyerere felt the need to defend the East Africa region at large.[240] Also, and again unlike many members of the African Association who since the 1930s had argued the cause for blacks in Africa only,[241] he refused to take the position that the majority black Africans should have the lion's share of political representation. In his manuscript he wrote instead of the need to 'build up a society in which we shall belong to east Africa and not to our racial groups'.[242] This more moderate position was one shared by the Oxford undergraduates 'with East Africa links' – probably code for whites and Asians, as well as blacks, and perhaps influenced by Fabian Colonial Bureau editors – who in 1952 declared that they did 'not consider that it is in the interests of any one community to strive for a dominant political position, as this could not fail in the long run to react to its own disadvantage'.[243] Later, at the United Nations in 1956, Nyerere nevertheless insisted that Tanganyika must be declared a primarily African state.[244] Come 1960, while he still wished to avoid discrimination amongst any Tanganyika citizens, political pressure forced him to give Africans priority in civil service recruitment.[245] He maintained his personal stance on non-racialism for many years however, still making it clear much later that 'the purpose of socialism is the service of man, regardless of colour'.[246]

The Scotsman soon gave coverage to the United Nations' increasing criticism of British rule in Tanganyika. One of the most persistent stories from the territory was the failure of the hugely expensive Groundnut Scheme, a disastrous attempt by the colonial authorities to produce vegetable oil (for manufacturing margarine in the British welfare state) in an area subject to drought.[247] This was followed by a report on a similarly fraught 'eggs-for-U.K.' scheme in The Gambia that must have left any educated African reader questioning their colonial rulers' mastery of techniques of which his brothers and sisters were supposedly incapable.[248] The 'Tragedy of East Africa' – the title given to an article by the newspaper's special correspondent in Nairobi – was about just these educated Africans across the region, where

> young men, after a taste of education and a glance at local government, believe that they are ready to run the country and that anyone who tries to delay them is moved by pure selfishness. The few African political leaders here – educated in Britain – appear to be lonely, unhappy, and bitter men who lash out at any sort of authority, and the mass of the people is affected by a deep and wordless suspicion of our motives and believes surprisingly little of what we say.[249]

While claiming to speak for East Africa as a region, the journalist Patrick O'Donovan then proceeds in the article to comment exclusively on Kenya, extrapolating his (perhaps limited) experience in this one country to also hold for Tanganyika and Uganda. It is not difficult to imagine what effect such comments would have had on the likes of Nyerere, whose thoughts on Tanganyikan nationalism would only have solidified against such blatant disrespect of the political abilities of the educated African. He may well have also speculated whether for his article O'Donovan had interviewed Jomo Kenyatta. Kenyatta first arrived in London in 1929 to impress on the British government the Kikuyu Central Association's views on land alienation, and he stayed in Europe for sixteen years, interrupted only once by a return journey to Kenya. By 1934 he had reinvented himself as a student and an informant to linguists on Kikuyu, first at University College and then at the LSE. The two never met in the United Kingdom, since Kenyatta had returned to Kenya before Nyerere arrived in London.[250]

Despite some 'definite progress in rural local government',[251] as another article in *The Scotsman* put it, the national-level inspiration for those future African leaders who were still undergoing their education

Scotland: Great Conceptions

in Britain was from their continent's western shores. Much ink in the newspapers was given over to developments in the Gold Coast, where one journalist from *The Scotsman* proclaimed that 'it is more likely that the surge of African nationalism will break the vessels that are intended to contain it'.[252] The focus was on Kwame Nkrumah's impending release from prison, with one article adopting the same Biblical language that Ghana's independence leader himself used: 'Election time in Gold Coast: African prisoner seeks to 'free' his people. Britain's bold policy'. The author was once more *The Scotsman*'s man in Africa, Patrick O'Donovan, who wrote from Accra with his ever-present casual racism:

> The Colony that until recently was looked on as the most friendly and gentle in the British Empire has turned alien and sour – at least on the surface – since the end of the war. To satisfy this sudden dissatisfaction, the four million inhabitants of this gold and cocoa-rich colony on the west coast of Africa have been offered the power to choose themselves a government. They have a new constitution in which the-man-in-the-jungle will have more control than anywhere else in Africa – and that includes Ethiopia and Liberia. It is not self-government, but it is not far off. … Every man today in the Gold Coast to-day [*sic*] is nationalist. There is a large and extreme element who demand self-government now. … By far the most important of the Nationalist parties is the Convention People's Party.[253] Its leader, Kwame Nkrumah, is the prisoner who dominates the election …. Nkrumah is a very remarkable man. He has created a party in the last two years and outstripped all others. Educated by Catholic missions, he went to Britain and America to study without any great scholastic success, and returned to the Gold Coast to 'free' his people. … One of the secrets of his power is his utter personal honesty. He is eloquent in a Hitlerian sort of way. … In the Gold Coast Britain has taken a leap in the dark. Officials believe they can work with the new men. They have done a bold thing, but only bold measures could conceivably satisfy this suddenly awakened people.[254]

Some of the parallels between Nkrumah and Nyerere are palpable. A few short months after the publication of this article, at the opposite side of the continent, Nyerere went on to begin a similar course in shaping Africa's history.

6
Edinburgh & Uhuru
Politics, Philosophy & Economics

Socialism is about people, and people are the products of their history, education, and environment.

Julius Nyerere, *Freedom and Socialism*[1]

This chapter begins by revealing the contact that Nyerere had with fellow Tanganyikans, especially those with him in the United Kingdom at the same time. It details an early sign of political differences that arose in a London meeting between Nyerere and representatives from the territory. It then charts Nyerere's political activities in Edinburgh, where publicly he focused on the proposed Central African Federation. The chapter discusses the influence of Fabianism, which leads into an examination of the key political economy and moral philosophy texts that he studied for his degree. Emphasis is placed on Nyerere's understandings of religion, traditional society, freedom and democracy, and how he saw that these could be applied to his homeland. The chapter draws on interviews with John Keto, co-author with Nyerere of a hitherto uncited political article that the two Tanganyikans wrote together in Edinburgh. It also provides analysis of other Africa-related content in *The Student* magazine, and reflections on Nyerere's unabridged version of 'The Race Problem in East Africa' article that he completed in Edinburgh. The final treatment is on the works of classical and later European philosophers who Nyerere studied, and his appreciation of the position taken by authors such as Jean-Jacques Rousseau and John Stuart Mill, T.H. Green, Bernard Bosanquet and Harold Laski.

Thirteen Tanganyikans

While his political views at the time were put to paper, Nyerere never became much of a platform politician in the University itself. He did speak publicly in Edinburgh on the Central African Federation, but those who knew him in the city did not remember him as a student politician of vocal prominence.[2] As Shepperson put it in a later BBC interview: 'We at Edinburgh were … very surprised, in the mid-1950s when Dr. Nyerere's name became widespread throughout the world press. We never felt when he was here that he was going to become a leading politician.'[3] Nyerere was certainly politically aware in the early 1950s. From Edinburgh he is said to have maintained regular correspondence – 'almost like a newsletter' – with the few other Tanganyikans in Britain, informing them about and discussing with them the situation back home.[4] Before his departure from Tanganyika, the African Association had discussed the need for a delegate to be sent to Europe to request African points of view in international affairs.[5] This is a role that Nyerere now assumed, at least informally, when writing to other Tanganyikan students in the United Kingdom.

There is some small indication that Nyerere was receiving at least some information from political activists in Tanganyika. This is shown in a letter that was written to him by his Makerere and Tabora friend Hamza Mwapachu, who at the time of writing in early 1952 was working as a welfare officer on Ukerewe Island in Lake Victoria – probably a form of exile as punishment for his involvement with a group of political activists, among them Abdulwahid Sykes, Steven Mhando, Dr Kyaruzi and Dr Seree, who in 1950 had produced a memorandum that basically called for political independence. The document is said to have been secretly handed over to the first United Nations Mission responsible for Mandated Territories when it visited Tanganyika to determine how the British administration was dealing with the future of the trustee territory. When the Tanganyika colonial regime's Special Branch became aware of Mwapachu's involvement, the medic was quickly sent to the Lake Victoria outpost. From Ukerewe the exiled Mwapachu is said to have written to Nyerere to inform him of regional political developments, and of the value of the general manager of the Victoria Federation of Co-operative Unions, a young man from Musoma called Paul Bomani.[6] Bomani was one of a new group of political leaders emerging in Lake Province, among them Saadani Abdu Kandoro, Said Maswanya and Bhoke Munanka.[7] All of these men had interacted with Nyerere when he was a student at Tabora Boys, either as students themselves and co-debaters in the English Debating Society or, in the case of Saadani Kandoro, in the April 1940 African Association meeting. The Mwapachu letter to Nyerere in Edinburgh is now thought to be lost.[8]

More concrete signs of Nyerere's interest in communicating about political activities with Tanganyikans while he was in the United Kingdom are evidenced in his continuing correspondence with Lieutenant Colonel W.V. Crook. At the beginning of Nyerere's final year in Edinburgh he wrote to Crook asking for the names of 'all the

Nyerere

Tanganyika (African) Students in Britain'.[9] Over the last year, so Nyerere informed the Liaison Officer, the Tanganyika students had lost touch with one another. Exactly how many Tanganyikan students Nyerere had earlier been communicating with is unknown, although he later said that there were seventeen Tanganyikan students in the United Kingdom at the same time as him. Among them were four Colonial Development Welfare Scheme scholars.[10] Since seventeen is the figure that Nyerere remembers, that is probably around the number of students that he was in touch with, although we know that at the time there were officially 47 Tanganyikan students (forty male, seven female) in the capital city alone.[11] London is where Nyerere met with most Tanganyikans, and when he visited the city he caught up with his fellow nationals in the British Council hostel at 1, Hans Crescent, and in East Africa House. The latter, known by the students as 'The Club', was the official centre for East African students in Britain, and catered for East Africans of all races. The majority of the members appear to have been Asians and Europeans. In the case of Tanganyika, this reflects the racial representation of students who were studying in the United Kingdom. It probably also explains, in part, why Nyerere only remembered seventeen Tanganyikan students.[12] After all, and despite his racial sensitivity, Nyerere's interest was in communicating with 'Tanganyika (African) Students'. Writing about relations between racial groups of students from East Africa in the United Kingdom at this time, Carey states that there was no hostility, but they tended to keep apart. A black Kenyan student, for example 'cannot remember ever having a conversation with a European at this centre'. Whites from East Africa normally joined British unions, notes Carey, while the East African unions run by black students had a briefer lifespan.[13]

In Nyerere's case, organising meetings with Tanganyikans was particularly difficult because in Edinburgh he was geographically distant from the England-based majority. Writing letters was the next best option, although this posed its own problems because Crook, in response to Nyerere's request, claimed that he was not at liberty to disclose addresses. All he could offer was thirteen names: G.J. Kiletta, F. Mfundo, R.B. Nyauli, T. Wagi, J.B. Matovu (a CDWS scholar at the Institute of Education, London), D.A. Omari (Education, Aberystwyth),[14] J.A. Sawe (Geography, Aberystwyth),[15] P.S. Mwinyipembe (Durham), F.L.N. Mongi, M.M. Mushi, G. Rutabanzibwa (Co-operative College, Nottinghamshire), J. Keto (already in Edinburgh with Nyerere, and also a CDWS scholar), and C.M. Gerrard[16] – presumably not the kind of 'Tanganyika (African) Student' Nyerere had in mind. It is not known with whom from the list Nyerere then corresponded, and no letters have yet come to light.[17] That Nyerere attempted to communicate with his fellow Tanganyikans at all, however, is evidence of his interest in territorial matters.

Some of the Tanganyikan students on Crook's list met five months earlier. Nyerere wrote to Crook in June 1951 asking him for assistance, apparently on behalf of all of the Tanganyikans studying in Britain, so that some of them could meet the African chiefs who were imminently coming to the Festival of Britain in July.[18] Conceived of as an official celebration of Britain's recovery from the war, the Festival ran for five months, with colonial exhibits and trade fairs that continued to tour the country until further into the early 1950s.[19] Nyerere travelled to London however, where the Festival exhibition on the South Bank focused on metropolitan Britain. Among those Africans who attended the celebrations were the Kabaka (King) of Buganda (in Uganda) and the Nabagereka (the Kabaka's wife), three paramount chiefs from Sierra Leone, and a number of Nigerians of high standing.[20] Also present were Kojo Botsio, then Gold Coast Minister of Education; Kwame Nkrumah, Leader of Government Business, Accra, Gold Coast; and Abdulla Hasham Gangji, a Member of the Zanzibar Legislative Council since 1948.[21]

Chief Kidaha Makwaia – 'the governor's favourite African'[22] – was among the Tanganyika chiefs who travelled to London for the Festival of Britain. Accompanying him was Marangu's Petro Itosi Marealle, uncle to the future Chagga Paramount Chief Thomas Marealle and a man who later became a respected elder of the Tanganyika African National Union (TANU) – which replaced the Tanganyika African Association (TAA) in 1954.[23] The 1951 celebrations in London were the first time that Nyerere met with Chief Petro Itosi Marealle,[24] who also travelled on to Bristol with other 'Tanganyikan tribal dignitaries' for the city's 'Our Way of Life' exhibition.[25] Nyerere had previously met with Chief Makwaia as early as 1947 when the chief had clashed with Nyerere and other African Association intellectuals over Colonial Paper 210.[26] Chief David Kidaha Makwaia then spent part of 1949 and 1950 studying at Oxford, but there is no evidence to suggest that the two resolved their differences during that time.

Whatever Nyerere had discussed with Makwaia before or during the Festival of Britain, the deal turned sour in London. John Keto was among the East African students who had been invited to East Africa House at 36, Great Cumberland Place, and he recalls that the students met there with the new Governor of Tanganyika, Sir Edward Twining.[27] Twining wanted to give the students a gift upon the visit of his friend Chief Kidaha Makwaia. The students were lined up as if on parade, and the Governor walked along exchanging pleasantries and shaking their hands. When Twining reached Nyerere he stopped, was introduced to him, and, leaning forward, he said softly, 'Ah Nyerere, I've read about you. … But I disagree with you on one point …'. The Governor then walked on to chat with the other students as if nothing had happened in this the first meeting between Twining and Nyerere.[28] Keto vividly remembered the silence as, still on parade, he could see that Nyerere was trying to fathom what exactly the one point was on which Twining disagreed with him. Perhaps it was something the young Tanganyikan had written in his draft of 'The Race Problem of East Africa' and which he had sent to Twining for comment. Nyerere simply stood trembling, Keto relates, and was wondering what issue in the many articles he had written had so irked the Governor. Twining promptly departed, by which time Nyerere's fear had turned to rage. Keto approached him and asked why he was now so quiet, and what Twining had said. Nyerere's silence quickly turned to anger, and in a clipped tone he simply said to Keto: 'Chief Kidaha has betrayed me!' The two left East Africa House and hurried to Kidaha's hotel, but the chief could not be found.[29]

At the time, Makwaia was the most prominent of all Tanganyikan chiefs.[30] He was the first African to be appointed to the Legislative Council, and in its meetings he purposefully refrained from referring to the (Tanganyika) African Association. He regarded the association as more of a social club than a political organisation. Nyerere later called Makwaia 'our Hamlet' because he could never make up his mind whether to join the nationalists.[31] In the eyes of the British establishment, the Tanganyika-based Makwaia and Shangali represented the views of Africans. Indeed, Makwaia was rumoured to be such good friends with Twining that he had a bedroom in Government House. But in Nyerere's eyes Makwaia and Shangali were simply nominated members of the Legislative Council, toadies to the British. They 'were not, or meant to be, the delegates of the Africans of Tanganyika', Nyerere wrote at the time.[32] It is not known what exactly Makwaia had done that so angered Nyerere at the London festival to celebrate all things British. He may have felt that the connected Makwaia could have done more to help influence the Tanganyika Committee on Constitutional Reform, which recommended a 7-7-7 system of representation for the Africans, Asians and Europeans.[33] It is clear that the two had very different opinions on the course of Tanganyika's political future. After independence Makwaia joined the opposition Tanganyika African National Congress (or at least he pretended to join it) and later, under the same Preventative Detention Act that he applied to Kasella Bantu, Nyerere had Makwaia rusticated to the remote Tunduru District. The Oxford-educated ex-chief never troubled the President again.[34] Nyerere, still based in his own outpost in Edinburgh at the time of the London incident with Twining, already saw Makwaia as a threat to his growing political ambitions.

African Affairs

Reverend MacKenzie was also of the belief that in the early 1950s Nyerere 'learned a great deal in the rough and tumble of the political fight against the Federation [of the Rhodesias and Nyasaland] which was being proposed by the British government'.[35] Though no record of Nyerere's addresses to Scottish groups at this time appear to have survived, his deep concern with the threat of increasing white-domination over the emerging Central African Federation (CAF) was echoed in sentiments he offered to George Shepperson, then a lecturer in History at Edinburgh, after an address to the student members of the Cosmopolitan Club for overseas students in late 1949.[36] In the rooms of Reverend Cattanach, the young Tanganyikan warned Shepperson that the creation of such a white-dominated Federation without the establishment of democratic constitutions in its three territories would be a disaster.[37]

As British interest in the CAF grew, so a couple of Tanganyikans were invited to the United Kingdom on a short visit 'to study British life "at all levels"'.[38] One of the invitees was Erasto Mang'enya, who initially took the purpose of the visit at face value. Shortly before he left for Britain, however, Mang'enya was approached in Tanga by Daniel Mfinanga, a former colleague at Old Moshi School, who whispered to him,

> although you have not been told the real object of the visit [to the United Kingdom], the African Association is well informed of the purpose of the visit. The purpose is to discuss the issue of the Central African Federation. ... The stand of the African Association on this issue is to postpone the Federation until the Africans are ready for it.[39]

According to Mang'enya, his informant then revealed that the white settlers both in East and Central Africa were contemplating extension of the idea of Federation to East Africa. If Mang'enya's account is correct, then it could suggest that while Nyerere was in the United Kingdom he was in touch with the Tanganyika African Association who had informed him of the possible extension of the Federation to East Africa. Another source of news from home was the *East African Standard* newspaper, copies of which Nyerere managed to obtain in Edinburgh and, suggests Keto, may have been why his focus was regional. Describing Nyerere's political concerns at the time concerning his homeland, Keto says that in Edinburgh 'Mwalimu was talking about independence for Tanganyika, but this was within limits. He was talking more of an East African Federation – although this wasn't the term he was using. The events in East and in Central Africa, these were a hot

Nyerere

potato for him.'[40] Indeed, as we have seen in Nyerere's 1946 letter to Arthur Creech Jones, issues of regional federation had been a burning issue for some time. Reverend MacKenzie, describing Nyerere's engagement with African politics when he was in Edinburgh, later wrote that at this time Julius,

> took a prominent and active part in opposing the proposed Central African Federation. An informal, international and inter-confessional group used to meet at Bill Cattanach's flat. I remember that I was given the opportunity of addressing them and I took as my subject the white papers published in June, 1951 on this controversial subject.[41] ... I well remember crossing the Firth of Forth with [Nyerere] one spring evening on the old Granton Ferry ... to address a weeknight meeting in the old parish kirk [church] of Burntisland. It was quite a well attended meeting, especially when the subject didn't have the drama and public appeal which it developed later.[42] ... He talked with great interest and with his quiet conviction about the future of Tanganyika. He made the point that although its administration was and appeared more liberal than that of Northern Rhodesia, where I had been working, yet it contained similar problems. It had no legal colour bar but it had a powerful conventional one. He spoke strongly but without bitterness about accommodation and facilities in hospitals.[43]

A truly unique insight into Nyerere's opinions on the Central African Federation while at Edinburgh has recently been unearthed in a hitherto unquoted article. Co-authored with John Keto, the piece is one of few overtly political contributions to be published in *The Student* magazine during Nyerere's time in Edinburgh. At two-and-a-half pages, the article is unusually long for the magazine, it is written with a persuasive eloquence that counters the position of Sir Godfrey Huggins, then Prime Minister of Southern Rhodesia, who the authors quote as declaring: 'It is time for people in England to realise that the white man in Africa is not prepared, and never will be prepared, to accept the African as an equal, socially or politically.'[44] Nyerere and Keto's argument begins by outlining African opposition to federation, especially the Southern Rhodesia's Land Apportionment Act, which divided the colony chiefly into well-watered, fertile areas for Europeans, and remote, poor quality land with inadequate water resources for Africans. The authors also outline the Industrial Conciliation Act, which effectively protected European skilled workers against African competition. The main thrust of the Tanganyikan students' argument is in their attack of the proposed constitution for the federation, where Southern Rhodesia were to have seventeen representatives in a Legislative Assembly of thirty-five members, of which only four were to be Africans. The African position, Nyerere and Keto argue, is that federation involves such grave dangers to their freedom 'that no safeguards short of full participation in the Government of their country are adequate'.[45] Nyerere later applied this argument when negotiating the liberation of his own people.

Nyerere and Keto's political submission to *The Student* magazine was published at a time when most students' contributions were either light-hearted stories, a few verses of mediocre poetry or, in a story entitled, 'High Jinks at the English Boys' School from School', faintly humorous tales from the Christmas dance. The raising of a very serious political matter in a magazine that devoted much space to student gossip suggests that Nyerere and Keto were slightly out of touch with many of their European counterparts who read *The Student*. Yet their success in pushing for the publication of their piece points to a commitment to bring African issues to an audience comprised largely of educated young Scots. The matters the Tanganyikans raise are broadly similar in content to a twenty-five page memorandum written in London three years earlier by Hastings Banda and Harry Nkumbula 'on behalf and on the authority of Nyasaland and Northern Rhodesian Africans in the United Kingdom'.[46] It is possible that Banda supplied them with a copy of the memo in advance of the 'Politics on the Zambezi' meeting in Edinburgh. The tenor of Nyerere and Keto's piece however, and the different statistics they draw on, suggest that in the main they composed the argument themselves.

In the same year as Nyerere and Keto's 'Central African Federation' piece, 1951, a flurry of stories relating to Africa began to be published. One, 'King of the N'gombali', is a short tale of the ruler of the 'N'gombali' tribe in a country called 'Central Africa' 'where Rome had never reached'.[47] In the story, the king and his English District Commissioner (D.C.) are very close, such that when the D.C. dies he offers to leave his house and all his possessions to the king. Sometime before the D.C.'s death the two friends discuss the ongoing European war and the D.C. advises the king that he should resist the desire for his young men to travel until at least eleven years, and even then they should not all to be allowed to go far: 'Your people have lived in one place for many years now; they would lose much if they became wanderers.'[48] Upon the D.C.'s death the king refuses to allow his son to lead an expedition until he is on his own deathbed. He advises his son to 'get rid of all but a few wives', and then teaches him the doxology to the Lord's Prayer. The new king burns down the D.C.'s house as per his father's wishes, carouses with villagers and heads south to the white man with his tribe, 'the most civilised people in the world'.[49]

The author of the story is given as a 'Jonathan Leanstrait', although the name is not listed as an Edinburgh graduate during the 1951–54 period. It is quite possibly a pseudonym adopted by an African student (some details in the story suggest familiarity with the continent), or it could be the pseudonym adopted by various students for different submissions to the magazine. The story itself is a bit of a disappointment for a reader interested in Africa, one of whom was Nyerere. Yet the inclusion of the doxology, found in the Anglican version of the

Nyerere

Photo J. John Keto (standing, fourth from right) with African students, George Square, University of Edinburgh, c.1953. The gentleman sitting second from left also appears in Photo N (p.195, standing far left). (*Reproduced by kind permission of the late John Keto*)

Lord's Prayer and not in the Catholic version, makes it unlikely that Nyerere wrote the piece.[50] Whoever the author is, the point seems to be that African culture is to be guarded against that of the European – something Nyerere later wrote about himself[51] – and that travel to foreign places should be undertaken with great caution. Interestingly, upon the death of the ruler the house is destroyed (a custom some Zanaki and other nearby tribes performed), and the question of multiple wives is discussed. Chief Nyerere Burito, of course, had over twenty wives – a subject that is also the focus of a 1951 piece in *The Student* called 'A Man with Twenty Wives'. The author is a 'J.K. Yankson', who is also not listed in the list of graduates during the 1951–54 period.[52]

Further evidence has recently come to light to suggest that, whilst dealing with many contemporary issues of African politics during his time in Edinburgh, Nyerere may well have had meetings in the city with southern Africans of influence. A 1951 article in *The Student* magazine entitled 'From Darkest Africa' reports a meeting at which a 'Mr Chirwa of the Nyasaland National Congress and Mr Katilungu of Northern Rhodesia's T.U.C. spoke of federation in the Men's Union'.[53] The author summarises the speeches and the discussion (described as 'almost frivolous at times'), which returned to the familiar issue of race: 'Why are

Africans and whites differently paid for equivalent responsibilities?' There is little doubt that Nyerere would have attended the meeting, which was held in immediate proximity to his classes and concerned a matter so close to his heart.

We also know that Nyerere heard the London-based medical doctor Hastings Banda speak in Edinburgh.[54] Being at the time two of only a handful of people from east and central Africa in the city, it is quite possible that Nyerere and Banda spent some time together north of the border. The occasion was a February 1952 mass meeting on the possible imposition of the Central African Federation. Held in the Church of Scotland Assembly Hall, the meeting was organised by the World Church Group, a 'rather loosely organised and mainly student group … [that] took to circularising petitions, running protest meetings, sending out speakers, lobbying M.P.s, writing to the press, etc'.[55] Nyerere was an executive member of the Edinburgh World Church Group, and would have spent time with the Chair, an ex-colonial governor called Sir Gordon Lethem, as well as the Bishop of Edinburgh, academics and other leaders of the Scottish churches who flanked him at the meeting.[56] Entitled 'Politics on the Zambezi', the advertisement for the meeting was made at the end of the Nyerere and Keto 'Central African Federation' article in *The Student* magazine, and was probably written by one, or both, of them. They billed it 'a critical examination of the proposals for Central African Federation', and described it as a matter of significance 'far beyond Central Africa, [for] the eyes of Asia and Africa are on it'. The call described the meeting in terms of race – by now an emerging theme in Nyerere's politics while in Edinburgh – and students were asked to 'come and hear why this may be a "test case" of Britain's attitude in racial relationships'.[57]

More than 1,100 people crowded into the venue, and Kenneth Little, by this time Reader in Social Anthropology at the University of Edinburgh, presided over the guest speakers: Reverend Kenneth MacKenzie, described by Nyerere as a 'Missionary in Central Africa', John Hatch, 'well-known broadcaster and writer on African matters' (and by this time lecturer in African Studies at the University of Glasgow), and Dr Hastings Banda, 'Representative in Britain of the Nyasaland African Congress'. Banda's speech was summarised the following day in *The Scotsman*:

> Dr Banda said that the federation of these territories was not in the best interests of the people. They had many reasons for opposing it. The British Government had been telling the world that the British purpose was to train Africans, and train them for the day when they would be able to stand on their own feet. Federation would produce a situation where they would lose the right to form their own Government within the Commonwealth. … The attitude of the British people and government in this country was that the African was a human being and as such entitled to the same rights and privileges which people of every race claimed for themselves.[58]

Nyerere

When the floor was given, Nyerere angrily denounced the proposed federation between the two Rhodesias and Nyasaland. In rebuke, he condemned it as yet another example of white domination over Africans. The meeting unanimously passed a resolution condemning closer association between the three African territories 'without the free consent of the African peoples'. It led to the creation of the ad hoc Scottish Council on African Questions, set up to combat racism and colonialism in Africa. Nyerere also addressed this council.[59]

There appears to be nothing to suggest that Nyerere and Banda developed any further relationship while in Edinburgh. The two educated Africans very likely met when Nyerere was in London, where the future father of the Malawi nation was then practicing medicine. Mang'enya, still on his short study visit, tells of a meeting with Tanganyikans at the time of one of Nyerere's trips to the English capital. The group dined with Banda, 'who talked much against the Central African Federation and referred to Sir Roy Wellensky as "the architect of the infamous Central Federation". [Banda] swore that he would see to it that the Federation did not materialise. If it did he would see to it that the Federation would not last.'[60]

Banda was captivating company for the young Tanganyikans. As a medical doctor with his own practice in the suburbs and a European secretary, Banda owned a comfortable house in Brondesbury Park and had a standard of living higher than that enjoyed by many of his white neighbours.[61] The young Tanganyikans would have known this – Banda was not renowned for his modesty – and African friends who visited him at his home were said to have been impressed by his adjustment and the ease with which he had assimilated British attitudes.[62] Certainly Banda's British mannerisms and dress – he favoured a black homburg hat and carried a rolled umbrella – would have been conspicuous when they met. Yet there is little about Nyerere that at any time suggests he also wished to mimic the British. In Nyerere's eyes, Banda was a man who in the United Kingdom of the 1950s had reached the top, a man with a respected position of authority as a professional, and (at this time) a man who claimed to be a voice of his people. More importantly, Banda was one of the very few Africans with direct experience of parliamentary democracy in practice. His campaign on Federation saw him mobilise his political contacts in the Labour Party so that he could discuss the issue face-to-face with Creech Jones. While Nyerere did not manage to reach the Colonial Secretary, he did on occasion – and following Banda's lead – discuss politics with the Fabian Bureau.[63]

The groups with whom Nyerere mixed most when in Edinburgh were Nigerians and West Indians.[64] The most dynamic African colonial student organisation in Britain was the London-based West African Students' Union (WASU). WASU promoted African nationalist aspirations and opposed racial discrimination.[65] It is not known if Nyerere attended their meetings in Edinburgh, nor of their vibrancy in the city. Edinburgh's West Indian society was certainly in full flourish at the time.[66] The West Indian Students' Association, as it was known, aimed to promote a 'better understanding of the life and peoples of the Caribbean Territories'. It did this through 'co-operation with kindred societies ... [such as] the E.U. Cosmopolitan Club'. We have seen that Nyerere attended the latter. It is quite possible that he also attended meetings of the West Indian Students' Association since Mavis Anderson, its Secretary, lived in the same intimate residence as Nyerere.[67] As noted, 2 Palmerston Place was also the meeting place of the (Edinburgh) African Association. The group is not listed in the *Student's Handbook* until 1954, so we cannot be sure that it was in existence in Nyerere's days. This could be for many reasons: perhaps because the committee did not enter their details to the publishers on time, or for other reasons the existence of the Association was not known to the editors. In any case, by 1954 Nyerere's contemporary, John Keto, was an active member of Edinburgh's African Association, and he features in a photograph in the *Student's Handbook* as one Tanganyikan alongside ten West Africans. Despite the Nigerian and Gold Coast majority, the Association was open to all African students pursuing studies at Edinburgh University and its extramural schools.[68] The Association aimed to promote closer co-operation among African students in Great Britain and Ireland, to foster the spirit of international brotherhood between African students and students of other nationalities, and to provide scope for social and other activities. Activities included lectures, debates and discussions relating to Africa.[69]

Attitude to Africa

Nyerere seems to have focused primarily on his studies. He did take up invitations to spend time with tutors outside the classroom, including an 'at home' with his Moral Philosophy tutor Axel Stern, author of *The Science of Freedom*.[70] He was good friends with the black Jamaican Sydney Collins, an Assistant Lecturer in Anthropology who wrote one of the earlier books on the colour bar in Britain.[71] Nyerere's discussions with Collins, who wrote of the intermediary (and sometimes highly-esteemed) role that some white women in the United Kingdom assumed in marriage across racial lines, may well have influenced his 'Race Problem in East Africa' manuscript.[72] Nyerere seems to have spent much time on the issue of race when in Edinburgh. Jean Wilson recalled that he often commented on Africans, Asians and Europeans in his continent, once stating – when perhaps guided by the then conventional

Nyerere

African ethos of respect for one's seniors, and showing tact and politeness to an older woman – that 'there is plenty of room for all of them in Tanganyika'.[73] In his Edinburgh writing on race, Nyerere suggested a more proactive approach, representing Europeans as the problem and Africans as the solution: 'I appeal to my fellow Africans to take the initiative in this building up of a harmonious society. The Europeans have had the initiative and all the opportunities for over 200 years and everywhere they have succeeded in producing inter-racial chaos.'[74] He went on to adopt a more conciliatory tone:

> The Africans and all the Non-Africans who have chosen to make east Africa their home are the people of east Africa and frankly we do not want to see the Non-Africans treated differently either to our advantage or disadvantage … We must build up a society in which we shall belong to east Africa and not to our racial groups … We appeal to all thinking Europeans and Indians to regard themselves as ordinary citizens of Tanganyika … We are all Tanganyikans and we are all east Africans.[75]

A few years later Nyerere commented that in the forty-four-page handwritten essay, 'I expressed for myself what I have since been trying to put into practice.'[76]

That Nyerere tried to get this manuscript on race in East Africa published is perhaps an indication that by 1951 he was thinking seriously about having his political views heard on the wider international stage. His targeted audience for this paper was the Fabian Colonial Bureau, to whose *Venture* journal Nyerere submitted his piece for 'criticism and suggestion'.[77] He received just that in a thorough and frank reply from the editor, Marjorie Nicholson, who felt the document was 'very excellent' but not suitable for publication. In part this was because an inter-racial group of East African students at Oxford University had already been promised publication of a paper on East Africa. The refusal was because his article lacked detail: 'A general dissertation on race relations hardly comes within our field', wrote Ms Nicholson in reply.[78] The sticking point for the editor, however, was more the accuracy of some points Nyerere used to support his arguments – arguments at which both Chief Kidaha and Governor Twining flinched when Nyerere asked them for their comments on the same manuscript.

Nyerere was polite in his reply to Nicholson's scathing critique of his work, and – having read over it again – he confessed that,

> the tone in which I have expressed myself is so provocative that if the manuscript was read in East Africa it would almost certainly antagonise the Europeans there. This and other considerations make me feel that unless I am prepared to produce something much more satisfactory I must not try to publish what is undoubtedly an unsatisfactory effort.[79]

Nyerere also acknowledged that his manuscript 'gives an incomplete picture of political development at home'. He admitted that his aim in writing it was apparently 'not only to discover to myself what ideas I had on the subject of race relations, but … to conciliate European opinion if such ideas should ever get into print'.[80] Ever keen to engage in debate, he then proceeded to take the opportunity to confirm to Nicholson his views on the Tanganyikan constitution. The constitution, he stated, 'will only be fair as long as it insists on racial representation when it gives more representatives to the Indians, for instance, than it gives to the Europeans, whatever the Europeans as a community may stand for'.[81]

The editor of *Venture* did not dismiss Nyerere completely, and asked him to write a short review on a recently-published Penguin book of essays entitled *Attitude to Africa*. The publication was the outcome of a small group of left-leaning activists, among them Arthur Creech Jones and Margery Perham, who were concerned with colonial affairs and soon formed what became known as the Africa Bureau. The emergence of the Bureau serves again to illustrate the growing importance of Africa's position in British colonial affairs, this time in the eyes of United Kingdom progressives.[82] The wide-ranging *Attitude to Africa* included contributions from Colin Legum and the St Lucian-born and LSE-educated Arthur Lewis (who was later awarded a Nobel Prize in economics).[83] It covered such timely topics as 'The Revolution in Africa', 'African Communism' and 'African Nationalism'. Nyerere used the tiny amount of space allotted for the review to pick up on what were now firmly his most consuming issues: education for all, service to the people, racial equality, and independence.[84]

The *Attitude to Africa* writings by Fabian authors in the early 1950s certainly resonate with Nyerere's later pronouncements on the basic equality that he felt all the people of independent Tanzania should attain. Yet there is little direct evidence to suggest that the Fabian Society deserves to receive quite so much credit for apparently being such a great influence over Nyerere during his formative years.[85] He was in Scotland's capital for the vast majority of his time in the United Kingdom, but the minutes of the Edinburgh Fabian Society make no mention of a Julius Nyerere.[86] Granted, the Fabian Colonial Bureau was in touch with some Tanganyikan nationalists and they discussed shared interests. But for Nyerere their support was sometimes little more than acting as a (at times quite patronising) sounding board. He did read the organisation's publications for many years, and he occasionally wrote for them.[87] If he was 'sharpened by the politics of the Fabian Society during his student days in Britain', as Mohammed Said surmises, it was through literature.[88] Many of the central underpinnings of Nyerere's later writing and speeches, especially in relation to *ujamaa*, can be traced back more explicitly to prescribed texts that he read at university. These include the writings of Immanuel Kant and

Nyerere

John Stuart Mill, both of whom influenced later understandings of welfare liberalism and Fabian socialism taken up by recent contemporaries such as Harold Laski.[89] The bookish Nyerere may well have interacted with left-leaning activists. But his engagement was more with the original western philosophical texts upon which Fabian socialism was built.

Much like the lack of questioning over the (unsubstantiated) influence on Nyerere of the Fabian Colonial Bureau, however, an analysis of the academic literature that informed his later intellectual and political arguments has never really taken place. In part this is because, as Evaristi Cornelli has noted, Nyerere's writings 'have no footnotes, references or bibliography, and for that reason it is not easy to determine the sources of his ideas, particularly those which fed into *ujamaa*'.[90] It is also because those studies that have attempted to analyse the influences that particular thinkers may have had on Nyerere have almost all looked first at his political philosophy and, glancing backwards, then supposed – sometimes accurately – what he might have read.[91] Others have simply made reference to a catch-all 'classical political theory'.[92] Using the 'books recommended' for the various courses that we know Nyerere took in Edinburgh, here we consider the literature to which he was exposed in Edinburgh. Drawing links from this theoretical grounding, the remainder of this chapter looks forward to how the literature then informed his later writing and speeches.

The weakness of this approach, however, is that we cannot know for sure whether Nyerere actually read all of the books that his lecturers recommended in the reading lists that were published in the University calendar. His undoubted curiosity towards progressive academic European views on Africa, the fact that certain books were set for examination, and his thirst for reading, all suggest that he did. Certainly at Edinburgh Nyerere was much freer than ever before to read whatever he liked. Indeed on some courses, such as Moral Philosophy, students were 'expected to undertake independent reading'.[93] In this university city, with its excellent libraries and well-stocked bookshops, Nyerere purchased many of the requested titles on his course reading lists, along with many other extracurricular books. Hand-dated from the 1949–52 period, the fact that many of Nyerere's books have annotations in his handwriting confirms that he studied them. What is more revealing, however, are the parallels between Nyerere's own writing and the writings of many academics he read and heard in Edinburgh.

Principles of Political Economy: Work and Co-operation

Sir Alexander Gray's Political Economy course taken by Nyerere in his first year is the obvious starting point in this small survey of the literature that influenced the political beliefs of the '£1 million scholar'. Nyerere purchased two volumes of Frank Taussig's *Principles of Economics* as background reading for Gray's introduction to the fundamentals of political economy. Students were examined on classical texts by Enlightenment philosophers. One was Adam Smith's *The Wealth of Nations* (1776).[94] In his 'Ujamaa' paper, Nyerere touched on Smith's treatise on the production of wealth. Whether it was 'by primitive or modern methods', Nyerere explained that Tanzanians already possessed what Smith saw as the essential requisites to prosperity. Tanzanians had land (given by God), tools (Nyerere's list being predominantly agricultural), and human exertion (that is to say, the 'hard work' he perpetually exhorted).[95]

Gray also examined his students on John Stuart Mill, whose *Subjection of Women* Nyerere had studied while at Makerere. Like Smith, Mill's *Principles of Political Economy* also considers the means of production, and begins with the key statement that 'the requisites of production are two: labour, and appropriate natural objects'.[96] Both were central to Nyerere's writing on *ujamaa*. The TANU constitution states that 'People' (who control 'the major means of production') and 'Land' are the first prerequisites to national development. The Arusha Declaration outlines hard work as a condition for these two prerequisites to flourish.[97] The emphasis of *ujamaa*, Nyerere explained, was on Tanzania's rural-based population of farmers and agricultural labourers – be the person 'a peasant working on his own *shamba* [smallholding], a member of a co-operative farming group, or a woman looking after her small children and the family home'.[98] For these majority Tanzanians, and all other workers (for 'a socialist society… will consist of workers, and only of workers'[99]) there was 'no alternative to hard work'. Nyerere regarded hard work as the labourer's 'duty to society'.[100] Tanzanians' 'duty to work' brought about the well-being of all citizens, which Nyerere saw as central to their future development.[101] He directly linked Mill's two basic requisites of production – the people and the land – to the wealth of the nation. Tanzania's resources, Nyerere observed, 'are the land and the people, and it is through the organized exploitation of these two that we shall have to make progress'.[102]

Co-operation was the third requisite in Mill's *Principles of Political Economy*.[103] As was the case for Smith, so Mill was also inspired by the efficient practices of urban factories. This form of co-operation was clearly inconsistent with Nyerere's idea of traditional African co-operative labour which 'did not have the "benefit" of the Agrarian Revolution or the Industrial Revolution'[104] Yet while Nyerere's philosophy was at odds with Mill's in many ways – the Englishman was a staunch defender of private property and private ownership – Mill still advocated the establishment of co-operatives as combining the best of capitalism and socialism. Mill's support for collective work raised in Nyerere's mind the potential of harnessing the first two requisites of production; his nation's land, and its labour. If co-operation worked for the 'civilized nations', then it could surely work for 'the half-civilized', as Mill explained:

> Works of all sorts, impracticable to the savage or the half-civilized, are daily accomplished by civilized nations, not by any greatness of faculties in the actual agents, but through the fact that each is able to rely with certainty on the others for the portion of the work which they respectively undertake. The peculiar characteristic, in short, of civilized beings, is the capacity of co-operation.[105]

Nyerere was surely rankled by Mill's pejorative tone. But it served to strengthen his resolve in proving that co-operation was long-established on his continent and was inherently African.[106]

The 'traditional' African society that so strongly influenced Nyerere's ideas on African socialism and African democracy motivated him personally. His image of traditional African society was clear enough to convince him that the Eurocentric philosophers he studied in Edinburgh were misinformed on the 'savage' societies they so often disparaged. This is evidenced in Nyerere's explanation of some of the basic principles that were discussed in Gray's political economy course: 'We don't need to read… Adam Smith', Nyerere told his audience in 1967, 'to find out that neither the land nor the hoe actually produces wealth. And we don't need to take degrees in Economics to know that neither the worker nor the landlord produces land. … But we do know, still without degrees in economics, that the axe and the plough were produced by the labourer.'[107]

Nyerere also used tradition as a motivational tool to stir the people of Tanzania into supporting African democracy and *ujamaa*. Tradition was the foundation of Nyerere's 'reconstruction of an idealized past as the basis for present and future political activity', as Paul Nursey-Bray has put it.[108] Herein lay a contradiction, for harking back to the past was in fact incongruous with Nyerere's claim that Africa's traditional moral strength 'must be free from the ties of history'.[109] But Tanzanians seldom questioned the 'tradition' since these images from the past were being handed down by a highly-educated and respected teacher. Nyerere made no attempt to provide proof for his traditional society.

He was satisfied to use his pronouncements merely as 'an axiom of his political thought'.[110]

Macmurray's Socialism

Nyerere's political thought is also clearly influenced by authors covered in Professor John Macmurray's Moral Philosophy courses. Nyerere took the first course in the first half of his final year at Edinburgh. It offered an understanding of 'the moral structure of Western civilisation through a study of its origins…. with special reference to Plato and Aristotle, Stoicism and the Bible.'[111] These were the philosophical foundations on which Nyerere built the structure that he felt was appropriate to the Tanzanian environment. He later made reference to classical institutions in one of his many explanations of the suitability to Tanzania of his particular form of African democracy: 'the City States of Ancient Greece' practiced democracy, he observed, although he only used this to emphasise the hypocrisy of the rulers, who would 'boast of "democracy" when more than half the population had no say at all in the conduct of the affairs of the State'.[112] When choosing his courses Nyerere was drawn to Moral Philosophy I and its special reference to the Bible. Macmurray was a member of the Christian Left Movement and in his political philosophy argued that 'the religious voice cannot be excluded'. By this he meant not the voice of an institutional interest group, but 'the voice shaped by a belief in the deepest possible ontological ground for understanding human persons'.[113] Nyerere regularly read the scriptures and was exposed to the Word when worshiping at church, usually every day. In his speeches he frequently quoted passages from the Bible, and as early as his JUKANYE article he was employing Biblical language. The authors that Macmurray used in Edinburgh for his discussion of metaphysics and the existence of God are not recorded, but it must be here that Aristotle and Cicero featured. We can be more sure of Nyerere's ontological reflections that developed from these classes. He stated this later in his writing on socialism:

> There is not the slightest necessity for people to study metaphysics and decide whether there is one God, many Gods, or no God, before they can be socialist. … What matters in socialism and to socialists is that you should care about a particular kind of social relationship on this earth. Why you care is your own affair. There is nothing incompatible between socialism and Christianity, Islam, or any other religion which accepts the equality of man on earth.[114]

The Bible and Greek philosophy undoubtedly had their appeal to Nyerere. The introduction to modern philosophy that came towards the end of his first course in the work of Immanuel Kant was less inspiring for him.[115] As engaged as Nyerere was with metaphysics, ethics and political philosophy, it is hard to believe Cornelli's assertion that Nyerere 'had Kant's text in front of him' when formulating and articulating *ujamaa*.[116] Other criticisms of Cornelli's thesis aside, the association he makes between Kant's explanation of (external and internal) freedom and Nyerere's use of the term 'freedom' does not fit as neatly as Cornelli would have his reader to believe.[117] Granted, there may well be Kantian roots in some of Nyerere's philosophy; the right to dignity and respect, for example, is indeed a summary of Kant's discourse on the concept of personal right.[118] But Nyerere went on to study texts that, while often inspired by Kant and other less accessible philosophers, were presented in a more digestible language. In the second Moral Philosophy course that he took with Macmurray he was exposed to works such as T.H. Green's *Principles of Political Obligation* and Bernard Bosanquet's *Philosophical Theory of the State*. The course offered 'a study of the development of political theory from Hobbes to the present day'.[119] Macmurray had taught a similar course when he was at Oxford University, where 'he told the students that both the individualism and the socialism of the west are still sub-human – conceived respectively in mere mechanical and organic terms, and therefore being acted out in the world as distortions of the ideal of genuine individuality and genuine social life'. This was Macmurray's philosophy of the personal; a focus on man.[120]

Among the key themes in Nyerere's writing and speeches during the struggle for independence were unity, equality, human dignity, and freedom in its various forms. They remained with him well into the post-independence period. But until independence it was freedom that was the absolute goal. After 1961 it cannot be said conclusively which of unity, equality, human dignity and freedom Nyerere saw as the priority. In part this is because Nyerere's writing suggests that in some way or another these issues are always inter-related. Underpinning them all, however, was a focus on *wananchi*, the people, and their role in society: 'The Purpose is Man', he announced a few months after the Arusha Declaration.[121] This was a reaffirmation of his independence address to the United Nations in 1961, in which he declared that 'the individual man and woman is the purpose of society. All great philosophies in the world do agree on this simple statement. The way they differ is how to carry out this principle in actual practice.'[122]

The statement clearly shows Nyerere's willingness to engage with the philosophy he grew to love. This was in no small part thanks to the enthusiasm of John Macmurray and Axel Stern. The charismatic Macmurray was not a distant, dull and abstract author who was forced upon students to read. Macmurray, and Stern the tutor, were approachable philosophers in the flesh with whom students could interact. In Macmurray's case in particular, this was helped by an ability to avoid specialised philosophical jargon.[123] Even before Macmurray and Nyerere first met there is evidence that they shared similar beliefs. Both felt that capitalist greed was a significant cause of the Second World War, for example, and European countries' self-centred perspective on national identity led to their exploitation of African resources.[124] Macmurray had a soft spot for his students from Africa, a continent that he visited many times. He was vocal in his support for blacks in the South Africa he had lived in, he had lectured in Kenya, and when he first lectured Nyerere he had recently returned from separate trips to the Gold Coast and Nigeria in his capacity as Edinburgh University's representative on the Inter-University Council for Higher Education in the Colonies.[125] Macmurray's African students in Edinburgh were an embodiment of his unstinting affirmation of the freedom of individuals. This attitude struck a chord with Nyerere, as did Macmurray's conception of democratic polity that 'balances equal participation for all with a strong sense of a common good for all'.[126] Macmurray was of a school of political philosophers who advocated the inclusion of a multiplicity of voices engaged in a fully democratic debate over the nature of the formation of social policies; Nyerere quickly subscribed. In a philosophy that Nyerere later echoed in 'Democracy and the Party System', Macmurray argued that different voices engaged in a common conversation can bring out the elements of the unique contributions of distinct persons, while at the same time they reign in the centrifugal tendencies present in many liberal democratic societies to produce 'factions' aiming only at the satisfaction of their own interests.[127] Nyerere similarly argued that political 'factionalism… is, by definition, self-interest'.[128] 'Politics must be more than a contestation of and for power among disparate and fundamentally hostile groups', Macmurray then continued.[129] One can imagine the Scotsman at the front of a packed and smoky Edinburgh lecture theatre, making this point by an analogy between point-scoring opposing parties and 'trivial football politics'.

Nyerere continued to develop his thoughts on socialism during the decade or so following independence. He decried Engels' 'scientific socialism', in particular Marx and Lenin[130] – although this did not stop him quoting *Das Kapital* for a sympathetic audience.[131] He spared little more time for proponents of the so-called 'utopian socialism', naming in his *Freedom and Socialism* the French early socialist Claude Henri de Rouvroy, and Robert Owen, the Welsh early promoter of the cooperative movement.[132] While valuable in some of their motivations, Nyerere felt that the efforts of these authors were simply not relevant to the Tanzanian situation:

> Knowledge of the work and thinking of these and other people may help a socialist to know what to look for and how to evaluate the things he sees; but it could also mislead him if he is not careful. Equally, a knowledge of history may help him to learn from the

experience of others; a knowledge of economics will help him to understand some of the forces at work in the society. But if he tries to use any of these disciplines and philosophies as a gospel according to which he must work out solutions he will go wrong. There is no substitute for his own hard work and hard thinking.[133]

Nyerere's message is that he had thought deeply about philosophy, history and economics, and he had prepared very hard for the classes he was to give to the people of Tanzania. The teacher had a valuable lesson for his pupils. They were to learn his original thoughts on how socialism was inherently African, and they better listen hard. But this being a primary school class for the uneducated, Nyerere the teacher did not worry about the small details of referencing his sources. In explaining his ideas on African socialism he did not feel the need to acknowledge that he borrowed freely from the ideas of many authors.

A reliance on the work of others is not unusual for politicians, and many successful speeches make no reference to those who have influenced the thoughts of the speaker. The studies that Nyerere drew on are themselves situated in living disciplines where the subject matter evolves. Nyerere's ideas on African socialism evolved in the same fashion. They began at least by the time of JUKANYE's earliest published thoughts on African socialism, written in 1943 when Nyerere was a young Makerere student scorning 'those selfish capitalists who have mainly caused this abominable war'. They eventually evolved into his critique of scientific and utopian socialism, given in 1968, by which time Nyerere was unquestionably Africa's philosopher-king (or Tanzania's 'teacher-President'). The hitherto unacknowledged thinkers who nurtured the evolution of Nyerere's philosophical and political thought were the authors of works on the reading list for Moral Philosophy II that Nyerere took at Edinburgh. The texts that Macmurray recommended were almost exclusively written by philosophers of the later European liberal tradition. The likes of Rousseau and Mill had a profound influence on Nyerere, and he appropriated many of their ideas for his vision of a future Tanzania. As has been observed of John Locke – another philosopher studied on Macmurray's second course – so the same can be said of Nyerere: he sought 'to demonstrate every point by considering it rationally, without reference to what his predecessors had said…. But while he tried, and appeared, to approach each point afresh, he had undoubtedly pondered and absorbed the views of a wide variety of earlier writers.'[134]

Central to Nyerere's argument on the misfit of European-inspired socialism to the Tanzanian setting is that non-African authors did not concern themselves with the history of 'colonial domination' – at least not from the African perspective.[135] Under colonial rule, Nyerere argued, the 'whole existence' of Tanganyikans was 'controlled by people with an alien attitude to life, people with different customs and beliefs'.[136] As he wrote in 1943, the foreign rulers were 'very reluctant to accept' socialistic principles, and their European 'attitude to life' was not socialist but 'capitalist' and 'individualistic'.[137] This attitude was implicit in much of Tanganyika's independence constitution – which the British had a strong hand in writing – and was perpetuated until Nyerere announced the refusal of his country to put itself in 'a straitjacket of constitutional devices'.[138] Nyerere rejected the Western model, stating that 'it was not appropriate for our circumstances'.[139] In replacing the British system, he held, 'there is no model for us to copy'.[140] Yet while Nyerere did not copy any models per se, the influence of Rousseau is already evident in the argument that all forms of government do not suit all countries: 'Every good legislative system needs modifying in every country in accordance with the local situation', wrote Rousseau in *The Social Contract*.[141] This was one of the most influential works of political philosophy in the Western tradition, and it was certainly instrumental to Nyerere's thinking. Rousseau himself was building on Thomas Hobbes' *Leviathan* – one of the earliest examples of social contract theory – and on Locke's *Second Treatise of Government*.[142] Nyerere studied all three works under Macmurray.[143]

A year after independence Nyerere announced that his country was to be a republic, the only rightful rule of law. He could be confident in this decision since it was approved by Rousseau's statement: 'Every legitimate government is republican.' By this Rousseau meant 'any government directed by the general will, which is the law'.[144] An extension of his *Discourse on Political Economy*, in *The Social Contract* Rousseau defined the State's real being as the 'General Will' of its members: 'Every society should be governed by the general will, the common good.'[145] Nyerere frequently employed Rousseau's 'common good' when speaking of African socialism. The *ujamaa* village, for example, was a place where 'people live together and work together for their common good',[146] and their educational system aimed to 'foster the social goals of living together, and working together, for the common good'.[147] Again Nyerere's focus was on humanity: 'The service of man, the furtherance of his human development, is in fact the purpose of society itself', he wrote. He then usually added that the other basic characteristic of a socialist society is the equality of man. The two were frequently accompanied in Nyerere's writing with the need for human dignity.[148]

Nyerere began with the issue of equality in an early written expression of his rejection of the two-party system. As was so often the case when he sought to legitimise a point, Nyerere looked to the past. Dismissing Tanganyika's most stratified and authoritarian societies in the West Lake Region, and ignoring the Swahili coastal dynasties, Nyerere insisted that there can be no 'doubting the African's sense of equality, for aristocracy is something foreign to Africa'.[149] He continued

Nyerere

his attack on aristocracy in 'Democracy and the Party System', and added his condemnation of the (British) monarchical system for sustaining inequality.[150] Similar criticism of both aristocracy and monarchy were made by Rousseau.[151] As is evident in his JUKANYE letter from Makerere, Nyerere had for many years before independence agreed with the Geneva-born philosopher's abhorence of inequality. Nyerere may not have read Rousseau at that stage, but he continued to express the same sentiment after he left Edinburgh, as demonstrated in a piece he wrote only a few short years after completing Macmurray's moral philosophy courses in which Rousseau featured: 'Government belongs to all the people as a natural and inalienable possession', Nyerere held, 'it is not the private property of a minority, however élite or wealthy or educated, and whether uni- or multi-racial.'[152]

Nyerere continued the following year to state his desire to level out the '"haves" and "have-nots"', as he frequently described the inequality that he then saw in his society.[153] 'Our position is based… in the equality of citizens, in their right and duties as citizens', Nyerere announced. He supported his statement with a section from the preamble of the United States Declaration of Independence: 'All men are created equal', Nyerere quoted, this being a phrase with roots in Locke's *Second Treatise of Government* that he studied with Macmurray.[154] The sentiment was expressed in what he regarded as Africa's 'own Declaration of Independence' against colonial rule.[155] It was enshrined in the TANU Constitution: '…all human beings are equal… every individual has a right to dignity and respect… every citizen is an integral part of the nation'.[156] Nyerere acknowledged that in the struggle against colonial domination he was inspired by the Declaration of Independence made by American colonies, and by the principles defined during the French Revolution.[157] The revolution was strongly influenced by the political philosophy of Rousseau.[158]

In Nyerere's attempt to define a balance between the free individual and his responsibilities in a larger society, he adopted Rousseau's ideas – albeit to far less extreme ends than Robespierre. With implicit acknowledgement of the influence of the western philosophers he had studied, Nyerere asks:

> Where does society, or the state draw the boundary of its rights and obligations; and where does the individual? … Our problem is just this: How to get the benefits of European society – the benefits which have been brought about by an organization of society based on an exaggerated idea of the rights of the individual – and yet retain the African's own structure of society in which the individual is a member of a kind of fellowship?[159]

Nyerere shows his appreciation of both aspects of traditional African society and certain aspects of European society that he admired. It led him back to the Rousseauian problem, discussed in *The Social Contract*, that arises from the quest for an individual and community good that is simultaneous and equal.[160] Rousseau, along with Green and Bosanquet – all of whom Nyerere studied – are in search of whether there can be a legitimate political authority.[161] Building on Rousseau's declaration that 'Citizens, by the social contract, are all equal',[162] Nyerere then borrowed heavily from Rousseau's explanation of how the existence of the State can be reconciled with human freedom. The solution in the African context comes with tradition, for it is 'fortunate that there is still to be found on our continent a form of organization of society which fundamentally solves the conflict between individual and society'. Nyerere's answer for Africa's legitimate political authority comes in the form of *African* socialism.[163]

In his numerous speeches justifying the appropriateness of *ujamaa* to African society, Nyerere became a modern equivalent to Rousseau's legislator, the one who first defines the system on which a State will operate. As Cranford Pratt puts it, Nyerere 'hoped that he could lead his people by example, by leadership and by teaching, but without coercion'.[164] Or as T.H. Green summarised the quest: 'Will, not Force, is the Basis of the State.'[165] To some extent, however, Nyerere's persistent explanations of how society should function forced his own will into the minds of citizens. But by his emphasis on unity, '*umoja*', his teaching served to focus the struggle against foreign domination, both before and after independence. Nyerere's will was the will of a people unified around the common desire for freedom. Here was a figure who could articulate the frustrations of Africans in a language that they understood. Simultaneously, because he was able to use the logic of their own philosophy, here was a figure who could challenge European domination. As Nyerere put it in his own words, European colonial powers 'know that domination is contrary to the democratic principles they profess, and they therefore do not like to acknowledge that they have been – and still are in other places – guilty of it'.[166] Yet, much like the philosophers he drew upon, Nyerere's speeches and writing also read like the aspirations of an idealist – or the 'long-term optimist' that he later admitted to being when it became evident that *ujamaa* was not being embraced as readily as he had first hoped.[167] Green and Bosanquet, writing much closer (than Rousseau and Kant) to the time that Nyerere first studied them, were both idealists,[168] as was Macmurray who, like other British idealists, blended Hegel and Kant with his Christian faith.[169] Following their lead, Nyerere could also refer to 'the *ideal* society… based on human equality and on a combination of the freedom and unity of its members. There must be equality…. There must be freedom.'[170]

Nyerere wrote the above in 1966, summarising his thoughts on freedom and unity, the rallying cry of the independence struggle. The central idea that Africans were opposed to, as he explained in the late 1950s, was that of 'a small minority... appointing itself the masters of an unwilling majority'.[171] Shortly after independence was realised he then referred to *uhuru* as a 'struggle for freedom from foreign domination'.[172] A number of the philosophers covered in Macmurray's second course dealt with the various forms of freedom. Few were more concerned than T.H. Green with the issue of 'freedom from external control' and the 'domination of a foreign power'.[173] Writing in the late 1880s, Green discussed British rule in India, which to Nyerere had parallels with British rule in Tanganyika. Green noted how in India the British presented themselves as 'the maintainer of customary law, which, on the whole, is the expression of the will', and he quickly added that the reality was that Britain was merely a 'tax-collecting military power'.[174] Green then referred to the 'duty' of 'resistance to a despotic government'.[175] This clearly resonated with Nyerere who, as we have discussed, recalled the influence that events in India had on him, especially with India's independence shortly before he arrived in Edinburgh.[176]

Green identified two freedoms: freedom from external control, and personal freedom. One naturally lead to the other, he determined, for 'the realisation of freedom in the state can only mean the attainment of freedom by individuals.'[177] Nyerere said much the same in his Presidential inaugural address, explaining that 'the freedom we demanded was not mere independence from colonialism; what we sought was personal freedom for all the people of Tanganyika'. He followed this by then pressing home his familiar message that the people of Tanganyika 'determined to build a country in which all her citizens are equal; where there is no division into rulers and ruled, rich and poor.'[178]

Uhuru, much like *umoja*, was a key word for an independent Tanganyika.[179] Freedom was something with which Nyerere was keen to be associated, as is evident in the title of each of his three major compilations of writings and speeches: *Freedom and Unity*, *Freedom and Socialism*, and *Freedom and Development*.[180] Freedom was certainly on Nyerere's agenda prior to reaching Edinburgh, for he wrote of the freedom of women while at Makerere. He had also apparently lectured his own students on Africa's freedom when teaching at St Mary's. But his most intense exposure to European notions of freedom came during his studies as an undergraduate. Of the courses he took at Edinburgh, Macmurray's Moral Philosophy I and II are the most prominent examples. Moral Philosophy II, in particular, was seemingly devoted to little more than an analysis of European philosophical notions of liberty.

Nyerere's understanding of freedom has its roots in Kantian liberalism. It was Mill's rendition of freedom that he followed most closely in his own writing. To Mill, as to Nyerere, the purpose of the State is to promote liberty, to take for granted man's free activities, and to use its power to promote and not to hinder freedom. Mill concludes his introduction to *On Liberty* with his three basic freedoms:

1, the freedom of thought and emotion; 2, the freedom to pursue tastes (provided they do no harm to others); and 3, the freedom to unite (so long as no harm is done to others).[181] Nyerere refers to all of these in various speeches, but in his own collection of three essentials to African socialism he considered freedom, equality and unity to be paramount.[182] Nyerere's lists of three essentials changed depending on his argument, and his claims for 'the most important' in relation to *ujamaa* are frequently followed by different terms. 'The freedom and well-being of the individual', for example, is the first essential to democracy, and is also an 'essential characteristic of a socialist society'.[183] Nyerere then expanded upon his understanding of freedom to explain away many points or to introduce what he saw as a linked theme. So when his rhetorical question was 'what do we mean when we talk about freedom?'[184] Nyerere first discusses freedom as *uhuru*, or 'national freedom; that is, the ability of citizens of Tanzania to determine their own future'. To this he adds 'freedom from hunger, disease, and poverty' as his second liberty. He finishes his triumvirate by following Green's second stage of freedom, the 'freedom for the individual'. Green sees this as following naturally from freedom from external control; Nyerere's *uhuru*. Nyerere then expands on individual freedom, and inevitably brings his listener back to the now-familiar 'right to live in dignity and equality with all others, his right to freedom of speech, freedom to participate in the making of all decisions which affect his life'. Nyerere's third, all-encompassing freedom – the freedom of every individual who 'really wants… freedom to pursue his own interests and his own inclinations'[185] – is basically Mill's freedom to pursue tastes. By Nyerere's generous definition it could equally be Mill's freedom of thought and emotion.

Nyerere used the equality of man in justification for his form of African democracy. He supported this by linking it to the rationality of man, another common theme in the philosophy he studied at Edinburgh. Rational knowledge is discussed in both Kant's *Metaphysics of Morals* and Mill's *Utilitarianism*. Mill also ends the first chapter of *Representative Government* with the 'rational choice'. Later Nyerere used rational choice as the title of a speech in which he presented the argument (yet different from Mill's overall point) that socialism was new nations' only rational choice.[186] Despite Nyerere's opposition to the two-party system, he nevertheless emphasised his advocacy of democracy as a principle, referring both to man's rationality and his equality: 'Given that Man is a rational being, and that all men are equal, democracy – or government by discussion among equals – is indeed the only defensible form of government.'[187] In the same piece Nyerere then establishes that democracy in Africa, as anywhere else, is 'Government by the people'. 'Ideally', he announced, 'it is a form of government whereby the people – all the people – settle their affairs through free discussion.'[188] This is an only slightly altered version of the definition of democracy given by the transcendentalist and reforming clergyman Theodore Parker. Nyerere made acknowledgement of this later for, as was so often the case, he reinforced the same point in a subsequent speech. This time he offered a direct quotation, with reference to Parker, as the source for his definition of democracy. Democracy, Nyerere explained, was 'Government of all the People by all the people, for all the people'.[189]

Some years before Independence Nyerere had stated his understanding of the basic principles of governance. He insisted that the many 'must inevitably be genuinely consulted, and the just powers of government derived from them'. This, he concluded, was 'government by representatives'.[190] By much later then announcing that 'Tanzania shall remain a republic with an executive head of state',[191] and that it would be a representative democracy,[192] Nyerere returned to Kant and his assertion that 'every true Republic is and can only be constituted by a Representative System of the People'.[193] In supporting his case for representative democracy under a one-party system, Nyerere also again borrowed from Rousseau, this time in the philosopher's attack on mixed governments.[194] In Nyerere's constant desire to express his favoured form of democracy in simple terms, however, he returned to the triplet, again in a slightly different form: 'These three, then, I consider to be essential to democratic government: discussion, equality, and freedom.'[195]

Discussion was a key concept to which Nyerere frequently referred. In his 1961 independence message to TANU he stated that 'the people can and must express their worries to the Government'.[196] He continued to reinforce the point in subsequent speeches, linking it wherever possible to his other key themes, especially to freedom: 'Free debate must continue. It is an essential element of personal freedom.'[197] As with equality and freedom, the discussion that Nyerere encouraged also had its roots in the philosophy that he studied at Edinburgh. Mill, for example, spent much time on the liberty of thought and discussion. As Nyerere, Mill regarded representative government to be government by discussion.[198] Discussion was essential to create public policy, Nyerere argued, and this relied on an environment that allowed for the open exchange of ideas from all citizens. Mill made a similar point, and followed it by calling for voice to be given to those who could challenge 'the tyranny of opinion'. To help avoid such oppression, Mill argued, 'it is desirable… that people should be eccentric'.[199] The same point was made for Tanganyika: 'The "eccentric"', Nyerere echoed, 'stops society from ceasing to think, forces it to make constant re-evaluations and adjustments.'[200]

Nyerere's further ideas on representative democracy continue to provide evidence of the influence of the European philosophers he read at Edinburgh. 'The two essentials for "representative" democracy', Nyerere announced, 'are the freedom of the individual, and the regular opportunity for him to join his fellows in replacing, or reinstating, the government of his country by means of the ballot-box.'[201] This follows the ideas on voting and elections put forward by Rousseau, and later by Green. Both emphasised the absurdity of the English electoral system.[202] Nyerere then went on to explain that voting and elections were to be supported by institutions, which 'safeguard and promote both unity and freedom' and 'build attitudes which promote universal human dignity and social equality'.[203] Here, finally, Nyerere acknowledges the influence that John Stuart Mill had on his philosophy.[204]

Mill is one of the most evident philosophical influences on Nyerere. He is joined by Rousseau, who Nyerere mentions in his introduction to *Freedom and Unity*.[205] Rousseau resonates with Nyerere at many levels. *The Social Contract* begins with the issue of freedom: 'Man is born free; and everywhere he is in chains.'[206] It then considers societal roots that bear similarities to Nyerere's image of traditional Africa: 'The most ancient of all societies, and the only one that is natural, is the family.' Rousseau continues: 'The family then may be called the first model of political societies: the ruler corresponds to the father, and the people to the children; and all, being born free and equal.'[207] Following from Rousseau, Nyerere also saw the first political society as the family. He extended this to *ujamaa*, which he translated as 'familyhood':[208] 'In his own traditional society the African has always been a free individual, very much a member of his community, but seeing no conflict between his own interests and those of his community. This is because the structure of his society was in fact, a direct extension of the family.'[209]

Paul Nursey-Bray is correct in his assertion that there is no evidence that Rousseau's ideas have been *directly* borrowed by Nyerere. Yet the many similarities in their writings make it indisputable that the leader of Tanzania appropriated many of the Swiss-born philosopher's ideas and applied them to *ujamaa*.[210] But the question cannot be which philosopher had the greatest influence. Most of the authors who Nyerere was exposed to as an undergraduate, especially in Moral Philosophy II, were of the same later European liberal tradition. Many of the texts on Macmurray's course addressed common themes, and they often started with slavery. Together they resonated with Nyerere's ideas on freedom, thoughts that he had been developing prior to studying at Edinburgh. The point is rather that Nyerere was influenced by a succession of philosophers of the European liberal tradition who share a common heritage. He read those authors advocating positive liberty, such as Mill, Green and Bosanquet, as well as those earlier writers such as Rousseau and Kant who presented their concerns about natural rights and utilitarianism. They in turn were influenced by Enlightenment philosophers such as Hobbes and Locke. Nyerere studied them all at Edinburgh. But his exposure expanded well beyond classical philosophy and the later development of social contract theory that informs much of his earlier writing and, ultimately, to his justification of *ujamaa*.

Only Nyerere knew which philosophical ideas stuck with him as he developed his thoughts on African socialism. Certainly his references to Rousseau, Mill and their predecessors of the classical tradition suggests that they were among those he felt the need to cite (sometimes critically) in order to state his case. But it would be remiss to ignore the philosophers who are less obviously present in Nyerere's writings – T.H. Green, many of whose ideas paralleled those of the Fabian Society, being one of them.[211] We know that Nyerere spent much time on *Principles of Political Obligation* because it formed the basis of Macmurray's class lectures and was an examination text.[212] Nyerere may not have agreed with all of Green's proclamations, but the Oxford philosopher's systematic breakdown of issues fundamental to governance in a tolerant society free of foreign domination offered something of a blueprint to the fundamentals of a new state. Like Nyerere, Green dealt centrally with liberty and rights, family and property, and considered the necessity of public spirit to maintain a peaceful nation.[213] At the time that Nyerere studied *Principles of Political Obligation* he was questioning British rule in Tanganyika. Green's more contemporary writing – relative to Kant, to whose central doctrines Green was clearly sympathetic – cannot but have had an impression on Nyerere.[214] *Principles of Political Obligation* was readable in its logic and straightforward use of his native English. In it Green addresses concerns that spoke to Nyerere and played on his mind.[215]

The same could be said of Green's student Bosanquet. Bernard Bosanquet's political philosophy was both a response to, and a continuation of, nineteenth century thought. It was a response to the utilitarian positivism of Mill; and it was a continuation of earlier idealist philosophy found in Green, and the tradition that Bosanquet traced through Kant and Rousseau, and back to Aristotle and Plato.[216] Bosanquet adopted many of the ideals of the liberal tradition, and explains them in a language more similar to Nyerere's than perhaps any other of the philosophers he studied in Edinburgh. As Nyerere, Bosanquet emphasised the importance of autonomy and self-government (which implied representative, democratic rule) and was concerned to promote the improvement of character and the self-realisation of the individual, and saw that limits must be imposed on the state to prevent it from interfering with this development.[217] Bosanquet insisted on liberty as the essence and quality of the human person. As one of the most contemporary philosophers that Nyerere read, Bosanquet's writing confirmed to Nyerere that human liberty was still an issue of immense relevance in the twentieth century.[218] More practically for Nyerere's purposes, Bosanquet was a cutting-edge, modern day philosopher who succinctly summarised Macmurray's entire Moral Philosophy II course.[219]

The other later philosopher who should not be ignored is the English socialist Harold Laski, an LSE lecturer whose *Grammar of Politics* was the most recently-written work that Macmurray had his students study.[220] While published some two decades before Nyerere read it, Laski follows Green in providing an overview of contemporary European attitudes to socialism and his (usually contrary) perspective on mainstream United Kingdom politics. Criticised by Churchill and eventually disavowed by the Labour Party, Laski was on the executive committee of the Fabian Society. *Grammar of Politics* discussed Fabian socialism at length, and detailed Laski's suggested reorganisation of British industrial life to reflect those ideals.[221] The state was where citizens went to realise themselves, whether 'barristers or miners, Catholics or Protestants, employers or workers'.[222] The role of the state, as Laski saw it, was to make it possible for each citizen to be his 'best self'.[223] As was Nyerere's aspiration, so too for Laski the state, in a revival of the older Fabian principle of 'civic minimum', was to enable each citizen to achieve a sufficient share of the primary material wants: food, shelter, health, education and work.[224] The individual was the starting point, and free speech was essential to this. In words that could have been written by Nyerere, Laski stated that 'the citizen must be left unfettered to express either individually, or in concert with others, any opinions he happens to hold…. he is entitled to speak without hindrance of any kind.'[225] Similarly, Laski went on to argue that opinions need to be 'related to the government if the decisions of the latter body are to be wise…. It means weighing their opinions, seeking their criticism, meeting their special needs.'[226] Laski could have been writing for newly-independent Tanganyika.

Laski is said to have been a significant influence on not only Jawaharlal Nehru, the first Prime Minister of independent India, but a number of other students at the LSE who went on to become postcolonial leaders in Asia and Africa. Laski supported Indian independence because, like Nyerere's view of exploitative and 'selfish capitalists', his socialist reading of imperialism was that its oppression was derived from the search for markets.[227] It is not known if Nyerere met Laski when he was in the United Kingdom, nor whether he read any of Laski's works other than *Grammar of Politics* – 'one of the few fundamental "texts" of English Socialism', as Ralph Miliband called it.[228] Laski presupposed familiar issues of rights and equality that we know Nyerere was concerned with. He introduced the right to education, which features less in the earlier texts on moral philosophy that Nyerere studied but became a central feature of Tanzanian domestic policy under his leadership.[229] Yet the impact of *Grammar of Politics* on Nyerere was less 'in any original contribution which it makes to modern thought', as a reviewer at the time put it, 'but in the co-ordinated review which it supplies of the newer ideas which are increasingly shaping British politics'.[230] With the outline Laski presented in *Grammar of Politics*, Nyerere was able to contextualise contemporary views of socialism, 'the politics of the moment' that surrounded him in the United Kingdom.[231] He could then contrast those views with his own impression of traditional African society.

Nyerere's critique of the authors of the socialist tradition that he studied with Macmurray – and, for that matter, his critique of European-inspired economics and historical record that he studied under Arthur Birnie and Richard Pares – was essentially that the content was of only limited use to his homeland. The result, as Cranford Pratt has argued, is that in his attempt to marry the beliefs of western philosophers with what he understood to be traditional African concepts of socialism and democracy, Nyerere made a transition from a 'young, anglicized intellectual to a profound African thinker'.[232] This started in Edinburgh. When Nyerere returned to Tanganyika he clearly then continued to develop his ideas in the period immediately before independence, and many years after. They culminated in The Arusha Declaration of 1967.

Nyerere's contribution to socialism was to make it African; and, in his eyes at least, to bring 'traditional' communal societies into the modern world. Whether *ujamaa* was a success or a failure is another issue. What is at issue when reflecting on the development of Nyerere's political philosophy is the influence of the lecturers who guided him towards a reflexive study of European traditions. Alexander Grey, Axel Stern and, especially, William Macmurray, played a hitherto unacknowledged role in moulding the political mind of their ambitious and inquisitive Tanganyikan student. By extension, the lecturers unknowingly contributed to charting the course of the history of the nation that Nyerere went on to govern. As noted by Isaac Kramnick and Barry Sheerman, the LSE at the time was described as 'the most important institution of higher education in Asia and Africa'. This was in no small part because Harold Laski 'moulded the minds of so many future leaders of the new majority' of unaligned nations.[233] A less prickly character of this age in British academia was Edinburgh's William Macmurray, 'the best kept secret of British philosophy in the twentieth century'.[234] Through encouraging Nyerere to study those philosophers who mattered, as a lecturer in Edinburgh Macmurray was one of Tanzania's understated equivalents to Laski at the LSE. In the next chapter we turn to another lesser-known academic influence on Nyerere, a social anthropologist called Ralph Piddington.

7
Edinburgh & Ujamaa
History & Anthropology

A nation which refuses to learn from foreign cultures is nothing but a nation of idiots and lunatics.

Julius Nyerere, Inaugural address to Parliament, 10 December 1962[1]

This chapter shifts from the philosophy that Nyerere studied at Edinburgh to the history and anthropology that he was exposed to there. It refers to the instruction he received on collectivity and political systems in Africa, and continues to relate this to his later writings on *ujamaa*. It outlines the Christian environment in Edinburgh, and considers how this impacted on Nyerere's religious views. It also deals with the literature he studied on educated Africans and political ambition. Further analysis is offered of Nyerere's relationship with Edinburgh academics, culminating in his decision over his post-Edinburgh calling. The chapter conducts a first study linking Nyerere to the original texts relevant to African societies that he read in Edinburgh, as well as a section on peasant life in China. The analysis includes reference to some of the original books annotated by him. The chapter also draws on Nyerere's personal communication with Christian mentors to whom he turned for advice concerning his future life.

Social Anthropology: Collectivity in Africa and China

On the face of it, Ralph Piddington's Social Anthropology option is a less likely place than Moral Philosophy and Political Economy courses to find links to Nyerere's later political writings. Piddington's course closely followed his own *Introduction to Social Anthropology*, which provides a treasure trove of pointers.[2] Nyerere purchased a first edition immediately after its publication in Edinburgh in early 1950, and (at some point) he underlined sections of particular interest.[3] His annotations give an

Nyerere

intriguing insight into the influence of Piddington's teaching on the collectivity that Nyerere later embraced. Nyerere highlighted a passage on 'derived needs' (those man 'derived from the conditions of his collective life').[4] Piddington then discusses examples of 'a universal process whereby the *need for the organization of collective activities leads to traditionally defined systems of co-operation, to leadership and to forms of political authority*' (original emphasis).[5] Piddington thus establishes co-operation as traditional to the people, and that co-operation bolsters the power of the leader. The anthropologist then explains that human need 'is founded upon two universal characteristics of human social behaviour'. His first characteristic (with a '1' circled next to it in Nyerere's hand) is that 'human beings satisfy their needs collectively – they band together in groups and carry out activities determined by certain explicitly formulated purposes and traditionally defined rules'.[6] Piddington's explanation of human need essentially serves as an introduction to Nyerere's three basic assumptions of traditional life, characteristics that in African society 'were not questioned, or even thought about'.[7] Nyerere outlines these in 'Socialism and Rural Development', where it is evident that Piddington's first characteristic of human need bears close relationship to his own first principle of *ujamaa*. Where Piddington (in 1950) affirms that 'human beings satisfy their needs collectively', Nyerere likewise affirmed (in 1968) that Africans hold 'a recognition of mutual involvement in one another.... Each member of the family recognized the place and the rights of the other members.'[8] Piddington's collectivity of primitive societies is Nyerere's mutual involvement among African peasants.

The similarities between Nyerere's later speeches on *ujamaa* and his Edinburgh lecturer's writing on collectivity continue. Mutual involvement does not arise spontaneously, explains Piddington, but is 'governed by cultural traditions which create institutions'.[9] Institutions are Piddington's second universal characteristic of human social behaviour (beside which Nyerere has circled a '2'). Borrowing from Malinowski, Piddington defines an institution as 'a group of people united in a common task or tasks, bound to a determined portion of the environment, wielding together some technical apparatus, and obeying a body of rules'.[10] Nyerere's second basic assumption of traditional life bears some resemblance to Piddington's in as much as it describes the commonality of basic goods and their availability for all in production, such that 'no one could go hungry while others hoarded food'.[11] 'Food and Wealth' is the chapter heading that follows Piddington's analysis of institutions. In a section on 'Production', the academic departs from some of the day's more familiar 'primitive peoples' of anthropological investigation and takes his undergraduate readers to a little-known African territory called Tanganyika:

> The interest in primitive work is increased, and its drudgery mitigated, by the fact that it is often co-operative.... Thus, in Hehe agriculture much of the cultivation is done individually or by small family groups. But at the time of the annual hoeing of the ground, it is customary for a man to announce that on a certain day his wife will brew beer. His relatives and neighbours attend, help with the hoeing, and are rewarded with beer.... Under this system, each man helps others and is helped by them in turn.[12]

The co-operative labour system of the Hehe is essentially the *eriisaga* of the Zanaki, or its equivalent by a different name elsewhere. To Nyerere, co-operation was not an exclusively Zanaki trait. Like the 'universal hospitality' to which both Piddington and Nyerere refer,[13] co-operation was also a characteristic common to other ethnic groups in Tanganyika Territory. Nyerere would have learnt something of these other societies from friends of different ethnic backgrounds who he met in Tabora, Kampala and on his other travels. It is evident that he also absorbed much from Piddington's discussion of Chagga, Masai and Nyakyusa societies – he used exactly these three tribes in 'Socialism and Rural Development' as his own examples of traditional African society.[14] Piddington continues with the Hehe to emphasise that 'each individual helps and is helped in turn', to then explain that laggards who are 'consistently slack in rendering assistance... become the object of public condemnation'.[15] The laggard – or 'the loiterer, or idler' – later became one of Nyerere's favourite targets, a 'modern parasite' who he claimed did not exist in his traditional Africa, where 'loitering was an unthinkable disgrace'.[16]

The work that the loiterer shirked relates to the third characteristic of traditional life that Nyerere created – and one that, in the '*uhuru na kazi*' slogan, also accompanied Tanzania's independence. On his writing about freedom and work,[17] Nyerere again draws very closely on Piddington's study of primitive societies. In a section on land tenure (which Nyerere has heavily marked in his personal copy), Piddington discusses what he terms 'the fiction of primitive communism'.[18] He then proceeds to tear apart characteristics of co-operation in the socio-economic organization of society that Nyerere later went on to present as 'traditionally African'.[19] Piddington then lists the different possible emphases of communism '*in modern civilized society*' (emphasis added): equality in social status and standards of living; the organisation of production by social planning in contradistinction to individual enterprise; the ownership of the means of production of the community; the way in which political authority is organised and exercised.[20] All are key tenets of *ujamaa*, or the 'socialistic principles' which, as early as 1943, Nyerere declared drove 'the indigenous native [who] knows no other way of living.... and who is not by any means a communist'.[21] Piddington's remaining characteristic of communism is 'the obligation to work, and the conception of productive effort as constituting the only valid claim to a share of the common income'.[22] This is co-operative labour, be it Zanaki, Hehe, Tanganyikan or 'African'. It is also Nyerere's third characteristic of his image of traditional African life that informed *ujamaa*: 'everyone had an obligation to work', echoed Nyerere.[23] He was of course writing decades after he first read his lecturer's social anthropology primer, but there is little doubt that he drew on Piddington's work where it suited him. Where it did not, he persisted nonetheless with his own understanding of the perfect pre-colonial society that best suited the nation that he wanted to create. Nyerere chose to ignore Nkrumah's observation that

> the phrase 'African socialism' seems to espouse the view that the traditional African society was a classless society imbued with the spirit of humanism and to express a nostalgia for that spirit. Such a conception of socialism makes a fetish of the communal African society.... Colonialism deserves to be blamed for many evils in Africa, but surely it was not preceded by an African Golden Age or paradise.[24]

Meyer Fortes and Edward Evans-Pritchard's *African Political Systems* helped provide Nyerere with some of the proof about the traditional Africa to which he frequently harked back in his later writings. Their introduction classified two groups of African societies, A and B, the latter of which lacked centralised authority, and had no sharp divisions of rank, status or wealth.[25] Nyerere's experience of Zanaki society fitted most closely with Fortes and Evans-Pritchard's 'Group B', in which kinship ties played a prominent role and distinctions of rank and status were of minor significance.[26] Within these societies 'there are common material interests such as the need to share pastures or to trade in a common market-place', the celebrated anthropologists summarised, 'or complimentary economic pursuits binding different sections to one another.'[27] As we have seen, this was later one of the central tenets of the *ujamaa* unit – based on Nyerere's understanding of traditional African society – in which 'the basic goods were held in common, and shared among all members'.[28] The doctrine of *ujamaa* was to bind the nation, as was a common language – a unifying force that Fortes and Evans-Pritchard identified as capable of creating a strong feeling of community across different societies.[29]

Among the other recommended reading for the course that Nyerere took on Social Anthropology was a second book that Piddington authored (with John Graham) entitled, *Anthropology and the Future of Missions*. One of its central themes is consideration of 'the lack of adjustment of native education to native needs' in a future Africa.[30] 'A carefully planned educational policy', they argue, would include 'a careful consideration of claims of the mass of natives against the "favoured few"'[31] – of which Nyerere was one, as he earlier acknowledged in his 1946 piece for the *Makerere* magazine. As the title of their book suggests, Graham and Piddington made a case for the important role that they believed missionaries had to play in a future Africa governed by Africans. Nyerere would have read his lecturer's opinion that the missionary should,

> co-operate increasingly in the administration of Indirect Rule, and will help to prevent the degeneration of this policy into *laissez faire*. He will assist in developing it from its 'protective' to its 'constructive' phase, from a limited policy of preserving native institutions to a remoulding of these institutions to meet new problems. He will help to make it clear that Indirect Rule, properly conceived, is not a puppet government or a means of 'keeping the native in his place', but means the setting up of forms of local government which are adapted to immediate requirements, but which may well survive and prove useful when more comprehensive forms of native self-government become possible.[32]

Yet while this may have been a new opinion for Nyerere to be reading from published Europeans – one of whom was his tutor, who he could now personally engage in discussion – it is worth noting that in reality the authors' position is perhaps not as radical as it may first appear. Underlying the emancipatory argument from Piddington and Graham is the assumption that the wise paternal hand of enlightened white religious humanitarianism would necessarily be there to guide black people into an indefinite future.[33] To a certain degree this was the case for Nyerere, at least for the next few years in his friendship with missionaries such as Father Richard Walsh.

Piddington and his co-author's beliefs on self-government for Africans were influenced by Lucy Mair. They repeatedly reference her *Native Policies in Africa*, which was another of Piddington's 'books recommended'.[34] In it Mair also addresses African education, at one stage raising the point about privilege that Nyerere had made himself in his *Makerere* article. On 'the educated African', she asks whether 'his superiority over his fellows [is] so great as to justify their sacrifice to his interests?' and goes on to point out that 'a transformation of native society on lines admittedly felt as desirable by only a small group must mean the sacrifice of the rest'.[35] Mair also considers the great potential of the educated African, at times almost as if she is writing of – or to – Nyerere himself:

> There is, as we are constantly reminded, an important factor to be reckoned with in forecasting the future – the demands of the educated African. ... It is said that all reforms have come from thinking minorities; that this class represents an *élite*, as is proved by their ability to profit by European education; that their ultimate triumph is inevitable. ... For an African to complete a course of education provided in his country, and perhaps proceed to a British university, may require greater perseverance than is called for in societies where a long period spent at school and college is taken for granted. ... For some it may represent financial sacrifice; for many the accident of wealthy parentage, rather than individual merit, makes higher education possible. To pass in English the examinations taken by English students is certainly an intellectual achievement showing great ability; but is this necessarily the type of ability called for in the political field?[36]

Another of Nyerere's recommended books carried on with the theme of politics that some commentators felt was the inevitable course for the educated African. William Macmillan wrote in his updated (1949) discussion of political trends in British Africa, entitled *Africa Emergent*:

> A leading African governor has put it that 'the submissive savage' is a thing of the past. We are witnessing what our own rule has brought to life, the struggle of Africans towards self-expression. The ceaseless questioning of methods and purposes of government is the birth of African politics – our trusteeship is arriving at the point where it must stand and answer: 'Quis custodiet ipsos custodes?'.[37] Our aim and hope should be that Africa will continue on the lines our own experience has taught and proved, its ultimate goal self-government in the best Western tradition.[38]

Professor Pares, Nyerere's Edinburgh lecturer in British History, also appears to have had some impact on his political thought. Nyerere's notebook for his second-year course contains a series of essays which may have been taken by dictation, and might well reflect the 'bland and brilliant' nature of its source.[39] Bjerk's analysis of the notebook suggests that it is from this course in British History that the kernel of Nyerere's theory of villagization may have arisen.[40] From Pares, Bjerk supposes, Nyerere 'learned that the Romans had imposed towns on rural areas "as a method of pushing ahead Roman civilization" and that "the existence of towns must have stimulated economic activity. They were artificial collections of consumers."'[41]

It is tempting to accept this conclusion because the text that Bjerk offers from the Tanganyika student's notebook fits so conveniently with Nyerere's later policy of villagization. But while the Britain that the Romans ruled was geographically close to Nyerere in Edinburgh, it was temporally very distant. Tacitus' *Agricola* and *Germania*, prescribed reading for Pares' 'British History to 1939' course that Nyerere took, was unlikely to inspire any but the most fanatical scholar of imperial expansion in ancient Europe.[42] As paradoxical as it may seem, what was more relatable to the young Tanganyikan was the society that Hsiao-Tung Fei described in his *Peasant Life in China*, another of the far more exciting books that Piddington recommended to his students.[43] Fei's study area was the village of Kaihsienkung in the Yangtze Valley, set in a country that – like Tanganyika at the time Nyerere was reading – was still struggling with the legacy of colonial occupation, and which at the time of the research (1936) found itself at a stage of economic development that was not too far removed from the rural life Nyerere had left in Tanganyika. Unlike bygone Roman Britain, the young Nyerere could somehow relate to Kaihsienkung's serendipitous similarities. It was a world of local spirits and the supranatural kingdom of local taboos,[44] and of family trees to keep alive the memory of ancestors to whom sacrifices should be offered.[45] *Peasant Life in China* was the first time that

Nyerere was exposed to a non-European's detailed commentary of a society outside Europe or Africa. It chimed with great clarity, congruous with the romantic view of the African continent that Nyerere's mind was creating while far away in Edinburgh. Fei describes the 'Chia', the expanded family who farm a common property and who, through division of labour, co-operate together to pursue a common living.[46] Chia emphasises inter-dependence, notes Fei, and it gives security to the old who are no longer able to work. Chia ensures social continuity and co-operation.[47] In some respects, Fei's actual Kaihsienkung could be Nyerere's utopian Butiama of the past; or an *ujamaa* village of the future. But it is in the institution of village government in Kaihsienkung where the most uncanny resemblances to the later *ujamaa* villages can be found. Households were associated together to form larger local groups that superimposed on each other without the need for hierarchy. The village, separated from others by a considerable distance, was governed by a headman who received outsiders with a warm welcome. 'The visitor will be impressed', Fei proudly announces, by the headman's 'heavy burden of work.' This included responsibility for the local co-operative.[48] Yet while the headmen 'have no direct economic reward, they enjoy prestige'[49] – undoubtedly with great modesty.

Kaihsienkung's headmen, Mr Chen and Mr Chou, would have been able to live without complaint in Nyerere's vision of socialist Tanzania, because *ujamaa* 'has nothing to do with the possession or non-possession of wealth'.[50] They would certainly have agreed with Nyerere that 'acquisitiveness for the purpose of gaining power and prestige is unsocialist'.[51] As in the Yangtze Valley, Nyerere's 'traditional African socialism' was based on a 'predominantly peasant society', inhabited by the 'extended family' in which the land 'was always recognized as belonging to the community' and where 'the basic goods were held in common, and shared among all members of the unit'.[52] In Nyerere's Tanzania, peasants 'would live together in a village; they would farm together; market together; and undertake the provision of local services and small local requirements as a community' – a common living through 'division of labour', because there was 'no alternative but to combine their efforts'.[53] 'The old' of Africa, as in Kaihsienkung, were 'looked after by the village as a whole' and 'only in relation to work discipline would there be any hierarchy'.[54] In the *ujamaa* village the headman, or 'manager' – adhering, like all others in the traditional African society, to 'universal hospitality' – worked with a 'governing committee'.[55] All peasants were motivated to carry a heavy burden, including the headman, for nobody was exempt from hard work.[56] If the similarities to Nyerere's writings on *ujamaa* are not enough, there is an eerie coincidence in the career of the headman of Fei's village: he is a scholar who 'at the beginning of the Republic…. started his career as a schoolmaster'.[57]

Nyerere

Fei continues with an account of an imposed administrative system in which the villagers were 'told to arrange their houses in a manner prescribed by the district government'[58] – a similar system to *ujamaa* villages, although these were 'governed by those who live and work in them', instead of being 'created from outside, nor governed from outside'.[59] Like *ujamaa* villages, the Yangtze Valley villages 'were subdivided into self-governing units',[60] overseen by 'the members' self-government in all matters'.[61] Another governance system that Fei describes involved ten households that form a larger unit of ten – the ten house cell system, or '*nyumba kumi*' that Nyerere later encouraged.[62] These were instigated in the rural Yangtze Valley so to help 'to organize the people'[63] in a 'system of mutual responsibility'[64] – or in Tanzania later, to assist 'rural economic and social communities where people live together and work together for the good of all'.[65]

Fei's historical and contemporary accounts of administrative rule in the Yangtze Valley up to the 1930s, while dated by the time Nyerere read *Peasant Life in China*, provided him with some ideas, if not a blueprint, for peasant life in Tanzania. Conversely, his vision of Tanzania was barely illuminated by Richard Pares' teachings on the ancient Roman Empire of the North. After all, Nyerere later wrote dismissively, when 'its legionnaires retreated to their homeland, the fine roads and buildings were left to rot because they were irrelevant to the people of the occupied areas'.[66] The affinities of village life in the East, on the other hand, struck a chord with Nyerere in Edinburgh and remained with him for many years to come. Decades after he first read Fei, Nyerere was still keen to study another village's efforts in 'the great anti-imperialist, anti-feudal revolution which transformed China'. He read *Fanshen*, William Hinton's account of the Chinese revolution.[67] China, perhaps more so than any other country in the late 1960s, was where Nyerere felt he could learn most directly about the values of *ujamaa*.[68] It was not from Roman Britain that the kernel of Nyerere's theory of villagization arose. It was from his reading in 1950 about peasant life in China.

The Vocation

Those who knew Nyerere in Edinburgh recall him as 'not the usual type', 'a very decent fellow',[69] 'of a very independent turn of mind',[70] 'a delightful person; a student with a clearly evident awareness of opportunity to learn; a quiet, likeable young man of integrity',[71] and 'a quiet, unassuming person … who drew no attention to himself in the way some students do'.[72] One of Nyerere's friends at Edinburgh, the Reverend Kenneth MacKenzie, said that he stuck him as 'a very humane and gentle man; a man who was sensitive to human suffering. Julius liked people and

Julius was always very critical of policies that might involve violence.'[73] There are no descriptions of Nyerere's character given by his European student contemporaries. He was quiet and fairly unremarkable, and therefore forgettable. The other portrayals were made in retrospect, and those who collected them may have omitted any less flattering descriptions. Students from the West Indies are said to have almost unanimously described Nyerere as 'intense'.[74] John Keto, who claimed not to have spent much time with his fellow Tanganyikan when they were studying in the city at the same time, describes him as a man who 'didn't mince his words'.[75] There is little to suggest, as Herbert Neve assumes, that as a student at Edinburgh Nyerere suffered problems of self-esteem.[76] He may have been low-key (or as low-key as a black African could be in 1950s Edinburgh), but the picture is rather one of an unobtrusive and quietly competitive young man who kept his ambitions to himself.[77] At the same time, Keto adds, Nyerere was 'religious, honest, kind, considerate to others – this is the reason why, when [later in Tanganyika] he started a political party; *ujamaa* was about helping others'.[78]

If John Keto is correct that '*ujamaa* was about helping others' – and everything Nyerere wrote about it confirms that it *was* about helping others, to achieve human equality[79] – then it is reasonable to suggest that the architect of *ujamaa*, a devout Catholic, would at some point in its design have allowed his relationship with God to seep in. Much like Neve's claim that Nyerere lacked self-esteem, his conclusion that there is 'no reason for thinking that his political views are motivated by his personal religious faith' is equally misleading.[80] As Harvey Glickman notes in his analysis of the 1958 'Mali ya Taifa' speech concerning the basis of the right of owning property, Nyerere's pronouncement then very obviously 'fits the teaching of the Roman Catholic church' of which he was a member.[81] Yet the clearest indication that disproves Neve's claim that Nyerere's politics were not motivated by his Christianity is in the President's 1970 address to a congress of sisters at the Headquarters of the Maryknoll Mission[82] – the same mission that his old friends Fathers Arthur Wille and William Collins served under. Foregrounding his speech on the issue of human equality, and after quoting from the Bible, Nyerere suggested that 'the Church should accept that the development of peoples means rebellion'.[83] He then went on to argue that unless the (Catholic) Church participates

> actively in the rebellion against those social structures and economic organizations which condemn men to poverty, humiliation and degradation, then the Church will become irrelevant to man and the Christian religion will degenerate into a set of superstitions accepted by the fearful.[84]

Careful to transcend religious boundaries, towards the end of his address Nyerere added a brief line – which almost reads as an afterthought – that non-Catholics and non-Christians must also be working to promote social justice.[85]

Among the common themes in Nyerere's writing on (in)equality were the need for tireless labour,[86] and the need to avoid 'the anti-social effects of the accumulation of personal wealth'.[87] As discussed, he saw 'no alternative to hard work', and later stated that the Arusha Declaration was 'a commitment to the belief that there are more important things in life than the amassing of riches'.[88] While undoubtedly motivated in some way by his Christianity however, Nyerere did not go so far as to directly link such pronouncements to his personal faith: clearly a strong work ethic need not necessarily be an exclusively (Protestant) Christian trait, and a life of austerity is not the preserve of monasticism alone. When Nyerere did use the name of God – who is mentioned at no fewer than ten instances in the six-page abridged version of 'Mali ya Taifa'[89] – it could equally have been applied to deity worshiped in other mainstream world religions. This fitted with Nyerere's belief in the 'necessity for religious toleration'.[90] Even so (and the address to the Reverend Chairman of the Maryknoll Mission headquarters notwithstanding), Nyerere's message surrounding *ujamaa* was more often a deliberately areligious one. No doubt aware that some of the many Muslims and adherents to other faiths in Tanzania might accuse him of being unduly biased by his Catholic beliefs, Nyerere insisted that 'socialism is secular'.[91] It is not 'any business of socialism if an individual is, or is not, inspired in his daily life by a belief in God, nor if he does, or does not, attend a place of religious worship – or pray elsewhere'.[92] This was ostensibly a lesson for Tanzanians to apply to their fellow citizens of other faiths. But the wording equally applied to those who might have questioned how a society could be truly secular when the policies that citizens were to live by were largely articulated by a practicing Catholic. In this respect Nyerere's comment on the secularism of *ujamaa* was a personal statement to any doubting Thomases about his own motivations: 'Socialism is concerned with man's life in *this* society', he insisted. 'A man's relationship with God is a personal matter for him and him alone; his beliefs about the hereafter are his own affair.'[93]

In spite of the stated secularism of *ujamaa* and Nyerere's apparent desire to keep his faith private, Christians in particular were still familiar with many of the expressions that he used.[94] His remarks that 'wealth tends to corrupt those who possess it', for example, is essentially the Apostle Paul's 'love of money is the root of evil'.[95] Other direct quotations were more obviously from the Bible, even when they did not fit particularly well with the point being made. Nyerere's pronouncement that 'Man does not live by bread alone', from the Gospel of Matthew, for example, is not a particularly logical link in his call for the need for mutual respect and harmonious living to achieve economic development.[96] Nyerere was a man who strove to live by Christian values, and the central role that the Bible played in his life brought the Word into his writings and speeches. In this respect there are parallels to the moral philosophy of the English theologian and philosopher Joseph Butler, whose *Fifteen Sermons Preached at the Rolls Chapel* Nyerere studied at Edinburgh.[97] The writings of both make rich use of passages from scripture and introduce familiar Christian stories and concepts, but make little reference to – and depend little on the reader having – any particular religious commitments. Indeed, as has been noted of Butler, many of Nyerere's arguments do not rest on the reader having any religious commitments at all.[98]

There is less in Nyerere's earlier writing that overtly points to his Christian instruction. There are, however, some subtle connotations that would resonate with a reader of the same faith as him. In Nyerere's 1943 'African Socialism' article, for example, he stated that the 'indigenous native…. will always help his neighbour' – a similar statement to Jesus' second greatest commandment, to love thy neighbour.[99] In the same vein, Nyerere's views on monogamy, as expounded in his 'Uhuru wa Wanawake' of 1944, were likely influenced by the Christian message to create a single enlightened family – something he was to embark upon with Maria, his devout Catholic fiancée, shortly after returning from Edinburgh.

Nyerere's relationships with white Christians while in Edinburgh was more than an amplification of his interaction with their counterparts in Tanganyika. Prior to Edinburgh he had little social integration with Europeans. With the rare example of small clubs such Hamsa u Ishirini, colonial East African social circles outside the workplace were racially restricted.[100] If Christians of different races worshipped together, then the unity often only lasted as long as the service. Nyerere's more meaningful engagement with fellow believers before he left for the United Kingdom was with a number of priests: Father Walsh; Father James, the padre at Tabora Boys;[101] the Swiss-born Father Edgar Maranta, formerly Vicar Apostolic and then Catholic Archbishop of Dar es Salaam; Father William Collins, a Maryknoll missionary who had arrived in Musoma in 1946; and Father Wille, a nationalist sympathiser who was also of the Maryknoll Fathers who later helped in the registration of a number of TANU branches.[102] Whether in Nyerere's earlier years he consciously sought the counsel of these learned men cannot be said for sure, although he did spend much time in their company. He was well aware of the wisdom that learned men could impart. Once again quoting Booker T. Washington, for example, Nyerere wrote the following in his notes for a presentation on the man: 'I am convinced [that] there is no education which one can get from books and costly apparatus that is equal to that which can be gotten from contact with great men and women.'[103] Nyerere spent time with older women in his extended family, but none were Christian. His closest Catholic female companion before he left for the United Kingdom was Maria.

Nyerere was in the racial minority in Edinburgh, but in the University's Catholic and ecumenical chaplaincies there was considerable interaction between British and foreign students. This was also the case for Hastings Banda who, writing from Edinburgh University, told another friend that the people of Britain 'treat me just as anybody else. I go to church with Europeans every Sunday, and sit on the same seats with them. I go to the theatres and picture houses when I want to, and sit right next to Europeans. ... [T]hey are kind and respect me.'[104]

Banda's church experience was with Presbyterians, but there is no reason to believe that, on the whole, Nyerere would not also have been warmly received by his fellow Catholics. It is more likely that in the Church – be it at the University or in the city – Nyerere was not so aware of racial antipathies as he was aware of the strong Catholic-Protestant enmity that prevailed in Edinburgh at the time. Indeed, while Nyerere was on good terms with his fellow Tanganyikan John Keto, the Muheza-born student later explained that he could give no details about the Wilson's house that Nyerere sometimes stayed at. The Wilson's was not a home that he was familiar with, Keto explained: 'Mwalimu was Catholic, and I am Anglican, so I never visited there.'[105]

Nyerere appears to have transcended the sectarian tensions through his friendship with the Protestant Chaplain to Overseas Students, the Reverend Dr William Cattanach, in whose rooms he was a frequent visitor.[106] The religious bigotry of the time appears to have been nothing but a human construction to Nyerere. It was not an obstacle to friendship. He was also good friends with the Church of Scotland missionary Reverend Kenneth MacKenzie, and he was close to the historian Donald Nicholl, whose presentation on the 'Catholic Conception of the State' Nyerere attended at Edinburgh.[107] Like Mrs Wilson – with whom Nyerere was such good friends that she and her son took him to spend Christmas with their relatives[108] – there would have been other open-minded Scots (and undoubtedly some 'well-intentioned cranks') who had spent time in East Africa and were curious to meet a bright young man with whom they could chat about their experiences. When Mang'enya visited the United Kingdom in 1952, for example, he met the Reverend Cullen Young, a missionary anthropologist who had co-edited *Our African Way of Life* (1946) with Hastings Banda.[109] As with Banda, Nyerere was free to meet with missionaries and other returned Scots expatriates and 'discuss the old days and debate the shape of the new'.[110]

Suddenly in Edinburgh, and in great contrast to Tanganyika, Nyerere was welcomed into the lives of more than missionaries alone. Outside formal tuition he also spent time with University academic staff, and this sympathetic student-staff relationship may have had some part in moulding his multi-racial outlook.[111] Along with Axel Stern and Sydney Collins, Nyerere spent much time with Kenneth Little. At a meeting of the colonial students' Cosmopolitan Club he discussed with Little the roots of colonial rule.[112] A distinguished social anthropologist, Little wrote many publications on race (among them *Negroes in Britain*, 1947, with its emphasis on the colour bar), and supervised both Alexander Carey's doctoral thesis on colonial students in London and (with Ralph Piddington) Collins's thesis on Gold Coast and West Indian communities in Britain. Little was also on the Advisory Committee to the Fabian Colonial Bureau and – along with John Hatch in Glasgow – acted as its contact with Reverend Cattanach's Edinburgh World Church Group that Nyerere attended and went on to Chair.[113] Nyerere also was on good terms with the communist Victor Kiernan, lecturer in European history.[114] All these white academics treated him with respect, as did Sydney Collins, possibly the first senior black academic that Nyerere spent much meaningful time with. There were doubtless many less welcoming lecturers. But it is the positive experiences with his Edinburgh tutors and fellow churchgoers that Nyerere kept close to his heart when writing on race.

There is scant detail on Nyerere's involvement in Catholicism while studying for his degree. The detail of his personal relationship with God was something he more often reserved for those who were close to him, especially other practising Catholics. These were young men of his own generation, and older figures in the Church, in particular White Fathers and Maryknoll missionaries. Kenneth Mackenzie's recollection is that his Tanganyikan friend's faith was not something that he wore on his sleeve:

> Julius often reminded me of some people whom I knew in the Highlands. They wouldn't discuss theology too much … and yet their beliefs were clear and simple and profoundly personal. For example, I remember Julius discussing with me points about Lutherism and Roman Catholicism and his ideas I thought were very clear and definite but accompanied with a very real toleration.[115]

We know that in Edinburgh Nyerere used to find peace by sitting alone in church.[116] This would undoubtedly have been one of the city's many Catholic churches. University church services were held regularly at St Giles' Cathedral on the Royal Mile,[117] but this being the High Kirk of Edinburgh – the principal place of worship for the Church of Scotland in Edinburgh – it would not have been a place that Roman Catholics gravitated towards.[118] None of the sources suggest that Catholicism was merely a habit to Nyerere, or anything less than a living faith. As stated, it is highly likely that he joined the Catholic Students'

Union, which met at The Chaplaincy at 23, George Square.[119] It may have been here that Nyerere was gifted *The Confessions of St Augustine* – famed for the author's prayer that God 'Grant me chastity and continence, but not yet' – a copy of which Nyerere acquired as soon as he arrived in the city.[120] Mass was on Sundays and weekdays, and Benediction was held most days at The Chaplaincy. This was less than fifteen minutes from Nyerere's Palmerston Road residence, and only five minutes' walk from his classes in Old College (at the highest point of which, incidentally, a large gold figurine holds a flame that bears a striking resemblance to the *Uhuru* torch). Nyerere may have spent time in prayer or reflection at The Chaplaincy, or simply as a place to take a break during his studies, for it boasted the luxury of a well-furnished and heated common room, and held social evenings on Sundays.[121] The late Father Anthony Ross, who was brought up a Free Presbyterian and converted to Catholicism when he studied at Edinburgh the decade before Nyerere attended, described the Catholic students at the University as 'varied and stimulating. They loved argument, and my combination of pacifism, socialism, and "Home Rule for Scotland"'.[122]

Had Nyerere indeed been attracted to the Catholic Students' Union, then during his first few days as a student at Edinburgh they offered a Freshers' Tea Party as an opportunity for students to introduce themselves, along with another Freshers' Social a few days later at St Columba's Hall, situated immediately below the city's imposing Edinburgh Castle at the top of the Royal Mile.[123] Should he have not got enough of debating in secular contexts, yet more could be had with the Catholic Students' Union's own debating society. Visiting speakers provided further extra-curricular challenge. These included the well-known Oxford priest, theologian and writer Monsignor Ronald Knox, and the distinguished author Evelyn Waugh, whose talk was entitled 'Those Convert Writers'.[124] Again, it is not known for sure if Nyerere attended addresses by the likes of the prominent Catholic converts Knox and Waugh. There is, however, some evidence that Nyerere contemplated ordination while in Britain.[125]

According to Father Arthur Wille, from Edinburgh Nyerere wrote to Father Richard Walsh, the Director at St Mary's and his mentor, to tell him that he was considering becoming a priest. His rationale, apparently, was that he felt he 'could do a lot of good for people'. Walsh then wrote back to tell the young Nyerere that he did not have a vocation for the Church.[126] The letters that the two exchanged are now lost, so we can only speculate about the effect of Walsh's advice. Certainly it now forced Nyerere to ask himself what exactly he was going to do after Edinburgh. It would also have caused him to think carefully about his personal faith. At some point he may have shared with Walsh or other Catholics his surprise at the extent to which the Christian message was honoured in

Photo K. Father Richard Walsh, Director when Nyerere was teaching at St Mary's, and later his mentor. The photograph hanging behind Walsh is of his young protégé in December 1961 as the first Prime Minister of independent Tanganyika. (*Reproduced by kind permission of Archives de la Société des Missionnaires d'Afrique (Pères Blancs), Rome, Italy*)

the United Kingdom. It was probably less than he had thought before he arrived. Nyerere might well have been prepared for this by missionaries in Tanganyika, but in the white-man's land he had witnessed at first hand a British population that, in the main, was either composed of practicing Christians who were bitterly divided along sectarian lines, or was completely secular. Whether this strengthened his own faith or caused him to question it will remain unknown. We can be much more sure that Nyerere was a devoted Christian who at some point in Edinburgh felt drawn to serve God, and this featured in his decision-making as to what he was going to do when he returned to Tanganyika.

The more sceptical view, on the other hand, is that by raising his interest in the priesthood Nyerere was angling for a further scholarship from his benevolent friends in the Catholic Church. To put it another way, and equally sceptically, Nyerere was hedging his bets so that he would have more time to reflect on his future while taking another degree. Certainly Nyerere's earlier repeated threats to return home from Edinburgh provide evidence that he was willing to play the system. In a letter to Father Leonard Marchant, who was formerly Superior of the Brother Postulants at St Boswell's before he was appointed to Tabora,[127] Nyerere wrote of his wishes to extend his stay 'for a few more years'.

Nyerere

He outlined one of the forces on his mind: 'Should I really decide to stay many people would be very disappointed, if not quite angry with me, and one of them would undoubtedly be my Mother. However, at the moment I have a very strong desire to stay and I would like to feel that at least I have the Church's blessing.'[128] Nyerere then expressed his desire to meet either Father Marchant or Father Stanley. He did not say why he wanted to remain in the United Kingdom, and the precise attraction for Nyerere to stay is still unknown. We do know from other sources that he had initially applied to stay in order to take a Diploma in Education after his degree. That was refused. The grounds were insufficient funds, along with his existing Teacher's Diploma from Makerere, and the wish of his employers at The White Fathers Mission 'Voluntary Agency School' for him to return to teaching duties. The entry in the Colonial Office minutes file reads, 'they want him back'.[129] This did not stop him discussing with Father Walsh the pros and cons of taking a further degree, this time in law.[130]

The cynical position, that Nyerere expressed an interest in becoming a priest because it might provide an opportunity for further study in the United Kingdom, should be discarded. He had spent sufficient time with missionaries to know what devoting a life to God's work entailed. He was fully-aware that he could not be half-hearted in his commitment to the Church. More likely Nyerere had at one stage toyed with the idea of ordination, mentioned it to Walsh, and had been told that he required a vocation. Nobody questioned that Nyerere was motivated by honest conviction, but more than one fellow Christian may have thought that he did not have a vocation. Few knew this better than Richard Walsh, with whom Nyerere was still sharing his new-found attraction to law. If the two bachelors shared their more intimate thoughts, Nyerere would also have shared with Walsh the increasing pull of politics back home.

The lack of primary sources documenting the relationship between Walsh and his acolyte make it difficult to judge how much influence the Catholic priest exerted over the young man. If Nyerere was going to discuss his thoughts about the Church, it was obviously best to do so with a man of the cloth. Walsh 'afforded special guidance to Julius Nyerere from 1946 until the time he gave up teaching for a political career'.[131] At this great crossroads in Nyerere's life, his mentor was the obvious choice for him to turn to. But there is nothing to suggest that the White Father wanted to squeeze Nyerere into a mould. Rather, there seems to have been a mutual respect and fondness between the two. Bound by a shared Catholicism, theirs was the brotherly Christian love that Nyerere never fully attained with Edward Wanzagi. Given the closeness between Walsh and Nyerere after some six years, and their shared left-leaning social and theological outlook, there is every chance that at some junctures their discussions turned to future politics in Tanganyika.

Not long after this correspondence with Nyerere, Walsh was writing elsewhere about the merits of an essentially socialist economic ethic for government. He urged for laws 'to guarantee … a reasonable standard of comfort' for all people as a 'sacred right'. The context, notes Bjerk, was the disruptions in African society in the twentieth century.[132] The clergyman argued for the adaptation of African culture to the changing circumstances of its people. The text, Bjerk continues, evinced probing conversations between Nyerere and his mentor:

> In the history, languages and folklore of Africa is found reflected the genius and soul of the African people. … It is by seeking first what is good in these that we can hope to lay lasting foundations for the Africa of tomorrow. We might just mention in this connection the strength of family ties and tribal organization, the respect for laws, custom, authority and native wisdom, intolerance of injustice and the universal belief … in a Supreme Being … Just as a child can scarcely survive much less develop normally without the combined care of father and mother united in family, so the family needs the assistance of other families to carry out its essential tasks. And so it is nature herself which urges families to seek the mutual support of other families; thus we find people grouped into clans, tribes, and, ultimately, into that more highly organised society we call the State … The State is in fact a commonwealth of families.[133]

Walsh's position emerged from the left-leaning social theology that came to prominence after the election of Pope John XXIII. The pontiff's own theology reflected the development of Catholic dogma in conversation with European philosophy. In turn this reflected Mill's *Utilitarianism* that Nyerere had studied at Edinburgh.[134] It was almost as though the mentor, having discouraged his student from the priesthood, was still in conversation with him over what lay ahead in the secular world.[135] Nyerere probably already knew that his vocation was elsewhere:

> There was no moment when it all clicked into place. It wasn't a sudden inspiration, I didn't suddenly see the light. It was not like the call of the Christian, 'I've been called!' At Edinburgh, I was certain I was coming back [to Tanganyika] to get myself involved in full-time politics. I had made up my mind that my life would be political.[136]

8
London & Pugu
Teaching & Politics

Beyond the family, there are groups and relationships ... where such sacrifices as we may make for others are nevertheless undergone for a group with which we are already identified.

The Socialist Tradition by Alexander Gray,
Nyerere's Political Economy tutor at Edinburgh[1]

This chapter covers the period between Nyerere's graduation until his resignation from Pugu. A final section then outlines the continuation of his ties with Edinburgh until shortly before his death. The chapter opens at the time Nyerere was based in London, months when he experienced intense interaction with African nationalists. It brings to light the racial motivations that determined his journey back to Tanganyika, and covers his marriage to Maria Waningu. Reflections are made on the tensions that impinged on Nyerere's political activity in Uzanaki, and on the development of his relationship with political activists who held territorial-level ambitions. The chapter ends with Nyerere's resignation from teaching and his entry into full-time politics. It continues to draw on the Colonial Office file that was kept on Nyerere, as well as archival material from Rome that illuminates his correspondence with Catholic priests. The chapter also uses further interview material in which Nyerere outlined the circumstances that led to his decision to enter politics.

The Race Problem

Nyerere graduated from Edinburgh on 4 July 1952 with an Ordinary Degree of Master of Arts.[2] A little more than a week later he left the city, according a letter to Father Marchant.[3] Having successfully completed his undergraduate studies – a time that he described as the happiest in his life[4] – Nyerere was 'anxious to get back to work as soon as possible'.[5]

Before returning home, however, he was granted a short British Council Visitorship to study educational institutions in England. Foregoing a trip to Europe, his stay in Britain was lengthened so that he could see the schools in operation during term time.[6] Nyerere would only have been interested in this if he was serious about becoming a teacher. It appears that he may have been anticipating a longer stay however, for in the same letter to Father Marchant, Nyerere emphasised his concern that he was 'going to add to the never-ending difficulty of the shortage of teachers'.[7] The lack of indigenous school teachers was an issue in Tanganyika, as announced in a lengthy report on the state of the territory: 'One of the major problems still to be faced in the programme of African educational advancement is the shortage of teachers.'[8] It was also a serious issue in the United Kingdom, where the most pressing educational need after the war was to provide 600,000 new school places and 70,000 new teachers.[9] Nyerere was not to deprive his own country for long, for although the Colonial Office cancelled his departure on the S.S. *Mantola* on 23 August 1952, he was still to return to Tanganyika that same year.[10] In the process of the rearrangements a W.G. Loltgen, an official from the Passages Department, telephoned Carmichael at the Welfare Office in Edinburgh explaining the proposed itinerary. Lacking a crystal ball, Carmichael 'thought we could accept as Nyerere was not the man to defy his Government'.[11]

From mid-July 1952 until at least the end of September Nyerere was based in London. From there he took short visits to Oxford and Cumberland (surrounding Carlisle, on the border with Scotland) as part of his Visitorship.[12] In the capital he again stayed at the British Council's Hans Crescent Colonial Centre hostel. Nyerere was now living in the social and cultural centre for London's colonials. There were over 200 young Africans and other foreign students on his doorstep.[13] Some students went to Hans Crescent specifically for the politics, the hostel being the city's hotbed for politically-active students with an interest in colonial affairs.[14] The atmosphere was so infectious that even the less politically-inclined quickly became exposed to fresh and radical perspectives on the future of Africa. Around the same years Nyerere stayed at the hostel, a young Kenyan student of law noted that some of his West African student friends at Hans Crescent had given him 'a new outlook on social and political affairs'.[15] A thirty-seven-year old school teacher from Tanganyika, who spent most of his time in the company of other East African students at the Colonial Centre, was similarly exposed there to complaints from African students about difficulties in Britain.[16]

It was at this same location of Hans Crescent, now lodgings to Dunstan Omari, that Erasto Mang'enya says that the African Association was discussed among Tanganyikans. They included Dunstan Omari, Mathew Ramadhani, Joseph Adolf Sawe and, shortly after he graduated

Nyerere

Photo L. Julius Nyerere, an unknown woman and the Nigerian Agwu Okereke Uche after their graduation, University of Edinburgh, 4 July 1952.
(Reproduced by kind permission of Godfrey Madaraka Nyerere)

from Edinburgh, Julius Nyerere.[17] Against the tiny number of Tanganyikan students at the time however, were some 2,000 Nigerians, some of whom lodged at the same residence. As well as being lodging for Omari, Hans Crescent was also headquarters to both the West Indian Students' Union and the Nigerian Union.[18] Nyerere recalls an incident with one radical Nigerian student after he returned from voting in a British general election: 'I asked him, "Have you voted?". He said "Voted what? You mean you voted?" I said yes. He said "Foolish man! These people don't allow me to vote in Nigeria, and they think I should come and vote here?" I felt ashamed.'[19] It was incidents such as this – more often with the greater number of forward-thinking London-based Africans from outside Tanganyika than with the small number of his own countryfolk – that Nyerere was exposed to the shared experience of injustice both in the United Kingdom and back home. The grievances usually boiled down to race, an issue that continued to confound Nyerere for the remainder of his stay in London.

In the main the Colonial Office in London went to some lengths to facilitate Nyerere's time in Britain. They allowed him to extend his stay for further training and they put pressure on the obstinate Tanganyika government with its 'high moral line' when his dependents' allowance payments were late. In contrast, the Union Castle Line, providers of his passage home, were far less accommodating. Nyerere was booked to sail on 3 October 1952 aboard the S.S. *Kenya Castle*. In what is the only known recorded incident explicitly involving Nyerere's ethnicity during this period, issues of his race (and which bore a striking similarity to those in East Africa that he wrote about while at Edinburgh) now reached the surface.[20] The Union Castle Shipping Company would not refuse outright to accept 'coloured' people on their boats but, Loltgen of the Colonial Office relayed, they wished black Africans to be accommodated together and separate from whites. Nyerere was due to travel alone. In this case the shipping company's policy, explained Loltgen, was that 'for odd individuals, unless they have accommodation available, such as a berth in 2 or 4 berth cabin, where they have already sat coloured persons, they will not accept. This would appear to be the situation where Nyerere was concerned.'[21]

Again the Colonial Office stepped in on Nyerere's behalf. It asked the company for an official declaration of their policy as regards 'coloured students'. The Union Castle Shipping Company replied that they were 'not prepared either to have a half empty cabin or to double up white and coloured individuals.'[22] Lieutenant Colonel Crook offered an additional African student in order to obviate the difficulty. He received a flat refusal from the shipping company, and a categorical statement that 'because Nyerere was coloured, his booking had been cancelled'.[23] The records relating to Nyerere do not reveal this, but the company's overtly racist position may be explained by the fact that the *Kenya Castle* served apartheid South Africa.[24] The matter was finally settled when Crook gained authority from the Government of Tanganyika to use air travel instead. On 7 October 1952 Nyerere took a flight from London to Nairobi and on to Dar es Salaam.[25] His departure was noted by the British authorities and 'Mr. Nyerere's name deleted from the "List".'[26]

Julius Kambarage Nyerere, now thirty years old, arrived at Dar es Salaam airport on 9 October 1952. He was met by Father Walsh, who drove him to the residence of the city's Catholic Archbishop, Edgar Maranta.[27] Later he met with his fiancée at the convent in Msimbazi, Dar es Salaam, where Maria Waningu was 'living under the custody of the nuns', as she puts it.[28] Maria recalls how, naturally, she was pleased to see her fiancé, 'but we did not discuss his [Edinburgh] studies because, academically, we were at different levels. And there was an age difference too. In those days it wasn't so much in the culture to discuss studies.'[29] Well aware that Nyerere's United Kingdom education now made him an even more eligible bachelor, Maria was concerned that he was still interested in a future together.

While Nyerere's friends and family closely observed if he had changed after his three years in Europe, one question surely on their minds was what the teacher was now going to do with himself. The matter of how his studies influenced his future choice of career is one that was put to him by a journalist almost exactly thirty years later. The then President's reply bears full transcription as it nicely summarises – albeit in hindsight – Nyerere's mindset before he left for the United Kingdom. It points also to what he felt were the major influences on him while he was in 'Europe':

> I had intended to be a doctor but then in one of my sudden decisions I said to myself: 'No, I am not going to be a doctor, I am going to be a teacher.' Had I become a doctor it would have been for the same reason: to help our people. At that time, quite frankly, I think in my mind the idea of 'my people' was very limited. To be honest, I was talking about my little tribe. The vision became wider and, after Europe, one's attitudes began to change. Yet those attitudes had begun to alter before Europe, because after Makerere, the fact of the Kenya situation with the settlers there and their racial discrimination, one already had a clearer view of things. But I was not a radical as a student. I had been to college with radicals. When they returned, however, I was surprised how they became very good civil servants. Yes, I was no radical at all, but I had started the campaign while in Europe to stop the creation of the Central African Federation. Then, of course, there was Ghana. That was another eye-opener. Ghana got its self-government led by Nkrumah. Nkrumah had been locked up and this was something to talk about among the African students in the hostels and the universities. Suddenly, the boys from Ghana became different. They had changed overnight – they were no longer like us. I was coming back to [Tanganyika to] teach, but I came back with a very firm decision that I was going to teach for a short time only and then I would engage myself completely in politics. I would teach for five years, that was my idea of a short time.[30]

Tanganyika: The Energies of the Intelligentsia

Reunited with Maria, Julius briefly sojourned in Butiama. His unparalleled education notwithstanding, the now politically-ambitious Nyerere apparently showed no signs of being supercilious with those he had left in the village. He surprised many people by doing things that they considered inconsistent with both his academic achievement and with his social status as a son of a chief. Selemani Kitundu wrote: 'the European influence had not spoiled him.'[31] This attitude could perhaps be contrasted with a more brash and cocky personality such as Godfrey Kayamba. That said, there is actually little hard evidence to suggest that any Tanganyikan returnees came back with a new sense of arrogance. Nevertheless, village neighbours seemed to have expected some changes in Nyerere's character. Yet they recall how there appeared to be none whatsoever: 'He was still comfortable in the village. He first saw his mother in Butiama for a few days. She removed the goats, swept the house and they ate in the same place, using their hands to eat the *ugali* [stiff porridge].'[32]

After mealtimes Julius was still used to helping wash the cooking utensils, as he did when he came back from Uganda. 'People would say, "But you are a Makerere graduate, you should not be doing these things!" And he still did this later on, when he returned from Edinburgh', recalls Jack Nyamwaga.[33] After his long period away in the United Kingdom, another friend described Nyerere thus: 'still humble; he gained much admiration from the elders for his humility. Despite his education he still lived a simple life. He would never look down on people, which could have the effect that those who bragged would be more humble.'[34] Nyerere's enduring humility was something that he is said to have shared with his half-brother Chief Edward Wanzagi: 'Wanzagi wore his chiefly gown for special occasions but, like Mwalimu, he would usually dress simply. Wanzagi and [Julius] Nyerere were not ostentatious. The modesty of both came from their father. They were both educated, very modest and lenient. … They never looked down at anybody.'[35] There may of course be an element of truth in all these rhapsodic pronouncements. But it would be wise, as ever, to take them with a pinch of salt. Those who have offered such laudatory remarks were well aware that doing so also reflected well on them as welcome accomplices to the image of Nyerere, man of the people.

As in the days prior to his departure from Uzanaki to the United Kingdom, local politics were again coming to the fore. A couple of days before Nyerere's return to Uzanaki, Chief Ihunyo was accused of corruption and incited his followers to riot in consequence. Edward Wanzagi and some colonial officials were chased by the hostile crowd, which the police sought to disperse by firing shots in the air. Ihunyo's supporters then responded with spears. The District Commissioner, Arthur Hodgson, is said to have grabbed Nyerere's half-brother out of the melee, which apparently contributed to saving his life.[36] After the dust had settled, Wanzagi became the chief of the Zanaki.[37] Not everyone in the district were supportive of this change however, for to many Zanaki local politics were still dominated by the institutions, practices and cultural formations surrounding rain. As Jack Nyamwaga explains:

> Ihunyo had been elected as paramount chief of Buzanaki. He was *mwami*, a rainmaker. But he proved incompetent [in the eyes of the British, because he had been involved in corruption]. So Wanzagi was elected, but he was unpopular because he was not a rainmaker. Wanzagi was very progressive in constructing roads and dams, but the Zanaki wanted somebody who could bring the rains.[38]

The concerns of those who supported Ihunyo reached beyond applied meteorology. His followers were well aware of the immense influence of the rainmaker in Uzanaki – and this one was chief to boot.[39] Ihunyo, unusually, straddled what Steven Feierman has identified as one of the central paradoxes of British rule: they installed chiefs who could help ensure their own legitimacy, working on the assumption that peasants' respect for the chief's rain, combined with ancient habits of deference, would lead to smooth acceptance of their orders. Yet in practice, notes Feierman, the chiefs with the greatest reputation for rainmaking were those in the strongest position to resist colonial orders – these chiefs knew that they held the loyalty of their subjects, even without colonial support.[40] This was the case in post-war Ugogo and, with Ihunyo as both *mwami* and paramount chief, it was now very much the case in Uzanaki. The highly educated Nyerere was returning to a land where rainmaking was still a strong idiom in the language of political power, and where it continued to clash with bureaucratic authority.[41]

This was nothing new to Nyerere. He had been brought up in an environment where religious and cultural institutions were closely bound to the local structures of authority. Indeed, the persistence of rainmaking was brought home to him when, not long after he returned to Butiama, the foreign-educated scholar went to neighbouring Ikizu to pay a visit to his father's friend Chief Mohamed Makongoro – the man who is said to have encouraged Chief Nyerere Burito to send his *orusoro*-playing son Kambarage for a primary education. On receiving the good news that the young man had now returned to Tanganyika with a university education, a group of elders are said to have spontaneously began a celebratory chant that lasted several minutes. The sky was clear and sunny but, so the account goes, before they completed their congratulatory incantations a thunderstorm emerged and rain poured down for several minutes on the chief and his guests. Recalling much later what he witnessed there in Ikizu, Julius Nyerere neither said he believed nor that he doubted that the rain was caused by the chants of the elders.[42] Whatever the reason for the downpour, the point is that the Catholic convert found himself squarely back in what he regarded as the uncomfortable world of magico-religious belief and ritual.[43] Informed now by an even wider world view, however, Nyerere was impatient with the parochial disputes of an opaque politics where men such as his late father's chiefly friends and their companions continued to hold considerable influence. Having taken the decision to soon engage himself completely in politics, Nyerere knew that now was the time to start acting on his convictions on a grander scale, and to transcend the limitations of local politics over which he would have less control. If this is the case, then we should conclude that all the earlier narratives about Nyerere's consideration of building up Uzanaki are simply fables and retrospective lip service to his honourable commitment to family and local people; but one that could not be met given his enormous talents. Having had the chance in Edinburgh to think carefully about the bigger picture, Nyerere now had his sights set on a greater challenge. He may not have calculated it at the time but, by deciding not to engage in politics in Uzanaki, his lack of a political base there – nor in any other region or with any social group – was to become an asset.[44]

Under the auspices of a 'Youth Social Club', some young men of Musoma town held a party to honour Nyerere's return home. They hosted a similar party years before upon his return from Makerere, and this time, as then, Nyerere took the opportunity in his remarks to repeat the theme of unity. Kitundu notes that at this second gathering Nyerere had 'introduced an idea that was somewhat strange to us: the formation of a political party to wage a struggle for independence.'[45] Similar comments came through when after his return from Edinburgh Nyerere spoke with Jackton Nyambereka and some other friends: 'He explained how the British seemed to use due process of law, but the Germans beat people. So he started talking about the right way to change things. He started talking about forming a party, and about our independence.'[46]

Nyerere then stayed at Oswald Marwa's home, where he told the family how in Europe some people were also poor, and that some people also farmed the land.[47] One of these experiences (probably during the Easter break in 1951) was when he picked potatoes with a group of students in the Welsh countryside. Much like Aminu Kano's trip to the same country, Nyerere likely gained similar impressions of 'observing and running the combine-harvester, milking cows, and so on, always thinking of possible applications back home.'[48] Julius may also have mentioned to his friends and family when he returned to Tanganyika that he had lived with a Scottish family who were miners. Father Wille recalls how Nyerere 'was very much impressed how hard the men worked in the mines.'[49] These manual workers in the United Kingdom, Adam Marwa notes, 'would have provided a sharp contrast to the Europeans he saw living in Tanganyika who, especially around Musoma, were usually office-bearers such as District Commissioners and the like.'[50] This opinion seems quite valid in demographic terms. The 1948 population census records 117 Europeans and 677 Indians across the whole of Musoma district, which compared to 2,344 Africans in Butiama village alone.[51] Marwa's observation is also supported by Carey: 'more so than other groups, East Africans express their surprise at seeing Europeans do manual work; and while the experience of equality is greatly welcomed, it makes them more conscious than before of inequalities existing in their own countries.'[52]

When later visitors of Nyerere's generation arrived in Britain they were surprised by the reality of social life. The few accounts available to them before their departure were nearly always very favourable towards the metropole. Mang'enya's explanation for the uncritical account is that the likes of Makwaia, Francis Lwamugira and Martin Kayamba (father of Godfrey and son of Hugh) could not comment adversely on the country of their masters because they were guests of the British government, sitting on a London committee considering the possibility of a joint East African colony.[53] The favourable accounts were not simply because they were guests, but because the British censored their visitors' reports. In some cases the colonial authorities even wrote the documents themselves and, according to Mang'enya, they then made the 'author' sign them. He adds that matters were aggravated by Martin Kayamba's account of his visit to Britain in his book *The Story of Martin Kayamba Mdumi, M.B.E., of the Bondei Tribe*,[54] which includes a vivid account of the journey, but no gist of the official business: 'Instead', Mang'enya writes, Kayamba 'described at length tea parties which he attended in the United Kingdom; but never commented on the shortcomings of the daily life in Britain. He did not even comment on the uncertainty of the British weather.'[55] The cold and the rain aside, Nyerere described his first-hand experience of the 'the land of milk and honey' thus: 'One of the things I felt immediately that was of great help to me and a boost to my morale, was the demystification of the British.'[56]

The colonial administration soon became aware of Zanaki responses to their government. Witness notes were prepared by Hans Cory in his capacity as Tanganyika Government Sociologist. They were submitted to the East African Royal Commission on Closer Union of 1953. At this time Nyerere – who the same year assumed the presidency of the TAA – was still in close proximity:

> The energies of the intelligentsia, small though this is as yet, are not in harmony with Government and its policies are tending to become a hostile force. The Lake Province, in the more leisurely past, was never reckoned among the more 'politically' difficult of the Tanganyika Province. ... With the advance of education and communications, political feeling has become apparent. ... Throughout the major part of the province, relations between the intelligentsia, or at least some of the more politically-conscious element of it, and the Government and the Native Administration are becoming tense. ... The more clamant and vocal among these 'embryo politicians' by no means represent the voice of the people. But they are gaining in influence over people and will continue to do so until Government, aided by the responsible elements of society, can regain the initiative.[57]

On the Edge of the City

Back in Butiama it was time for Julius to pay the bridewealth for his fiancée. The cattle that had been deposited by his father for Magori Watiha had now been returned.[58] For Maria the usual bridewealth of ten cows was increased by her mother, Hannah. She argued that the educated man should pay twelve cows.[59] This created a problem for the ex-student, whose finances were depleted such that he had to borrow the bridewealth from Father William Collins.[60] A bodyguard to Chief Wanzagi and Julius's cousin delivered the cattle to Maria's family.[61] Nyerere began the construction of a house as a wedding present for his wife-to-be. Assistance in the building was given by his mother, other chiefs' wives and their siblings. The plans had been drawn by Oswald Marwa, who was district foreman and he helped his friend Julius make and lay the bricks. The house was topped with *mabati* roofing, and was complete by the end of 1952 in time for the wedding.[62]

Julius Kambarage Nyerere and Maria Waningu Gabriel Magige were married on 21 January 1953 by Reverend Father Alphonse Schiavoul. The ceremony took place in Musoma Roman Catholic church, known as Musoma Mwisenge. Nyerere wrote these details in the family record section of his personal Bible that he purchased in Edinburgh.[63] Father William Collins witnessed the marriage, Oswald Mang'ombe Marwa was best man, and the bridesmaid was his wife Bona. Maria had been friends with Bona ever since she was taught by her at primary school on Ukerewe Island.[64]

The following month, February 1953, the newlyweds moved to a house awaiting them in Pugu, Kisarawe, a few miles inland from Dar es Salaam. When Julius first arrived in the city from the United Kingdom he had received an offer from the Government to teach in one of their Secondary Schools, but he quickly secured the job at St Francis College, Pugu. The offer first came around the time when he graduated from Edinburgh, and was made by Father Richard Walsh, formerly his Director at what Nyerere at the time called 'good old St Mary's'.[65] Pugu, then run by Irish Spiritan (or Holy Ghost) Fathers,[66] was one of the leading schools for Africans in the territory. Father Wille described it as 'the first territorial secondary school set up by the Roman Catholic hierarchy for Tanganyika. It was the elite Catholic secondary school that got the selection of all the best students when they completed middle school.'[67]

Nyerere later claimed that when he left Edinburgh he was absolutely certain that politics was his primary motivation.[68] It raises the question as to why he taught at all. Missionaries were an influence over some rising stars deciding to become teachers. This was the case for both Tom Mboya in Kenya and Kenneth Kaunda in Southern Rhodesia who – so hoped the missionaries – would then go on to become seminarians.[69] Whether or not Walsh had supported Nyerere's decision to teach, teaching fitted neatly with both his education and his employment to date. Unlike politics, teaching was hardly a radical suggestion. As with Aminu Kano, so too for much of Nyerere's young life he could not consider politics as a career choice anyway, because the opportunities were so limited.[70] Becoming a teacher, on the other hand, was a much more common aspiration. At the time that Nyerere decided to go to Makerere and study teaching there were few more prestigious, or achievable, ambitions. So like the most highly educated young men with a Makerere degree, the *mwalimu* re-entered the classroom.[71] With priest-

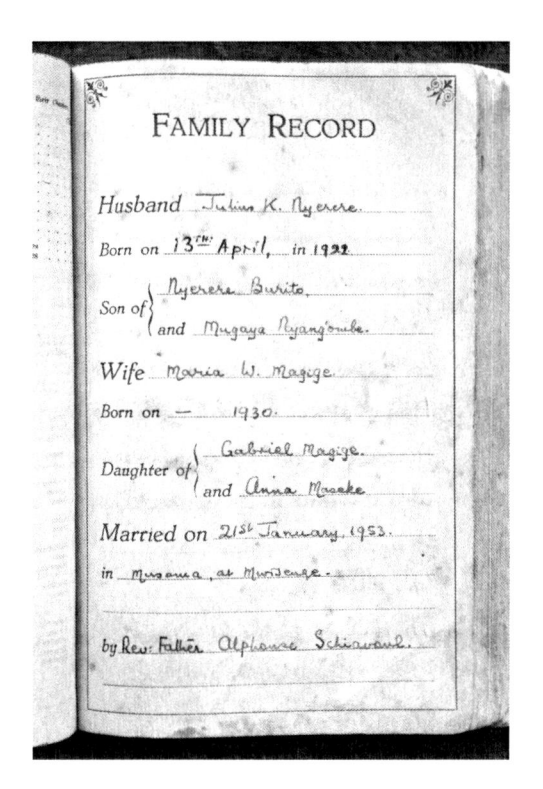

Photo M. Julius Nyerere's family record, in his own hand, recorded in his personal Bible. His birthday has been revised, presumably after Mtokambali Bukiri offered the new date from his own records. (*Photograph by author*)

hood now out of the question, and with politics not holding great prospects of putting food on the table, the decision to return to teaching after Edinburgh was virtually made for him.

But why choose Pugu when he now had roots in Tabora, where he could have slipped easily back into a job at one of the town's leading schools? This is where, in part, the politics creeps in. Tabora was not the seat of territorial politics in 1952, and political activity in Dar es Salaam had cooled off towards the end of 1951. Lake Province was the place to be for radical politics.[72] But being in the centre of the political action was not Nyerere's primary ambition at this stage. If it was, then a government school in Dar es Salaam would make more sense than the more physically remote Pugu, set some distance from the city. The pull of St Francis' was threefold. The first and probably most important factor is a very practical one that should not be underestimated: the post at Pugu was pretty much assured. With a recommendation from Walsh, the job was being offered on a plate at little risk of it being snatched away. Nyerere was now married and had a good chance of needing to provide for children in the near future. St Francis' offered the couple a secure income after Nyerere's three lean years as a student. Secondly, the religious motivations of teaching in a Catholic school were important to Mr and Mrs Nyerere alike. Both were quietly firm in their faith, but in this new location they appreciated the security of the Church and the ability to worship and live with others in a familiar Catholic environment. The third pull factor is the political one: Nyerere had existing political links in both Lake Province and Tabora, and this was now an opportunity to branch out and share his ideas with a new cohort.[73] Pugu's relative proximity to senior African Association members in Dar es Salaam allowed him to make new political contacts on the less familiar coast. In all three of these respects, the new St Francis' school on the outskirts of Dar es Salaam exerted a powerful attraction. Pugu was only ever going to be a stop-gap.

Politics increasingly became a stronger pull. Until Pugu, Nyerere had proceeded with his education almost seamlessly, with few breaks (mostly spent reading) at home. Following on from the intellectual challenges of Edinburgh, teaching schoolboys was a cakewalk. With few more advanced academic achievements to strive towards, Nyerere's restless thoughts now focussed on the issue of colonial rule that had been simmering in his mind while he was in the United Kingdom. But where previously he threw himself headfirst into new ventures that excited him – and he often entered with a loud splash – this time he was more prudent. Nyerere had matured in Edinburgh, where he had had the time to carefully assess the enormity of territorial issues. Now he slowly directed his energies towards the task ahead. A man of quiet reflection, Nyerere decided to ease himself gently into the treacherous waters of politics. As John Iliffe has put it, 'Nyerere could have been a great teacher, and had he not lived in the Africa of the 1950s he might well have remained one.'[74] His long-term aim was now politics, but it absorbed him sooner than he thought.

Despite being the only Tanganyikan at the time with (what was understood to be) a Masters degree, the government offered Nyerere a salary of only £300. This was the salary for a Bachelor's degree level teacher.[75] It was increased to £450 (plus a 30 per cent cost of living allowance) after several interventions by Father Walsh. The sum still represented only three-fifths of what Nyerere would have received had he been a European teacher in Tanganyika.[76]

Much like Mwalimu's own teacher, James Irenge, Nyerere taught History. And also like his own instructor – and possibly recalling the message of the illicit evening meetings in Mwisenge – he engaged himself in the '"special" subject of politics'. On occasions during these Pugu days Nyerere's mother stayed with her son for some time. This was when she first began to know about his political activities. Mugaya Nyang'ombe later recalled that 'every day a man called Dosa [*sic*] Aziz came to our house and he would talk with Julius for a long time.'[77] The family of Dossa Aziz was very close to the influential Sykes family in Dar es Salaam, and Hamza

Mwapachu knew both families intimately ever since he had first lodged with them in the early 1930s. Later, at Makerere, Mwapachu became very close to Nyerere, and there is every chance that he talked to his older political acquaintances in Dar es Salaam about his gifted and politically-aware Zanaki friend. The same can be said of Kasella Bantu at the time, who also knew Nyerere from Makerere and had political connections that could have been exploited in the coastal city.

Whoever first linked Dossa Aziz and Nyerere is a moot point.[78] Certainly the fact that Hamza Mwapachu knew very well both the political elite Sykes family (one of whom, Kleist, was a founder member of the African Association in the territory's capital city) and also Nyerere (formerly in the leadership of the Makerere and then the Tabora branch of the same organisation, which communicated with headquarters) does suggest that the Aziz and Sykes families may have been aware of the gifted young Zanaki for some time. According to the late Ally Sykes in an interview published shortly after his death, however: 'Nyerere came to Dar es Salaam as a teacher at St. Francis College.... [and] before this time we had never heard about him.'[79] Mzee Sykes' comment perhaps rings hollow because of the political context of the African Association when Nyerere entered Dar es Salaam in 1952. The Association had made significant advances in Nyerere's absence.[80] Here came a smart and much talked-about young man to steal the show from the uneducated or semi-educated notables who had risen to ranks of leadership in the 1930s and early 1940s. Some now found themselves challenged by college-educated men. One of the most prominent was Vedastus Kyaruzi, leader of a group of Makerere graduates who had aligned with the Sykes brothers, and who staged a coup that took control of the TAA headquarters in Dar es Salaam.[81] Nyerere was another threat to their authority over the party they had established. He was now back having learnt even more about the political game. Recalling her son's daily conversations with Aziz, Mugaya Nyang'ombe went on:

> One day I overheard them talking about taking over the government from the Europeans. I became afraid. Later I asked Julius if what I heard was true. When he said yes I became frightened. I told him that what he was doing was bad. God had given him a job [as a teacher] and now he wanted to spoil it. But he said that what he was doing would benefit not only us but everyone in the country.[82]

Julius and Maria came to Butiama during the Pugu vacations, one holiday being at Christmas 1953 in Nyigina when the couple brought their first son, Andrew, who was three months old.[83] They returned the following year, five months after the establishment of TANU, for the Christmas of 1954. By this time Nyerere's activities were being closely monitored. With violence and terror just across the border in neighbouring Kenya, Jack Nyamwaga recalls that, the British were furious with Mwalimu because they thought that he was planning another Mau Mau [in Tanganyika].[84] So the District Commissioner and the CID [Criminal Investigation Department] were visiting the Chief and asking him about Mwalimu's movements. This tired Mwalimu, to see harassment, to see his people now being brought in to all of this. So on 22nd March 1955 Mwalimu resigned teaching at Pugu.[85]

The resignation was also influenced by Nyerere's principal at the school, who told him that 'politics and teaching did not mix.'[86] Caught between two commitments to which he was equally devoted, the demands of TANU had finally superseded the demands of the teaching profession that he had committed himself to for so long. After years spent instructing young pupils, the time had come for change. Nyerere had finally decided to apply his knowledge and plans to master the people of Tanganyika in the politics that he now dedicated his working life to.

Epilogue: Return to 'my Scotland'

Edinburgh continued to play a part in the ensuing forty or so years of Nyerere's life. He stayed in touch with the Wilson family who welcomed him into his home during his undergraduate days. Indeed, it may have been the Wilson's to whom Nyerere referred when he remarked in an interview that the family unit was strong in 'my Scotland.'[87] When independence was attained in 1961 he insisted that only his friends the Wilson family would be invited to stay in his official residence during the Dar es Salaam celebrations.[88] Mrs Jean Wilson was also invited to the Republic celebrations in 1962, and President Nyerere met her and her son Walter when they arrived at the airport in Dar es Salaam.[89] Mrs Wilson then went on to work for a short while in Nyerere's private office and in State House. She was also his guest in Butiama, after which she was asked whether Julius had changed over the years. Her reply was, 'No, he is just as he was, but I think he'll be wiser now.'[90] Later, when Joan Wicken vacationed in England, Nyerere asked her to visit Mrs Wilson on two occasions. In 1986 he visited Mrs Wilson at her home, a year before she died.[91]

Nyerere returned to Edinburgh in 1959,[92] and maintained contact with its students. One of the University students interviewed him in Dar es Salaam in 1961. The recently discovered film footage of the interview has the young interviewee ask 'Mr Nyerere' – then either Chief Minister or Prime Minister – his thoughts on Britain's contribution to education in Tanganyika, and specifically in scholarships to universities such as Edinburgh. In reply, Nyerere called for teachers from English-speaking countries to work in Tanganyika. 'For sentimental reasons,' he added, 'I would like to see a large number of teachers coming from the

University of Edinburgh.'[93] Nyerere returned to Edinburgh the following year to receive the Honorary Degree of Doctor of Laws from the University.[94] In the recommendations put forward by academics to the Dean of the Faculty of Arts and on to the Honorary Degrees Committee, the anthropologist Kenneth Little reflected on Nyerere's resignation as Prime Minister in January 1962 to concentrate on reshaping TANU from a nationalist movement into an institution of government:

> Mr. Nyerere's very obvious courage in resigning at this moment seems to me to strengthen the case for an award to him. Quite clearly he is going to have many difficult battles ahead of him in the attempt to keep racialism under control in Tanganyika. Recognition of his work from his old University would, I am sure, encourage him enormously at this stage. If the University decides to honour Mr. Nyerere, it would of course be giving him the degree on the basis of past achievements, which in perspective seem as great as ever. Nevertheless, if one tries to look into the future, it seems to me that his stature will be enhanced rather than diminished by the courageous step which he took this week.[95]

The considerable support from some of the University academics saw the Honorary Degrees Committee approve Nyerere's Honorary LL.D. The invitation came from The Principal and Vice-Chancellor, Sir Edward Appleton, to whom Nyerere replied using the bold letterhead of TANU Headquarters, Lumumba Street, Dar es Salaam: 'I am as delighted as a child to receive this honour. It is, I suppose, natural that one should regard one's own University with special veneration and pride. To receive the honour of an honorary degree from Edinburgh will give me such immense pleasure.'[96]

The ceremony took place in the University's McEwan Hall, where the Dean gave the laureation address and quoted *Uhuru na Kazi*.[97] The text of the official script of the address ends with reference to a famous speech made two years earlier by the then British Prime Minister, Harold Macmillan: 'The wind of change has altered and will alter much in its relations between Africa and Britain', said the Dean, 'but it has not blown away or chilled the affection and pride we feel for our graduate in Arts who now stands before you as a graduand for the highest degree we can offer.'[98]

In Appleton's dinner speech he referred to the four new Doctors of Laws as four 'Modern Greats':

> Dr. Nyerere is a 'Modern Great' who has addressed himself to what must be the greatest problem of today, the task of government. It could be said that he has presided over the birth of a nation; and, with that characteristic breadth of vision which has rightly compelled the admiration of the world, he has devoted his energies to its healthy development. ... We extend to him ... a warm welcome in token of our sense of pride in both his aims and his achievements.[99]

London & Pugu: Teaching & Politics

Photo N. Julius Nyerere and guests after the Honorary Degree of Doctor of Laws ceremony, University of Edinburgh, 5 July 1962. The guests include Sophia Mustafa, Christopher Kasanga Tumbo, Samuel Chamshama, Peter Bwimbo (Nyerere's bodyguard), George Shepperson, Jean Wilson, Samson Mwambenja and Walter Wilson.
(Reproduced by kind permission of Marian Somerville, on behalf of the late Jack Fisher)

The following year, 1963, Nyerere stood as a candidate for the University of Edinburgh's post of Rector. At the time the Rector directly represented the students, and was (and still is) the chair of the court that governs the University; an integral function in shaping the institution's agenda. While already President of Tanzania, for this proposal Nyerere had 'given an undertaking to be in Edinburgh whenever he is required.'[100] One of the members of the Nyerere team who were campaigning on his behalf while he was in Tanzania was Norman Clark, then reading for a Masters in Economics. Clark authored an article in *Umoja! The magazine of the Nyerere Rectorial campaign committee*, in which he wrote:[101]

> To those who know [Nyerere] best he is, like most great people, a quiet and unassuming man with simple tastes. He combines great personal dignity with compassion but beneath his gentleness, there is a strong determined character, sincerely dedicated to the cause of African nationalism. At the same time, however, he is not a racialist as can be seen by the masterly way in which he brought Tanganyika to independence last year with the promise that 'we are not seeking a privileged position for the Africans, but equality with the other races on the basis of the individual.' Indeed, he has won the respect of all nations, all classes and creeds, for his tact, his patience, his quiet good humour and above all, I think,

for his unwavering determination in following a cause in which he passionately believes. … Such a man would be an obvious choice for our Rector even if he did not have such unique links with Edinburgh. … In an article in the Scotsman a few weeks ago the Universities Correspondent said that 'He would be an illustrious Rector and a symbol of the University's many links with Africa.' We believe this too.[102]

The Nyerere Rectorial campaign committee was also supported in speeches given by George Shepperson and the anti-imperialist Labour Member of Parliament, Fenner Brockway, who the same year had his *African Socialism* book published.[103] The Nyerere team were up against stiff opposition in the form of four individuals from the literary world and entertainment: the actor, writer and playwright, Peter Ustinov; Yehudi Menuhin, the distinguished violinist; Sean Connery, the Edinburgh-born actor who by this time had made only one notable film, *Dr No*, in which he played James Bond for the first time; and another actor, James Robertson Justice. In the voting Nyerere, Menuhin and Connery were eliminated early from the count, and Ustinov was runner-up to Robertson Justice.[104] The actor was a popular Anglo-Scottish thespian who regularly drank with the student men in the 'males only' Students' Union and had recently featured in and narrated *The Guns of Navarone*. Informing Nyerere of his defeat, his friend George Shepperson added with derision that, 'It looks as if the young gentlemen of Edinburgh University (unlike their equivalents at Glasgow who elected Chief Luthuli last year) prefer to go on electing film actors and people of this sort.'[105] The failed campaign to make Nyerere Chancellor could have knocked confidence of many. His reaction was to ignore Edinburgh for many years and to concentrate on the job in hand at home.

Edinburgh was persistent, however, and a decade later the then Rector, the student Gordon Brown – later Chancellor of the Exchequer and then Prime Minister of the United Kingdom – wrote to Nyerere in a bid to unseat the then Chancellor of the University, none other than the Duke of Edinburgh. This time the President made it clear that he was unable to cross the Rubicon.[106] Nyerere was very busy as Head of State, but he would also have been mindful of his lack of success in the 1963 Edinburgh Rectorial campaign and was keen to focus his energies at home. In the same period the University wrote to Nyerere asking for a contribution towards its Southern Africa Scholarship fund. Joan Wicken replied that 'the President's numerous contributions in this field can be most appropriately utilized within Tanzania. We do in fact have a number of Southern African students at the University of Dar es Salaam and at other educational institutes in the country.'[107]

Nyerere returned to Edinburgh in July 1987, this time to the Department of History for a conference on 'The Making of Constitutions and the Development of National Identity'. Papers were presented in honour of the bicentenary of the American Constitution, which

Nyerere had studied under Lawrence Saunders. Nyerere's attendance was not for the subject matter, however, as he made clear when replying to the organisers:

> I am trying to reduce to the absolute minimum my visits outside Tanzania, and in particular to confine my speech making on such occasions to the few subjects on which I feel qualified to make a contribution – in particular the Liberation of Southern Africa and the need for a New International Economic Order. On the other hand, you have made the request from Edinburgh University – and I cannot forget my three years as a student there, nor the honour given to me in 1962. And you are proposing to honour Professor George Shepperson, to whom I am personally indebted. Those two facts encourage me to bend my own rule.[108]

The event took place in the University's McEwan Hall, where Nyerere had received both his Edinburgh degrees. 'Never has anybody been in that remarkable place who ever fulfilled its sense of academic and spiritual leadership', recalled one of the organisers of Nyerere's presence at the conference.[109] 'The Chairman of *Chama cha Mapinduzi*' gave the opening address entitled, 'Reflections on Constitutions and African Experience', to which he added a subtitle: 'A tribute to Dr George Shepperson upon his retirement'.[110] 'The paper was delivered with very firm grace',[111] with Nyerere blaming the early fall of democracy in post-independent Africa on 'the lack of a predominant sense of nationhood to match the establishment of an independent state.'[112] Nyerere argued that decolonisation gave birth to governments that were recognised internationally but which were not similarly crowned by large segments of the population over which they ruled.[113] Nyerere 'was telling a collection of [Europeans] what they must do', remarks an organiser of the conference, 'and one could imagine how, in the same way, he would also hold respect in an African village.'[114]

The following morning a party in honour of Tanzania's first president was held at the now-defunct Edinburgh University Settlement. Arranged by Nicholas Flavin, Director of the Settlement and a former missionary priest in Nigeria, the programme included Scottish harp and fiddle music, Gaelic singing and traditional Highland dancing, all part of what in Scotland is known as a *ceilidh*. The University staff magazine described the event at Potterrow as 'A Highland Gathering for Dr Nyerere'.[115] Flavin met Nyerere for the first time at the *ceilidh*, but recalls that talking with him 'was as if you had known him always. It was as if talking with your friend. ... He was the essence of humility; totally gracious.'[116]

Nyerere's final trip to his alma mater was in 1997 to deliver the Lothian European Lecture. He also taught and conducted seminars at the Centre of African Studies. In his lecture, 'Africa: The Third Liberation', he castigated neo-colonialism and appealed for African countries to be allowed to develop their own forms of democracy.[117] On 14

Photo O. Julius Nyerere giving the Lothian European Lecture, 'Africa: The Third Liberation'; Playfair Library, University of Edinburgh, 9 October 1997.
(*Reproduced by kind permission of the University of Edinburgh*)

December 1999, exactly two months after his death in London, the University held a 'Celebration and Thanksgiving for the Life of Mwalimu Julius Nyerere'.

The University of Edinburgh now honours its first Tanganyikan alumnus with three Julius Nyerere Masters Scholarships. The entrance to the University's School of Social and Political Science at 15A George Square now bears a plaque, unveiled by retired President H.E. Ali Hassan Mwinyi at the two-day celebration of the life of Julius Nyerere, held at the University in conjunction with the Tanzania High Commission to mark ten years after the Father of the Nation's death. The plaque reads: 'In Honour of Mwalimu Julius Nyerere, 1922–1999, African Statesman, first President of the United Republic of Tanzania, Graduate of the University'.

9
The Early Years
Legacy & Reappraisal

What a wee little part of a person's life are his acts and his words! His real life is led in his head, and is known to none but himself. ... Biographies are but the clothes and buttons of the man – the biography of the man himself cannot be written.

Mark Twain[1]

The new evidence provided here has offered much-needed depth to the sparsely-informed and predominantly uncritical account of Julius Nyerere's early life. In doing so it serves to correct some frequently-cited inaccuracies concerning his formative years. This study has revealed the dubious foundation upon which the dominant history of Uzanaki is based, allowing the case to be made for a lesser role of Zanaki influences on *ujamaa* than is currently accepted. It has documented the Tanganyikan predecessors who studied in the United Kingdom before Nyerere, and it has determined why exactly he ended up studying certain subjects in Edinburgh.

This study has also given volume to some silences about Nyerere's early years. While he is often depicted as Tanganyika's *wunderkind*, he still failed in his first attempt to gain a scholarship to study in Europe. Seemingly minor details such as this have their significance. Nyerere's decision to reapply for a scholarship, for example, suggests a certain perseverance when faced with disappointment. Further, while Maria Waningu is usually regarded as his only marital partner, the detail that has been given here on the union with his child bride Magori Watiha reveals more than those who have criticised the inclusion of this hushed relationship are prepared to consider. The circumstances of the marriage points to the local custom that surrounded Nyerere in Butiama. His reaction to Chief Nyerere Burito's imposition of the marriage serves as an example of the young man's resolve to take an independent stand – this time against the traditional Africa that he frequently applauded in his later speeches and writings. The period also marks a time when Nyerere entered a wider world. As he travelled further, he was increasingly exposed to influences that led him to question the status quo in his homeland. Fertile of mind and eloquent in speech, he positioned himself to become the educated African leader of the movement against hegemonic rule in the territory in which he was born. With the help of many others, the movement ultimately led to the downfall of the colonial state in Tanganyika. Nyerere went on to have an immense influence over his independent nation, and he continues to wield his power from the grave. Further afield, he is remembered as one of Africa's most respected statesmen.

Nyerere's political life has certainly been the subject of much scrutiny. But to an outside observer the lack of serious inquiry into his formative years is surely baffling. The history of the thirty years leading to Nyerere's formal entry into politics – scant as it is – was long ago laid to rest as indisputable fact. As a result, many Tanzanians have been happy to go along with received wisdom: the invincible '*Baba wa Taifa*' grew up in a humble rural abode, so the account goes, he excelled in his studies, and single-handedly conquered all in his path. He fathered the nation and guided its people with the integrity and commitment of a dedicated teacher. The inaccuracies and silences that have been revealed here are a symptom of the unexplored history of this early period in the man's life.

Many portrayals of Nyerere were made in retrospect, shaped by the knowledge of what he became. Similarly, those descriptions collected in the past from Nyerere's peers tend to have omitted the less flattering accounts that at least a small number of those informants surely offered. Apparently impartial sketches of Nyerere's character can also be tainted. For example, the contemporary account given in Chapter 4 by John Stanley, headmaster when Nyerere was working at St Mary's, describes the Zanaki teacher as 'an excellent young man: intelligent, enthusiastic, industrious and conscientious to a very high degree … a fine type of character, open as a book'. The context, however, is that Father Stanley had been asked to submit a character reference as part of Nyerere's application for a prestigious scholarship to study in the metropole. The reference was a rare opportunity for the liberal Stanley to influence the future of his blue-eyed boy, undoubtedly in the hope that he would return to St Mary's with greater knowledge and yet more shining credentials. It was in the school's interests for Stanley to praise Nyerere and to exclude any shortcomings, of which he was surely aware.

New sources unearthed by this study suggest that some depictions of the more positive aspects of Nyerere's character are indeed accurate. As a young man he was down-to-earth, principled, and had a strong sense of fairness. He was modest and unpretentious. In contrast to a good number of his contemporaries at Tabora Boys, he was neither arrogant nor conceited. While among the more privileged at Makerere, he was not one of the 'presumptive elite'. As a student he was keen, reflexive and at times original. As a teacher he was enthusiastic, diligent, persuasive and collegial. He was unconcerned with personal financial gain, but more motivated by a desire to improve the lives of others. Yet the dogged eye for Nyerere's virtues and admirable principles consistently stifles a more complicated and human portrait.

Further evidence that has been revealed here helps the formulation of a more balanced character description. Had someone shadowed Nyerere during the formative years, a candid character reference would have included some of the more critical traits of his personality. An independent character, the young Nyerere was personable when he chose to be, but tended to be distant and detached when engrossed in issues he regarded as important. He could give the impression of being self-absorbed. Bookish and driven, he worked hard at his studies and was sometimes outstanding. The mischievous and less academically-inclined students called him a swot. Others, especially at Makerere when as a student he gave informal lectures, felt the diminutive Tanganyikan was a touch precocious. Those who did not know him well thought he was a bore. Others considered him too intense to spend much time with. Nyerere sought to keep a low profile, but he regularly led public debates. Confident in his skill as a debater, he was an entertaining and voluble speaker to listen to, but an intimidating opponent. He could be cooperative with his fellows when he felt it was required, but he was not always a team player. Manipulative at times, increasingly shrewd with experience, and always tenacious, the young Nyerere shared his personal issues only with those who could help him. He kept much to himself. He developed these personality traits during his early life, and carried them into his political career.

The new sources that have been discussed in this study also reveal something of the influences that Nyerere was exposed to in his formative years. For a young man who was exposed to such varied influences relative to many of his Zanaki contemporaries, arguments that seek to promote one influence as paramount are fruitless. Rather, many factors formed Nyerere's world view. As he himself asserted: 'This is one thing I can say: all the changes I have experienced have been gradual.'[2] Mwisenge, Tabora Boys and Makerere – let alone his mentors outside school, college and university – were clearly all major, if unquantifiable, influences that had a huge bearing on his early life. But for a youth who had apparently spent much of his earlier years hunting wild animals and raising goats and sheep, one can only speculate on the barrage of multifarious new impressions that he suddenly faced in his first few months at Tabora Boys, 'the Eton of Tanganyika'. Later, having been exposed in Tabora to the trappings of the English public school, the differences were immense between a Makerere where Nyerere rubbed shoulders with the sons of Tanganyika's elite, and Edinburgh, one of Britain's ancient universities where at the time the vast majority of students were from literate Scots families.

It is very difficult to demonstrate a definite instrumental link between Nyerere's educational career and choices and the development of his political ideology, but it is possible to argue for a non-instrumental link. He studied in institutions where opinions could be expressed – first Makerere, but never more so than in Edinburgh. At university he encountered several academics who used their knowledge to further progressive politics, without being improperly prescriptive. Nyerere came to read for an M.A., but he got far more: an opportunity to study extra subjects and to discuss his ideas in a sympathetic, engaging and challenging environment. Under these conditions a naturally bright young man with increasingly big ideas was able to thrive. Tabora Boys, for all its fagging, sportsmanship and fair play, had taught the use of ploughs. At Edinburgh Nyerere was now expected to become aware of 'great conceptions', and their utility for the betterment of humanity – the mid twentieth century extension of the (ideal) principles of Scotland's eighteenth-century enlightenment. The focus at Edinburgh was largely on Europe, but Nyerere took the opportunity to express his developing ideas on the relevance of the great conceptions in relation to Africa. He wrote about service to the people, racial equality and independence.

In Europe, Nyerere increasingly felt that he was duty-bound to serve his countrymen. With time this emerged into a need to challenge the colonial state. At some level race certainly influenced his desire to achieve self-rule for Tanganyika. In the United Kingdom, as in East Africa, the prevailing context of race relations was one of European feelings of superiority over Africans. We know that Nyerere experienced lower pay than teachers who were European, even though he had higher qualifications than many of them. He was exposed to racism as much as any other African. There were likely other injustices that are not recorded and which piled up over time. That they remain a further silence of Nyerere's early life is indicative of his liberal stance towards other races – and, later, of his ability to influence the people of Tanzania. He was friends with a number of missionaries before he left Tanganyika, and he knew how to behave in their presence. He asked the right questions, and developed the avuncular charm of the witty clergyman. In the United Kingdom he was close to many white people who welcomed him into their homes. These positive experiences played a significant role in moulding Nyerere's multi-racial outlook. He clearly detested colonialism, but from his positive experiences with Europeans he was well aware that not all whites were colonialists and racists. As the struggle for Tanganyika's independence gained momentum, Nyerere's pragmatic participation in multi-racial politics contrasted with the more hard-line position taken by many other nationalists.[3]

When looking at the influences from Nyerere's early years on his later political life, one must be careful not to focus too much on Edinburgh just because much new detail is now available from his time there. As Sanders has explained, it is important to show that Nyerere also received an education from his African Association contemporaries before he ever left for Europe.[4] It was during the fervent Kampala days when, alongside other 'educated Africans' from outside Tanganyika, Nyerere began to think in terms of nationalities, and he gained his first direct experience of political organisation. The growing nationalist momentum was sustained when he taught in Tabora. There he protested against the proposed East African Federation. It was also during his time in Tabora that a delegate of the United Nations Trusteeship Council Visiting Mission spoke at St Mary's to inform his listeners that they were the young men who must lead the country. In Edinburgh he embraced the development of his political philosophy more fully than he engaged in direct political action. He matured intellectually while in Scotland's capital, which marked an important stage in his political socialisation. London then played a significant part in broadening his outlook, exposing him to nationalist sentiments from across Africa. With distance from the precarious and unpredictable vagaries of his ancestral home, Nyerere was able to view Tanganyika's future through a wider lens than ever before. In the United Kingdom he had the time and space to take stock and to strategise.

It is also important to consider the role of educational choice on Nyerere's political ideology.[5] The evidence presented here suggests that as he progressed from school to college and on to university, Nyerere gained autonomy in his decision-making and increasingly made important decisions himself concerning his educational path. This is no different from many of his contemporaries whose education took a similar trajectory. They were a tiny minority of the young men – and far fewer young women – who were born in East Africa in the 1920s. As one of the elite, Nyerere was able to make choices over his studies and to realise the educational opportunities presented to him both at home and then abroad. This is where one of the most significant overlooked aspect of his formative life lies. Despite Nyerere's best efforts in his later years to play it down, he was immensely privileged when compared to so many of the other young boys of his generation in Tanganyika Territory.

Many aspects of Nyerere's upbringing were no different from those of the majority of his peers. But from the start there are other features of his life that were distinctly atypical. Nyerere's education may not have occurred in the first place had he not been the son of a compliant government chief. Chief Nyerere Burito secured his status through his relative cooperation with European colonialists. His son Kambarage did much the same with European missionaries. Even before his interaction with the White Fathers, however, Kambarage was surrounded from birth by the structures of power. There is no doubt that he was both clever and charismatic. But his intelligence was nurtured by the education that initially he was only able to obtain because of his father.

As a politician, Nyerere's charisma and force of personality helped seduce people into accepting the stories about his apparently humble upbringing. Nor did people question his authoritative account of African tradition. At times he relied on detention to enforce his will, but his ruthless streak to dissenters is frequently also swept under the carpet. In the main, however, Nyerere could persuade his people to accept his position through force of argument. His skill at debating was his key political gift, and was very much at the centre of his national and international career as a politician and statesman. From a young age he was a minor celebrity of the debating circuit, where he gained confidence and proved himself to be increasingly adept at using against his colonial masters their own weapons of democratic doctrines and parliamentary skill. The independence struggle that relied in part on his talents, and the Tanzania that emerged after *Uhuru*, would have been quite different had Nyerere not experienced the education he received. That he performed well in his studies was down to natural intelligence and the hard work that he constantly urged others to embrace. Nyerere the student did not absorb reading and lectures passively. He reflected on and developed his thoughts in both the short and the long terms, and articulated his sometimes complex ideas in a simple and logical style of speechwriting.

As Nyerere progressed through his studies his education was increasingly liberal. His Edinburgh degree provided him with the opportunity to explore his nationalist ambitions. He was encouraged by some of the academic greats of the day to read books that discussed the potential of the African educated elite. His exposure in the United Kingdom to progressive politics was through the original western philosophical texts upon which Fabian socialism was built. This ranged from some of the earliest works by authors of the liberal philosophical tradition, to the latest writings of the day. The direct influence of Fabian organisations on Nyerere's later political life is probably not as great as many of the unsubstantiated claims suggest. His largely theoretical experience of socialism in the metropole occurred at a time of immense change there. Nyerere the emerging nationalist was in the United Kingdom to witness the advent of the great political issues of race and African liberation. He gained confidence from the energies of fellow Africans from other parts of his continent who were driven by a determination to realise their dreams. Meanwhile, Scottish nationalism was discussed much in

The Early Years: Legacy & Reappraisal

Edinburgh University politics, and the calls for home rule intensified. Westminster rule was even being questioned in the metropole.

Alongside his studies, the other highly significant influence of Nyerere's years in Edinburgh was the demystification of the colonial masters. As one of his contemporaries put it, 'colonialists eulogized their country, praised their culture, sang the glories of their achievements, and aggrandized their war victories'.[6] Nyerere soon realised that the United Kingdom was not as united as it had appeared from Tanganyika, and that the British were not so great. Before he left Tanganyika he had met precious few Africans who outranked white men. Then in the United Kingdom he met ambitious young Africans from across the continent whose shared experience was largely one of dissatisfaction with their subordinate position, and who were desperate to challenge hegemonic rule. Nyerere had been on good terms with some European teachers and missionaries in Tanganyika, but many settlers were unfriendly to Africans and presented themselves as superior. Then in the United Kingdom he observed – and, through the Wilson family, got to know – white manual workers engaged in employment that back home was usually reserved for Africans. This made the young Nyerere more conscious than before of the inequalities between black and white on his continent. Yet British officialdom in Tanganyika remained persistently aloof. Few Africans would dare present themselves to high-ranking office bearers, and the governor was almost completely detached from his subjects. What little respect that Nyerere may have had for his colonial superiors was shattered when he met the governor in London. All Twining could offer Nyerere was a cryptic warning about his political activities. Nyerere took this as a personal threat, and it only strengthened his resolve to challenge the authority of the colonial state. He was frustrated that both in Tanganyika, and now in the United Kingdom, it was nearly always the case that another European trumped the African to a position of authority. So when Nyerere met with Banda, the Nyasaland doctor provided him with a powerful example that the African could succeed at the white man's game. Nkrumah, Kenyatta and other political leaders who had spent time as activists in London also proved to Nyerere that the organised efforts of Africans could effectively challenge the colonial state back home.

In the eyes of nearly all Tanganyikans, Nyerere's experience of living in the white man's land meant that when he returned to the territory he was able to make claims with greater authority. A captivating storyteller, he came back with a message from the wider orbit of the modern world. He did not return as a messiah though. He was only known in tiny pockets of the territory: chiefly around Uzanaki, the towns of Musoma, Mwanza and Tabora, and by a few men here and there who had met through their shared education or limited (but growing) political activity in particular towns in the territory. Nyerere returned from the United Kingdom as a modern progressive man with much intellectual capability and almost no financial means. The picture is one of an approachable and affable country priest, pushing his bicycle around the village, with some personal warm words for individual parishioners. This image of Nyerere is influenced by his fundamental decision in early life to become a Roman Catholic. But the image of Nyerere the righteous Christian with a playful sense of humour should not disguise his authoritarianism. As an academic at the University of Dar es Salaam noted of his later political days:

> the notion of 'mwalimu' of the nation has always seemed to have particularly missionary resonance: the shepherd and his flock, perhaps combining with certain aspects of patri-archal authority in indigenous culture…. [T]he way he handled 'critical' questions [was]… very much in the manner of the tolerant but potent teacher/leader, adjudicating what could be said and how.[7]

Nyerere was brought up in a deeply political milieu. From birth he was surrounded by local-level authoritarianism. This developed in his interaction with missionary discipline. Like many of his contemporaries at boarding school, he soon became accustomed to the clear hierarchy of authority. This experience later helped him to cope with British officialdom. At Tabora Boys he assumed the responsibility that came with leadership roles as a prefect and in the Boy Scouts, and he threw himself wholeheartedly into debating. In doing so he acquired some of the basic skills of political organisation, and a self-confidence that his way was the right way. He had tasted influence over others, and quickly developed a hunger for authority. His ambition never waned. In time he developed the firm control required for political success. When he reached the ultimate position of authority he was then faced with challenges to power that are commonplace in politics anywhere. He possessed a certain grit from a young age, and he learnt through experience to be more vigorous in the implementation of his will. As much as he harked back to a traditional African democracy where 'elders sit under the big tree, and talk until they agree', Nyerere was well aware of the threat to his authority posed by consensual democracy.

Much as Tanganyikans rarely questioned the official line on Nyerere's humble upbringing, and none felt it worthwhile to cast aspersions on his authoritative account of African tradition, nobody challenged his view on the faults of the democratic system in post-war Britain. Very few Africans had travelled beyond their own local territory, let alone to the metropole. Fewer still were both capable of engaging with Europeans in reasoned debate and also of expressing the independence message in a way that resonated with Tanganyikans. None had an appetite to challenge Nyerere's position anyway, for it fitted so well with the nationalist movement that had grown in Tanganyika while he was away in the United Kingdom. In the years after his return, the teacher had an ever growing class of keen students willing to listen to his thoughts on fundamental change. It took those many uneducated Tanganyikans, men and women, Christians, Muslims and those with other beliefs – who did not have the fortune of so much education – to help turn Nyerere's theoretical lessons into a practical movement capable of challenging colonial rule.

*

The *Modern Tanzanians* collection mentioned in the Introduction aimed to encourage the recording of the stories of those who for the fifty years up to independence provided leadership in different parts of Tanganyika. Some of them were lesser-known figures of the independence movement. A reading of these biographies now is inspiring. They act as an example of the strong foundation of historical scholarship produced by talented young Tanzanians at the time. They also serve as a reminder of the sacrifices taken by some of the country's less celebrated personalities so that *Uhuru* could be realised. John Iliffe's statement in the Introduction to that book, written close to forty years ago, still holds true today: 'The task of recovering Tanzania's history is too big and too important to be left to necessarily small numbers of professional historians.'[8] As the research conducted for this study has shown, Tanzanians have a role to play in identifying 'missing' documents relating to the local, regional and national past. Tanzanians also have a role to play in recording the life histories of the men and women of older generations who lived through the vanishing days of *Uhuru*.

Select Biographies, Bibliography & Sources

Select Biographies

Baker, E.C.
District Officer in Musoma for six years during the 1920s, and compiler of the *Musoma District Book* 'Early History' section that includes the Zanaki.

Baker, G.W.
Member for Social Services, The Secretariat, Dar es Salaam. Wholly unsympathetic to Nyerere's concern that his dependants' allowance was not paid to his family for many months.

Bantu, J.K.
From Nzega in the then Western Province, Joseph Kasella Bantu taught with Nyerere at St Mary's Secondary School in the 1940s. Also a member of TAA and instrumental in the founding of TANU, he left his teaching job in Tabora, joined opposition politics for a period, then moved to Dar es Salaam to join the radio Tanganyika Broadcasting Corporation (TBC).

Bomani, P.L.
Paul Lazaro Bomani was born in Ikizu in 1925, attended Tabora Boys for a short period and Minaki Secondary School. He studied co-operatives in Uganda and in 1953 undertook a course offered by the Co-operative College, Nottinghamshire, before becoming general manager of the Victoria Federation of Co-operative Unions, Africa's largest agricultural marketing co-operative. He served as head of various ministries and went on to ambassadorial positions, and died in 2005.

Buhoro
An *omurwazi* (one who acts as a 'whip'), Buhoro was appointed by the Germans as 'first Chief of Butiama' sometime in the late nineteenth century or early twentieth century.

Select Biographies, Bibliography & Sources

Burito, N.
Julius Nyerere's father, Chief (Nyerere) Burito was born in 1860 to Burito Mazembe and Wakuru Malima, and was given the name 'Nyerere', meaning 'caterpillar' in Zanaki, after a plague of army worm caterpillars that attacked the countryside at the time of his birth. He was an 'assessor' to Ihunyo, the senior chief of the Zanaki Federation, and was appointed 'chief of Butiama' by the Germans. Well-liked by British administrators relative to other Zanaki chiefs, Chief Nyerere Burito was an animist and polygamist with some twenty-two wives. He died in 1942.

Cameron, Sir Donald
Governor of Tanganyika from 1925 to 1931 while the United Kingdom administrated the territory as a League of Nations Mandate, he revamped provincial administration, formed the (unelected and unrepresentative) Legislative Council and established indirect rule.

Carmichael, D.D.
Area Welfare Officer, Colonial Office, Edinburgh.

Chamshama, S.S.
A Native Treasury clerk, Samuel Seyid Chamshama founded the Usambara Association and who was appointed a chief minister in Shambaai. He served as Regional Commissioner of Arusha.

Cohen, A.
Sir Andrew was a Colonial Office official who became Governor of Uganda (1952–57) and Permanent Secretary at the Overseas Development Agency (1964–68).

Cory, H.
Born in Austria in 1888 as Hans Koritschoner, he came from Tanganyika before the First World War, during which he was wounded while fighting under von Lettow-Vorbeck. He became a temporary District Officer under the British administration, and in 1943 took up the post of government sociologist.

Crook, W.V.
A retired Lieutenant Colonel, Crook was Liaison Officer for East African Students at the Colonial Office in London, and was continuously supportive of Nyerere when at Edinburgh he faced a lack of co-operation from Colonial Service administrators in Tanganyika.

Eliufoo, S.N.
Born in Machame in 1920, Solomon Nkya Eliufoo graduated from

Makerere in 1943, then taught at the college for two years. He then worked for the Lutheran Church, and later (1956) studied at Bristol University. He held ministerial posts and was heavily involved in Chagga politics. He passed away in 1971.

Fundikira, A.S.
Chief of the Nyamwezi, Abdallah Saidi Fundikira was born in 1921 and educated at Tanga Government Secondary School and then Makerere, where he was friends with Nyerere. He matriculated at Caius College, Cambridge, but was denied a UK scholarship. In 1957 he was elected unopposed to the Legislative Council. Fundikira served in various ministries, but resigned in 1963 in protest against one-party rule and later formed the Union for Multiparty Democracy (UMD). He lost the 1993 presidential elections to Benjamin Mkapa, who appointed him a Member of Parliament.

Hodgson, A.B.
(Arthur) Brian Hodgson served in the Tanganyika administration from 1939. In 1945 he was appointed Secretary of the Legislative Council, and in 1952 became District Commissioner in Musoma. From 1958 he was Principal Secretary (Establishments), at the Office of the Prime Minister. Hodgson was appointed a CMG in 1962.

Ihunyo, M.
One of Nyerere's best childhood friends, Marwa Ihunyo claims to be the only surviving rainmaker in Uzanaki, where his residence is the headquarters of rainmaking and a school for future rainmakers.

Jaberi
A Ganda government agent working for the colonial authorities in Uzanaki, in 1917 he was put in charge of the central section of Musoma District to supervise the chiefs. He was allegedly removed from his position the following year after being duped into committing murder.

Jones, A.C.
Trade union official and politician. A protégé of Ernest Bevin, Arthur Creech Jones was elected to Parliament in 1935 and served in the Colonial Office in the Labour Government of 1945–60.

Junker, A.
A French-born White Father, Father Aloysius Junker baptised Julius Nyerere in the chapel of the Nyegina Catholic Mission on 23 December 1943.

Kandoro, S.A.
A Manyema born in Ujiji in 1926, Saadani Abdu Kandoro studied teaching and worked as a clerk for the native treasury in Uyui, Tabora. He later turned to trade, when he began to work towards the establishment of native welfare and co-operative unions. In 1952 he took up the post as TAA's full-time secretary in Lake Province, and was one of the seventeen founders of TANU. Kandoro held various political positions. In 1969 Tanzania's Academy of Letters appointed him Poet Laureate, and the following year he retired from active politics to take up farming.

Keith, J.L.
Head of the Colonial Office's Welfare Department and Director of Colonial Scholars in London since 1941, John Keith had served as Native Commissioner in Namwala, Northern Rhodesia, where he had known the Northern Rhodesia nationalist Harry Nkumbula. A left-leaning liberal, Keith was awarded an OBE.

Keto, J.E.
Born in Magita, Muheza in 1917, John Ernest Keto graduated from Makerere with a Diploma in Education. He then taught at Korogwe Middle School and Minaki, after which he was awarded a CDWS scholarship to study at the University of Edinburgh, where he published an article with Nyerere on the proposed Central African Federation. He became Chairman of TANU in Minaki District, then Member of Parliament for Tanga Province. He was Chairman of the Public Service Commission, worked in the postal service in Nairobi and Kampala, and upon retirement became Headmaster of Hegongo Secondary School, then served as Councillor of Korogwe District. Shortly before his death in 2012 he was still local Chairman of the Council of CCM Elders.

Könen, M.
A German national, Father Matthias Könen was approached by Nyerere for baptism at Nyegina mission in late 1942 or early 1943, but the Missionaries of Africa pastor insisted that Kambarage first be prepared for baptism by the catechist Petro Maswe Marwa.

Kunambi, G.P.
Born in Matombo, Morogoro in 1919, (George) Patrick Kunambi attended Tabora Secondary School and Makerere University College. The Waluguru chief was a member of TANU since its foundation in 1954, and the following year led the meeting that resolved to send Nyerere to New York to press the United Nations for Tanganyika's independence. He died in 2011.

Select Biographies, Bibliography & Sources

Kyaruzi, V.K.
Born in 1921, Vedastus Kyalakishaija Kyaruzi played an active role in TAA and the formation of TANU. He studied at the White Fathers School at Kajunguti, Bukoba, St Mary's Tabora, and Makerere University College, where he obtained a degree in Medicine. When president of the TAA he was posted to Kingolwira Prison Hospital near Morogoro, then to the even more remote Nzega. Kyaruzi later attended the University of Edinburgh, was awarded a Diploma in Public Health, and in 1964 was admitted (in absentia) a Member *qua* Physician of the Royal College of Physicians and Surgeons of Glasgow. He went on to become the first Tanganyikan Permanent Representative to the United Nations, and after independence became the country's Permanent Secretary for Foreign Affairs and Defence. Dr Kyaruzi died in 2012.

Loltgen, W.G.W.
Colonial Office official in London who dealt with Nyerere's stuttering return travel arrangements to Tanganyika in 1952.

Makwaia, D.K.
Born in 1922, David Kidaha Makwaia was a Makerere student from 1941 to 1944. He succeeded to the Chieftainship of the Sukuma on the death of his father and did not complete college. He was the first of two Africans appointed to Tanganyika's Legislative Council, and was elected paramount chief of the Sukuma Federation in 1949, the same year that he matriculated at Lincoln College, Oxford, to read a Diploma in Public Administration. Makwaia was then appointed to the Tanganyika Executive Council, and to the Central Legislative Assembly of East Africa. He resigned as chief of Usiha in 1954, and took up a post in the Social Welfare Department in Dar es Salaam. A convert from Islam to Roman Catholicism and married to a woman of mixed race, Makwaia was viewed with such esteem by the British that he was invited to the coronation of Queen Elizabeth, who awarded him an OBE two years later. Makwaia is said to have facilitated Nyerere's political rise by winning him British support as well as by securing the allegiance of Sukuma chiefs to TANU. At independence Nyerere abolished the role of chiefs, and temporarily banished Makwaia to a remote outpost. He then left politics, and died in 2007.

Mang'enya, E.
Born in 1915, Erasto Mang'enya authored the autobiographical *Discipline and Tears*, one of the few written accounts recorded by a Tanzanian of events in the United Kingdom and Tanganyika during a time that runs roughly parallel to Nyerere's own travels in both these countries. Mang'enya went on to become Speaker of the National Assembly.

Select Biographies, Bibliography & Sources

Marwa, O.M.
A Zanaki and schoolmate of Nyerere's from Mwisenge, after school Oswald Mang'ombe Marwa joined South Mara District Council (Musoma) and, following independence, became the first District Commissioner of South Mara District Council. Marwa was best man at Nyerere's wedding, and his wife Bona Anicet Musoga was bridesmaid. He died in 1970.

Masubugu, M.
Chief Nyerere Burito's first wife, Magori automatically became the senior wife of the twenty-two.

Maswanya, S.A.
A Nyamwezi from near Tabora, Said Ali Maswanya was an active member of Tabora Boys' English Debating Society. He joined TAA in 1952, and later became Provincial TANU Secretary in Tabora. Said Maswanya served in multiple ministries.

Matovu, J.B.
A teacher at Dar es Salaam Central School, Matovu was awarded a CDWS scholarship to study a Teaching Course at the Colonial Department of the Institute of Education, University of London. He was close to finishing his degree when in 1952 Nyerere sought the names of 'all the Tanganyika (African) Students in Britain'.

Msuguri, D.
Age-mate of Nyerere, General David Msuguri entered the military in 1942, served with the King's African Rifles in Madagascar and rose through the ranks in the Tanzanian army. He reached Chief of Defence Force in 1980, a position he held until 1988. He still lives near Butiama.

Munanka, B.I.M.
A Kuria from near Singida, Bhoke Isaac Muller Munanka completed a two-year clerical course at Tabora Boys. In 1950 he drafted the memorandum that TAA Mwanza branch submitted to the Constitutional Committee demanding that government should prepare Africans for independence. He resigned his government post in 1952 to devote more time to politics, was later voted president of the TAA, and after independence was appointed Minister of State in the President's Office. Steadfastly loyal to Nyerere, during the 1964 mutiny he refused at gunpoint to disclose the President's whereabouts. Munanka became Personal Assistant to Nyerere. He died in 2008.

Select Biographies, Bibliography & Sources

Mustafa, S.
Born to Kashmiri parents in India in 1922, Sophia Mustafa was raised and educated in Nairobi. She moved with her husband to Tanganyika, and became the first elected non-white female legislator in Africa. Refusing to join the Asian Association because it was run on racial lines, she was nominated as a Member of Parliament in 1963, and served TANU until she retired from politics in 1965. She passed away in 2005.

Mwapachu, H.K.B.
Hamza Kibwana Bakari Mwapachu was born in 1913 and studied at the Sewa Haji teaching hospital in Dar es Salaam. There he stayed with Aziz Ali and was introduced to political activists such as Kleist Sykes and his family, Thomas Plantan and Dossa Aziz. He graduated as a Medical Assistant and practised briefly before undergoing further training in Mwanza, where he met Juliana Volter, a half Polish/German, half Sukuma woman whom he married in 1937. He read Medicine at Makerere College, where he met Nyerere and Andrew Tibandebage and helped establish a student welfare association that became the roots of an African Association branch. Mwapachu was posted to the Government Hospital in Tabora, where he became President of the African Association. He studied Social Work at the University College of South Wales, and on his return to Tanganyika was posted (read exiled) to Ukerewe Island, where he continued meetings with the likes of Abdulwahid Sykes, Ali, Mwinyi Tambwe and Paul Bomani. Mwapachu is said to have informed Sykes and Aziz that Nyerere was the right man to lead TAA and the struggle for independence. He died in 1962.

Nyamwaga, J.
Son of the driver to Chief Nyerere Burito (hence 'Jack'), Nyamwaga studied at Tabora Boys and taught at Musoma Alliance Secondary. He went on to become Assistant Secretary at the TANU Youth League headquarters, and later held the post of Butiama *ujamaa* village secretary. He reached CCM Assistant Secretary in the Musoma Regional Office before his retirement in 1988. Born in 1937, Jack Nyamwaga continues to act as a local historian in Butiama.

Nyerere, E.W.
Chief Edward Nyerere Wanzagi was born in 1910, attended the Native Administration School, Musoma in 1924 and earned a place at Mpwapwa Teacher Training College, but his father Chief Nyerere Burito instead posted him as a clerk for Chief Utagirga, the chief of Nata. Wanzagi succeeded his father as chief of Butiama, and is recorded as having organised a co-operative shop in the chiefdom. He later became

chief of the Zanaki, and was hugely supportive of efforts to educate the young. At his funeral in 1997 his half-brother Julius acknowledged that Wanzagi was responsible for him attending school.

Nyerere, J.K.B.
Joseph Kizurira Burito Nyerere studied at St Mary's, and was at St Francis, Pugu, when his half-brother Julius taught there. A leader of the TANU Youth League with Rashid Kawawa and Lawi Sijaona, Kizurira went on to become Regional Commissioner of Mwanza. Some of his knowledge of Zanaki traditional political organisation is recorded in Mustafa's (1975) 'Concept of Authority and the Study of African Colonial History'.

Nyerere, J.M.
Born in 1928, Joseph Muhunda Nyerere accompanied his half-brother to Tabora when Julius Nyerere taught at St Mary's. He returned to Butiama with the unhappy young Magori Watiha.

Omari, D.A.
Dunstan Alfred Omari was born in 1922, and attended Makerere and then the University of Aberystwyth to read a Diploma in Education. In 1959 he was the first African to be appointed as a District Officer, and as a District Commissioner in Tanganyika (1958–61). At independence he was appointed as the first Tanganyika High Commissioner in London (1961–62), he then became Permanent Secretary in Nyerere's office, and was later Secretary-General of the East African Community. In 1972 Omari became a naturalised Kenyan. He died in 1993.

Ramadhani, M.D.
Born in Zanzibar in 1915, Mathew Douglas Ramadhani was educated at St Paul's, Kiungani and St Andrew's College, Minaki, followed by Makerere. He attended the London Institute of Education on a CWDS scholarship, obtained a Teachers' Professional Certificate in 1948 and then in 1951 a B.A. (Econ) from the University of Sheffield – making him the first African Tanganyikan/Zanzibari to receive a UK degree. Ramadhani returned to Tanganyika and served in education. During yet further study in the UK he died in a train accident at Guidebridge Station, Ashton-under-Lyne in 1961. He is buried in Manchester.

Rutabanzibwa, G.M.
Born in Bukoba in 1921, Gosbert Miarcell Rutabanzibwa attended Catholic mission schools, then proceeded to Tabora Boys where he was in the same class as Nyerere, and then studied Botany at Makerere. He joined the Bukoba Co-operative Union and travelled to the United

Select Biographies, Bibliography & Sources

Kingdom where he attended the Co-operative College in Nottinghamshire. Rutabanzibwa became the Bukoba Co-operative Union marketing manager, before being co-opted by Nyerere to help organise the transition of power from the British. At independence he was appointed Head of Protocol in the Foreign Ministry, and later headed several foreign missions. He died in 1997.

Sawe, J.A.
Born in Nronga, Machame in 1921, Joseph Adolf Sawe met Nyerere while studying at Tabora Boys. He went on to Makerere College, and then enrolled for a B.A. in Geography at Aberystwyth University when Nyerere was in the United Kingdom. Sawe taught at Mpwapwa Teacher Training College and Tabora Boys, where his students included Jack Nyamwaga, Joseph Butiku and Theophilus Mlaki. In 1968 he was appointed to create the Joint Inspection Unit of United Nations, which reports to General Assembly, and served the body until 1982. He died in 2003.

Shepperson, G.
Born in the same year as Julius Nyerere, Professor George 'Sam' Shepperson served during the Second World War with the King's African Rifles in both Kenya and Tanganyika. In 1948 he was appointed as a Lecturer at the University of Edinburgh, where he became friends with Nyerere (although he never formally taught him). He was awarded a CBE for his contribution to the Commonwealth, and lives in Peterborough, England.

Stanley, J.S.
Born in Ireland in 1910, Father John Sydney Stanley was headmaster at St Mary's, Tabora from 1944 until 1949. He wrote a strong reference for Nyerere's application for a Scholarship to study in the United Kingdom. He died in 1962.

Tibandebage, A.K.
Andrew Kajungu Tibandebage was born at Kasheshe village in Kagera Region in 1922. In 1939 he went to St Mary's Tabora, and then on to Makerere College where he first met Nyerere and was integral in the formation of the African Association branch. Upon graduation with a Diploma in Education Tibandebage returned to St Mary's, shortly before Nyerere did so. He later joined London University College as a Tutorial Assistant for two years. At independence Nyerere appointed Tibandebage an ambassador, and he was posted to various countries, including the United Kingdom. He died in 2011.

Select Biographies, Bibliography & Sources

Tumbo, C.K.
A Tanganyika Railway Workers' Union leader and TANU activist, Christopher Kasanga Tumbo's strong support for Africanisation unsettled Nyerere and other party moderates. Realising his appointment as High Commissioner to London was a form of political exile, he quickly resigned, left TANU and announced his leadership of the People's Democratic Party. Tumbo continued to take a racialist stance and was effectively rusticated to his village near Tabora. He returned to the political scene in 1992 and registered the Union for Multi-Party Democracy (UMD). Tumbo fell out with Chief Abdullah Fundikira, the UMD Chairman, and returned to the ruling party shortly before his death.

Twining, E.F.
Sir Edward Francis was Governor of North Borneo (1946–49) and Governor of Tanganyika (1949–58). The highly decorated diplomat and former army officer was a member of the Twining tea family.

Walsh, R.M.
Born in Kerry, Ireland in 1910, Father Richard Mortimer Walsh studied Philosophy in Belgium, made his novitiate at Maison Carrée, and completed his studies at Carthage, where he was ordained in 1937. He was appointed to Tabora Diocese and taught at St Mary's. He became headmaster in 1944 and at the same time Education Secretary for the Diocese, and took Nyerere on his staff. Nyerere remained in touch with Walsh while he was in Edinburgh, and Walsh discouraged Nyerere from joining the priesthood but instead encouraged his political ambitions. Nyerere stayed at the White Fathers' House in Dar es Salaam many times when Father Walsh was there, but the two were in less proximity from 1957 to 1967, when Walsh was a General Assistant in Rome. Walsh later returned to Tanzania where he was briefly parish priest of Oyster Bay, Dar es Salaam, and Nyerere then made him Chaplain to the University of Dar es Salaam. Nyerere visited Walsh's grave after his death in Ireland in 1979. Andrew Tibandebage named his son Richard after the Irishman.

Watiha, M.
Chief Nyerere Burito married Magori Watiha to his son Kambarage at a very young age, but she recalls little of the brief union, which was formally annulled when Nyerere became engaged to his fiancée Maria Waningu Gabriel Magige. Magori later remarried, and attended Nyerere's burial in Butiama. She still lives in Butiama.

Wicken, J.
Born in London in 1925, Joan Wicken enrolled at Ruskin after the war, taking a degree in Philosophy, Politics and Economics at Somerville

Select Biographies, Bibliography & Sources

College, Oxford. Wicken first met Nyerere in 1956 when he visited the Labour Party headquarters, and she helped him meet Labour Party leaders, to visit local constituency party meetings, and to learn about the organisation of the party. She first visited Tanganyika in 1957 to set up the Tanganyika Education Fund, the main task of which was to found Kivukoni College. Wicken served as Nyerere's personal assistant from 1960 until 1994. She died in 2004.

Wille, A.
Born in St Louis, Missouri in 1925, Father Arthur Wille attended Moreland Notre Dame Academy. He passed through the Maryknoll education process, after which he was ordained a priest at Maryknoll Seminary, New York, and was then assigned to the Maryknoll Mission in the Prefecture of Musoma, where he was to assist in building the Komuge Mission among the Sumbiti. Wille was then assigned to open a new mission among the Zanaki, and in 1955 first met Nyerere, who taught him the Zanaki language. He remained in the Musoma area for many years, later serving as Vicar General of the Diocese of Musoma. He lives in the United States.

Wilson, J.W.
Jean Wilson acted *in loco parentis* to Nyerere during his time in Edinburgh. Nyerere was friendly with her son Walter, and both were invited to stay in his official residence during the independence celebrations in Dar es Salaam. Mrs Jean Wilson was also invited to the Republic celebrations in 1962. Nyerere personally visited Jean Wilson at her home in Edinburgh in 1986, the year before she died.

Sources

Individual papers and files, newspaper articles, unpublished manuscripts, typescripts, and non-interview personal communication ('pers.comm.') are given in the appropriate note references.

Primary sources
Archives de la Société des Missionnaires d'Afrique (Pères Blancs), Rome. ('ASMA'.)
Edinburgh Fabian Society minutes, National Library of Scotland, Edinburgh. ('EFS'.)
Hans Cory papers, East Africana section, University of Dar es Salaam library. ('CORY'.)
Fabian Colonial Bureau papers, Bodleian Library of Commonwealth & African Studies at Rhodes House, Oxford. ('FCB'.)

Select Biographies, Bibliography & Sources

Lincoln College archives, University of Oxford.
Ramadhani Kilongola papers, Mwalimu Nyerere Foundation, Dar es Salaam. ('Kilongola'.)
Colonial Office files, National Archives, Kew, London. ('NACO'.)
Shepperson Collection, Special Collections, Edinburgh University Main Library, Edinburgh. ('Shepp.Coln.'.)
Tanzania National Archives, Dar es Salaam. ('TNA'.)

Author's personal collection
Cattanach, W.D. November 2000. Personal letter to author.
Kyaruzi, V.K. n.d. 'A Muhaya Doctor: First Tanzania Ambassador United Nations'. Bukoba. Extracts from unpublished typescript obtained from Juma Mwapachu.
MacKenzie, K. in 'Portraits of Our Time', 'No.2: Julius Nyerere', a BBC broadcast on 12 July 1964. Transcript of broadcast.
Shepperson in 'Portraits of Our Time', 'No.2: Julius Nyerere', a BBC broadcast on 12 July 1964. Transcript of broadcast, p.2. Facsimile in author's possession.
Shepperson, G. 4 November 2000. Personal letter to author.
Tibandebage, A. 1996. 'The Life of a Near-Failure'. Karagwe. Extracts from unpublished typescript held by the Richard Tibandebage.
Wicken, J. 14 March 2001. Personal letter to author.

Written communication
Alexander, Peter. 4 and 6 March 2012, and 7 March 2014.
Aucoin, Fr. Pierre. 24 October 2011.
Billingsley, Maurice. 3 November 2011.
Brokensha, David. 15 March 2012.
Clark, Norman. 21 August 2011.
Finn, Peter. 31 October 2011.
Killingray, David. 18 June 2012.
Koren, Shem. 10, 12 and 17 March 2014.
McCracken, John. 25 April 2012.
Meyers, Lauren. Woodson Research Center, Fondren Library, Rice University. 15 and 22 February 2012.
Moore, Sally F. 28 and 29 March 2012.
Mustafa, Fawzia. 11 August 2012.
Mustafa, Kemal. 12 August 2012.
Mwapachu, Juma. 2 September 2011, and multiple January and February 2012.
Owens, Geoffrey. 7 August 2012 and 10 May 2013.
Palmer, Geoffrey. 29 May 2012.
Sanders, Ethan. 18 July 2013.
Saul, John. 3 August 2012.

Select Biographies, Bibliography & Sources

Shorter, Aylward. 30 November 2011.
Tibandebage, Richard. 22 January 2012 and 1 February 2012.

Other personal communication
Barron, Tom. 13 September 2012, Edinburgh. Discussion.
Dudley Edwards, Owen. 31 August 2012, Edinburgh. Discussion.
Flavin, Nicholas. 3 September 2012, Edinburgh. Discussion.
Iliffe, John. 22 August 2012, Oxford. Discussion.
Nyerere, Magige. 20 May 2010, Mwitongo, Butiama. Discussion.
Nyerere, Makongoro. 1 July 2011, Mwitongo, Butiama. Discussion.

Interviews
A series of interviews were conducted with key informants. All but one (with George Shepperson) took place in Tanzania. Interviews were semi-structured, and some subsequent meetings were even less formal, often taking the form of casual discussions, either covering a small number of follow-up questions or simply as unplanned conversations on the subject. The meetings were either in English or Swahili or, on occasions, a mixture of both, especially when questions asked in Swahili would be answered in English or vice versa. Interviewees sometimes replied in Zanaki, at which point I relied even more than normal on the considerable skills of Mwalimu Jack Nyamwaga.

Daily discussions took place throughout July 2011 with Madaraka Nyerere and, occasionally, with Mama Maria Nyerere and Rose Nyerere. More pointed discussions in Mwitongo, Butiama, took place with Mwalimu Jack Nyamwaga throughout the same month in 2011, 2012 and 2013. To save space, the exact dates for specific comments are not given in the interview references. These are available on request from the author.

Ihunyo, Marwa. 29 July 2011, Busegwe (with assistance from Jack Nyamwaga).
Irenge, James. 21 May 2010, Mwisenge, Musoma (with assistance from Madaraka Nyerere).
Keto, John Ernest. 24 and 25 May 2010, Korogwe.
Marwa, Adam. 29 June 2011 and 29 June 2012, Msasani, Dar es Salaam.
Msuguri, David. 27 July 2011, Butiama (with assistance from Jack Nyamwaga and Madaraka Nyerere).
Mwambenja, Rehema. 11 July 2012, Ilala, Dar es Salaam.
Nyambeho, John. 29 July 2011, Kiyabakari (with assistance from Jack Nyamwaga).
Nyambereka, Wakirya Sondobi. 20 May 2010, 14 July 2011 and 8 July 2012, Butiama.

Select Biographies, Bibliography & Sources

Photo P. Jack Nyamwaga and Jackton Nyambereka Nyerere, Butiama, July 2011. Nyambereka is holding hand-written family records of significant events, including births and deaths, passed down through the generations. (*Photograph by author*)

Nyamwaga, Jack. 20 May 2010, Mwitongo.
Nyerere, Jackton Nyambereka. 20 May 2010, 14 July 2011 and 8 July 2012, Butiama.
Nyerere, Joseph Muhunda. 20 May 2010, 10 and 17 July 2011, Mwitongo.
Nyerere, Maria Waningu Gabriel Magige. 17 May 2010, Msasani, Dar es Salaam and 3 August 2011, Mwitongo (with assistance from Rose Nyerere).
Nyerere, Rosemary Victoria Octavia. 28 June 2011, Upanga, Dar es Salaam.
Rutabanzibwa, Patrick. 6 August 2011, Oyster Bay, Dar es Salaam.
Sawe, David. 28 June 2011, Upanga, Dar es Salaam.
Sawe, Dinah. 6 August 2011, Upanga, Dar es Salaam.
Shepperson, George. 2 November 2000 and 22 August 2012, Peterborough, United Kingdom.
Tibandebage, Richard. 26 June 2012, Ilala, Dar es Salaam.
Warioba, Elias Nyang'ombe. 20 May 2010, Muryaza; and by Madaraka Nyerere, 20 August 2012, Muryaza.
Warioba, Fanis Makonjio Nyang'ombe, by Madaraka Nyerere, 20 August 2012, Muryaza.
Watiha, Magori. 21 May 2010, Butiama (with assistance from Madaraka Nyerere, and Zanaki translation by Magembe Nyambereka Nyerere).

221

Bibliography of select secondary sources

Space limitations prevent the full listing here of all secondary sources, which exceed 550 and are already given in the appropriate notes. The following are key texts.

Bischofberger, O. *The Generation Classes of the Zanaki (Tanzania)*. Fribourg: University Press, 1972.

Bjerk, P. 'Julius Nyerere and the Establishment of Sovereignty in Tanganyika'. Unpublished Ph.D. thesis, University of Wisconsin-Madison, Madison, 2008.

Bosanquet, B. *The Philosophical Theory of the State*. South Bend, IN: St Augustine's Press, 2001 (1899).

Brennan, J.R. *Taifa: Making nation and race in urban Tanzania*. Athens, OH: Ohio University Press, 2012.

Brennan, J.R. 'Julius Rex: Nyerere through the eyes of his critics, 1953–2013'. Paper presented at the Centre of African Studies seminar series, University of Edinburgh, 27 February 2013.

Carey, A.T. *Colonial Students: A study of the social adaptation of colonial students in London*. London: Secker & Warburg, 1956.

Costello, J.E. *John Macmurray: A biography*. Edinburgh: Floris, 2002.

Edinburgh University. *Edinburgh University Calendar: 1949–1950*. Edinburgh: James Thin (and subsequent publications of the same from 1950 to 1963), 1949.

Fei, H.-T. *Peasant Life in China: A field study of country life in the Yangtze Valley*. London: Kegan Paul, Trench, Trubner & Co., 1939.

Feinstein, A. *African Revolutionary: The life and times of Nigeria's Aminu Kano*. Boulder, CA: Lynne Rienner, 1987.

Fortes, M. and E.E. Evans-Pritchard (eds). *African Political Systems*. London: Oxford University Press, 1940.

Geiger, S. 'Engendering and Gendering African Nationalism: Rethinking the case of Tanganyika (Tanzania)'. In *In Search of a Nation: Histories of authority and dissidence in Tanzania*, ed. Maddox, G, Giblin, J, Oxford, Dar es Salaam, Athens Ohio: James Currey, Kapsel, Ohio University Press, 2005, pp.278–89.

Graham, J.M., Piddington, R. *Anthropology and the Future of Missions*. Aberdeen: The University Press, 1940.

Green, T.H. *Lectures on the Principles of Political Obligation*. London: Longman, Green and Co., 1948 (1895).

Hatch, J. *Two African Statesmen: Kaunda of Zambia and Nyerere of Tanzania*. London: Secker and Warburg, 1976.

Iliffe, J., ed. *Modern Tanzanians: A volume of biographies*. Nairobi: East African Publishing House (for the Historical Association of Tanzania), 1973.

Iliffe, J. *A Modern History of Tanganyika*. Cambridge: Cambridge University Press, 1979.

Laski, H.J. *A Grammar of Politics*. London: George Allen & Unwin, 1950 (1925).

Listowel, J. *The Making of Tanganyika*. London: Chatto and Windus, 1965.

Lohrmann, U. *Voices from Tanganyika: Great Britain, the United Nations and the decolonization of a Trust Territory, 1946–1961*. Münster: LIT Verlag, 2007.

Mill, J.S. 'On Liberty'. In *Utilitarianism, Liberty, Representative Government*, pp.63–170. London: Dent, 1972 (1859).

Mill, J.S. 'Representative Government'. In *Utilitarianism, Liberty, Representative Government*, pp.175–393. London: Dent, 1972 (1861).

Mills, D. 'Life on the Hill: Students and the social history of Makerere'. *Africa*, 76 (2) 2006, pp.247–66.

Mkirya, B. *Historia, Mila na Desturi za Wazanaki*. Peramiho: Benedictine Publications Ndanda, 1991.

Mustafa, K. 'The Concept of Authority and the Study of African Colonial History'. *Kenya Historical Review: The journal of the Historical Association of Kenya*, 3 (1) 1975, pp.55–83.

Mwakikagile, G. *Nyerere and Africa: End of an era*. Pretoria and Dar es Salaam: New Africa Press, 2010.

Nyerere, J.K. 'Attitude to Africa book review from Tanganyika'. *Venture: Journal of the Fabian Colonial Bureau*, 3 (11) 1951, pp.6–7.

Nyerere, J.K. 'The Entrenchment of Privilege'. *Africa South*, 2 (2), 1958, pp.85–90.

Nyerere, J.K. 'Africa's Place in the World'. In *Symposium on Africa*, ed. Barnette Miller Foundation, pp.148–63. Wellesley, MA: Wellesley College, 1960.

Nyerere, J.K. 'Tanganyika Today: II. The Nationalist View'. *International Affairs*, 36 (1) 1960, pp.43–7.

Nyerere, J.K. 'One Party Government'. *Transition* (2) 1961, pp.9–11.

Nyerere, J.K. 'The Challenge of Independence'. *East Africa and Rhodesia*, 38, 1961 (1939), pp.339–40.

Nyerere, J.K. 'Democracy and the Party System'. Dar es Salaam: Tanganyika Standard Limited, 1963.

Nyerere, J.K. *Freedom and Unity: Uhuru na Umoja. A Selection from Writing and Speeches, 1952–65*. Dar es Salaam: Oxford University Press, 1966.

Nyerere, J.K. *Freedom and Socialism: Uhuru na Ujamaa. A Selection from Writing and Speeches, 1965–67*. Dar es Salaam: Oxford University Press, 1968. Nyerere, J.K. 'A Call to European Socialists'. *Third World*, 1 (3) 1973, pp.5–7.

Nyerere, J.K. *Freedom and Development: Uhuru na Maendeleo. A Selection from Writing and Speeches, 1968–1973*. Dar es Salaam: Oxford University Press, 1973.

Nyerere, J.K. 'The Rational Choice' (speech). Dar es Salaam: United Republic of Tanzania, 1973.

Select Biographies, Bibliography & Sources

Nyerere, J.K. 'Reflections on Constitutions and African Experience'. In *Constitutions and National Identity*, ed. Barron, T., Dudley Edwards, O., Storey, P.J., pp.8–19. Edinburgh: Quadriga, 1993 (1987).

Nyerere, J.K. 'Africa: The Third Liberation'. Occasional Paper 70, Centre of African Studies, University of Edinburgh, Edinburgh, 1997.

Nyerere, J.K. *Uhuru wa Wanawake*. Dar es Salaam: Mwalimu Nyerere Foundation, 2009 (1944).

Nyerere, J.K., Keto, J. 'Central African Federation'. *The Student*, 1951–52, 48 (7), pp.278–80, 1951.

Piddington, R. *An Introduction to Social Anthropology*. Volume 1. Edinburgh: Oliver and Boyd, 1950.

Pratt, C.R. *The Critical Phase in Tanzania, 1945–1968: Nyerere and the emergence of a socialist strategy*. Nairobi: Oxford University Press, 1978.

Rousseau, J.J. 'The Social Contract'. In *The Social Contract and Discourses*, pp.1–116. London: Dent, 1947 (1762).

Sanders, E.R. 'The African Association and the Growth and Movement of Political Thought in Mid-Twentieth Century East Africa'. Unpublished Ph.D. thesis. University of Cambridge, Cambridge, 2012.

Shetler, J.B. *Telling Our Own Stories: Local histories from South Mara, Tanzania*. Dar es Salaam: Mkuki na Nyota, 2003.

Shetler, J.B. *Imagining Serengeti: A history of landscape memory in Tanzania from earliest times to the present*. Athens, OH: Ohio University Press, 2007.

Smith, W.E. *Nyerere of Tanzania*. London: Victor Gollancz, 1973.

Stöger-Eising, V. '"Ujamaa" Revisited: Indigenous and European influences in Nyerere's social and political thought'. *Africa*, 30 (1) 2000, pp.118–43.

Vaillant, J.G. *Black, French, and African: A life of Léopold Sédar Senghor*. Cambridge, MA: Harvard University Press, 1990.

Notes

Introduction
1. *The Nationalist* (Dar es Salaam). 5 September 1967; cited in Saul, J. 'Tanzania Fifty Years On (1961–2011): Rethinking *ujamaa*, Nyerere and socialism in Africa', *Review of African Political Economy*, 39 (131) 2012, pp.117–25, p.119.
2. For a discussion of 'anthropologist as hagiographer', ghost-writer and biographer, see Zeitlyn, D. 'Life-History Writing and the Anthropological Silhouette', *Social Anthropology*, 16 (2) 2008, pp.157–8.
3. Durand, P. 'Is a Catholic Saint Concealed Within the Ranks of African Head of States? A positive answer from Tanzania as the beatification process of Servant of God Julius Nyerere has opened!' 2009. www.africamission-mafr.org/Julius_Nyerere_gb.pdf, 24 February 2014. See also Wille, A. 'From President to Saint?' *Mission Today*, London: Association for the Propagation of the Faith, 2007, pp.4–5; Fouéré, M.-A. 'La Fabrique d'un Saint en Tanzanie Post-Socialiste: Essai d'analyse sur l'église, l'état et le premier président Julius Nyerere', *Les Cahiers d'Afrique de l'Est*, Institut Français de Recherche en Afrique, Nairobi, 2008; Mesaki, S., Malipula, M. 'Julius Nyerere's Influence and Legacy: From a proponent of familyhood to a candidate for sainthood', *International Journal of Sociology and Anthropology*, 3 (3) 2011, pp.93–100.
4. Denoon, D., Kuper, A. 'Nationalist Historians in Search of a Nation: The 'New Historiography' in Dar es Salaam', *African Affairs*, 69 (277), pp.329–49, 1970, p.348.
5. Iliffe, J. *A Modern History of Tanganyika*, Cambridge: Cambridge University Press, 1979, p.508, note 4.
6. Kyaruzi, V.K. 'A Muhaya Doctor: First Tanzania Ambassador United Nations'. Bukoba: Extracts of unpublished manuscript of Vedastus Kyaruzi's memoirs, n.d., p.1. For biographies of less well-known actors in the development of nationalism in African countries see, for example, Ranger, T. *Are We Not Also Men? The Samkange family and African politics in Zimbabwe, 1920–64*, London: James Currey, 1995; Macola, G. *Liberal Nationalism in Central Africa: A biography of Harry Mwaanga Nkumbula*, Basingstoke and New York: Palgrave Macmillan, 2010. For earlier biographies of Tanzanian nationalists see Mutahaba, G.R. *Portrait of a Nationalist: The life of Ali Migeyo*, Nairobi: East African Publishing House, 1969; Frederick, 'Joseph Kimalando', pp.21–8, and the compilation of biographies on the likes of Kleist Sykes, Ali Ponda and Hassan Suleiman in Iliffe, J., ed. *Modern Tanzanians: A volume of biographies*, Nairobi: East African Publishing House (for the Historical Association of Tanzania), 1973. Anonymised biographical data covering the background and attitudes of a section of Tanzania's elite in the late 1960s is given in Hopkins, R.F. *Political Roles in a New State: Tanzania's first decade*, New Haven, CT and London: Yale University Press, 1971, p.64–107. For 'ordinary' life histories see Bozzoli, B., Nkotsoe, M. *Women of Phokeng: Consciousness, life strategy, and migrancy in South Africa, 1900–1983*, Portsmouth, NH: Heinemann, 1991. Also van Onselen, C. *The Seed is Mine: The life of Kas Maine, a South African sharecropper, 1894–1985*, Cape Town: David Philip, 1996. Lives less ordinary, but falling broadly into this period and genre, are those of Chief Birifu Naa Gandah I and his son S.W.D.K. Gandah, author of *The Silent Rebel*,

Notes for Introduction, pp. 1–9

      Legon-Accra, Ghana: Sub-Saharan Publishers, 2004, about his father's life. On the former, see Gandah, S.W.D.K. (submitted by Lentz, C). 'Gandah-Yir: The House of the Brave: The biography of a northern Ghanaian chief (ca. 1872–1950)', *Africa*, 82 (3) 2012, pp.356–67. For the latter see Lentz, C. 'S.W.D.K. Gandah (1927–2001): Intellectual and historian from northern Ghana', *Africa*, 82 (3) 2012, pp.343–55.
7. Smith, D.J. *Young Mandela*, London: Weidenfeld & Nicolson, 2010; Benson, M. *Nelson Mandela: The man and the movement*, Harmondsworth: Penguin, 1994; Meer, F. *Higher Than Hope: The authorized biography of Nelson Mandela*, New York: Harper, 1990; Meredith, M. *Nelson Mandela: A biography*, New York: St Martin's Press, 1998.
8. Sherwood, M. *Kwame Nkrumah: The years abroad, 1935–1947*, Accra: Freedom, 1996; Birmingham, D. *Kwame Nkrumah: The father of African nationalism*, Athens, OH: Ohio University Press, 1998; Davidson, B. *Black Star: A view of the life and times of Kwame Nkrumah*, Oxford: James Currey, 2007 (1973); James, C.L.R. *Nkrumah and the Ghana Revolution*, London: Allison & Busby 1977.
9. Murray-Brown, J. *Kenyatta*, London: George Allen & Unwin, 1972. Also Arnold, G. 1974. *Kenyatta and the Politics of Kenya*, London: Dent; Lonsdale, J. 'Kenyatta's Trials: Making and breaking an African nationalist', in *The Moral World of the Law*, ed. Coss, P. Cambridge: Cambridge University Press, 2000, pp.196–239; Lonsdale, J. 'Jomo Kenyatta, God, and the Modern World', in *African Modernities: Entangled meanings in current debate*, ed. Deutsch, J-G, Probst, P. et al., Oxford: James Currey, 2002, pp.31–66.
10. Interview, John Keto.
11. Smith, *Young Mandela*, p.1.
12. For recent examples see *The Citizen* (Tanzania), 19 October 2013, 'Citizens recall the good old Nyerere days' and 'Nyerere: Bribery enemy of justice'. pp.2, 13.
13. Gevisser, M. 19 June 2010. Book review: '*Young Mandela* by David James Smith'. *The Guardian Review* (London), p.7.
14. Iliffe, J. *Obasanjo, Nigeria and the World*, Oxford: James Currey, 2011, p.ix.
15. Esperanza Brizuela-Garcia considers the accounts of the lives of Ofori Atta, Thompson Samkange and Kas Maine to have reached this objective, adding that none of the biographies he reviews fall neatly into the categories of 'pure', 'literary' or 'analytical' biography as classified in Oates, S.B. (ed.), *Biography as High Adventure*, Amherst, MA: University of Massachusetts Press, 1986. Brizuela-Garcia, E. 'The Past Never Stays Behind: Biographical narrative and African colonial history', *Journal of Historical Biography*, Autumn (2) 2007, pp.63–83, p.64–6.
16. Brizuela-Garcia, 'The Past', p.64–5.
17. Macola, *Liberal*, p.1.
18. Kyaruzi, 'Muhaya', p.42. This period, and up until the aftermath of *ujamaa*, is covered in James Giblin's chronology of the life course of men and women in and around Njombe District. Giblin, J. *A History of the Excluded: Making family a refuge from state in twentieth-century Tanzania*, Oxford: James Currey, 2005.
19. Iliffe, *Modern Tanzanians*.
20. ibid., p.iv.
21. Geiger, S. 'Tanganyikan Nationalism as 'Women's Work': Life histories, collective biography and changing historiography', *Journal of African History*, 37 (3) 1996, pp.465–78; Geiger, S. *TANU Women: Gender and culture in the making of Tanganyikan nationalism, 1955–1965*, Portsmouth, NH and Dar es Salaam: Heinemann and Mkuki na Nyota, 1997. But see also Mustafa, S. *The Tanganyika Way: A personal story of Tanganyika's growth to independence*, London: Oxford University Press, 1962.
22. Said, M. *The Life and Times of Abdulwahid Sykes (1924–1968): The untold story of the Muslim struggle against British colonialism in Tanganyika*, London: Minerva, 1998; Hajivayanis, G.G., Mtowa, A.C., Iliffe, J. 'The Politicians: Ali Ponda and Hassan Suleiman', in Iliffe, *Modern Tanzanians*, 1973, p.228; Mutahaba, *Portrait*. Susan Geiger's focus on women in the nationalist movement largely covers Muslim women. See, for example, Geiger's 'Women in Nationalist Struggle: TANU activists in Dar es Salaam, *International Journal of African Historical Studies*, 20 (1), 1987, pp.1–26; Tanganyikan', pp.465–78; *TANU*

Women: Gender and culture; 'Engendering and Gendering African Nationalism: Rethinking the case of Tanganyika (Tanzania)', in *In Search of a Nation: Histories of authority & dissidence in Tanzania*, ed. Maddox, G, Giblin, J, pp.278–89, Oxford, Dar es Salaam, Athens, OH: James Currey, Kapsel, Ohio University Press, 2005.
23. Wicken to Molony, 14 March 2001, p.3. Unless stated otherwise, all correspondence in notes is by letter.
24. See Listowel, J. *The Making of Tanganyika*, London: Chatto and Windus, 1965, p.426.
25. Listowel spells his name 'Kamberage' (*Making*, p.170), and claims Chief Burito Nyerere was buried in Muhunda (p.173). Burito Mazembe was buried in Masaba, but under the orders of Chief Burito Nyerere, his corpse was later exhumed and reburied, it is thought, 'somewhere in the vicinity of Mwitongo'. Interview, Nyamwaga. Chief Burito Nyerere is buried in Mwitongo. The biography by Shirley Graham (Du Bois) is equally suspect: Graham, S. *Julius K. Nyerere: Teacher of Africa*, New York: Julian Messner, 1975. Written in places as if informed by Nyerere, it lacks reference to any sources and is essentially a storybook without the illustrations.
26. See Brennan, J. 'Julius Rex: Nyerere through the eyes of his critics, 1953–2013', paper presented at the Centre of African Studies seminar series, University of Edinburgh, 27 February 2013, pp.11–12.
27. See Brennan, 'Julius Rex', who notes Listowel's later cooling towards Nyerere.
28. Iliffe, *Modern History*, p.508, note 4; Iliffe, J. Review of *The Making of Tanganyika* by Judith Listowel, *Journal of Modern African Studies*, 4 (2) 1966, pp.270–2.
29. Iliffe, *Modern History*, p.508, note 4.
30. Wicken to Molony, 14 March 2001, p.3.
31. Kirkpatrick, E.G. *John Macmurray: Community beyond political philosophy*, Oxford: Rowman & Littlefield, 2005, pp.157–8 and http://johnmacmurray.org/further-reading/discovering-john-macmurray, accessed on 5 February 2014.
32. Nyerere, J.K. Opening speech at the International Congress of African Historians, University of Dar es Salaam, October 1965; cited in Ranger, T.O., ed. *Emerging Themes of African History*, Proceedings of the International Congress of African Historians, Dar es Salaam, October 1965, Nairobi: East African Publishing House, 1968, p.3.
33. Joan Wicken to Rex Collings, 29 June 1964, Shepperson Collection (hereafter 'Shep.Coln.'), Special Collections, Edinburgh University Library (EUL), CLX-A-16/1. Unless stated otherwise, all EUL are held in Special Collections.
34. Joan Wicken to Rex Collings, 17 May 1965, CLX-A-16/1, Shep.Coln. Nyerere is said to have agreed shortly before he passed away for Haroub Othman to prepare a proposal to write his biography. Yahya-Othman, S., ed. *Yes, in My Lifetime: Selected works by Haroub Othman*. Dar es Salaam: Mkuki na Nyota, 2014, p.7. See also 'Death Puts Nyerere Biography in Limbo', allafrica.com/stories/199910260101.html, accessed on 3 June 2013.
35. Smith, D.R. *The Influence of the Fabian Colonial Bureau on the Independence Movement in Tanganyika*, Athens, OH: Ohio University Center for International Studies, 1985, p.47.
36. Hatch, J. *Two African Statesmen: Kaunda of Zambia and Nyerere of Tanzania*, London: Secker and Warburg, 1976, p.5.
37. On the sidelining of Nyerere's detractors, see Brennan, 'Julius Rex'. For a brief discussion on the best biographer for a given subject, see Schorer, M. 'The Burdens of Biography', in *Biography as High Adventure: Life-writers speak on their art*, Oates, S.B. ed., Amherst, MA: University of Massachusetts Press, 1986, pp.77–92, p.82–3.
38. Nyerere, J.K. *Freedom and Unity: Uhuru na Umoja – A Selection from Writing and Speeches, 1952–65*, 1966; *Freedom and Socialism: Uhuru na Ujamaa – A Selection from Writing and Speeches, 1965–67*, 1968; *Freedom and Development: Uhuru na Maendeleo. A Selection from Writing and Speeches, 1968–1973*, 1973 – all Dar es Salaam: Oxford University Press. See Becker on the different ways that the memory of Nyerere has been constructed. Becker, F. 'Remembering Nyerere: Political rhetoric and dissent in contemporary Tanzania', *African Affairs*, 112 (447) 2013, pp.238–61.
39. Feinstein, A. *African Revolutionary: The life and times of Nigeria's Aminu Kano*, Boulder, CA: Lynne Rienner, 1987, p.34.

40. For discussion of the contrast between authorised and non-authorised biography, see Dunaway, D.K. 'Telling Lives: The aftermath', *Journal of Narrative and Life History*, 2 (1) 1992, pp.11–18, who argues that anticipated response from family, community and (when alive) subject inevitably shapes the work, before publication, by prior censorship.
41. These observations draw on discussion with Nadia Davids and Joost Fontein.
42. For an examination of biography as a method of research and field of enquiry in the social sciences, history, and literature, and also where it has been an arena for the production of memory outside the academy, see Rassool, C.S. 'The Individual, Auto/biography and History in South Africa', Unpublished Ph.D. thesis, University of the Western Cape, Cape Town, 2004.
43. Geiger, S. 'Engendering, p.286. The term 'Nyerere-philia' has also been used. Fouéré, M.-A. 'Hero', p.1.
44. Public memory emerges from the intersection of state-sponsored 'official memory' and ethnic, and regional 'vernacular memory'. Bodnar, J. *Remaking America: Public memory, commemoration, and patriotism in the twentieth century*, Princeton, NJ: Princeton University Press, 1992 p.13–14. Both are influenced by what Maurice Halbwachs calls 'historical memory', the written and other records to which we no longer have an 'organic' relation. Halbwachs, M. *On Collective Memory*. Chicago, IL: University of Chicago Press, 1992. See also Thomson, who explores changing interactions over time between experiences, memories and identities of the Anzac (Australian and New Zealand Army Corps) legend. Thomson, A. *Anzac Memories: Living with the legend*, Oxford and Melbourne: Oxford University Press, 1995.

Chapter 1

1. Press release, issued by the Information Services Division, Ministry of Information and Tourism, United Republic of Tanzania, CLX-A-16/7, Shep.Coln..
2. Also said as 'Abakabwege'. Julius Nyerere's father, Chief Nyerere Burito, was of the Abhakibhage ('Abakibagwa') clan. Author's interview with David Msuguri. (Unless otherwise stated, all interviews were conducted by the author. Full interview details are listed in Select Biographies) Hans Cory records that Chief Wanzagi, Julius's brother, was of the 'Abakibagara' clan. Cory, H. 1945. 'Report on the pre-European tribal organizations in Musoma (South Mara) District', Appendix Buzanaki, p.2, file 173, Hans Cory papers, East Africana section, University of Dar es Salaam library (hereafter 'CORY'). See also Mkirya, B. 'Jumuiya ya Ukoo', in Mkirya, B., ed. *Historia, Mila na Desturi za Wazanaki*, Peramiho: Benedictine Publications Ndanda, 1991, pp.32–3.
3. Wille, A.H. 'Recollections on President Julius Kambarage Nyerere by Father Arthur H. Wille', 2005, p.2. Available at www.scribd.com/doc/8498811/Fr-Willes-Recollections-on-Mwalimu-Nyerere, accessed on 14 December 2013. Tanzania census data no longer includes ethnic classifications, although the 1957 census indicates that the Zanaki ranked sixty-ninth in population size in Tanganyika. In a speech in 1960 Nyerere put the Zanaki population at 35,000. Nyerere, J.K. 'Africa's Place in the World', in *Symposium on Africa*, ed. Barnette Miller Foundation, Wellesley, MA: Wellesley College, 1960, pp.148–63, p.161.
4. Nyerere, G.M. 'A chat with Madaraka Nyerere at his eagle's nest in Butiama'. *Vodacom World*, 9, 2011, pp.34–45, p.38.
5. Nyerere's personal library holds a copy of Gaddafi's *Green Book*, in which the author had signed his name and, some five months before Nyerere's death, professed his 'gratitude and appreciation'. All of Nyerere's personally held literature referred to here can be found in his private library in Mwitongo.
6. See Bischofberger, O. *The Generation Classes of the Zanaki (Tanzania)*, Fribourg: University Press, 1972, p.23.
7. Audax Mabulla and Emanuel Kessy, pers.comm., 10 July 2012, University of Dar es Salaam, Dar es Salaam. (Hereafter all personal communication with author is abbreviated to 'pers.comm.'.) For a description and interpretation of similar art, see Mabulla,

Notes for Chapter 1, pp. 11–36

A.Z.P. 'The Rock Art of Mara Region, Tanzania', *Azania* (40) 2005, pp.19–42.
8. Interview, Nyamwaga.
9. Shetler, J.B. *Imagining Serengeti: A history of landscape memory in Tanzania from earliest times to the present*, Athens, OH: Ohio University Press, 2007, p.77.
10. Bischofberger, *Generation*, p.14.
11. ibid., p.77.
12. For an approximate diagram, see Mkirya, *Historia*, p.47.
13. Wicken to Molony, 14 March 2001, p.4.
14. Graham, J.M., Piddington, R. *Anthropology and the Future of Missions*, Aberdeen: The University Press, 1940, p.12.
15. Interview, Rose Nyerere.
16. Wicken to Molony, 14 March 2001, p.4. In the account by Kirwen (the missionary) of the diviner (Riana), the diviner explains that the sun is not worshiped in the sense understood by Westerners, but is given respect as a symbol of God. Kirwen, M. *The Missionary and the Diviner: Contending theologies of Christian and African religions*, Maryknoll, NY: Orbis Books, 1987, p.4–5. For a summary of the general pattern of African ancestor worship, see Kopytoff, I. 'Ancestors as Elders in Africa', *Africa*, 41 (2) 1971, pp.129–42, which draws on the work of Meyer Fortes.
17. Interview, Nyamwaga.
18. Jack Nyamwaga was informed by his forefathers that *eryoobha* worship faded away with the introduction of Christianity. He reports that *abhakuru* are particularly old men, normally over the age of eighty. This section on *amasaambwa* is largely based on a series of discussions with Jack Nyamwaga, in May 2010 and throughout July 2011 and July 2013.
19. Bischofberger, *Generation*, p.22–3.
20. Shetler, *Imagining*, p.106.
21. For detail on the consultation, see Bischofberger, *Generation*, p.57–8.
22. This incident should not be confused with the accidental shooting down, at the same time and in the same region, of another fighter plane.
23. Bischofberger, *Generation*, p.57.
24. Interview, Nyamwaga. Nyerere had been aware of his illness for some time, and in August 1999 visited his lifelong friend Marwa Ihunyo who remembers: 'It was as if he was saying goodbye.' Interview, Marwa Ihunyo. At the time of Nyerere's burial a minor earthquake is said to have taken place, followed by strong rain showers. On rumours surrounding this time, see Pels, P. 'Creolisation in Secret: The birth of nationalism in late colonial Uluguru, Tanzania', *Africa*, 72 (1) 2002, pp.1–27, p.457.
25. Also known as age/generation-sets or -classes. Piddington, R. *An Introduction to Social Anthropology* Volume 1, Edinburgh: Oliver and Boyd, 1950, p.176.
26. See Nursey-Bray's notes 4 and 28 on *ujamaa*, 'family' and 'socialism' in light of Ferdinand Tönnies' definition of Gemeinschaft. Nursey-Bray, P. 'Consensus and Community: African one-party democracy', in *Democratic Theory and Practice*, ed. Duncan, G, Cambridge: Cambridge University Press, 1983, pp.96–111.
27. Moore, S.F. *Anthropology and Africa: Changing perspectives on a changing scene*, Charlottesville, VA and London: University Press of Virginia, 1994, p.13.
28. Bischofberger, *Generation*, p.94.
29. Stöger-Eising, V. '"Ujamaa" Revisited: Indigenous and European Influences in Nyerere's Social and Political Thought', *Africa*, 70 (1) 2000, pp.118–43, p.120.
30. Stöger-Eising, 'Ujamaa', pp.124–140.
31. Mustafa, K. 'The Concept of Authority and the Study of African Colonial History', *Kenya Historical Review: The journal of the Historical Association of Kenya*, 3 (1) pp.55–83, 1975, p.76, note 3.
32. Stöger-Eising, 'Ujamaa', p.121. The point was made in Nyerere, J.K. 'The African and Democracy', in *Freedom and Unity: Uhuru na Umoja – A Selection from Writing and Speeches, 1952–65*, Dar es Salaam: Oxford University Press, 1961. pp.103–6.
33. Baumann, O. *Durch Massailand zur Nilquelle: Reisen und forschungen der Massai-Expedition,*

Notes for Chapter 1, pp. 11–36

     des deutschen Antisklaverei-Komite in den jahren 1891–1893, Berlin: Reimer, 1894.
34. Stöger-Eising, 'Ujamaa', p.120.
35. Maluki, E.I. 'The Influences of Traditionalism upon Nyerere's "Ujamaa-ism"', unpublished Ph.D. thesis, University of Denver, Denver, 1965, pp.279–80.
36. Mustafa, K. 'The Development of Ujamaa in Musoma: A case study of Butiama ujamaa village', M.A. dissertation, University of Dar es Salaam, 1975.
37. For example, Nyerere, J.K. 'Ujamaa: The basis of African socialism', in *Freedom and Unity: Uhuru na Umoja: A selection from writing and speeches, 1952–65*, Dar es Salaam: Oxford University Press, 1962, pp.162–71, p.170.
38. Pratt, C.R. *The Critical Phase in Tanzania, 1945–1968: Nyerere and the emergence of a socialist strategy*, Nairobi: Oxford University Press, 1978, p.72.
39. Interview, Nyamwaga. Bischofberger, *Generation*, pp.60–61 describes the procedures as told to him in the 1960s. See also Mkirya, *Historia*, p.59–62.
40. Interview, John Nyambeho.
41. Shetler, *Imagining*, p.131. Also Fouéré, M.-A. 28 June 2013. 'He Was a Hero Man; Everyone Should Act Like Him: Julius Nyerere as a national hero in contemporary Tanzania'. Paper presented at Fifth European Conference on African Studies, 27–29 June 2013, Lisbon, Portugal, passim.
42. Shetler, J.B., 'The Landscapes of Memory: A History of Social Identity in the Western Serengeti, Tanzania', unpublished Ph.D. thesis, University of Florida, 1998, p.399, 437; cited in Bjerk, P. 'Julius Nyerere and the Establishment of Sovereignty in Tanganyika', unpublished Ph.D. thesis, University of Wisconsin-Madison, Madison, 2008, p.84.
43. Interview, Nyambeho.
44. Bischofberger, *Generation*, p.59.
45. Butiama informants were not familiar with the term '*kukerera*', perhaps because it is used in Nata and Ikoma, where it is similar to a more symbolic practice in Ishenyi and Ngoreme. See Shetler, *Imagining*, p.102, 118–19, and Bjerk, 'Establishment', p.84. Also Bischofberger, *Generation,* p.59–60.
46. Bischofberger, *Generation*, p.16 spells the term '*ekiaro*'. There are similarities between the Zanaki *ekyaaro*, the Swahili *taifa* (nation/race) and the at-times interchangeable *kabila* (tribe). See Brennan, J.R. 2012. *Taifa: Making nation and race in urban Tanzania*. Athens, OH: Ohio University Press, pp.119–21, especially notes 12 and 13.
47. Interview with David Msuguri; cited in Bjerk, 'Establishment', p.376–7. Note, however, that the Zanaki do not use 'l'; hence 'ikuru'. Shem Koren, pers.comm. 10 March 2014.
48. Shetler, *Imagining*, p.131. For detail on the *okung'atuka* retirement ceremony, see Bischofberger, *Generation,* p.39–42, and Mkirya, *Historia*, pp.33–4, 39–42, 44. *Kung'atuka* is now widely used throughout the nation to refer to retirement, and is assumed by many to be a 'Swahili' word, not one of Zanaki origin. Upon announcing his retirement from Parliament on 29 July 1985 Nyerere finished with the words: 'To pass on the tongs is to sustain and perpetuate the blacksmithery', which may have been a further reference to tradition among the Zanaki who, one account suggests, were formed when the Turi (blacksmiths) arrived in Uzanaki. On the Turi, see Bischofberger, *Generation,* p.12, and Bischofberger, O. 'Die soziale und rituelle Stellung der Schmiede und des Schmiede-Klans bei den Zanaki (Tanzania)', *Paideuma* 15, 1969, pp.14–23.
49. That the question came from Jita is quite plausible since their alphabet has no letter 'z', but uses 'j' in its place. The reverse is true for the Zanaki, who use 'z' instead of 'j' – Julius, being a foreign name; thus, '*Baza na ki*'. Interview, Nyamwaga.
50. Cited in Bischofberger, *Generation,* p.11–12.
51. Société des Missionaires d'Afrique (Pères Blancs), Visitations Book, Nyegina, Mwanza 1, 1931–32, pp.67–69, White Father's Regional House, Nyegezi, Mwanza; cited in Shetler, *Imagining*, p.139–40, note 15. Shetler attributes chiggers for the foot sores associated with the 'famine of the feet'.
52. Bischofberger, *Generation,* p.14.
53. Société des Missionaires d'Afrique, *Rapport Annuel*, 1910–11, 383; L. Bourget, Trip Diary, 1904, 'Report of a Trip from 1904 from Bukumbi to Mwanza, Kome? Ukerewe, Kibara,

Notes for Chapter 1, pp. 11–36

Ikoma–Mara Region, together with some stories' (n.p., n.d.), M-SRC54, Sukuma Archives; cited in Shetler, *Imagining*, p.140, note 17. See also Shorter, A. *Cross and Flag in Africa: The 'White Fathers' during the colonial scramble (1892–1914)*, Maryknoll, NY: Orbis, 2006.

54. Admiralty War Staff Intelligence Division. *A Handbook of German East Africa*. London: His Majesty's Stationery Office, 1916, p.96; 'Musoma (Sub-District 1916–27)', p.65, *Musoma District Book*, Tanzania National Archives. The *Musoma District Book* (hereafter '*MDB*'), a collection of British administrative records ranging from 1917 to 1960. It is now located in the Tanzania National Archives (hereafter 'TNA') and in the School of Oriental and African Studies, University of London.
55. Shashi is a term sometimes used for multiple Mara tribes. Interview, Nyamwaga.
56. Cory, H. 'The People of the Lake Victoria Region', *Tanganyika Notes and Records*, 33, 1952, p.27. Hans Cory created one of the earliest written record of Zanaki history from a series of interviews in 1945 with two elders from each of the Musoma chiefdoms. Cory did not give the names of his informants but, according to Joseph Kizurira Burito Nyerere, Chief Edward Wanzagi was one of them. Mustafa, 'Development', p.70 and p.80, note 1.
57. CORY, 'Report', Appendix Buzanaki, p.2. See also Mkirya, B. 1991, chapters 'Utangulizi' and 'Historia ya Wazanaki'. In *Historia, Mila na Desturi*, pp.5–6, 7–14, respectively.
58. Shetler, J.B. *Telling Our Own Stories: Local histories from South Mara, Tanzania*, Dar es Salaam: Mkuki na Nyota, 2003, pp.10–12.
59. Nyerere, W. 'Asili ya Wazanaki', in Chuo cha Elimu ya Watu Wazima Tanzania, ed. *Hadithi za Kizanaki*, 1974, pp.1–2. Dar es Salaam: East African Literature Bureau, pp.1–2. See also Mkirya, 'Uhusiano wa Zanaki na Makabila Mengine', in *Historia, Mila na Desturi*, pp.71–4.
60. CORY, 'Report', Appendix Buzanaki, pp.2–3.
61. Bischofberger, *Generation*, p.12.
62. *MDB*, Early History, Sheet 4.
63. Sutton, J.E.G. 'The Archaeology and Early Peoples from the Highlands of Kenya and Northern Tanzania', *Azania*, 1, 1966, pp.37–57, p.49.
64. Kuper, A. *Anthropologists and Anthropology: The British school, 1922–1972*. London: Allen Lane, 1973, p.129.
65. Kuklick, H. 'The British Tradition', in Kuklick, H, ed. *A New History of Anthropology*, Oxford: Blackwell, 2008, pp.52–78, p.68.
66. Moore, *Anthropology*, p.9.
67. Austen, R. 'The Official Mind of Indirect Rule: British Policy in Tanganyika, 1916–39', in Gifford, P., Roger Louis, W.M., ed. *Britain and Germany in Africa: Imperial Rivalry and Colonial Rule*, New Haven, CT: Yale University Press, 1967, p.592.
68. These are recorded in the *Musoma District Book*.
69. Maguire, 1969. *Toward 'Uhuru' in Tanzania: The politics of participation*, Cambridge: Cambridge University Press, G.A, p.10. See also Walsh, M. 3 October 2010. 'Bad Swahili and Pidgin Swahili in Hemingway'. *Tanzania Notes and Records*. Available at http://notesandrecords.blogspot.co.uk/2010/10/bad-swahili-and-pidgin-swahili-in.html, accessed 3 August 2012.
70. Miller, N.N. 'Tanzania: Documentation in Political Anthropology – The Hans Cory Collection', *African Studies Bulletin*, 11 (2) 1968, pp.195–213, p.195.
71. Kuper, *Anthropologists*, p.137.
72. Miller, 'Hans Cory', p.195.
73. Cory, H. 'Reform of Tribal Political Institutions in Tanganyika', *Journal of African Administration*, 12 (2) 1960, pp.77–84, p.77.
74. Spear, T. *Mountain Farmers: Moral economies of land and agricultural development in Arusha and Meru*, Oxford: James Currey, 1997, p.198, also pp.199, 207.
75. Chiume, M.W.K. *Kwacha: An autobiography*, Nairobi: East African Publishing House, 1975, p.309.
76. Bischofberger, *Generation,* p.17. See also p.15, note 1. Falk Moore rightly describes the study as one 'of closed description' and 'a kind of timeless abstraction'. Moore,

Notes for Chapter 1, pp. 11–36

Anthropology, p.13. For further criticism, see Beidelman, T. 'Review of *The Generation Classes of the Zanaki (Tanzania)* by Otto Bischofberger', *Africa*, 44 (2) 1974, pp.206–7.
77. Mustafa, 'Concept', p.73.
78. Shetler, *Imagining*, p.65.
79. Evans-Pritchard, E.E. 'The Political Structure of the Nandi-Speaking People's of Kenya', *Africa*, 13 (3) 1940 pp.250–67, p.251; cited in Bischofberger, *Generation*, p.15.
80. Bischofberger, *Generation,* p.15. Mustafa includes Maganna to a list of eight districts which were autonomous chiefdoms during some periods of colonial rule, and excludes Buturu and Buzahya. Mustafa, 'Concept'.
81. Dobson, E.B. 'Comparative Land Tenure among Ten Tanganyika tribes', *Tanganyika Notes and Records*, 38, 1955, pp.31–9.
82. Shetler, *Imagining*, p.74.
83. Bischofberger, *Generation,* p.15.
84. ibid., p.17.
85. ibid., p.22.
86. Joseph Kizurira Burito Nyerere adds that it is possible that *abhagaambi* is the Kuria equivalent of the Zanaki *aburwasi*. Mustafa, 'Concept', p.69.
87. ibid. Communal activities in the form of co-operative labour (*eriisaga*) can take place when people of several adjacent homesteads help one another with tasks. Bischofberger, *Generation,* p.14.
88. Interview, Nyamwaga.
89. These are the terms used by Mustafa, based on terms used by colonial officers in their records. The current Swahili terms would be, respectively, *chifu* (pl., *machifu*), *mtemi* (pl. *watemi*) and, principally for the Great Lakes region, *mkama* (pl., *wakama*). Mustafa, 'Concept', p.70.
90. Shetler, *Telling*, p.32.
91. For detail on rule in German East Africa (later Tanganyika), see Iliffe, J. *Tanganyika Under German Rule: 1905–1912*, Cambridge: Cambridge University Press, 1969; Hopkins, R.F. *Political Roles in a New State: Tanzania's first decade*, New Haven, CT and London: Yale University Press, 1971, p.13–16 for a summary.
92. Shetler, *Imagining*, p.170.
93. Diare de la Station de N.D. de la Consolation, entry on 10 June 1913; cited in Huber, H, *Marriage and the Family in Rural Bukwaya (Tanzania)*, Fribourg: The University Press, p.16. On the growth of Asian shop keeping during this period, see Iliffe, *Modern History*, pp.138–4.
94. Admiralty War Staff, *Handbook*, p.96–7; Iliffe, *German Rule*, p.180.
95. Section 8c Control of Arms Act, in *MDB*, p.100.
96. Maillot, P. 1909/10. Letter to his Superior about his and P. Van Thiel's Journey from Ukerewe to North Mara in December 1909/January 1910; cited in Bischofberger, *Generation*, p.11. The Zanaki also later (if not also at this time) had a reputation for cattle theft involving violence, as detailed in Tanner, R.E.S. 'Cattle Theft in Musoma, 1958–59', *Tanganyika Notes and Records*, 65, 1966, pp.31–42.
97. CORY, 348. 'Schweinezeug' is a word creation that literally means 'pig-matter'. The phrase was not likely written for public consumption, since the politically-correct German colonial discourse was by this time dominated by the idea that Africans were human and could be civilised. I thank Wolfgang Zeller for this interpretation.
98. Schnee, H. *German Colonization, Past and Future: The truth about the German colonies*, London: George Allen and Unwin, 1926, p.162.
99. Shepperson, G.A. 'Erratum and addendum', *Edinburgh University History Graduates Association Newsletter*, 33, October 2000, p.14.
100. Dawson, W.H. 'Introduction', in Schnee, *German Colonization*, Schnee, pp.9–46, p.23.
101. *MDB*, H.C. Baxter, Tribal History and Legends, Bakwaya Sheet 1.
102. Interview, Nyamwaga.
103. J.L. Fairclough, as D.O., dropped the name 'Akidas' in favour of 'Government Agents', a job that saw 'Jabere' [sic] stationed in Musoma, from where he could be 'sent to report

on any area or to explain any new law that may come into force.' *MDB*, Chief Barazas, Sheet 6, p.47, 11 February 1931.
104. Mustafa, 'Concept', p.80.
105. Hopkins, *Political*, p.16.
106. Cameron, J., Dodd, W.A. *Society, Schools and Progress in Tanzania*. Oxford: Pergamon Press, 1970, p.39.
107. Bischofberger, *Generation*, p.14.
108. *MDB*, Chief Barazas, Sheet 6, p.47, compiled 11 February 1931 by J.L. Fairclough.
109. Austen, R. 1968. *Northwest Tanzania Under German and British Rule: Colonial policy and tribal politics, 1889–1939*. New Haven, CT and London: Yale University Press, pp.126–7.
110. This section is influenced by Iliffe, *Modern History*, pp.318–41 and Mamdani, M. *Citizen and Subject: Contemporary Africa and the legacy of late colonialism*, Princeton, NJ: Princeton University Press, 1996, pp.62–108, 138–41. For further discussion on indirect rule, see Spear, T. 'Indirect Rule, the Politics of Neo-Traditionalism and the Limits of Invention in Tanzania', in Maddox & Giblin, *In Search of a Nation*, pp.70–85; Berman, B. *Control and Crisis in Colonial Kenya: The dialectic of domination*, London: James Currey, 1990, pp.208–9; and Feierman, S. *Peasant Intellectuals: Anthropology and history in Tanzania*, Madison, WI: University of Wisconsin Press, 1990, pp.120–53. Willis provides counter-example to the presentation of a body of district administrators dedicated to indirect rule: Willis, J. 'The Administration of Bonde, 1920–60: A study of the implementation of Indirect Rule in Tanganyika', *African Affairs*, 92 (366), 1993, pp.53–67, p.63. Austen covers the emergence of indirect rule at the territorial level, and also examines its application in Bukoba and Mwanza: Austen, *Northwest*. Indirect rule in Sukumaland (due south of Musoma) is also covered in Maguire, *Toward*, pp.5–8. On the 'creation' of tribes throughout Africa see Vail, L., ed. *The Creation of Tribalism in Southern Africa*, Berkeley, CA: University of California Press, 1991. For the role of anthropologists (with a focus on Hans Cory) in indirect rule, see Bjerk, 'Establishment', pp.106–7.
111. Friedland, W.H. 'The Evolution of Tanganyika's Political System'. In Diamond, S., Burke, F.G., ed. *The Transformation of East Africa: Studies in political anthropology*, New York and London: Basic Books, 1966, pp.241–311, pp.257–9.
112. Bischofberger, *Generation*, p.11.
113. Berman, *Control*, p.210.
114. Smith, *Influence*, p.2.
115. CORY, 'Report', Appendix Buzanaki, p.3. Note that in Cory's submitted report he had not yet visited Zanaki, his remarks being 'based on the details of historical facts and native opinions'. CORY, Cory to Provincial Commissioner, Mwanza, 5 July 1945.
116. Interview, Nyamwaga.
117. *MDB*, p.51, compiled 11 February 1931 by J.L. Fairclough, when Acting D.O. He refers to the two as brothers, but this is likely a mistake. Although Mustafa does not offer the origin of his claim, he refers to Buhoro and Nyerere Burito as cousins. Mustafa, 'Concept', p.72. Those considered to be authoritative oral sources in Butiama also refer to them as cousins, as does Cory: CORY, 'Report', Appendix Buzanaki, p.3. See also Enahoro, P. 'The Private and Public Nyerere: Special interview', *Africa Now*, 32, 1983, pp.97–125, p.108. Fairclough later confirms that Chief Nyerere Burito was appointed to the chiefdom of Butiama in 1915 (*MDB*, p.59).
118. Interviews, Jack Nyamwaga and Jackton Nyambereka Nyerere.
119. In the language of the Mang'anja of southern Malawi, Nyerere is 'a small ant; the smallest ants found in a house and everywhere in great numbers': Scott, D.C.R. *A Cyclopaedic Dictionary of the Mang'anja Language spoken in British Central Africa*, Edinburgh: Church of Scotland, 1892, p.483. It is also an ant '(small, black)' in Chewa/Nyanja, the national language of Malawi, and spoken elsewhere in the region. Paas, S. *English Chichewa-Chinyanja Dictionary*, Blantyre: Christian Literature Association in Malawi, 2003, p.21.
120. *MDB*, p.91.

Notes for Chapter 1, pp. 11–36

121. Iliffe, *Modern History*, p.116.
122. Mwigura Kanyonyi, personal communication with Stöger-Eising, May 1996; cited in Stöger-Eising, 'Ujamaa', p.124.
123. The text given in Mustafa, 'Concept', p.74–5 differs slightly from that given here, copied verbatim from the typed text of H.C. Baxter's account in *MDB*, The Chiefs of South Mara: Character Studies, 17 May 1941, Sheet 24, p.71. Nyerere Burito's grievances about his boundaries may explain his insistence on the maintenance of *orukobha*, to cover all the boundaries of his territory.
124. CORY, 173.
125. Government Printer, *Annual Report of the Provincial Commissioners*, Dar es Salaam, 1943, p.30; cited in Mustafa, 'Concept', p.76.
126. *MDB*, H.C. Baxter, The Chiefs of South Mara: Character Studies, 17 May 1941, sheets 23–25, pp.70–72.
127. TNA, 'Musoma (Sub-District 1916–27)', p.8. A partial view of some men's attitude to the opposite sex is available in the Zanaki story told by Mtokambali entitled, 'Beware of Women': Bukiri, M. 'Jihadhari na Wanawake', in Chuo cha Elimu ya Watu Wazima Tanzania, ed. *Hadithi za Kizanaki*, Dar es Salaam: East African Literature Bureau, 1974, pp.11–13.
128. Interview, Nyamwaga.
129. Ovchinnikov, V. 'Mwalimu Julius Kambarage Nyerere (1922–1999): Teacher, Politician, Poet', in Vinokurov, Y.N., Shlyonskaya, S.M., et al, ed. *Julius Nyerere: Humanist, Politician, Thinker*, Ndanda-Peramiho: Benedictine Publications, 2003, pp.69–76, p.70.
130. Wicken to Molony, 14 March 2001, p.2.
131. Smith, *Nyerere*, p.34 (and p.40).
132. Bunting, I. 'The Heart of Africa: Interview with Julius Nyerere on anti-colonialism', *New Internationalist* (309). 1999.
133. Nyerere, J.K. *Uhuru wa Wanawake*, Dar es Salaam: Mwalimu Nyerere Foundation, 2009 (1944), p.30. The book is a posthumous publication of the essay, and has been copied verbatim. The essay was originally written in Swahili, and the original manuscript is now held at the Mwalimu Nyerere Foundation in Dar es Salaam. In 2010 Makerere University produced an English translation, the subtitle of which refers to James Aggrey's 'Parable of the Eagle', which Nyerere recalls in the text: *Women's Freedom: Women are eagles, not chickens*. Kampala: Makerere University Female Scholarship Foundation. I refer to the work as an essay so to retain its original motive as a piece of assessed work. The quotations are translated by the author from the Swahili-language *Uhuru wa Wanawake* book, and there I use italics for the title.
134. Wicken says she was fourth wife of twenty-three to the chief, while both Ovchinnikov and Smith believe that she came fifth. Wicken to Molony, 14 March 2001, p.2; Ovchinnikov, 'Mwalimu', p.70; Smith, *Nyerere*, p.40.
135. Smith, *Nyerere*, p.40.
136. Interview, Maria Nyerere.
137. Fanis Makonjio Warioba Nyang'ombe, discussion with Madaraka Nyerere, 20 August 2012, Muryaza. As indicated in Figure 1, Wandiba was the son of Wanzira, who Salum Nyang'ombe Warioba had inherited from his brother. Mustafa says that Wandiba was 'from Nyerere Burito's family'. Mustafa, 'Concept', p.80. Unions did occur between the Nyang'ombe and Nyerere Burito families, but information on Wandiba's wives is not available and this affiliation cannot be confirmed. Madaraka Nyerere, pers.comm., 21 August 2012.
138. Interview, Rose Nyerere.
139. Austen, 'Official Mind', p.591.
140. Annual Report of the Education Department, Dar es Salaam, 1926, p.22; Thompson, A.R. 1968. 'The Adaptation of Education to African Society in Tanganyika under British Rule', Unpublished Ph.D. thesis, University of London, p.48, 50. Both cited in Cadogan, T.E. 2006. 'Students and Schools in the Southern Highlands: Education in Tanzania, 1890s to the present'. Unpublished Ph.D. thesis, School of Oriental and

Notes for Chapter 2, pp. 37–61

African Studies, London, pp.82–3.
141. Sir Donald Cameron, Address to the Empire Parliamentary Association, London, 1927, cited in Furley, O.W. 'Education and the Chiefs in East Africa in the Inter-War Period', *Transafrican Journal of History*, 1 (1) 1971, pp.60–83, p.62. See also Buell, R.L. *The Native Problem in Africa*. New York: The Macmillan Company, 1928, pp.463–4.
142. Mayhew, A. 'Native Administration Schools, The Education of Native Chiefs, and Agricultural Teaching in Tanganyika Territory', *Overseas Education*, 2, 1930, pp.41–44, p.42. The report is based on the *Education Report*, 1928, for Tanganyika Territory.
143. ibid., p.43.
144. Interview, Jackton Nyerere. Jack Nyamwaga believes it was 1912.
145. Thompson, 'Adaptation', p.172.
146. *MDB*, H.C. Baxter's report, 25 November 1941, pp.31, 33; Gazette Notice: No.208/1929.
147. ibid., p.31.
148. *MDB*, p.66. The District Officer was A.C. Davey (p.43).
149. Interview, Jackton Nyerere.

Chapter 2

1. Nyerere, 'Africa's Place', pp.155–156.
2. United Kingdom National Archives, London (hereafter 'NA') CO981/16556/20; First Matriculation, 1949–50, EUA IN1/ADS/STA/4, EUL.
3. Nyerere to Shepperson, 5 May 1960, CLX-A-16/1, Shep.Coln.
4. Interview, Maria Nyerere; Wicken to Molony, 14 March 2001, pp.1–2. Wicken adds that after learning of the 13 April, 'Mwalimu always had a private or close family celebration on that day; it was not a "public day" and indeed it was indicated to his staff that they should not publicise the date or any planned private or family event. One or two outsiders did get to know about it, but the only time there was any public celebration was on Mwalimu's seventy-fifth birthday.'
5. Interviews, Jack Nyamwaga, Joseph Muhunda Nyerere. Adam Marwa is of the opinion that Nyerere found his birth date from notes taken by his maternal uncle (his mother's brother), Wandiba Nyang'ombe. Wandiba was the second of the two 'highly literate men' in Butiama at the time.
6. Interview, Maria Nyerere. In his personal Bible, Nyerere has written his own birth date under the name 'Kambarage', along with those of Nyabikwabi [Nyakigi], [Sophia] Magori, [Joseph] Kizurira and [Josephat] Kiboko. The preceding text, in Nyerere's hand, reads, 'Tarehe za Kuzaliwa (Aliziandika Marehemu Wandiba na Mzee Mtoka)' (Birth dates (as written by the late Wandiba and the respected Mtoka[mbali])) – which suggests all of the above from Nyamwaga, Muhunda and Marwa, is correct.
7. Wicken to Molony, 14 March 2001, p.2. Wicken uses the Swahili word *mganga*, which is variously translated as herbalist, witchdoctor, diviner or soothsayer. Jack Nyamwaga uses the Zanaki word *omugabhu* here to mean diviner, the function of whom in this context was 'one who predicts'. Interview, Nyamwaga.
8. April is known in Butiama to be the time of *masika*, the heaviest rains, and so the timing fits with Kambarage's birth date as given in Mtokambali Bukiri's exercise book.
9. Interview, Maria Nyerere.
10. Wille, 'Recollections', p.2.
11. Bischofberger (*Generation*, p.18–19) does not give a date for 'earlier times'. Writing in 1899, Kollmann remarked that 'Tattooing is practiced sometimes, circumcision always, all over Ushashi.' Kollmann, P. 1899. *The Victoria Nyanza: The land, the races and their customs, with specimens of some of the dialects*. London: Swan Sonnenschein, p.187.
12. Interview, Nyambeho.
13. Interviews, Nyamwaga, Jackton Nyerere, Adam Marwa, Joseph Muhunda Nyerere, Nyambeho.
14. Hopkins, *Political*, p.70. Witness the title of Edwin Mtei's autobiography: *From Goatherd*

235

Notes for Chapter 2, pp. 37–61

      to Governor: The autobiography of Edwin Mtei, Dar es Salaam: Mkuki na Nyota, 2009.
15. Mbise, A.S. 'The Evangelist: Matayo Leveriya Kaaya', in Iliffe, J, ed. *Modern Tanzanians: A volume of biographies*, Nairobi: East African Publishing House, 1973, pp.27–42, p.28.
16. Bischofberger, *Generation*, p.15.
17. Interviews, Elias Nyang'ombe Warioba, Jackton Nyerere.
18. 'Sitaki Kutishwa Kwa Migomo', *Ngurumo*, 20 November 1961, p.1. I thank Paul Bjerk for pointing out this reference. See Bjerk, 'Establishment', p.151.
19. Enahoro, 'Private', pp.103–4.
20. ibid.
21. Hopkins, *Political*, p.200–1.
22. Enahoro, 'Private', pp.103–4. For evidence of Nyerere's knowledge of the roots of chiefly rule across East Africa, see 'Wanawake na Utawala wa Wenyeji' in *Uhuru wa Wanawake*, pp.44–53.
23. Macmillan, W.M. *Africa Emergent: A survey of social, political and economic trends in British Africa*, Harmondsworth: Penguin, 1949, p.263. For information on chiefs who supported TANU, see the TANU newspaper *Sauti ya TANU*, 28 February 1958, p.22. For critique of the ruling clans and the beginnings of rural nationalism, see Spear, 'Indirect Rule', p.70–85. For a case study from Unyamwezi on the evolution of traditional leadership, see Miller, N.N. 'The Political Survival of Traditional Leadership', and Skinner, E.P. 'The "Paradox" of Rural Leadership – A comment', – both from *Journal of Modern African Studies*, 6 (2) 1968,. pp.183–98 and pp.199–201.
24. *MDB*, H.C. Baxter, The Chiefs of South Mara: Character Studies, 17 May 1941, Sheet 24, p.71.
25. Nyerere, J.K. 'Democracy and the Party System', Dar es Salaam: Tanganyika Standard, 1963, p.15.
26. Listowel, *Making*, p.173.
27. Feierman, *Peasant*, p.147.
28. Iliffe, *Modern History*, p.508.
29. Bates, D. *A Gust of Plumes: A biography of Lord Twining of Godalming and Tanganyika*, London: Hodder and Stoughton, 1972, p.278; Eckert, A. 'Cultural Commuters: African Employees in Late Colonial Tanzania', in Lawrance, B.N., Osborn, E.L., Roberts R.L., ed. *Intermediaries, Interpreters and Clerks: African Employees in the Making of Colonial Africa*, Madison, WI: University of Wisconsin Press, 2006, pp.248–69, p.259.
30. Brennan, 'Short History of Political Opposition and Multi-Party Democracy in Tanganyika, 1958–64', in Maddox et al., *In Search of a Nation*, p.70. See also Tordoff, W. *Government and Politics in Tanzania: A collection of essays covering the period from September 1960 to July 1966*, Nairobi: East African Publishing House, 1967, pp.112–21.
31. Obe, A.O. 'The Teacher Leader', *Africa Forum*, 1 (1) 1991, pp.5–12, pp.5–6.
32. Nyerere, 'Democracy', p.1–2. On Guy Clutton-Brock, see Nyerere, 'The African', pp.103–4.
33. Stöger-Eising, 'Ujamaa'.
34. Hatch, *African Statesmen*, pp.3–4.
35. On the chief's duties under the Native Authority Ordinance (1926), see Mayhew, 'Native', pp.41–4.
36. Maguire, *Toward*, pp.46–7.
37. Enahoro, 'Private', p.104, 107.
38. On later (Western) frustration with Nyerere's 'exhibitionist modesty' see Brennan, 'Rex', pp.8–9, 17.
39. Goldthorpe, J.E. *An African Elite: Makerere students, 1922–1960*. Nairobi: Oxford University Press, 1965, p.48.
40. Enahoro, 'Private', p.104, 107. See also Nyerere, J.K. 'The Power of Teachers', in *Freedom and Socialism*, p.226.
41. In his 1945 notes for an essay 'On Self' (for submission to the Makerere *College Bulletin*) Nyerere wrote 'I entered school in 1934', and later he informs that he 'entered Musoma School in February 1934'. Nyerere, J.K. 'Uhuru wa Wanawake' notebook, Mwalimu

Notes for Chapter 2, pp. 37–61

   Nyerere Foundation, Dar es Salaam.
42. *MDB*, H.C. Baxter's report, 25 November 1941, pp.31, 33.
43. Nyerere apparently told this to Adam Marwa. Interview, Adam Marwa.
44. Obe, 'Teacher', p.5.
45. Hatch, *African Statesmen*, p.7.
46. Wicken to Molony, 14 March 2001, p.2. On Wanzagi, Wicken interjects here (pp.2–3): 'I am not certain that Wanzagi was the Chief's oldest son although Julius always spoke of him in such a manner. At any rate, he was the one who had attended school for 3 years, was more than literate, and was at that time already 'assisting' the Chief with his duties. Mwalimu always had high respect for Wanzagi (who was 12 years older than himself), liked him, and without question regarded him as Head of the Family after the Father's death.'
47. Charles Meek served as a colonial administrator in Tanganyika for twenty years. He later became Nyerere's Permanent Secretary and Secretary to the Cabinet in the run-up to independence. See Meek, C. and Meek I., ed. *Brief Authority: A memoir of colonial administration in Tanganyika*, London: Radcliffe Press, 2011, and *The Daily Telegraph*, 10 November 1999, p.31.
48. Meek, *Brief*, p.164–5.
49. Wille, 'Recollections', p.3. For more on the neighbouring chief, see Mbogoni, L.E.Y. *Aspects of Colonial Tanzania History*, Dar es Salaam: Mkuki na Nyota, 2013, pp.43–56.
50. Listowel, *Making*, p.175.
51. Mwenegoha calls Kambarage's friend 'Mwanangwa'. Mwenegoha, H.A.K. n.d. *Mwalimu Julius Kambarage Nyerere*. Dar es Salaam: Huduma za Maktaba, p.3. 'Mwanangwa' is a rank of headman, but Ihunyo's son Marwa believes it is he that Mwenegoha is referring to, adding that he had been at school for three months before Kambarage arrived. Interview, Marwa Ihunyo.
52. Interviews, Adam Marwa, Nyamwaga.
53. Department of Education (Tanganyika Territory) Report of 1934, p.9; cited in Ishumi, A.G. 'Inequities in the Distribution of Educational Opportunities: Origins and trends in Tanzania', in Ishumi, A.G., Maliyamkono, T.L., Darch, C., ed. *Education and Social Change: Readings on selected issues and cases*, Dar es Salaam: Black Star Agencies, 1980, pp.207–22, p.210.
54. Bouniol, J. *The White Fathers and Their Missions*. London: Sands & Co., 1929, pp.215, 219.
55. Department of Education (Tanganyika Territory) Report of 1934, p.40; cited in Ishumi, 'Inequities', p.211.
56. Department of Education (Tanganyika Territory) Report of 1934, separate table, p.40; cited in ibid., p.214.
57. Chiume, *Kwacha*, p.12.
58. Wicken to Molony, 14 March 2001, p.2; Interview, Adam Marwa.
59. *MDB*, H.C. Baxter's report, 25 November 1941, p.31.
60. Makongoro Nyerere, pers.comm., 1 July 2011, Mwitongo.
61. Kitundu, S. 'Reflections: 3', in Tanzania Standard, ed. *Nyerere: 1961–1985 – Passing on the tongs*, Dar es Salaam: Tanzania Standard, 1986, pp.47–8, p.47.
62. Kitundu, 'Reflections', p.47.
63. Interview, Adam Marwa.
64. Interview, Marwa Ihunyo.
65. Kitundu, 'Reflections', p.47.
66. Mwakikagile, G. *Nyerere and Africa: End of an era*. Pretoria and Dar es Salaam: New Africa Press, 2010, p.382. The references here to Mwakikagile's *Nyerere and Africa* that relate to James Irenge were written in Swahili in 1989 by Irenge himself, and published in *Rai*, 14 October 1999. The translation is by Godfrey Mwakikagile.
67. Irenge, in Mwakikagile, *Nyerere*, p.382.
68. Kitundu, 'Reflections', p.47.
69. Eckert, 'Cultural', p.249.
70. Irenge, in Mwakikagile, *Nyerere*, p.382.

Notes for Chapter 2, pp. 37–61

71. Kitundu, 'Reflections', p.47.
72. ibid.
73. ibid.
74. Nyerere, J.K. 'The Importance and Pleasure of Reading', speech at opening of printing works and book warehouse, Arusha, 29 November 1965; cited in Lema, E., Omari, I., Rajani, R., eds, *Nyerere on Education/Nyerere kuhusu Elimu*. Dar es Salaam: HakiElimu and E & D Ltd, 2006, p.22.
75. Wicken to Molony, 14 March 2001, p.4.
76. Wille, 'Recollections', p.3.
77. When Nyerere resigned from teaching he spent much of his time at Oswald's house, where he translated the Catholic catechism from Swahili/English to Zanaki. Oswald Marwa was appointed Regional Commissioner to Mara Region and was also Regional Commissioner in Mbeya, where he died on 25 January 1970. Oswald Mang'ombe Marwa High School in Buturgi is named after him. Interview, Adam Marwa. See also Wille, 'From President'.
78. Nyerere in, Smith, *Nyerere*, p.20.
79. Nyerere in ibid.
80. Neve, H. 'The Political Life of Julius K. Nyerere in Religious Perspective', *Africa Today*, 23 (4) 1976, pp.29–45, p.32.
81. Stanley, B. 'Conversion to Christianity: The colonization of the mind?' *International Review of Mission*, 92 (366) 2003, pp.315–31, pp.320 and 326.
82. Nyerere, J.K. 'Education for Self-Reliance', in *Freedom and Socialism*, p.278.
83. Ranger, *Not Also Men?*, p.1.
84. Shorter, A. *Chiefship in Western Tanzania: A political history of the Kimbu*, Oxford: Clarendon, 1972, p.106. See also the explanation of magico-religious beliefs in Piddington, *An Introduction*, pp.356, 366–7, sections of which Nyerere underlined in his personal copy.
85. On the 'social engineering' in training of an indigenous African priesthood, see Mudimbe, V.Y. *The Invention of Africa: Gnosis, philosophy, and the order of knowledge*, Bloomington, IN: Indiana University Press, 1988, p.48.
86. Cooper, F. *Africa Since 1940: The past of the present*, Cambridge: Cambridge University Press, 2002, p.27.
87. Oliver, R. *The Missionary Factor in East Africa*, London: Longman, 1970, p.283.
88. ibid., p.216.
89. ibid., p.181.
90. Cameron & Dodd, *Society*, p.64.
91. Horton, R. 'African Conversion', *Africa*, 41 (2) 1971, pp.85–108, pp.101, 103.
92. Ng'hosha, D.N.M. 'The Bishop: Jeremiah Kissula', in Iliffe, *Modern Tanzanians*, pp.209–26, p.211.
93. Bouniol, *White*, pp.71–2.
94. Hastings, A. *Church and Mission in Modern Africa*, London: Burns & Oates, 1967, p.565.
95. Sadleir, R. *Tanzania: Journey to republic*, London: Radcliffe Press, 1999, p.83.
96. Hastings made this point for the Baganda: Hastings, A. *The Church in Africa, 1450–1950*, Oxford: Clarendon Press, 1994, p.462.
97. Hastings, *Church and Mission*, p.119.
98. Lekgoathi, S.P., Mwakasekele, T., et al. 'Working with the Wilsons: The brief career of a 'Nyakyusa clerk' (1910–1938)', in Bank, A., Bank, L.J., ed. *Inside African Anthropology: Monica Wilson and her interpreters*, Cambridge: Cambridge University Press, 2013, pp.162–90, p.167, and pp.167–8 for further examples of the links between education and Christianity, as well as a summary of other reasons that African converts in the Rungwe District told Monica (Wilson) Hunter led them to Christianity. Also Marsland, R. 'Pondo Pins and Nyakyusa Hammers: Monica and Godfrey in Bunyakyusa', in Bank & Bank, *Inside African Anthropology*, on changes to Nyakyusa values that conversion brought.
99. Nyerere, 'Power of Teachers', p.224.
100. Hunter, M. 'An African Christian Morality', *Africa*, 10 (3) 1937, pp.265–92, p.280.

Notes for Chapter 2, pp. 37–61

101. Smith, *Nyerere*, p.45.
102. Interview, Nyambeho. This is also a phrase used by the David Msuguri in an interview with Paul Bjerk; cited in Bjerk, 'Establishment', pp.376–7. Msuguri (born on 4 January 1923) was of the same age-grade as Nyerere and underwent the procedure in 1938. Interview, Msuguri. Another version of Nyerere's teeth filing, told by Jackton Nyambereka, is that the procedure occurred sometime while Nyerere was on vacation from Mwisenge, and his father decided that his son follow the custom for Zanaki youth. Despite Kambarage's protests, the procedure was carried out nonetheless. Interview, Jackton Nyerere.
103. Kollmann documents the Zanaki fondness for tobacco, which 'is largely cultivated, as well it might be, seeing how addicted the Washashi are to the enjoyment of tobacco, both in smoking and in taking snuff'. Kollmann, *Victoria Nyanza*, p.201. A CIA report from 1963 described Nyerere as a chain smoker. Biographic entry of Nyerere, n.a., dated 10 July 1963, JFK Presidential Office File 124–13, JFK Presidential Library, Boston MA; cited in Brennan, 'Rex', p.5.
104. James Irenge, interview with Paul Bjerk, Musoma, August 2003. In Bjerk, 'Establishment', p.37.
105. ibid., p.44.
106. ibid., p.45.
107. Feinstein, *African*, p.80.
108. Chiume, *Kwacha*, pp.18, 23.
109. Sanders, E.R. 'The African Association and the Growth and Movement of Political Thought in Mid-Twentieth Century East Africa'. Unpublished Ph.D. thesis. University of Cambridge, 2012, p.74.
110. NACO981/16556/20.
111. Irenge, in Mwakikagile, *Nyerere*, p.387.
112. Drum, 'The Julius 'Mwalimu' Nyerere Story', in Smyth, A.., Seftel, A.., ed. *Tanzania: The story of Julius Nyerere through the pages of Drum*, Dar es Salaam: Mkuki na Nyota, 1998 (1966), pp.27–31, p.29.
113. Kitundu, 'Reflections', p.47.
114. Interview, Elias Warioba.
115. Hatch, *African Statesmen*, p.8.
116. NACO981/16556/20.
117. Anonymous interview quotation presented in Hopkins, *Political*, p.73.
118. 'Senior assistant secretary', randomly selected interview quotation in Hopkins, *Political*, pp.72–3.
119. Edinburgh University, *Edinburgh University Calendar: 1951–1952*, Edinburgh: James Thin, 1951, p.223.
120. Huxley, J. *Africa View*, London: Chatto and Windus, 1932, p.96.
121. Nyerere, quoted in Smith, *Nyerere*, p.45. Fagging was the boarding school practice of younger pupils acting as personal servants to the most senior pupils. The duties included preparing food and hot drinks, tidying rooms, cleaning clothing and footwear, and running errands. Failure to comply often resulted in harsh (and frequently physical) punishment.
122. Clarke, P. 'Notes on Pre-Independence Education in Tanganyika', Occasional Paper 34, Centre for Language Education, School of Education, University of Southampton, 1995, p.17.
123. Tanganyika Education Department, *Annual Report* 1925; cited in Furley, 'Education', p.63.
124. Huxley, *Africa*, p.96.
125. Hill, J.F.R., Moffett, J.P. *Tanganyika: A review of its resources and their development*, Dar es Salaam: Government of Tanganyika, 1955, p. 63.
126. Kilongola, R. 'Historia ya Mwalimu Julius Kambarage Nyerere: Mwalimu Julius K. Nyerere alipokuwa mwanafunzi wa Tabora School, 1937–1942' (hereafter 'Kilongola'), 'Kumbukumbu ya Nne: Masomo, Kazi na Michezo'. Usoke, Tabora. Unpublished

Notes for Chapter 2, pp. 37–61

      manuscript (held at Mwalimu Nyerere Foundation, Dar es Salaam), p.30.
127. Hatch, *African Statesmen*, p.8.
128. Kilongola, 'Kumbukumbu ya Tano', p.51.
129. Listowel, *Making*, p.183.
130. Kilongola, 'Kumbukumbu ya Nne', pp.111, 118, 129.
131. ibid., pp.89–92, 97, 108, 110, 115.
132. ibid., pp.86–87; 'Kumbukumbu ya Tano', p.107. See also Thompson, 'Adaptation', pp.149–50.
133. Listowel, *Making*, p.93.
134. It was not until the late 1940s, or 1950, that the Cambridge Overseas School Certificate was selected as the academic target in preference to the Makerere entrance examination. Clarke, 'Notes', p.17.
135. Goldthorpe, *Elite*, p.4.
136. See Ngugi wa Thiong'o on Kenya's Alliance High School, where he offers the summary that – like Tabora Boys – the school was 'to produce leaders who of course, had the necessary character and knowledge to faithfully but intelligently serve King and Empire': wa Thiong'o, N. *Moving the Centre: The struggle for cultural freedoms*, Nairobi: East African Educational Publishers, 1993, p.137.
137. Cadogan, 'Students', p.188.
138. ibid., p.189.
139. For example, Feinstein, *African*, p.80.
140. Stirling, L. *History of Scouting in Tanzania, 1917–1992*, n.d. (c.1990), n.p., cited in Parsons, T. *Race, Resistance, and the Boy Scout Movement in British Colonial Africa*, Athens, OH: Ohio University Press, 2004, p.137. See also Stirling, L. *Tanzanian Doctor*, Nairobi: Heinemann, 1977, pp.66–9.
141. Lugusha and Maruma both applied for the Colonial Development Welfare Scholarship that Nyerere was eventually successful in obtaining to study in the United Kingdom. NACO981/16556/2, 5, 8 and 13.
142. Interview, Adam Marwa.
143. Kyaruzi, in Mwakikagile, *Nyerere*, p.394. Among many other future influential figures in Tanzanian politics and society who attended Tabora Boys were George Kahama, Rashidi Kawawa, Oscar Kambona, Job Lusinde, Christopher Ngaiza and Amon Nsekela. Kahama, J.K. *Sir George: A thematic history of Tanzania through his fifty years of public service*, Beijing: Foreign Languages Press, 2010, p.4.
144. Kilongola, 'Kumbukumbu ya Tano', p.116.
145. Hall, minute, 15 September 1938, and Hall to PC Southern Highlands, 5 October 1938, TNA 18/12/11/120, 122; cited in Iliffe, *Modern History*, p.328.
146. For a European account of colonial Tabora town a little earlier, see Huxley, *Africa*, p.134–6.
147. Wille, 'Recollections', p.3.
148. Kitundu, 'Reflections', p.47.
149. Hopkins, *Political*, p.201. James Blumer was assistant headmaster in 1942, and went on to become headmaster. Memorandum of J.A.C. Blumer, Primary and Secondary Education in Six Selected African Territories, Bodleian Library of Commonwealth & African Studies at Rhodes House, Oxford, MSS. Afr. s. 1755 (114) (Box XXXIII).
150. Smith, *Nyerere*, p.46.
151. Wille, 'Recollections', pp.3–4.
152. Smith, *Nyerere*, p.46.
153. Tibandebage, A. 'The Life of a Near-Failure', Karagwe, 1996: extracts of unpublished manuscript of Andrew Tibandebage's memoirs. The document, sent to the author by Richard Tibandebage, has no page numbers. The section this reference comes from is entitled 'Makerere'.
154. Smith, J.S. *The History of Alliance High School*. Nairobi: Heinemann, 1973, p.107.
155. Chiume, *Kwacha*, p.17.
156. Hofmeyr, I. 'Reading Debating/Debating Reading: The case of the Lovedale Literary

Notes for Chapter 3, pp. 62–77

Society, or why Mandela quotes Shakespeare', in Barber, K, ed. *Africa's Hidden Histories: Everyday literacy and making the self*, Bloomington, IN: Indiana University Press, 2006, pp.258–77, p.265.
157. Listowel describes Nyerere's debating skill in *Making*, p.197.
158. See Rooney, D. *Kwame Nkrumah: The political kingdom in the Third World*, London: I.B. Tauris, 1988, p.9; Biney, A. *The Political and Social Thought of Kwame Nkrumah*, Houndsmill: Palgrave Macmillan, 2011, p.12; Goldsworthy, D. *Tom Mboya: The man Kenya wanted to forget*, Nairobi: Heinemann, 1982, p.8.
159. Kilongola, 'Kumbukumbu ya Nne', p.72.
160. Interview, Nyamwaga. The names of the chiefs who are present were later told to Joseph Muhunda Nyerere and Jack Nyamwaga. The latter does not recall the name of the representative from Bukwaya, but he believes that the chief did attend.
161. NACO981/16556/71. Baker to Crook, 23 August 1950.
162. Lawrance, B.N., Osborn, E.L. Roberts, R.L., eds, *Intermediaries, Interpreters, and Clerks: African employees in the making of colonial Africa*, Madison, WI: University of Wisconsin Press, 2006, p.4.
163. Vaillant, J.G. *Black, French, and African: A life of Léopold Sédar Senghor*, Cambridge, MA: Harvard University Press, 1990, pp.24–5.
164. NACO981/16556/20.

Chapter 3

1. Fortes, M. and E.E. Evans-Pritchard, eds, *African Political Systems*. London: Oxford University Press, 1940, pp.1–23, p.21.
2. Apostolic Delegation Mombasa, *A Catholic Directory of East Africa: 1950*, Dublin: Cahill and Co., 1950, p.113; Shetler, *Imagining*, p.139. Bouniol (*White*, p.217) puts the founding year as 1910. A photograph of the mission house in 1946 is available at http://digitallibrary.usc.edu/cdm/ref/collection/p15799coll123/id/14983/rec/3, accessed 24 March 2014.
3. Société des Missionaires d'Afrique, *Rapport annuel*, 1910–11, p.383; Bourget, L. *Trip Diary*, 'Report of a Trip in 1904 from Bukumbi to Mwanza, Kome? Ukerewe, Kibara, Ikoma–Mara Region, together with some stories' (n.p., n.d.), M-SRC54, Sukuma Archives, 1904; cited in Shetler, *Imagining*, p.140, note 17.
4. *MDB*, A.C. Davey's report, 28 June 1935, entitled 'List of Mission Stations', p.133, 136.
5. Fr. Matthias Könen was born in Germany in 1906. In 1949 he was superior at Sayusayu, Tanzania. He died aged 93 in Germany. Pierre Aucoin, pers.comm., 24 October 2011. See also Apostolic Delegation Mombasa, *Catholic Directory*, p.114.
6. The catechism is a doctrinal manual, often in the form of questions followed by answers to be memorised. See Westerlund, D. *Ujamaa na Dini: A study of some aspects of society and religion in Tanzania, 1961–1977*. Stockholm: University of Stockholm, 1980, p.78.
7. Wille, 'Recollections', p.4.
8. NACO981/16556/20.
9. Listowel, *Making*, pp.181–2; Hatch, *African Statesmen*, p.9.
10. NACO981/16556/20.
11. Wicken to Molony, 14 March 2001, p.4.
12. Wille, 'Recollections', p.4, who writes 'Juker'. Fr. Aloysius Junker was born in France in 1899. In 1949 he was at Mwanza, Tanzania. He died aged 70 in France. Pierre Aucoin, pers.comm., 24 October 2011. Photographs of 'Alsisi' Junker are available at http://digitallibrary.usc.edu/cdm/singleitem/collection/p15799coll123/id/14962/rec/1 and http://digitallibrary.usc.edu/cdm/singleitem/collection/p15799coll123/id/15571/rec/1, accessed 24 March 2014. Fouéré, who puts the year of baptism as 1942, notes how the dates differ among commentators. Fouéré, 'La Fabrique', p.55. Listowel, *Making*, p.177, who gets the date correct, says that Father Mathias Koenen [*sic*] was the priest.
13. Iliffe, *Modern History*, p.508.

Notes for Chapter 3, pp. 62–77

14. Interview, Nyamwaga. Oswald was the only Christian among his brothers, and at the time Christians among the Zanaki were still a small minority. By 1960 the population of 90,000 Zanaki included 1,282 Catholics. Apostolic Delegation Nairobi, *Catholic Directory of East and West Africa: 1961*, Entebbe: Marianum Press, 1961, p.164.
15. Hatch, *African Statesmen*, p.14.
16. Magige Nyerere, pers.comm., 20 May 2010, Mwitongo, Butiama. A copy of Trollope's *Commentaries of Cæsar*, hand-dated by Nyerere to May 1949, is kept in his personal library.
17. Interview, Nyamwaga.
18. Farmer, D. *The Oxford Dictionary of Saints*. Oxford: Oxford University Press, 2003; Watkins, D.B., ed. *The Book of Saints: A comprehensive biographical dictionary*. London: A&C Black, 2002 (1921).
19. Smith, *Nyerere*, p.40.
20. TNA 20/g/11, Accession 83: 1/14/43:1, 12/21/43:3, 1/2/46:1; cited in Fleisher, M.L. *Kuria Cattle Raiders: Violence and vigilantism on the Tanzania/Kenya frontier*, Ann Arbor, MI: University of Michigan Press, 2000, pp.24–25. See also Killingray, D. *Fighting for Britain: African soldiers in the Second World War*, Woodbridge: James Currey, 2010, p.58. On Tanganyikans in the Burma Infantry, see Said, M. *The Life and Times of Abdulwahid Sykes (1924–1968): The untold story of the Muslim struggle against British colonialism in Tanganyika*, London: Minerva, 1998, pp.50–9.
21. On the comparative imagination of African *askari* in South Asia, see Brennan, *Taifa*, pp.136–43.
22. Tibandebage, in Mwakikagile, *Nyerere*, p.400.
23. Tibandebage, 'Life'.
24. Iliffe, J. 'The Spokesman: Martin Kayamba', in Iliffe, *Modern Tanzanians*, pp.66–94, p.75. Kayamba joined from Alliance High School, Kenya, but in 1936 gave up his course in medicine to work at the District Commissioner's Office at Masaka, Uganda. Smith, *Alliance High School*, p.45–6, 88.
25. Uganda Education Department, *Annual Report*, 1929, p.9; cited in Macpherson, M. *They Built for the Future: A chronicle of Makerere University College, 1922–1962*, Cambridge: Cambridge University Press, 1964, p.13. Also Makerere University College, *Makerere University College Calendar, 1961–62*, Kampala: The English Press, 1961, p.14. On the origins of Makerere see Iliffe, J. *East African Doctors: A history of the modern profession*. Kampala: Fountain, 2002, pp.60–91.
26. Cunliffe-Lister to MacMichael, 15 August 1934, TNA 13658/1/115, and Mitchell to MacMichael, 1 November 1937, TNA 25401/1/5; cited in Iliffe, *Modern History*, p.446, note 5.
27. Mills, D. 'Life on the Hill: Students and the social history of Makerere', *Africa*, 76 (2) 2006, pp.247–66, p.250.
28. ibid., p.251.
29. See also Nyerere, J.K. 'Statement to the U.N. Fourth Committee, 1956', in *Freedom and Unity*, pp.40–4, p.42.
30. Chiume, *Kwacha*, p.39.
31. ibid., p.41.
32. Goldthorpe, *Elite*, pp.11–2, 26.
33. ibid., p.12.
34. Prewitt, K. 'Makerere: Intelligence vs intellectuals', *Transition* 6 (27) 1966, pp.35–9, p.37. See also 'Obligations Upon Students', in *East Africa and Rhodesia*, 1950, 26 (1324), pp.744–5.
35. Listowel, *Making*, p.182. Some sheets in Nyerere's handwriting listing pupils in a few classes at Tabora Boys (probably from 1944–1945) are stored with the manuscript of 'Uhuru wa Wanawake' at the Mwalimu Nyerere Foundation, Dar es Salaam.
36. Mwakikagile, *Nyerere*, p.395, 400. Kyaruzi mentions that during his time at Makerere the Kabaka of Buganda, 'King Freddie' (Mutesa II), attended, for whom John Crabbe, later headmaster at Tabora Boys, was his private tutor. Kyaruzi, 'Muhaya', p.25.
37. NACO981/16556/90. Nyerere to Crook, 20 June 1951.

Notes for Chapter 3, pp. 62–77

38. Kyaruzi, in Mwakikagile, *Nyerere*, p.395.
39. Drum, 'Nyerere Story', p.29.
40. Tibandebage, 'Life', p.x.
41. Tibandebage, in Mwakikagile, *Nyerere*, pp.400–1.
42. Kyaruzi, in Mwakikagile, *Nyerere*, p.395.
43. Tibandebage, in Mwakikagile, *Nyerere*, p.400. Aggrey had visited Tanganyika in 1924 as a member of the Phelps-Stokes Commission. For the influence of Aggrey on nationalists in Tanganyika, see Sanders, 'African Association', pp.38–49. Adam Marwa recalls how, after Nyerere returned from Edinburgh, 'Mwalimu read much in his spare time. He read a book on Gandhi. After he read it he told Oswald [Marwa Mang'ombe] about this strange man from India who is like Jesus.' Interview, Adam Marwa.
44. Tibandebage, 'Life', p.1.
45. Listowel, *Making*, p.183.
46. Macpherson, *Built*, p.36. The report is from three years prior to Nyerere's entrance to the college.
47. Kyaruzi, 'Muhaya', p.27.
48. ibid., p.27.
49. ibid., p.27.
50. ibid., p.26.
51. Nyerere, undated personal notes for a presentation while at Makerere College, pp.12–13. 'Uhuru wa Wanawake' notebook, Mwalimu Nyerere Foundation, Dar es Salaam.
52. See, for example, the discussion of the 1962 Study Conference on Pan-African Socialism at Kivukoni College, described as 'the occasion for the debut of Dr. Julius Nyerere's political theory', in Burke, F.G. 'Tanganyika: The search for ujamaa', in Friedland, W.H., Rosberg, C.G., ed. *African Socialism*, Stanford, C.A.: Stanford University Press, 1964, pp.194–219.
53. Friedland, W.H., Rosberg, C.G. 'Introduction: The anatomy of African socialism', in Friedland & Rosberg, *African Socialism*, pp.1–11, p.1. For a slightly earlier summary see Friedland, W.H. 'Four Sociological Trends in African Socialism', *Africa Report*, 8 (5) 1963, pp.7–10. Metz also accepts this timeframe. Metz, S. 'In Lieu of Orthodoxy: The socialist theories of Nkrumah and Nyerere', *Journal of Modern African Studies*, 20 (3) 1982, pp.377–92, p.337.
54. Schachter Morgenthau, R. 'African Socialism: Declaration of ideological independence', *Africa Report*, 8 (5) 1963, pp.3–6, p.4. See also Senghor, L.S. *African Socialism: A report to the Constitutive Congress of the Party of African Federation*. New York: American Society of African Culture, 1959.
55. JUKANYE, 'African Socialism', Kampala, *Tanganyika Standard*, 21 July 1943. James Brennan writes that the letter was published on 23 July 1943, although the University of Dar es Salaam library East Africana Collection archive of the original newspaper has the letter published on 21 July. Brennan, J.R. 'Youth, the TANU Youth League and Managed Vigilantism in Dar es Salaam, Tanzania, 1925–1973', *Africa*, 76 (2), 2006, pp.221–46, p.226. I thank Paul Bjerk for bringing Brennan's article to my attention.
56. The 21 July 1943 daily edition was published on a Wednesday, but the circulation of the weekly edition was wider throughout the territory. Hill, *Tanganyika*, p.117. Hill and Moffett also discuss the Swahili press, although they are writing a decade after Nyerere's letter was published.
57. Nyerere, 'Ujamaa', p.170.
58. Nyerere's letters, including those from this early period, are usually written in flawless English. The confusing syntax in this sentence may be a transcription error made by a typist at the newspaper. The original text could have been, '…they are still very reluctant to accept it. Will Europe, however? Whether socialism is accepted now or later on, it does not matter very much because…'.
59. On cotton at the national level, see Dawe, J.A. 'A History of Cotton-Growing in East and Central Africa: British demand, African supply', unpublished Ph.D. thesis, University of Edinburgh, 1993, pp.347–62. For a case study of an exploitative, export-oriented

Notes for Chapter 3, pp. 62–77

      export structure involving cotton at the district level, see Larson, L.E. 'A History of Mahenge (Ulanga) District, c.1860–1957', unpublished Ph.D. thesis. University of Dar es Salaam, 1976, pp.232–52.
60. Mustafa, 'Concept', pp.76–7. The Sheet 1 (Agriculture) that Mustafa references for this story is missing from the *Musoma District Book* that is held in the Tanzania National Archives. Mustafa adds that he was informed by Joseph Kizurira Burito Nyerere that the story was apparently believed by Chief Edward Wanzagi who, when Wanzagi became Chief of the Zanaki, restarted cotton production after realising that his fellows had duped the colonial administration.
61. Mang'enya, E.A.M. *Discipline and Tears: Reminiscences of an African civil servant on colonial Tanganyika*, Dar es Salaam: Dar es Salaam University Press, 1984, p.273–6.
62. Nyerere to Nicholson (re. 'The Race Problem in East Africa'), 4 September 1951, Fabian Colonial Bureau papers (hereafter 'FCB'), Rhodes House, MSS Brit. Emp. S 365, Box 6/2/87.
63. Prewitt, 'Makerere', p.37.
64. Rooney, *Kwame*, p.17. Nkrumah's work was published in 1962, using his 1945 foreword.
65. Sanders, 'African Association', pp.202, 211.
66. ibid., pp.113–124.
67. Smith, *Nyerere*, p.55.
68. ibid., p.46. In the 2009 reproduction of *Uhuru wa Wanawake* Nyerere makes reference to J.S. Mill's *The Subjection of Women* (1869), although in his preface (where, intriguingly, he refers to his work as a book, '*kitabu hiki*') it is not clear to which part of the main text the footnote is intended to refer. Nyerere, *Uhuru wa Wanawake*, p.26.
69. Stöger-Eising, 'Ujamaa', p.129.
70. Bunting, 'Heart'.
71. Durand, 'Catholic Saint', p.11.
72. Nyerere, J.K. 'Socialism and Rural Development' in *Freedom and Socialism*, pp.337–66, p.339.
73. Macpherson puts 1945 as the year of the admission of the first women at Makerere. Nyerere, writing in 1944, says that he had already been studying alongside women for a whole year. Macpherson, *Built*, p.42; Nyerere, *Uhuru wa Wanawake*, p.61.
74. Mills, 'Life', p.254.
75. Mang'enya, *Discipline*, p.16.
76. Kagoro, G. 'Life at Campus: The halls of residence and the cultures', *The MAK Alumni* 1. 2003, pp.10–12, p.11.
77. Nyerere, *Uhuru wa Wanawake*, p.61.
78. Extracts taken from Dean Alistair MacPherson's files of the 'Welfare and Discipline Committee'. Makerere library, Africana section; cited in Mills, 'Life', p.255.
79. Mang'enya, *Discipline*, p.5.
80. Goldthorpe, *Elite*, p.89.
81. ibid., p.14.
82. An undated Biology notebook, signed 'Mwalimu Julius K. Nyerere', is stored with the manuscript of 'Uhuru wa Wanawake' at the Mwalimu Nyerere Foundation, Dar es Salaam, as are excerpts of his notes for Elementary Chemistry, from July 1945.
83. Wille, 'Recollections', p.4.
84. ibid., p.5.
85. ibid., p.4.
86. For example, see Nyerere, J.K. 'The Church and Society', in *Freedom and Development*, pp.213–28, p.227–8.
87. Wille, 'Recollections', p.4. On Maritain and Nyerere, see Mgeni, P. 'Jacques Maritain's Conception of Democracy: Philosophical foundation and its importance in the contemporary world with examples from Tanzania', unpublished Ph.D. thesis, Holy Cross University, Rome, 2009. Nyerere's personal library holds a number of Maritain's works.
88. Pius XI to the President of the International Union of Catholic Women's League, 30 July

1928; cited in Mathias, L. *Catholic Action: Theory and practice*. Madras: Huxley, 1952, p.16.
89. Said, *Abdulwahid*, p.110; Listowel, *Making*, pp.183–184. Elsewhere the martyrs are named as Charles Lwanga (canonised in 1964 by Pope Paul VI) and Mathias Marumba (Mulumba Kalemba). See, for example, Abdy, D.C. *The Martyrs of Uganda*, London: Sheldon Press, 1928.
90. Listowel, *Making*, p.184.
91. Wille, 'Recollections', p.4, writes 'Ruboga'. Rubaga (Kampala) is where St Mary's Catholic Cathedral is located.
92. Vedastus Kyaruzi worked at the same hospital. Kyaruzi, 'Muhaya', p.37–8. This section based on the author's personal communication with Juma Mwapachu, 2 September 2011. See also 'The Life and Times of Hamza Mwapachu', www.vijana.fm/2012/09/18/the-life-and-times-of-hamza-mwapachu, accessed on 23 August 2013.
93. The Princess Margaret Hospital (since independence, Muhimbili Medical Centre) was inaugurated in 1956, signalling the end of Sewa Haji Hospital. One of the ward blocks at Muhimbili still carries the name of Sewa Haji. Mwaluko, G.M.P. 'Health Services in Tanzania: A historical overview'. In Mwaluko, G.M.P., Kilama, W.L., Mandara, M.P., Murru, M., Macpherson, C.N.L., eds, *Health and Disease in Tanzania*, London: Harper Collins, 1991, pp.1-7, p.2. Also Hill & Moffett, *Tanganyika*, p.87, which makes no mention of civil servants at Sewa Haji. On Sewa Haji, see Matson, A.T. 'Sewa Haji: A note', *Tanganyika Notes and Records*, 65, 1966, pp.91–4 and Tajddin, M.A.S.A. 'Sewa Haji Paroo (1851–1891)', in *101 Ismaili Heroes*, Karachi: Islamic Book Publisher, 2003, p.400.
94. 1929 is the official date of the African Association's formation, but Sanders ('African Association', pp.27–73) – the most detailed account of pre-independence political organisation in Tanganyika – considers evidence that its roots stretch further back. See also Brennan, *Taifa*, p.68–9; Austen, R. 'Notes on the Pre-history of TANU', *Makerere Journal* (9) 1964, pp.1–6; and Okoth, A. *A History of Africa, 1915–1995 Volume Two: African nationalism and the de-colonisation process*, Nairobi and Dar es Salaam: East African Educational Publishers and Ujuzi Educational Publishers, 2006, pp.47–8 on the role of Martin Kayamba, Cecil Matola, Ramadhani Ali and Kleist Sykes. More detail on the roles of Martin Kayamba (including the earlier Tanganyika Territorial Civil Servants Association), Kleist Sykes, Lulapangilo Zakaria Mhemedzi, Ali Ponda and Hassan Suleiman is available in the respective chapters of Iliffe, *Modern Tanzanians*. For popular politics in the provinces and especially north-east and Sukumaland as a precursor to TANU, see Iliffe, *Modern History*, pp.412–417, 485–520. On the evolution of TAA see Lonsdale, J. 'Some Origins of Nationalism in East Africa', *Journal of African History*, 9 (1) 1968, pp.119–46, pp.131–6; Ulotu, A.U. *Historia ya TANU*, Dar es Salaam: East African Literature Bureau, 1971, pp.10–14. For an insider's account of its internal politics, see Kyaruzi, 'Muhaya', p.25–42.
95. Drum, 'Nyerere Story', pp.29–30. This may also be the 'Social Society' that Nyerere is said to have also organised while at Makerere. Segal, R. *Political Africa: A who's who of personalities and parties*, London: Stevens & Sons, 1961, p.215.
96. Tibandebage, 'Life', p.x.
97. Bunting, 'Heart'.
98. Nyerere was at Makerere from 1943 to 1946. The AA became the TAA in 1948.
99. Listowel, *Making*, p.184.
100. Smith, *Nyerere*, p.43 and Sanders, 'African Association', pp.86, 217. Kyaruzi mentions that a branch was at Makerere in 1942. Kyaruzi, 'Muhaya', p.25. For the important part that the Nyakyusa clerk Edward Mwangosi played in this period of Tanganyika's political history, see Iliffe, *Modern History*, pp.413–25, passim.
101. Sanders, 'African Association', p.218.
102. ibid., p.86, note 60.
103. ibid., p.206, note 4.
104. Nyerere to Shepperson, 8 October 1955, CLX-A-16/1, Shep.Coln. See also Listowel, *Making*, pp.184–5; Hatch, *African Statesmen*, p.16–17.
105. CCM. n.d. *Mwalimu Julius Kambarage Nyerere katika Tanzania*. Dar es Salaam: Chama cha

245

Notes for Chapter 4, pp. 78–99

Mapinduzi, pp.1–2; Mwenegoha, *Mwalimu*, p.7.
106. Kyaruzi, in Mwakikagile, *Nyerere*, p.395. See also Kyaruzi, 'Muhaya', p.25–6; Chapter 4, note 104.
107. Hatch, *African Statesmen*, p.18.

Chapter 4

1. Nyerere's notes are for a presentation he was giving on the U.S. educator in either 1944 or 1945. The quote is located on page 4 of the draft (stored at the Mwalimu Nyerere Foundation, Dar es Salaam, and filed in Nyerere's 'Uhuru wa Wanawake' notebook from Makerere). The original quote is from Washington, B.T. *Up from Slavery: An autobiography*. Cambridge, MA: Riverside Press, 1928 (1901), p.37.
2. NACO981/16556/20. Makerere University College was under the University of London, and at the time only awarded up to diploma level.
3. Memorandum on the Problem of Relations Between Native Authorities and the Younger African Generation, 12 May 1945, Tanganyika Territory Secretariat minute paper 33136; cited in Maguire, *Toward*, p.59.
4. Hatch, *African Statesmen*, p.18.
5. Interview, Nyamwaga.
6. Andrew Tibandebage left Makerere at the end of 1944. Richard Tibandebage, pers.comm., 22 January 2012.
7. Tibandebage, 'Life', p.2.
8. Tibandebage, in Mwakikagile, *Nyerere*, p.401.
9. Kyaruzi, in Mwakikagile, *Nyerere*, p.396.
10. Tibandebage, 'Life', p.2.
11. Tibandebage, in Mwakikagile, *Nyerere*, p.401.
12. On King's College Budo see, McGregor, G.P. *King's College Budo: A centenary history, 1906–2006*, Kampala: Fountain, 2006.
13. Interview, Adam Marwa.
14. Mang'enya, *Discipline*, p.32.
15. Macola, *Liberal*, p.16.
16. Wille, 'Recollections', p.4. John R. Crabbe was headmaster at Tabora Boys from 1951 to 1962. Clarke, 'Notes', p.18; Cadogan, 'Students', pp.363–4. Fierce and bustling, Crabbe was 'the archetypal colonial headmaster', John Iliffe, pers.comm., 22 August 2012, Oxford.
17. Wille, 'Recollections', p.4. The following year Nyerere's salary at St Mary's was 130 shillings a month. NACO981/16556/Minute Paper entry 53. Unidentified signature to Crook.
18. NACO981/16556/20.
19. Tibandebage writes 'his younger brother Joseph Nyerere (also deceased)'. This was Joseph Kizurira Burito Nyerere, who was later joined in Tabora by Joseph Muhunda Nyerere. Interview, Joseph Muhunda Nyerere.
20. Smith, *Nyerere*, p.47. Other teachers at the same time were Fathers Emile Lacroix, John Crook, Cornelius Bronsveld and Raymond Beaudet. http://archdiocese-tabora.net23.net/history.html, accessed on 11 March 2014.
21. Hatch, *African Statesmen*, p.19.
22. Tibandebage, 'Life', p.2.
23. Listowel, *Making*, p.196.
24. ibid.
25. Listowel, J. 'Tanzania and Her Future: Problems of building African socialism', *The Round Table: The Commonwealth Journal of International Affairs*, 60 (239) 1970, pp.275–84, p.283. Coincidentally, Oscar Kambona was at neighbouring Tabora Boys when Nyerere was teaching at St Mary's. Kambona became Secretary General of TANU and Foreign Minister after independence, but fell out with Nyerere over ideological issues. He remained in exile in London from 1967 to 1992, and in his absence was charged with

Notes for Chapter 4, pp. 78–99

treason for an attempted coup. See Kunsanje, Hamisi. n.d. *Tanzania: La Défense Accuser: Differences between Oscar S. Kambona and President Julius Nyerere*. London: Debemoja. For Nyerere's justification of detention without trial, see Nyerere, J.K. 'Opening of the University College Campus', in *Freedom and Unity*, pp.305–15, pp.312–3.

26. Kyaruzi, in Mwakikagile, *Nyerere*, p.396. The branch opened in March 1945. Iliffe, *Modern History*, p.421. Vedastus Kyaruzi took up his post at Dar es Salaam's Sewa Haji Hospital in March 1949. Juma Mwapachu (reporting communication with Vedastus Kyaruzi on 12 February 2012), pers.comm., 13 February 2012.
27. Hatch, *African Statesmen*, p.19.
28. Juma Mwapachu, pers.comm., 2 September 2011. Tibandebage was later elected Provincial Chairman. Tibandebage, 'Life', p.2. It is stated elsewhere that Nyerere was the Assistant Secretary. Hajivayanis, G.G., Mtowa, A.C., Iliffe, J. 'The Politicians: Ali Ponda and Hassan Suleiman'. In Iliffe, *Modern Tanzanians*, pp.227–53, 1973, p.243. The authors suggest that Hassan Suleiman and Ali Ponda visited the Tabora branch in early 1945 and met with Nyerere, who was teaching at St Mary's at the time. As stated, the National Archive records suggest that he started at St Mary's in January 1946.
29. Iliffe, *Modern History*, p.431. See pp.406–12, Sanders, 'African Association' (especially pp.172–205), and Anthony, D. 'Culture and Society in a Town in Transition: A people's history of Dar es Salaam, 1863–1939', unpublished Ph.D. thesis, University of Wisconsin-Madison, 1983, for the association's early roots in Dar es Salaam and its strong support among Muslim men.
30. Iliffe, ibid., p.432.
31. Frederick, S.W. 'The Life of Joseph Kimalando', *Tanganyika Notes and Records*, 70, 1969, pp.21–8, p.25.
32. Sanders, 'African Association', p.170.
33. See ibid., pp.156–172 for discussion on the African Association and chiefs. For the claim that chiefs' authority was already on the wane by the late 1950s, see Cory, 'Reform', p.78. Also Shorter, *Chiefship*, pp.384–386 for the argument that, with the mid-1960s introduction throughout Tanzania of ten house cell system (*nyumba kumi*), some chiefs and chiefs' sons still essentially continued to fill the role of headman.
34. Owens, 'The Secret History of TANU: Rumor, Historiography and Muslim Unrest in Contemporary Dar es Salaam', *History and Anthropology* 16 (4) 2005, pp. 441–463, p.442. For an important perspective on Tanganyikan nationalism that focuses on Abdulwahid Sykes – 'an "enabler" for the young Nyerere in TAA and TANU', and 'the patriot the party chose to forget' – see Said, *Abdulwahid*. There is also a strong case for the key role that women played in the nationalist struggle, presented in Geiger, S. *TANU Women*. Through her accounts of the life history of women participants in TANU, Geiger challenges the view that the nationalism movement was led solely by men who were the products of Christian mission education. I thank Demere Kitunga for urging me to revisit Geiger's work.
35. Iliffe, *Modern History*, p.432.
36. Interview, Joseph Muhunda Nyerere.
37. Smith, *Nyerere*, p.47.
38. Interview, Joseph Muhunda Nyerere.
39. Mang'enya, *Discipline*, p.17.
40. Pearson, N. n.d. (c.1949). 'Trade Unionist on Safari', Rhodes House MSS Africa.s.394, 184; cited in Brennan, *Taifa*, p.108.
41. Mlahagwa, J.R. 'The Headman: Chilongola Jenga', in Iliffe, *Modern Tanzanians*, pp.133–55, pp.139–40.
42. Interview, Jackton Nyerere.
43. Irenge, in Mwakikagile, *Nyerere*, p.384.
44. Irenge (in ibid., p.385) calls her 'Magoni', and says that she was about eight years of age. Accounts given to the author in interviews with Joseph Muhunda Nyerere and Magori herself suggest that she was some years younger.
45. Nyerere, *Uhuru wa Wanawake*, p.26.

Notes for Chapter 4, pp. 78–99

46. Interviews, Magori Watiha, Jackton Nyerere, Joseph Muhunda Nyerere.
47. Wille, 'Recollections', pp.5–6. This is supported by H.C. Baxter, who in 1941 recorded that '[a] goat is killed at the marriage feast and occasionally a bullock and this must be returned with the bride price should circumstances occur which necessitate the return of the latter'. *MDB*, Laws, Manner and Customs: Zanaki tribe, Sheet 3, p.1.
48. Wille uses the English term 'dowry', which may be a mistranslation from Zanaki, which he spoke with much competence. The context of his discussion of the transfer of cattle suggests that he is indeed talking of bridewealth/bride price – an exchange from the groom's family to the bride's family – rather than the opposite dowry exchange from the bride's family to the groom's. Wille, 'Recollections', p.5.
49. Interview, Joseph Muhunda Nyerere.
50. Irenge in Mwakikagile, *Nyerere*, p.385.
51. ibid.
52. Interview, Magori Watiha. Another interpretation of *nyakisaho* is that it is derived from *esaho*, a pot for food (or water) used in the unexpected arrival of a guest. Shem Koren, pers.comm., 12 March 2014.
53. Wille, 'Recollections', p.5.
54. Richard Tibandebage, pers.comm., 22 January 2012.
55. Tibandebage, in Mwakikagile, *Nyerere*, p.401.
56. Duggan, W.R., Civille, J.R. *Tanzania and Nyerere: A study of ujamaa and nationhood*, Maryknoll, NY: Orbis, 1976, p.26.
57. Nyerere to the editors of *Makerere* magazine, November 1946, (headed with '*Makerere*, Vol. 1, No. 1. November 1946, p.35'); CLX-A-16/1, Shep.Coln. Also Hatch, *African Statesmen*, p.24–5.
58. Hatch, *African Statesmen*, p.24–26. Hatch does not explicitly use the term 'education for self-reliance', but the article he refers to deals principally with both themes.
59. Nyerere to Creech Jones, 1 August 1946, TNA 34905/50; cited in Chachage, C.S.L. 'Socialist Ideology and the Reality of Tanzania', unpublished Ph.D. thesis, University of Glasgow, 1986, chapter 5, p.1. Creech Jones became Secretary of State for the Colonies two months later.
60. Chiume, *Kwacha*, p.27.
61. See RH MSS. Arf.s. 1755 (114) Box 33, R.A.C. Blumer; cited in Cadogan, 'Students', p.279.
62. Chiume, *Kwacha*, pp.27–8. See also Michael Lukumbuzya's account in Listowel, *Making*, p.197.
63. Rashidi Kawawa; cited in Smith, *Nyerere*, p.48. On Kawawa, see Magoti, J.M.J. *Simba wa vita katika historia ya Tanzania: Rashidi Mfaume Kawawa*, Dar es Salaam: Matai, 2007.
64. Tibandebage, in Mwakikagile, *Nyerere*, p.401.
65. Interview, Joseph Muhunda Nyerere. Smith says the chief was Chief Haroun Msabila Lugusha. Smith, *Nyerere*, p.47. Lugusha was twenty-sixth chief of the Sikonge, near Tabora. He studied just before Nyerere at both Tabora Boys and Makerere, but was not recommended for the CDWS. NACO981/16556/2 and 5.
66. Juma Mwapachu, pers.comm., 2 September 2011.
67. Kyaruzi, in Mwakikagile, *Nyerere*, p.396.
68. See Taylor, J.C. *The Political Development of Tanganyika*, London: Oxford University Press, 1963, p.109–10.
69. Friedland, 'Evolution', p.277.
70. Iliffe, *Modern History*, p.568; Sanders ('African Association', p.166) lists Adam Sapi as the third African member.
71. Listowel, *Making*, p.198–199; Hatch, *African Statesmen*, p.22–3.
72. Nyerere to Nicholson, 15 September 1954, Box 121/3, FCB.
73. Sanders, 'African Association', p.221.
74. Mwapachu's letter was discovered by Richard Tibandebage (son of the late Ambassador Andrew Tibandebage) in Karagwe, Kagera Region, where it was stored within Nyerere's 'Education – Child Study and Psychology' subject notes – presumably notes

Notes for Chapter 4, pp. 78–99

he took while at Makerere. Tibandebage assumes that the notes were 'among Mwalimu's belongings left in the house at Gongoni [the location of Tibandebage's house in Tabora] when he left for Scotland in 1949'. Discussion, Richard Tibandebage and author, January 2011. This section also draws on multiple communication between Juma Mwapachu and the author, January and February 2012; Lauren Meyers, Woodson Research Center, Fondren Library, Rice University, pers.comm., 15 and 22 February 2012. I thank Ms Meyers for her research on the Juliette Huxley papers.

75. On the club, see Kyaruzi, 'Muhaya', p.38–9. For the non-racial 'Oracle' group, which may have emanated from Hamsa u Ishirini, see Listowel, *Making*, p.220. See also Twining's comment on 'highly educated Africans… the loneliest people in Tanganyika,' in Bates, *Gust*, p.222. On race relations in the early 1950s, see Longford, M. *The Flags Changed at Midnight*, Leominster: Gracewing, 2001, pp.30–41; on later inter-racial meetings, see Eckert, 'Cultural', p.257–8.
76. Said reports of a Wednesday Tea Club of young British-trained intellectuals who met in the evening once a week to discuss political issues.
77. Kyaruzi, 'Muhaya', p.38–9.
78. Iliffe, *Modern History*, p.430. See also Chidzero, B.T.G. *Tanganyika and International Trusteeship*. London and New York: Oxford University Press, 1961.
79. This section on Mousheng's visit is taken from Lohrmann, U. *Voices from Tanganyika: Great Britain, the United Nations and the decolonization of a Trust Territory, 1946–1961*, Münster: LIT Verlag, 2007, p.76. It cites Lamb, 'United Nations' Visiting Mission. Notes on First Itinerary', n.d., CO 537/3484, no.81, p.8. See also Clarke, 'Notes', pp.21–2.
80. See Lohrmann, *Voices*, p.498–503.
81. For an insight into the young Nyerere's knowledge of the practice of polygamy among various tribes, and his views on the subject, see 'Kuoa Wanawake Wengi' in *Uhuru wa Wanawake*, pp.28–34.
82. Subsequent correspondence on these issues between the Muslim Mwapachu and the Catholic Nyerere has not yet come to light, but there was certainly a mutual respect between the two that lasted until Hamza Mwapachu's untimely death in September 1962.
83. Unless otherwise stated, the following text on Maria Nyerere draws collectively on: an interview with Maria Nyerere conducted by Stanley Kamana, published in *Rai*, 14 October 1999, and translated by Godfrey Mwakikagile as presented in *Nyerere*, p.389–393; an account given by Father Wille in Wille, 'Recollections'; and the author's interviews with Maria Nyerere.
84. Wille calls Maria's mother both 'Anna' and 'Hanna' ('Recollections', p.1). Maria clarifies that her mother said that her name was Hannah, as one of two wives of Elkanah in I Samuel: 1–2. Interview, Maria Nyerere. In Julius Nyerere's personal Bible he has written her name as 'Anna Maseke'.
85. Educated Tanganyikan men seemed to be greatly concerned with the short supply of (formally) educated Tanganyikan women during this period, as Vedastus Kyaruzi explained of a discussion between members of the TAWA/African Association Makerere branch and the Catholic Archbishop of East Africa: 'We stressed that it was not going to be easy for educated young men from Tanganyika to find educated girls to marry.' Kyaruzi, 'Muhaya', p.25.
86. Wille, in Mwakikagile, *Nyerere*, p.401.
87. Irenge, in Mwakikagile, *Nyerere*, p.385. This is Bona Anicet Musoga.
88. Interview, Maria Nyerere.
89. Maria Nyerere, in Mwakikagile, *Nyerere*, p.391.
90. Interview, Maria Nyerere.
91. ibid.
92. ibid. In another account, Julius is said to have accompanied to Nyegina a friend named Wambura who was visiting his friend called Radigunda. Magige Nyerere, pers.comm., 20 May 2010, Mwitongo, Butiama. This may have been a later visit.
93. *MDB*, Laws, Manner and Customs: Zanaki tribe, Sheet 3, p.13.

Notes for Chapter 4, pp. 78–99

94. Interview, Maria Nyerere.
95. Interview, Rose Nyerere.
96. Wille, 'Recollections', p.5.
97. Interview, Nyamwaga.
98. Listowel, *Making*, p.199; Molony, T.S.J. 'Nyerere, the Early Years: A perspective from Professor G.A. Shepperson', In Molony, T.S.J., ed. *Nyerere: Student, Teacher, Humanist, Statesman*, King, K. pp.3–18. Edinburgh: Centre of African Studies, University of Edinburgh, 2000, p.8.
99. Duggan, *Tanzania*, p.49. As well as some major African nationalists and world statesmen, Duggan lists the former Catholic Archbishop of Dar es Salaam, Edgar Maranta, and the Anglican bishop of Masasi, Trevor Huddleston, as providing important inspiration to Nyerere. Duggan also lists the French philosopher and Jesuit priest Pierre Teilhard de Chardin, whose attempts to reconcile science and (Catholic) religion displeased certain officials in the Roman Curia. See also Nyerere, 'Church', p.222. A number of de Chardin's books are held in Nyerere's private library.
100. Listowel, *Making*, p.195.
101. First Matriculation, 1949–50, EUA IN1/ADS/STA/4, EUL.
102. NACO981/16556/9; Moral Philosophy class list, Da 35 MOR PHIL 17, in EUA-A-1000, EUL. Minute paper entry 8 to NACO981/16556 relates to Nyerere's examination results and includes a brief note ('Mrs. [Mitford-]Barberton: B.U. as requested') made on 12 May 1948 and signed by an Alan Paton. Emeritus Professor Peter Alexander believes that while Paton was very interested in African education and African development, in May 1948 the author was in Johannesburg enjoying the fame from his recent bestseller, *Cry, the Beloved Country*, a novel indicting the apartheid system. Alexander adds that Paton made many contacts during a tour of British borstals from July to November 1946, and speculates that someone dealing with Nyerere's file might have thought he could make a contribution to it. Paton's 'B.U.' may refer to Bristol University (see Chapter 5, note 53). How he signed Nyerere's London-based file sheet from Johannesburg remains a mystery.
103. Wille, 'Recollections', pp.4–5.
104. Unpublished paper of John Petro, Branch Secretary of the African Association/TAA, 1946–54; cited in Cliffe, L. 'Nationalism and the Reaction to Enforced Agricultural Change in Tanganyika during the Colonial Period', in Cliffe, L, Saul, J., ed. *Socialism in Tanzania* Volume 1: 'Politics', Nairobi: East African Publishing House, 1972, pp.17–24, p.21. But see also main text at Chapter 3, note 106.
105. Interview, Jackton Nyerere.
106. Bjerk, 'Establishment', p.126. Bjerk's source is James Irenge, '*Historia: Uhusiano kati ya walimu*,' p.5–6, James Irenge Papers, Mwalimu Nyerere Foundation (which were not available to this author) and an interview with Irenge. See also Irenge in Mwakikagile, *Nyerere*, p.386–7.
107. Wille, 'Recollections', pp.4–5.
108. Duggan, *Tanzania*, p.48.
109. Hill, *Tanganyika*, p.66, and p.6, which outlines that bursaries were also available for post-secondary studies abroad – but not for Africans. Also Iliffe, *Modern History*, p.437, 446. For a critique of the Act, see Zeleza, P.T. 'Colonial Developmentalism', in *Manufacturing African Studies and Crises*, pp.218–40. Dakar: CODESRIA, 1997.
110. NACO981/16556/20. Other sources given here suggest Walsh was headmaster. The Missionaries of Africa record Stanley as having 'taught at Central School, Tabora, from 1 October 1944 till 26 April 1949'. Pierre Aucoin, pers.comm., 7 March 2014.
111. ibid.
112. ibid./22.
113. Lee, J.M. 'Commonwealth Students in the United Kingdom, 1940–1960: Student Welfare and World Status', *Minerva*, 44 (1) 2006, pp.1–24, p.2.
114. Creech Jones became Chairman of the Colonial Bureau in 1940 after serving on the Fabian Society's Executive Committee from 1925. He played a key role in the forma-

Notes for Chapter 5, pp. 100–131

tion of the Labour Party's colonial policies, and was the initiator of the plan to end colonial rule and to form a Commonwealth of freely participating states. See 'Introduction to the Guide to the Papers of Arthur Creech Jones', Rhodes House.
115. Smith, *Influence*, p.4–7, and p.25. See also Iliffe, *Modern History*, p.447, note 2.
116. NACO537/2592, 'The Political Significance of African Students in Great Britain', Memo by G.B. Cartland, July 1947; cited in Hargreaves, J. 'African Students in Britain: The Case of Aberdeen University', *Immigrants and Minorities*, 12 (3) 1993, pp.129–44, p.131.
117. Lee, 'Commonwealth', p.9.
118. NACO981/16556/5a–5d and 6a–6c.
119. ibid./2, 5d, 24, 25 and 36.
120. Kitundu, 'Reflections', p.48.
121. Interview, Adam Marwa.
122. Interview, Jackton Nyerere.
123. Irenge; cited in Bjerk, 'Establishment', p.126.
124. CORY, hand-written manuscript (marked with both '-5-' and '2').
125. Bjerk, 'Establishment', p.127.
126. Kitundu, 'Reflections', p.48.
127. Interview, Adam Marwa.
128. NACO981/16556/25.
129. ibid./26.
130. Nyerere outlines these in the 1944 *Uhuru wa Wanawake*, p.20–2.
131. Hatch, *African Statesmen*, p.24.
132. Nyerere, 'Kutoa Mahari' in *Uhuru wa Wanawake*, pp.9–18.
133. ibid., p.15.
134. ibid., p.8–10.
135. ibid., p.16.
136. Interview, Maria Nyerere. Father Wille believes that Julius had customarily paid the cows to the family of his future bride, adding the detail that Oswald helped him to make arrangements for his marriage and to deliver the cows. Wille, 'Recollections', p.5. Jackton Nyerere is of the opinion that, after the death of Nyerere Burito, somebody in Butiama met with Magori's family and returned the bridewealth. Interview, Jackton Nyerere.
137. Issues of family adjustments when a student (invariably a husband) returned home were something that Mary Trevelyan, an adviser to overseas students at the University of London, was well aware of, and she raised the issue in a discussion when asked what the greatest problem a (West) African student had to face in the United Kingdom. Trevelyan, M. 1955. 'African Student at Home'. *African Affairs*, 54 (214). pp.37–41, p.41.
138. Colonial Office, *Education Policy in British Tropical Africa*, London: HMSO, 1925, p.8; cited in Eckert, 'Cultural', p.252.
139. Interview, Maria Nyerere.
140. Wille, 'Recollections', pp.4–5.
141. ibid., p.5.
142. Juma Mwapachu and Richard Tibandebage, pers.comm., January 2012.
143. Interview, Adam Marwa.

Chapter 5

1. www.granta.com/New-Writing/The-Magic-Place. Reproduced by permission of Kapka Kassabova; accessed 17 August 2012.
2. Williams, S. *Colour Bar: The triumph of Seretse Khama and his nation*, London: Penguin, 2006, p.60.
3. For example, Che-Mponda, A.H. 'Aspects of Nyerere's Political Philosophy: A study in the dynamics of African political thought', *African Study Monographs*, (5) December 1984, pp.63–74, p.65; Abdulrahman Kinana 'The Legacy of Julius Nyerere', 2011, http://youtu.be/pnklBcI1KPc (at 1 minute 11 seconds), accessed 4 January 2012.

Notes for Chapter 5, pp. 100–131

4. Cox to Murray, 30 September 1948, Student file 1949 (Makwaia), Lincoln College archives, University of Oxford. Also in the same collection: unnamed letter, 17 October 1948; Chamier to Murray, 25 January 1949. Makwaia matriculated at Lincoln College, Oxford on 18 October 1949 to read the Public Administration Diploma Course 'as a kind of Honorary Colonial Service Probationer.' The anthropologist David Brokensha met with Makwaia when the two were at Oxford and describes him as at the time being 'thoughtful, critical, reasonable, articulate and good company.' David Brokensha, pers.comm., 15 March 2012.
5. For example, Wintersgill, D. *The Rectors of the University of Edinburgh, 1859–2000*, Edinburgh: Dunedin Academic Press, 2005, p.144; Segal, *Political*, p.215; Brockway, F. *African Socialism*, London: The Bodley Head, 1963, p.27.
6. Iliffe, *Modern History*, p.447. See also Daily News, 2011, '50th Death Anniversary: Meet Mwl Mathew Douglas Ramadhani', www.dailynews.co.tz/feature/?n=17675, accessed on 29 May 2013.
7. Pratt, *Critical*, p.80, Marealle did not receive a degree: 'A New African Supreme Chief', *Recent Trends in Chagga Political Development*, Moshi: KNCU, 1952, pp.1–4; cited in Fisher, T. 'Chagga Elites and the Politics of Ethnicity in Kilimanjaro, Tanzania', unpublished Ph.D. thesis University of Edinburgh, 2012, p.125; and Tom Fisher, pers.comm., August 2011. Eckert puts the courses as 'social welfare' at the University of Wales in Aberystwyth, and courses in 'social government and administration' at the LSE: Eckert, 'Cultural', p.260.
8. Hopkins, *Political*, p.18; Said, *Abdulwahid*, p.64. Chief Balele of the extensive and populous Nera chiefdom, studied at an agricultural college in England. Maguire, *Toward*, p.48.
9. Editor, 'O.B. News: H. Martin and Hugh Peter Kayamba', *The Bloxhamist*, 58 (425), 1932, pp.3–5.
10. Editor, 'The Rev. H.R. Willimott', *The Bloxhamist*, 47 (389), 1921, p.5.
11. Iliffe's *German Rule*, pp.175–176 and *Modern History*, pp.229–30, 446–7.
12. Williams, *Colour*, p.22.
13. Appiah, J. *Joe Appiah: The autobiography of an African patriot*. New York: Praeger, 1990, p.159. See also Rooney, *Kwame*, p.23; Milne, J. *Kwame Nkrumah: A biography*, London: Panaf Books, 1999, pp.23–6; Birmingham, *Kwame*, p.7.
14. At some point during his London days Nyerere apparently sat at Padmore's feet: Iliffe, *Modern History*, p.509.
15. NACO981/16556/28 and NACO981/16556/Minute Paper entry 27.
16. Smith, *Nyerere*, p.26. NACO981/16556/29 and Minute Paper entries 27–28.
17. Goldthorpe, *Elite*, p.48.
18. For detailed figures, see Kelsall, R.K. Report on an Inquiry into Applications for Admission to Universities, London: Association of Universities of the British Commonwealth, 1957.
19. NACO981/16556/30a and b.
20. Cattanach, W.D. 'Nyerere: Some notes on Mwalimu as a student', in Molony, T.S.J., King, K. ed. *Nyerere: Student, Teacher, Humanist, Statesman*, Edinburgh: Centre of African Studies, University of Edinburgh, 2000, pp.19–21, p.20. See also Ross, *The Root of the Matter: Boyhood, manhood and God*. Edinburgh: Mainstream, 1989, p.114. Buchman was an open admirer of Hitler in the 1930s. His Moral Re-Armament Movement encouraged its members to be involved in political and social issues. Cattanach adds that 'Julius, who had been raised and educated as a Roman Catholic, and I, a Church of Scotland Minister, found we shared wariness of any or all sorts of potential manipulation from whatever quarter, and many animated conversations with him therefore ensued!' Cattanach to Molony, n.d. November 2000, p.1.
21. Feinstein, *African*, p.99; Appiah, *Joe Appiah*, p.146.
22. Carey, A.T. *Colonial Students: A Study of the Social Adaptation of Colonial Students in London*. London: Secker & Warburg, 1956, p.127.
23. Carey, *Colonial*, p.127.

Notes for Chapter 5, pp. 100–131

24. Mwapachu to Hinden, 4 December 1950, FCB. The animosity of the white community meant that Mwapachu refused to contribute articles on territorial events to *Venture*, a journal that he continued to receive until he died in September 1962. Similar reasons caused Thomas Marealle, Paramount Chief of the Chagga and member of the Legislative Council, from publicly expressing his views. Marealle file; cited in Smith, *Influence*, p.75, and Juma Mwapachu, pers.comm., 2 September 2011.
25. On 'the Communist threat', see Hakim, A. 'West African Students in Britain, 1900–60: The politics of exile', *Immigrants and Minorities*, 12 (3) 1993, pp.107–28, p.122–5; Trevelyan, 'African Student', p.41.
26. Nkrumah also registered in London as a student of law. He was admitted as a 'student member of Gray's Inn in November 1946. … He does not appear to have been Called to the Bar'. The Honourable Society of Gray's Inn to Sherwood, 23 October 1991; cited in Sherwood, *Kwame*, p.115.
27. Lee, 'Commonwealth', p.11–12. The extent of Communist influence on Nkrumah is uncertain. Biney, *Political*, p.33. On surveillance of foreign students see also Stockwell, A.J. 'Leaders, Dissidents and the Disappointed: Colonial students in Britain as empire ended', *Journal of Imperial and Commonwealth History*, 36 (3) 2008, pp.487–507, p.493–7, and also NA FO 371/73750.
28. 'Concerns in UK of risk of Communism in East Africa', *The Scotsman*, 23 January 1950, p.5. See also articles in various issues of *East Africa and Rhodesia*, such as 'Colonial Students in Britain' and 'Communism and the British Colonies', in 25 (1288), p.1272 and (1297), pp.1561–2 respectively, 1949. For the case of a British Communist Party member who had attempted to create industrial unrest at Dar es Salaam port, see Said, *Abdulwahid*, pp.70–9.
29. NACO537/2574, H.P. Elliott to Keith, Pte, 13 February 1948; cited in Hargreaves, 'African Students', p.132. The P.G. Wodehouse observation also belongs to Hargreaves.
30. Should suspicion have fallen on Nyerere, his later retort was: 'I am not a communist. I believe in God'. Wille, in Mwakikagile, *Nyerere*, p.406. Much later, in September 1978 on the campus of the University of Dar es Salaam, he apparently stated in no uncertain terms that he was not a Marxist but a 'bourgeois liberal'. Che-Mponda, 'Aspects', p.64. Many years later Shepperson met in Ibadan with a Nigerian who had been a doctoral student in Edinburgh when Nyerere was an undergraduate. The man told Shepperson that Nyerere listened to a Marxist group on a number of occasions, after which Nyerere would see a priest who would change his mind. Discussion, George Shepperson. See also Metz, 'In Lieu', p.371, note 1.
31. Lee, 'Commonwealth', p.7–8.
32. Andrew, W., ed. 1947. *Edinburgh University Student's Handbook, 1947–48*. Edinburgh: Students' Representative Council, p.31–2.
33. Keith, J.L. 'African Students in Great Britain', *African Affairs*, 45 (179), 1946, pp.65–72, p.69.
34. Cross, B.F. 'Colour Bar', *The Student*, 1950–51, 47 (6) 1950, pp.291. See also 'Colonial Students in Britain' and 'Students' Hostels Only Temporary', in *East Africa and Rhodesia*, 25 (1288), 1949, p.1272 (and p.1295), and p.1499 respectively.
35. As late as June 1953 it was still being proposed that all University hostels were to be opened to all races. Discussions on which University accommodation was suitable for 'African, Asian and West Indian' students continued until at least December 1954. There was no such issue for the 'Commonwealth and America' and 'European' categories of student. EUA IN1/ADS/SEC/A/34/1, EUL.
36. T.P. 'America in Transition: The Negro student in America', *The Student*, 1951–52, 48 (5), 1951, pp.200–1, p.200.
37. Carey, *Colonial*, p.77.
38. Keith, 'African Students', p.68.
39. Carey, *Colonial*, p.53.
40. Macola, *Liberal*, pp.20–1.
41. Keith, 'African Students', p.69.

Notes for Chapter 5, pp. 100–131

42. Carey, *Colonial*, p.56.
43. *Scotsman*, 3 January 1952, p.10, 'Mixed marriages'.
44. Anonymous East African student; cited in Carey, *Colonial*, p.68–9.
45. Lee, 'Commonwealth', p.9.
46. NA CAB 134/604, Memorandum by British Council, 13 August 1948; cited in Hargreaves, 'African Students', p.133–134. See also Carey, *Colonial*, p.117.
47. The case is taken from Lohrmann, *Voices*, p.178–9. The context of the report on Kayamba's background and character is important. It was drawn from a British investigation into the circumstances of an unauthorised document that he submitted to the United Nations visiting mission, apparently in the name of the Tanga branch of the TAA, calling for Tanganyika's self-government.
48. NACO981/16556/Minute Paper entry 3. See also NACO981/16556/6.
49. ibid./26.
50. ibid./27, 28, 33, 36. There is no evidence that Nyerere 'was compelled to go to Aberdeen for six months to study English', as claimed in Chachage, C., Chachage, C.S.L. 'Nyerere: Nationalism and post-colonial developmentalism', *African Sociological Review*, 8 (2), 2004, pp.158–79, p.161.
51. Anonymous retired University of Edinburgh staff member, pers.comm., 2012, Edinburgh.
52. This section based on NACO981/16556/32, 35, 36, 39, 42, 68, 69 and Minute Paper entries 11 and 36.
53. ibid./35, 36 and Minute Paper entry 11. David Carmichael had reported to Shepperson that Nyerere was due to go to Bristol University to study Biology, but Carmichael (who was based in Edinburgh for the Colonial Office), pushed for him to attend Edinburgh. Molony, 'Nyerere', p.8; Discussion, Shepperson. This chimes with the 'B.U.' of Chapter 4, note 102.
54. Graduates in Arts, 1952, EUA IN1/ADS/STA/5, EUL. See also 'Applicants whose fitness is attested by certificates awarded by examining bodies other than the Scottish Education Department', in Edinburgh University, *University Calendar: 1949–1950*, pp.100–104.
55. NACO981/16556/42a, b and c. Nyerere took the Scottish Universities' Examination Board's Special English examination anyway, as he indicates in First Matriculation, 1949–50, EUA IN1/ADS/STA/4, EUL, and in Graduates in Arts, 1952, EUA IN1/ADS/STA/5, EUL. See also Moral Philosophy class list, Da 35 MOR PHIL 17, in EUA-A-1000, EUL.
56. Nyerere to Director of Colonial Scholars, Colonial Office, 19 August 1949, NACO981/16556/37. While most of Nyerere's United Kingdom letters were sent from his Palmerston Road residence in Edinburgh, this early correspondence is addressed from the White Fathers', Broomhall [*sic*], Coldharbour, Dorking.
57. ibid./105 and 120.
58. Hopkins, *Political*, p.202. Hopkins writes that Nyerere received a scholarship from the Church. His main source of funding was certainly the CDWS fund, although it is possible that, as well as supplying contacts, the Roman Catholic Church also made a smaller contribution to cover some of Nyerere's expenses.
59. Maurice Billingsley, pers.comm., 3 November 2011.
60. Nugent, P. *Africa since Independence: A comparative history*, 2nd edn, Houndmills: Palgrave Macmillan, 2012, p.144. The parallel is also drawn by Schneider, L. 'Freedom and Unfreedom in Rural Development: Julius Nyerere, *ujamaa vijijini*, and villagization', *Canadian Journal of African Studies*, 38 (2), 2004, pp.344–92, p.367.
61. Edinburgh University. *1951–1952*, p.223. See also the satirical Msigwa, T. *Filosofa's Republic*, London: Pickwick, 1989.
62. NACO981/16556/39, 42 and Minute Paper entry 37; Graduates in Arts, 1952, EUA IN1/ADS/STA/5, EUL.
63. As a consequence of their history, the Scottish universities of Dundee and Heriot-Watt also award the Master of Arts degree to undergraduates, as do (with several material

Notes for Chapter 5, pp. 100–131

differences) the universities of Cambridge, Dublin and Oxford.
64. Ian Duffield, pers.comm., 18 May 2012.
65. Nyerere to Mrs P.M. Mitford-Barberton, 22 April 1949, PRO, CO981/34/11007/16556/32.
66. Munger, E.S. *Touched by Africa*, Pasadena, CA: Castle Press, 1983, p.252.
67. Sanders, 'African Association', p.203.
68. ibid., p.74.
69. Renwick, W.L. 'The Ordinary M.A. Degree', *University of Edinburgh Gazette*, 28 (October), 1960, pp.20–2, p.20. See also Drever, J. 'M.A. Ordinary', *University of Edinburgh Gazette*, 18, October 1957, pp.12–5; Drever, J. 'New Ordinary M.A. Regulations', *University of Edinburgh Gazette*, 27, May 1960, pp.20–5, p.20, who refers to the pre-1957 version of the degree that Nyerere would have taken as 'patched and limping'.
70. 'Report of the commission on higher education in the colonies, 1944–45', Cmd. 6647, IV (The Asquith report), p.15; cited in Ashby, E. *Universities: British, Indian, African – A Study in the Ecology of Higher Education*, London: Weidenfeld & Nicolson, 1966, p.217. For a contemporary defence of the Humanities against Science, see Warner, A. 'Shakespeare in the Tropics', inaugural address as first Professor of English, Makerere College. Oxford: Oxford University Press, 1954.
71. Ashby, *Universities*, p.217.
72. Shepperson, G.A. 'Edinburgh University's First African Prime Minister', *University of Edinburgh Gazette*, 28, October 1960, pp.22–6, p.23, note 3.
73. Wood to Shepperson, University of Edinburgh Faculty of Medicine, 1 July 1960, CLX-A-19/12/8, Shep.Coln.
74. *Scotsman*, 7 February 1951, p.3; Little, K. 'The Centre of African Studies', *University of Edinburgh Gazette*, 34, October 1962, pp.31–3, p.31.
75. Among the works on Horton by Christopher Fyfe, see *Africanus Horton, 1835–1883: West African scientist and patriot*, New York: Oxford University Press, 1972; 'Africanus Horton as a Constitution-maker', *Journal of Commonwealth and Comparative Politics*, 26 (2), 1988, pp.173–84. For a study of African students at another of Scotland's great universities, see Hargreaves, 'African Students', pp.129–44.
76. First Matriculation, 1958–59, EUA IN1/ADS/STA/4, EUL; Matriculation Album, 1958–59, EUA IN1/ADS/STA/2, EUL; Edinburgh University, *Edinburgh University Calendar: 1959–1960*, 1959, pp.761–762.
77. Cartwright, A., Thomson, J.G., Kyaruzi, V.K., et al. 'Young Smokers: An attitude study among schoolchildren –Touching also on parental influence', *British Journal of Preventive and Social Medicine*, 14 (1) 1960, pp.28–34.
78. Parliamentary Correspondent. 1964. 'News and Notes: Parliament'. *British Medical Journal*, 2 (1 (5391)), pp.1193–6.
79. Carey, *Colonial*, p.28–9. Carey does not specify if this was British East and Central Africa.
80. ibid., p.104.
81. NACO981/16556/15b.
82. Jawara, D.K. *Kairaba*. Haywards Heath: Jawara (self-published), 2009; p.159.
83. ibid., p.162.
84. ibid., p.163. Judith Listowel, whose later writing on Nyerere became more critical, reports that in 1969 the President had Shariff and Kassim Hanga, a former Minister, handed to Karume. They were believed to have been executed in Zanzibar. Listowel, 'Tanzania', p.283.
85. The records of the Dialectic Society are minuted for 1949–50 (but not for 1951–2), and make no mention of Nyerere: Dialectic Society Minutes, 1949–60, EUA-A-156, EUL.
86. Nyerere's complete 'Particulars of Attendance' course details are given in Graduates in Arts, 1952, EUA IN1/ADS/STA/5, EUL.
87. Bjerk, 'Establishment', p.22–3.
88. Edinburgh University, *University Calendar: 1950–1951*, p.664. Also listed was Agwu Okereke Uche, the Nigerian who graduated together with Nyerere. (See Photo L, p.182.)

255

Notes for Chapter 5, pp. 100–131

89. Moral Philosophy class list, Da 35 MOR PHIL 17, in EUA-A-1000, EUL.
90. Shepperson, G.A. 'The Bright, Good-humoured Student, *Africa Events*, October 1985, p.36.
91. Nyerere to Shepperson, 28 December 1963, CLX-A-16/1, Shep.Coln. Records suggest that the Shakespeare examination texts were *Antony and Cleopatra* and *Much Ado About Nothing*. Edinburgh University, *1949–1950*, p.173. Proofs of Nyerere's Swahili language translations of Shakespeare's plays are located in EUL. Note that for 'merchant', which could translate easily to *mfanyabiashara*, Nyerere instead uses the Gujarati-derived *bepari* – which translates as 'merchant', 'but served as the Swahili gloss for "capitalist"'. Brennan, *Taifa*, p.165 and note 31. On Nyerere's use of Shakespeare, see Mazrui, A.A., Mhando, L.L. *Julius Nyerere: Africa's Titan on a Global Stage*, Durham, NC: Carolina Academic Press, 2013, passim. For more on the 'socialist twist' of Nyerere's translation, see Shule, V. 'Mwalimu Nyerere: The artist'. In Chachage, C, Cassam, A, ed. *Africa's Liberation: The legacy of Nyerere*, Oxford: Pambazuka, 2010, pp.160–74, p.165–166. For the argument that Nyerere's Swahili was 'by the book' – correct and fluent, but lacking in familiarity with, or appreciation of, local idiom, see Geiger, S. 'Tanganyikan', p.471. For a wider discussion of Nyerere's relationship with the Swahili language, see Legère, K. 'Marehemu Julius Kambarage Nyerere and Kiswahili', *Kioo cha Lugha*, 5 (1) 2007, pp.38–53.
92. Nyerere studied *Julius Caesar* in preparation for his entrance to Edinburgh. Shepperson, G.A. 'The University of East Africa', *University of Edinburgh Gazette*, 37 (October). 1963, pp.37–40, p.39. The notebook filed with Nyerere's 'Uhuru wa Wanawake' shows that at Makerere he had also been exposed to works by Samuel Taylor Coleridge, Hilaire Belloc, Robert Louis Stevenson, and John Keats.
93. NACO981/16556/68.
94. Stirrat, E., ed. *Edinburgh University Student's Handbook, 1949–50*. Edinburgh: Students' Representative Council, 1949, p.112–15; Shepperson to Kalinjuma, 1 March 1988, CLX-A-16/4, Shep.Coln.; Shepperson, G.A. 'A Short Memoir'. *Edinburgh University History Graduates Association Newsletter*, 33 (October), p.14, based on Stables to Shepperson, 18 January 1960; Shepperson to Kalinjuma, 16 February 1988, both CLX-A-16/4, Shep.Coln.; NACO981/16556/unnumbered sheet between 97 and 102.
95. Shepperson to Hassan, 9 August 1985, CLX-A-16/4; Shepperson, 'Short Memoir', p.14; Nyerere to Shepperson, 5 May 1960, CLX-A-16/1, Shep.Coln.
96. K.A.B.S. 'Modern Historian', *The Student*, 1950–51, 47 (7) 1950, pp.312–3, p.313.
97. Interview, John Keto. It was certainly Pares who Keto was referring to, since he used the correct pronunciation: 'pɛːs' (as in the fruit).
98. Nyerere, 'Democracy', pp.8–9 and passim.
99. J.M.W. 'Constitutional Lawyer', *The Student*, 1952–53, 49 (5) 1952, pp.220–1, p.220.
100. ibid., p.220.
101. Hopkins, *Political*, p.207.
102. Fraser, W.I.R. *An Outline of Constitutional Law*, London: William Hodge and Co., 1948; Jennings, I. *The Law and the Constitution*, London: University of London Press, 1959 (1933); Wade, E.C.S., Phillips, G.G. *Constitutional Law: An outline of the law and practice of the constitutional and local government of the British commonwealth and empire*, London: Longmans, Green and Co., 1950; Edinburgh University. *1951–1952*, p.261.
103. Listowel, J. 'Nyerere Holds His Course', *Statist*, 187 (4543) 1965, pp.919–21, p.921.
104. Shepperson, 'Short Memoir', p.14; NACO981/16556/104.
105. Nyerere to Shepperson, 5 May 1960, CLX-A-16/1, Shep.Coln.
106. NACO981/16556/104.
107. Shepperson, 'First African', p.24.
108. Moral Philosophy class list, Da 35 MOR PHIL 17, in EUA-A-1000, EUL.
109. Graduates in Arts, 1952, EUA IN1/ADS/STA/5, EUL.
110. Kalinjuma, A.M.K. 'Adult Education Development and Political Change in Tanzania: 1961–2002', unpublished Ph.D. thesis, University of Southampton, 1989, p.31.
111. Stern to Shepperson, 21 August 1960, CLX-A-16/4, Shep.Coln.
112. ibid.

Notes for Chapter 5, pp. 100–131

113. Ian Duffield, pers.comm., 18 May 2012.
114. Moral Philosophy class list, Da 35 MOR PHIL 17, in EUA-A-1000, EUL.
115. Edinburgh University. *1951–1952*, p.223.
116. Stored in Nyerere's personal library in Butiama, this is one of the few books from his university days in which he had not written the acquisition date. See reference to Mill in Nyerere, 'The African', p.105.
117. J.B.B. 'Moral Philosopher'. *The Student*, 1950–51, 47 (2) 1950, pp.70–1.
118. Bjerk, 'Establishment', pp.128–9.
119. Molony, 'Nyerere', p.11.
120. For a sense of the cogent reasoning between Edinburgh students outside their formal classes, see Ross, *Root*.
121. Nyerere to Shepperson, 5 May 1960, CLX-A-16/1, Shep.Coln.
122. Nyerere, 'Democracy', p.27.
123. Brogan, D.W. *Politics and Law in the United States*, Cambridge: Cambridge University Press, 1941; Hawgood, J.A. *Modern Constitutions since 1787*, London: Macmillan, 1939; Swisher, C.B. *The Growth of Constitutional Power in the United States*, Chicago: University of Chicago Press, 1946; Edinburgh University, *1951–1952*, p.261.
124. Molony, 'Nyerere', p.13–14.
125. MacKenzie in 'Portraits of Our Time', 'No.2: Julius Nyerere', a BBC broadcast on 12 July 1964. Transcript of broadcast, p.1. Facsimile in author's possession.
126. NACO981/16556/47, 78 and 90.
127. ibid./Minute Paper cover sheet and /47. Nyerere to Director Colonial Scholars, Colonial Office, 9 January 1950.
128. Carey, *Colonial*, p.114.
129. Wicken to Molony, 14 March 2001, p.5; Interview, John Keto. Maria Nyerere recalls her husband telling her about this trip, which seems not to have been an unusual way for students to make money during the vacation. Interview, Maria Nyerere. See also Ross, *Root*, p.130–1 and Keith, 'African Students', p.69–70.
130. Maria Nyerere, in Mwakikagile, *Nyerere*, p.392. Note that in the verbatim translation of the Swahili here Mwakikagile uses Nyerere's pre-baptismal name 'Kambarage', one that Maria Nyerere does not use. Maria did not know her husband before he took on the name Julius. She tends to favour 'Mwalimu', or uses the third person.
131. See 'Drought in Tanganyika', in *East Africa and Rhodesia*, 1949, 25 (1296), pp.1544.
132. An indication of the severity of the famine can be seen in the case of Mugara Marasi, mother to Joseph Muhunda Nyerere, who was married to Chief Nyerere Burito. Mugara became the chief's seventeenth wife during the famine because her parents were desperate for food, which they were able to purchase with the bridewealth. Interview, Nyamwaga.
133. Nyerere, 'Ujamaa', p.164.
134. NACO981/16556/37. Nyerere to Director of Colonial Scholars, Colonial Office, 19 August 1949.
135. ibid./102. Hinchcliffe to Crook, 17 August 1951.
136. NACO981/16556.
137. ibid./48. Nyerere to Director of Colonial Scholars, 30 January 1950.
138. Keith, 'African Students', p.68; NACO981/16556/50. From Director of Colonial Scholars to Tanganyika, Record of Savingram, 13 February 1950. See also NACO981/16556/Minute Paper entry 49.
139. NACO981/16556/55. Nyerere to Director of Colonial Scholars, 1 May 1950.
140. ibid.
141. ibid./66. Baker to Crook, 17 June 1950; ibid./67. Crook to Nyerere, 26 June 1950.
142. ibid./76. Nyerere to Keith, 19 March 1951.
143. ibid.
144. ibid./Minute Paper entry 87. Crook to Keith, 5 June 1951. Nyerere's letter to which Crook refers is NACO981/16556/84.
145. ibid./88. C. Hinchcliffe, Acting Director of Education, Education Department, Dar es

Notes for Chapter 5, pp. 100–131

Salaam to Keith, 12 June 1951; ibid./89. Crook to Nyerere, 19 June 1951.
146. ibid./90. Nyerere to Crook, 20 June 1951. Maria confirms that she was the sibling being schooled in Uganda. Interview, Maria Nyerere.
147. ibid./90. Nyerere to Crook, 20 June 1951. Also ibid., Crook to Nyerere, 21 June 1951 and ibid./92. Crook to C. Hinchcliffe, Acting Director of Education, Education Department, Dar es Salaam, 21 June 1951.
148. ibid./102. Hinchcliffe to Crook, 17 August 1951.
149. ibid./87. C. Hinchcliffe, Acting Director of Education, Education Department, Dar es Salaam to Keith, 29 May 1951.
150. ibid./103. Crook to Nyerere, 30 August 1951.
151. ibid./Minute Paper entry 103, T. Rogers, 4 September 1951.
152. ibid., Keith to Mr T. Rogers, 4 September 1951. Hinchcliffe to Crook is ibid./102, 17 August 1951.
153. Goldthorpe, *Elite*, p.55.
154. NACO981/16556/Minute Paper cover sheet. See also Keith, 'African Students', p.68.
155. British Council, *How To Live in Britain: A handbook for students from overseas*, London: Longman, 1952, p.9.
156. See for example, Birmingham, *Kwame*; Rooney, *Kwame*.
157. Lwanda, J.L. *Kamuzu Banda of Malawi: A study in promise, power and paralysis*, Bothwell: Dudu Nsomba, 1993, p.29.
158. Many Colonial Office foreign student files were destroyed, apparently to free-up storage space. Nyerere's was retained because at the (unknown) time of the exercise he had already reached a position of prominence.
159. Interview, Nyamwaga. Mugara was mother to Joseph Muhunda Nyerere.
160. NACO981/16556/102. Hinchcliffe to Crook, 17 August 1951.
161. Nyerere, 'Why I Resigned', in *Freedom and Unity*.
162. Iliffe, *Modern History*, p.566.
163. 'Nyerere Threatens to Resign: Angry Intervention in Citizenship Debate,' *Tanganyika Standard*, 19 October 1961, p.1; Nyerere, J.K. 1961. 'The Principles of Citizenship'. In *Freedom and Unity*, p.128.
164. Nyerere, 'Resignation as Prime Minister', in *Freedom and Unity*, p.158.
165. Shepperson, 'First African', p.26.
166. Besson, W., Besson, J. *Caribbean Reflections: The life and times of a Trinidad scholar, 1901–1986*, London: Karia, 1989, pp.57–79.
167. Banda to Matako, 8 October 1938; cited in Morrow, S., McCracken, J. 2012. 'Two Previously Unknown Letters from Hastings Kamuzu Banda, Written from Edinburgh, 1938, Archived at the University of Cape Town'. *History in Africa*, 39. pp.337–54, p.349.
168. Jenkinson, J. 'The Glasgow Race Disturbances of 1919'. *Immigrants and Minorities*, 4 (2) 1985, pp.43–67.
169. Carey, *Colonial*, p.107.
170. ibid., p.105.
171. ibid., p.172.
172. ibid., p.321–2.
173. Interview, John Keto.
174. ibid.; *Scotsman*, 2 January 1952, p.8.
175. Nyerere to Westcott, 10 December 1987, CLX-A-16/1, Shep.Coln. Nyerere listed Palmerston Place as his residence when first matriculating, and when signing up to the Moral Philosophy course in his final year. First Matriculation, 1949–50, EUA IN1/ADS/STA/4, EUL; Moral Philosophy class list, Da 35 MOR PHIL 17, in EUA-A-1000, EUL.
176. Molony, 'Nyerere', p.8. The records show no evidence of Nyerere staying at the British Council Residence. Shepperson is more sure that Nyerere 'went there a lot; it was a social centre'. Shepperson, pers.comm., 22 August 2012, Peterborough.
177. Hatch, *African Statesmen*, p.28.
178. Brewin, D. 'A Brief Comment', BTS, ed. in *The Nyerere Years: Some personal impressions by*

Notes for Chapter 5, pp. 100–131

friends, pp.15–6. London: Britain-Tanzania Society, 1985, p.16; Molony, 'Nyerere', p.9.
179. Keith, 'African Students', p.70.
180. Carey, *Colonial*, p.72; Stirrat, *Student's Handbook*, p.47, 50.
181. Carey, *Colonial*, p.121.
182. Read, D.H.C. 'The Chaplain's Report', *University of Edinburgh Gazette*, 2, November 1952, pp.8–10, p.9.
183. Wicken to Appleton, 31 March 1962, EUA IN1/ADS/SEC/A/86, EUL.
184. Wicken to Molony, 14 March 2001, p.5. Here note previous comments in the Introduction on Wicken's dominant role in the 'authoritative' account of Nyerere's life.
185. Carey, *Colonial*, p.123. See also Collins, S.F. 1951. 'The Social Position of White and "Half-Caste" Women in Colored Groupings in Britain'. *American Sociological Review*, 16 (6). pp.796–802.
186. Carey, *Colonial*, p.239.
187. Williams, *Colour*, pp.14–15. An earlier marriage involving a man also to become an African Head of State was that between Jomo Kenyatta and Edna Clarke, which took place in West Sussex in 1942.
188. Munger, *Touched*, p.252.
189. Interview, Maria Nyerere.
190. Keith, 'African Students', p.70.
191. Hatch, *African Statesmen*, p.28.
192. Brewin, 'Brief', p.16.
193. Smith, *Nyerere*, p.50.
194. Nyerere to Shepperson, 5 May 1960, CLX-A-16/1, Shep.Coln. Also cited in Shepperson, 'First African', p.23.
195. Interview, John Keto; Smith, *Nyerere*, p.50.
196. Nicholson to Nyerere, 11 September 1951, Box 6/2/87, FCB.
197. Scotterlobber, 'Kwofe's Vote: A cynical parable of democracy', *The Student, 1951–52*, 48 (1) 1951, pp.52–3, p.53.
198. Nyerere's most detailed explanation is found in 'Democracy', extracts of which appear in *Freedom and Unity*, pp.195–203. For an earlier version, see Nyerere, J.K. 'One Party Government', *Transition* (2) 1961, pp.9–11. Also note 14 in Pratt for a bibliography of the interest in Tanzania's one-party democracy. Pratt, C.R. 'The Ethical Foundation of Julius Nyerere's Legacy', in McDonald, D.A., Sahle, E.N., eds, *The Legacies of Julius Nyerere: Influences on development discourse and practice in Africa*, Trenton, NJ and Asmara, Eritrea: Africa World Press, 2002, pp.39–52.
199. Nyerere, 'Democracy', p.14.
200. ibid., p.15, passim.
201. ibid., p.9. His understanding of the party system, whips and the like is close to that presented in Campion, G., Chester, D.N., et al. 1950. *British Government since 1939*. London: George Allen and Unwin, pp.16–23. Also Wade, *Constitutional*; Fraser, *Outline*, pp.33–54 on the House of Commons, and Jennings, *Law*, p.91 on 'Her Majesty's Opposition'.
202. Nyerere, 'Democracy', p.7.
203. Nyerere, 'Statement to the U.N.', p.44.
204. Iliffe, *Modern History*, p.572.
205. ibid., p.561–562.
206. Pratt, 'Ethical', p.44.
207. Nyerere, 'The future of African nationalism,' in *Tribune*, 27 May 1960; cited in Iliffe, *Modern History*, p.572.
208. Nyerere, 'The African', p.105.
209. ibid., p.105.
210. Mill, J.S. 'Representative Government', in *Utilitarianism, Liberty, Representative Government*, 1972 (1861), pp.175–393. London: Dent, p.228.
211. Jennings, *Law*, p.92.
212. ibid., pp.255–6, 267–9, 280–304.

Notes for Chapter 5, pp. 100–131

213. Brady, A. *Democracy and the Dominions: A comparative study in institutions*, London: Oxford University Press, 1947; Keith, A.B. 1938. *The Dominions as Sovereign States: Their constitutions and governments*. London: Macmillan.
214. Nyerere, 'The African', p.106.
215. ibid.
216. Nyerere, 'Democracy', p.1–2.
217. Nyerere, 'The African', p.106.
218. Wade, *Constitutional*, pp.361–362. Also Fraser, *Outline*, pp.265–279, 286–91; Edinburgh University. *1951–1952*, p.261.
219. For a recent example of its application, see Ben Taylor's http://mtega.com/2013/09/30/a-step-backwards-on-the-road-to-democracy, accessed 1 October 2013.
220. Nyerere, 'Democracy', p.10.
221. ibid., p.13, passim.
222. See 'Socialism Rejected', in *East Africa and Rhodesia*, 1950, 26 (1326), pp.792.
223. For discussion of the slow dialogue and differing opinions between London and Dar es Salaam on the social development of Tanganyikans at this time, see Eckert, A. 2004. 'Regulating the Social: Social security, social welfare and the state in late colonial Tanzania'. *Journal of African History*, 45 (3). pp.467–89.
224. NACO981/16556/84. Nyerere to Crook, 26 April 1951.
225. Nyerere, J.K. 'Arusha Declaration: Socialism and self-reliance', in *Freedom and Socialism*, pp.231–50, pp.232 (g) and 233 (j). Also Nyerere, J.K. 'Ten Years After Independence', in *Freedom and Development*, pp.262–334, pp.278–279.
226. By 1951 in Britain six nationalised industries produced a combined turnover equivalent to 17 per cent of gross domestic product and employed a total of 10 per cent of the employed workforce. May, T. *An Economic and Social History of Britain, 1760–1990*, Harlow: Longman, 1995, p.427; Shivji, I. 'The Silent Class Struggle'. In Shivji, I., ed. *The Silent Class Struggle*, Dar es Salaam: Tanzania Publishing House, 1973, pp.1–60, p.21.
227. Iliffe, *Modern History*, p.509.
228. *Scotsman*, 17 February 1951, p.8.
229. ibid., 12 February 1951, p.6.
230. ibid., 3 August 1950, p.5.
231. ibid., 3 January 1952, p.6, 'Points of View', 'Scottish and South African Nationalists: A reader's criticism'.
232. See, for example, 'Scottish Devolution' in *The Student*, 1949–50, 46 (11), p.476–7.
233. On Scottish home rule in the newspapers see, for example, *Scotsman*, 8 February 1951, p.4, 'Edinburgh students: Nationalism in University politics'. For one of many articles on the fate of the Stone of Destiny, see *Scotsman*, 2 January 1951, and Neat, T. 2007. *Hamish Henderson: A Biography. Volume I: The Making of the Poet (1919–1953)*. Edinburgh: Polygon, p.314–37 on Edinburgh-based Scottish nationalism.
234. Shepperson, 'Bright, Good-humoured', p.36.
235. NACO981/16556/80; Nyerere, J.K. 1997. 'Africa: The Third Liberation'. Occasional Paper 70, Centre of African Studies, University of Edinburgh, Edinburgh, p.2.
236. *Scotsman*, 15 August 1950, p.6.
237. The introduction to the abridged version in Nyerere's 1966 *Freedom and Unity* (pp.23–9) states that 'The Race Problem in East Africa' was written in 1952. Nyerere sent the manuscript to Nicholson in September 1951 (Box 6/2/87, FCB). Shepperson saved a typed version of the original, available in CLX-A-16/1, Shep.Coln. Listowel, *Making*, pp.201–4 provides a summary of the manuscript. For an expression of Nyerere's views on race around this time, see Nyerere, J.K. 1960. 'Tanganyika Today: II. The Nationalist View'. *International Affairs*, 36 (1). pp.43–7.
238. Chidzero, *Tanganyika*. The British perspective on their efforts towards increasing racial harmony and co-operative are given in Hill, *Tanganyika*, p.4–5.
239. Sanders, 'African Association', pp.202, 211.
240. Ethan Sanders, pers.comm., 18 June 2013.
241. Sanders, 'African Association', pp.115–116.

Notes for Chapter 6, pp. 132–162

242. Nyerere, J.K. 'The Race Problem in East Africa', CLX-A-16/1, Shep.Coln.
243. Oxford undergraduates with East Africa links. Fabian Colonial Bureau 1952. *East African Future: A report to the Fabian Colonial Bureau.* London: Fabian Publications and Victor Gollancz, p.13.
244. Iliffe, *Modern History,* p.554.
245. ibid., p.573–574. See Nyerere, J.K. 1960. 'Africanization of the Civil Service'. In *Freedom and Unity*, pp.99–102.
246. Nyerere, J.K. 'Socialism is not Racialism', in *Freedom and Socialism*, pp.257–61, p.258.
247. For an example of an article on the United Nations reports see *Scotsman*, 21 February 1950, p.8. On the Groundnut Scheme and the Overseas Food Corporation see, *Scotsman*, 13 June 1950, p.5; 10 January 1951, p.5; 2 March 1951, p.4.
248. *Scotsman*, 26 February 1951, p.6, 'Gambia poultry farm: Eggs-for-U.K. scheme "Almost abandoned"'.
249. ibid. 25 July 1950, p.6.
250. Bronisław Malinowski was instrumental in obtaining a scholarship for Kenyatta to study at the LSE. Kenyatta's ethnographic monograph, *Facing Mount Kenya: the Traditional Life of the Gikuyu* was an outcome of his Diploma dissertation, supervised by Malinowski, who wrote the Introduction. See Murray-Brown, J. 1972. *Kenyatta*. London: George Allen & Unwin, p.180–94. For a brief introduction on the relationship between Kenyatta and Malinowski, see Frederiksen, B.F. 2008. 'Jomo Kenyatta, Marie Bonaparte and Bronislaw Malinowski on Clitoridectomy and Female Sexuality'. *History Workshop Journal*, 65 (1). pp.23–48.
251. *Scotsman*, 3 August 1950, p.5. See also 'Government of Africa: Natives taking bigger part', ibid., 26 July 1950, p.5.
252. ibid., 12 February 1951, p.4, 'African Issues'.
253. The influence of the Convention People's Party on Nyerere should not be underestimated. The TANU constitution was later modelled on Nkrumah's party (and, according to Iliffe, Britain's Labour Party). See Hopkins, *Political*, p.19–20; Iliffe, *Modern History*, p.511.
254. *Scotsman*, 27 January 1951, p.8.

Chapter 6

1. Nyerere, Introduction to *Freedom and Socialism*, p.20.
2. Shepperson, 'First African', p.23.
3. Shepperson in 'Portraits of Our Time', 'No.2: Julius Nyerere', a BBC broadcast on 12 July 1964. Transcript of broadcast, p.2. Facsimile in author's possession.
4. George Shepperson; cited in Molony, 'Nyerere', p.9.
5. Sanders, 'African Association', p.201.
6. Bomani went on to become Minister of Natural Resources and Co-operative Development, among other ministerial and ambassadorial positions.
7. Iliffe notes of these four men: 'Whether they liked it or not, their local interests forced them to enter national politics, to become the most important men in the nationalist movement.' Iliffe, J. 'Tanzania Under German and British Rule', in Ogot, B.A., Kieran, J.A., eds, *Zamani: A survey of East African history*, Nairobi and London: East African Publishing House and Longmans, Green & Co., 1968, pp.290–311, p.303. On the local negotiation of concepts of (national) identity and imaginations of the state, see Pels, 'Creolisation', pp.1–27.
8. Juma Mwapachu, pers.comm., 2 September 2011.
9. NACO981/16556/106 Nyerere to Crook, 5 January 1952.
10. Obe, 'Teacher', p.6; Nyerere, 'Statement to the U.N.', p.42.
11. Carey, *Colonial*, p.31. One was Al Noor Kassum, who played a critical role in the run-up to Tanganyika's independence, and went on to serve Tanzania both at home and abroad. Kassum met Nyerere in London in the early 1950s when he was studying law at Lincoln's Inn. Kassum, A.N. *Africa's Winds of Change: Memoirs of an international*

261

Notes for Chapter 6, pp. 132–162

      Tanzanian, London: I.B. Tauris, 2007, p.5.
12. At the end of 1952 there were ten African students from Tanganyika studying in the United Kingdom, and fifty-five and thirty-three Asian and European students respectively. Hill, *Tanganyika*, p.66.
13. Carey, A.T. 'The Social Adaptation of Colonial Students in London, with special reference to West Africans and West Indians', Ph.D., University of Edinburgh, 1955, which focuses on West African and West Indian students in London but also includes the findings from interviews with students from East Africa and elsewhere in the Commonwealth. Carey interviewed informants outside London, and there is nothing in his methodology to suggest that none of his colonial student informants were in Edinburgh – the city where he was writing his thesis. Also Stockwell, 'Leaders', p.500.
14. Also Clarke, 'Notes', p.16.
15. Interview, David Sawe, Dinah Sawe. Thomas Marealle had also studied at Aberystwyth. Eckert, 'Regulating', p.487.
16. NACO981/16556/107 Crook to Nyerere, 7 January 1952. A number of these names appear in the CDWS sections of the NACO981/16556 file. A.S. Fundikira, the son of the Nyamwezi chief, who was refused a CDWS scholarship because his proposed course was too similar to his previous studies at Makerere, managed to secure some form of funding and is listed as a 1953 graduate of Caius College, Cambridge. Weber, M. 'Caius Lost – Where Are They?' *Once a Caiu...: The Newsletter of Gonville & Caius College Cambridge*, Michaelmas (2) 2005, pp.18–24, p.20. The name of the Makerere-educated Paulo Mwinyipembe had already been put forward to study at Oxford as early as 1935, but the proposal was opposed by Martin Kayamba, by this time Assistant Secretary in the Dar es Salaam Secretariat. Iliffe, 'Spokesman', p.83; Iliffe, *Modern History*, p.396, and NACO691/126/12. Mwinyipembe began a General Arts degree course at Durham a year before Nyerere started at Edinburgh, and had presumably graduated by the time Crook replied to Nyerere. As Nyerere, he was initially down to take teaching, NACO981/16556/2. See also NACO981/16556/6, 14, 18, 22.
17. ibid./107 Crook to Nyerere, 7 January 1952. Keto is mentioned as another University of Edinburgh Tanganyika student who was 'here at the same time as him [Nyerere]', in unattributed note, CLX-A-16/4, Shep.Coln.
18. ibid./94 Nyerere to Crook, 17 June 1951.
19. See MacKenzie, J.M. 'The Persistence of Empire in Metropolitan Culture', in Ward, S., ed. *British Culture and the End of Empire*, Manchester: Manchester University Press, 2001, pp.21–36, p.29.
20. NA WORK 25/7 and NA WORK 25/10.
21. ibid./10. For a brief biography on Adbulla Hasham Ganji (as he signed his name in the visitors book), see http://ismaili.net/heritage/node/20667, accessed on 5 February 2014.
22. Hatch, *African Statesmen*, p.91.
23. 'Chief Kidaha Makwaia, Shinyanga, Tanganyika, East Africa', signed his name thus in the Festival of Britain visitors book. NA WORK 25/10.
24. Moore, S.F. 'Post-Socialist Micro-Politics: Kilimanjaro, 1993', *Africa*, 66 (4) 1996, pp.587–606, p.590, and Sally Moore, pers.comm., 28 March 2012. Marealle later said that he did not want anything to do with TANU at the time of meeting Nyerere in London, but that he would not refuse to let recruitment take place on the mountain. In 1979 Marealle told the American anthropologist Sally Moore that he was an early member of TANU, but secretly, because it would have been suicide to belong to it during the days of the colonial government. Sally Moore, pers.comm., 29 March 2012. I thank Tom Fisher for pointing me to this detail from Moore's paper.
25. See www.flickriver.com/photos/brizzlebornandbred/2056126901 for an image of 'Tanganyikan tribal dignitaries' meeting members of the Dagenham Girl Pipers at the 'Our Way of Life' exhibition, Bristol, as part of the 1951 Festival of Britain. Chief Petro Itosi Marealle of Marangu is to the right (with feather headdress) and Chief Makwaia of Ushiha is second from right; accessed on 27 October 2013.

Notes for Chapter 6, pp. 132–162

26. On Makwaia's proceedings with the Legislative Council, see Maguire, *Toward*, pp.52–3. Makwaia's probing of the government suggests that, while a conservative, he was not always the lackey to the British that Nyerere's supporters often portrayed him to have been.
27. NACO981/16556/96.
28. Twining was sworn in as Governor in mid-April 1949, by which time Nyerere had left Tanganyika. Bates, *Gust*, p.202.
29. Interview, Keto.
30. This section leans on Maguire, *Toward*, pp.52–58 for detail on Makwaia's dealings with the Legislative Council.
31. Smith, *Nyerere*, p.53. Iliffe adds that Makwaia 'alienated nationalists by apparent acquiescence in the East African High Commission and Operation Exodus' (a 1951 scorched earth campaign inflicted on the Meru, also known as the Meru Lands Case). Iliffe, *Modern History*, p.535, 451. See also Lohrmann, *Voices*, p.337–342, and Spear, 'Indirect Rule'.
32. Nyerere to Nicholson, 4 September 1951, Box 6/2/87, FCB.
33. Oxford undergraduates, *East African*, p.8.
34. See Maguire, *Toward*, pp.354–6.
35. MacKenzie, 'Portraits', p.2.
36. The Cosmopolitan Club left no minutes, although it is known that among the speakers was the anti-apartheid campaigner Michael Scott. Cattanach to Molony, n.d. November 2000, p.1.
37. Shepperson, 'First African', p.23. The Edinburgh Fabian Society discussed the proposed Central African Federation only a few days after Nyerere had left the United Kingdom. See *The Scotsman*, *Evening Dispatch*, and *Edinburgh Evening News*, all 3 November 1952. Also Edinburgh Fabian Society, National Library of Scotland, Edinburgh (hereafter 'EFS'), Session Minutes 1951–52, Acc. 4977 (14), p.22.
38. Mang'enya, *Discipline*, p.250.
39. ibid., p.251.
40. Interview, Keto.
41. This meeting was attended by Nyerere and Keto. ibid.
42. For discussion on the CAF among East Africans and the British in England and Scotland, see Mang'enya, *Discipline*, p.263–270. Note though that Hatch, *African Statesmen*, p.29, states that the protest against federation was considerably stronger in Scotland than in England, with support from both the main national newspapers, *The Scotsman* and the *Glasgow Herald*.
43. Kenneth MacKenzie to Alison Truefitt, 11 March 1964, file 4, Shep.Coln.
44. Godfrey Huggins speaking to the Colonial and Overseas League in 1934; cited in Nyerere, J.K., Keto, J. 'Central African Federation', *The Student*, 1951–52, 48 (7) 1951, pp.278–80, p.278.
45. Nyerere, 'Central African', p.278.
46. Macola, *Liberal*, p.25. Nkumbula's name also appears on the 1951 version of the published pamphlet (National Archives of Zambia, Lusaka, HM 70/4/49/2), although McCracken claims it was written by Banda alone. McCracken, J. *A History of Malawi, 1859–1966*, Woodbridge: James Currey, 2012, p.327, note 129. I thank Giacomo Macola for making the pamphlet available to me.
47. Leanstrait, J. 'King of the N'gombali', *The Student*, 1951–52, 48 (1), 1951, pp.11–3, p11.
48. ibid., p.12.
49. ibid., p.13.
50. A Grasslands/Semi-Bantu-speaking sub-group among the Bamileke of Cameroon's West Region are known as the Ngombale, who are predominantly Roman Catholic. In a number of Bantu languages the apostrophe normally follows the 'g', as in 'ng'ombe' (cow) or 'okung'atuka' (retire; relinquish). The word may have been produced instead as a combination of the English 'go', and the Swahili '*mbali*', meaning 'far' (producing 'go far'); a very similar name to the Butiama *omugabhu* Mtokambali ('the one who comes

263

Notes for Chapter 6, pp. 132–162

from afar').
51. For example, Nyerere, 'Socialism', pp.340–341.
52. Yankson, J.K. 'A Man with Twenty Wives', *The Student*, 1951–52, 48 (6) 1951, pp.238. If a real name, and not a pseudonym, Yankson may have been from the Gold Coast. Paul Nugent believes that there was a Ghanaian railway workers' leader by the name in the early 1960s. 'Yank' may also refer to an anti-slavery position. The unusual 'J.K.' initials could, of course, have stood for 'Julius Kambarage'.
53. W.G.B. 'From Darkest Africa', *The Student, 1951–52*, 48 (10) 1951, p.412. 'Mr Chirwa' is most likely not Orton Chirwa, but Wellington Manoah Chirwa, a leading Nyasaland nationalist of the early 1950s who went on to become one of the two Malawians in the Federal Parliament. I thank John McCracken for the explanation. Mr Katilunga [*sic*] was probably Lawrence Chola Katilungu, who became president of the TUC. He was killed in a car accident in 1961, some say in suspicious circumstances: Meynaud, J., Salah-Bey, A. (trans. Brench, A.), *Trade Unionism in Africa: A study of its growth and orientation*, London: Methuen, 1967, p.179–80.
54. Cattanach, 'Some notes', p.20.
55. Kenneth MacKenzie to Alison Truefitt, 11 March 1964, file 4, Shep.Coln.
56. Cattanach adds that five chiefs from Central Africa were also in attendance. Cattanach to Molony, n.d. November 2000, p.1.
57. Nyerere, 'Central African', p.280.
58. *Scotsman*, 1 March 1952, p.5., 'Central African Federation: Traditional British Policy Reversed, Edinburgh Protest'.
59. Hatch, *African Statesmen*, p.29; Shepperson, 'First African', p.23. Referred to elsewhere as the Scottish Council for African Affairs, among the founders were Reverend Cattanach and Sinclair Shaw, Q.C.
60. Mang'enya, *Discipline*, p.269.
61. Short, P. *Banda*, London: Routledge & Kegan Paul, 1974, p.51–52.
62. ibid., p.51.
63. McCracken, *History*, pp.327–8. See Lwanda, *Kamuzu Banda*, p.27 for examples of later antipathy between Banda and Nyerere.
64. Molony, 'Nyerere', p.11.
65. Carey, *Colonial*, pp.89, 99. See Garigue, P. 'The West African Students' Union: A study in culture contact', *Africa*, 23 (1) 1953, pp.55–69; Sherwood, *Kwame*, p.111–188.
66. Molony, 'Nyerere', p.11. Note, however, that the *Edinburgh University Student's Handbook* for the last two years Nyerere was in Edinburgh has no record of the West Indian Students' Association, perhaps because it was not housed in University property at the time. See Besson, *Carribean*, p.143.
67. Stirrat, *Student's Handbook*, p.48.
68. Loudon, D., ed. *Edinburgh University Student's Handbook, 1954–55*, Edinburgh: Students' Representative Council, 1954, p.99.
69. ibid., p.100.
70. Stern to Shepperson, 21 August 1960, CLX-A-16/4, Shep.Coln.
71. Collins, S.F. 1957. *Coloured Minorities in Britain: Studies in British race relations based on African, West Indian and Asiatic immigrants*. London: Lutterworth.
72. Collins, 'Social'. Also Shepperson to Kalinjuma, 16 February 1988, CLX-A-16/4, Shep.Coln.
73. Wilson to Shepperson, 9 November 1960, CLX-A-16/1, Shep.Coln. Wilson went on to say: 'I wish the Congo, where I lived, could have had a leader like Julius Nyerere at this time.'
74. Nyerere, 'Race Problem'.
75. ibid.
76. Nyerere to Shepperson, 5 May 1960, CLX-A-16/1, Shep.Coln.
77. Nyerere to Nicholson, 4 September 1951, Box 6/2/87, FCB.
78. Nicholson to Nyerere, 29 August 1951, ibid./84–85, FCB. The article appears in Nyerere, *Freedom and Unity*, pp.23–9, as the first speech in the book. See also the 'Racial

Notes for Chapter 6, pp. 132–162

Disharmony in East Africa' chapter, authored by Oxford undergraduates in the 1952 *East African*, pp.25–9. For an insight into Fabian views on the race problem in East Africa, see 'Racial Inter-Marriage', in *East Africa and Rhodesia*, 1949, 26 (1307), pp.199–200.

79. Nyerere to Nicholson, 4 September 1951, Box 6/2/87, FCB.
80. ibid.
81. ibid.
82. Ross, G.A. 'European Support for and Opposition to Closer Union of the Rhodesias and Nyasaland, with special reference to the period from 1945–1953', M.Litt. University of Edinburgh, 1988, p.293–4.
83. Nicholson to Nyerere, 11 September 1951, Box 6/2/87, FCB. When during a speech at the University of Ghana some years later Lewis was asked why there were no African Fabian Societies, he said of his reviewer: 'of all Africa's so-called socialist writers, the only leader who sees this very clearly is Mr. Nyerere of Tanzania': Lewis, W.A. *Some Aspects of Economic Development*, London: George Allen & Unwin, 1969, p.69.
84. Nyerere, J.K. '*Attitude to Africa* book review from Tanganyika', *Venture: Journal of the Fabian Colonial Bureau*, 3 (11) 1951, pp.6–7.
85. For example, Kosukhin, N. 'Julius Nyerere: Statesman, Thinker, Humanist'. In Vinokurov, Y.N., Shlyonskaya, S.M., et al., ed. (trans. Petruk, B.G.), *Julius Nyerere: Humanist, Politician, Thinker*, Ndanda-Peramiho: Benedictine Publications, 2003, pp.11–20, pp.11–12; Pratt, *Critical*, p.63; Ishumi, A.G., Maliyamkono, T.L. 'Education for Self-Reliance', in *Mwalimu: The Influence of Nyerere*, Legum, C., Mmari, G., ed. Oxford, Dar es Salaam and Trenton: James Currey, Mkuki na Nyota, Africa World Press, 1995, pp.46–60, p.46.
86. Session Minutes 1951–52, Acc. 4977 (14), EFS.
87. The 1959 *New Fabian Colonial Essays*, edited by Arthur Creech Jones, for example, is held in his personal library (and sections of Lionel Elvin's 'Social Development' chapter are marked). For example of his writing for the Fabians, see Nyerere, J.K. 'A Call to European Socialists', *Third World: Socialism and Development*, 1 (3) 1973, pp.5–7.
88. Said, *Abdulwahid*, p.111.
89. McBriar, A.M. *Fabian Socialism and English Politics, 1884–1918*, Cambridge: Cambridge University Press, 1962, pp.152–153; Doyle, M.W. 'Kant, Liberal Legacies, and Foreign Affairs' Part I, *Philosophy & Public Affairs*, 12 (3) 1983, pp.205–35, p.208, note 4.
90. Cornelli, E.M. 'A Critical Analysis of Nyerere's Ujamaa: An investigation of its foundations and values', unpublished Ph.D. thesis, University of Birmingham, 2012 p.80, see also p.4, note 2.
91. Among the numerous examples are ibid., especially pp.79–106; Stöger-Eising, 'Ujamaa', pp.134–135. An exception is Bjerk, who mentions Fortes and Evans-Pritchard, *African Political Systems* and Bagehot, W., *The English Constitution*, Oxford: Oxford Paperbacks, 2001 (1867). Bjerk, 'Establishment', pp.22–23, 134–135.
92. For example, Metz, 'In Lieu', p.385; Mazrui, A.A. 'Tanzaphilia'. *Transition*, (31), 1967, pp.20–6, p.20.
93. Edinburgh University. *1951–1952*, p.223.
94. Edinburgh University, *1949–1950*, p.213.
95. Nyerere, 'Ujamaa', p.164.
96. Mill, J.S. *Principles of Political Economy with some of their applications to social philosophy*, London: Longmans, Green and Co., 1904 (1848), p.15.
97. Nyerere, 'Arusha Declaration', pp.233, 243–5.
98. Nyerere, 'Introduction' *Freedom and Socialism*, p.6.
99. ibid., p.5.
100. Nyerere, 'Socialism', p.358.
101. Nyerere, J.K. 'Guide to the One-Party State Commission', in *Freedom and Unity*, pp.261–5, p.263.
102. Nyerere, 'Opening of the University', p.307.
103. Mill, *Principles*, p.72.

Notes for Chapter 6, pp. 132–162

104. Nyerere, 'Ujamaa', p.170.
105. Mill, *Principles*, p.423.
106. Nyerere, 'Ujamaa', p.170.
107. ibid., p.164.
108. Nursey-Bray, 'Consensus', p.98. For discussion on the anthropological weakness of Nyerere's traditional society, see Metz, 'In Lieu'.
109. Nyerere, 'Africa's Place', p.152.
110. Pratt, *Critical*, p.72.
111. Edinburgh University. *1951–1952*, pp.222–3.
112. Nyerere, 'Democracy', p.1; Nyerere, 'The African', p.104.
113. Kirkpatrick, *Macmurray*, p.150.
114. Nyerere, Introduction to *Freedom and Socialism*, p.13.
115. One text was Kant, I. *Fundamental Principles of the Metaphysics of Morals*, Cambridge: Cambridge University Press1991, (1785).
116. Cornelli, 'Critical Analysis', p.4. Also pp.79–106.
117. ibid., pp.99–106.
118. Nyerere, 'Arusha Declaration', p.231; Nyerere, Introduction to *Freedom and Socialism*, passim; Kant, *Fundamental Principles*, pp.100–108; Cornelli, 'Critical Analysis', pp.56–8, 83–8.
119. Edinburgh University. *1951–1952*, pp.223.
120. Costello, J.E. *John Macmurray: A biography*, Edinburgh: Floris, 2002, pp.147–148.
121. Nyerere, J.K. 'The Purpose is Man', in *Freedom and Socialism*, pp.315–26..
122. Nyerere, J.K. 'Independence Address to the United Nations', in *Freedom and Unity*, pp.144–56, p.147.
123. Costello, *Macmurray*, p.181.
124. ibid., pp.158–9; JUKANYE, 'African Socialism'.
125. Costello, *Macmurray*, pp.103, 315.
126. Kirkpatrick, *Macmurray*, p.150.
127. ibid., p.149.
128. Nyerere, 'Democracy', p.22.
129. Kirkpatrick, *Macmurray*, p.149.
130. Nyerere, Introduction to *Freedom and Socialism*, pp.14–17.
131. A quote from Chapter 25 of Volume 1 appears in Nyerere, 'European Socialists', pp.5–7. It was removed from the version that appears in *Freedom and Development*.
132. Nyerere, Introduction to *Freedom and Socialism*, p.17. Nyerere later mentioned 'humanistic socialism' as a variation of socialism, but he did not expand his thoughts. Nyerere, J.K. 'The Rational Choice' (speech), Dar es Salaam: United Republic of Tanzania, 1973, p.2.
133. Nyerere, Introduction to *Freedom and Socialism*, p.17.
134. Gough, J.W., Introduction to Locke, J. *The Second Treatise of Government: An essay concerning the true original, extent, and end of civil government*, Oxford: Blackwell, 1966 (1689), p.xiii.
135. Nyerere, 'Democracy', p.1.
136. Nyerere, J.K. 'The Challenge of Independence', *East Africa and Rhodesia*, 38 1961 (1939), pp.339–40, p.339.
137. JUKANYE, 'African Socialism'.
138. Nyerere, J.K. 1972. 'Dissolving the Independence Parliament'. In *Freedom and Development*, p. 35–49, p.37.
139. Nyerere, Introduction to *Freedom and Socialism*, p.19.
140. ibid.
141. Rousseau, J.J. 'The Social Contract', in *The Social Contract and Discourses*, pp.1–116. London: Dent, 1947 (1762), p.42, also pp.64–8.
142. Hobbes, T. *Leviathan, or The Matter, Forme and Power of a Common-Wealth Ecclesiasticall and Civill*, Oxford: Oxford University Press, 2008 (1651); Locke, *Second Treatise*.
143. Edinburgh University. *1951–1952*, pp.223.
144. Rousseau, 'Social Contract', p.31, and note 1.

Notes for Chapter 6, pp. 132–162

145. ibid., p.20, and passim. The term is also discussed in Green, T.H. *Lectures on the Principles of Political Obligation*, London: Longmans, Green and Co., 1948 (1895), p.93–120. Bosanquet refers to general will (or 'Real Will'), which he links it to the common good: Bosanquet, B. *The Philosophical Theory of the State*, South Bend, IN: St Augustine's Press, 2001 (1899). His formulation was criticised as anti-democratic and devaluing the individual. Sweet, W. 'Bernard Bosanquet', in Zalta, E.N., ed. *The Stanford Encyclopedia of Philosophy*, Stanford, CA: Stanford University, 2012.
146. Nyerere, 'Church', p.224, also 219.
147. Nyerere, J.K. 'Freedom and Development', in *Freedom and Development*, pp.58–71, p.67.
148. For examples of these recurring themes, see Nyerere, 'Introduction', *Freedom and Socialism*, p.4; 'Principles and Development', in *Freedom and Socialism*, pp.187–206, p.193; 'Introduction', in *Freedom and Unity*, pp.4, 8, 15, 17; 'Independence Message to TANU', in *Freedom and Unity*, pp.138–43, p.139.
149. Iliffe, *Modern History,* p.25; Kimambo, I.N. 'The Interior Before 1800', in Kimambo, I.N., Temu, A.J., ed. *A History of Tanzania*, Nairobi: East African Publishing House, 1969, pp.14–33, pp.18–22; Nyerere, 'The African', p.103.
150. Nyerere, *Democracy*, pp.9, 15, 19–20.
151. Rousseau, 'Social Contract', p.56–63.
152. Nyerere, J.K. 'The Entrenchment of Privilege', *Africa South*, 2 (2), 1958, pp.85–90, p.87.
153. For example, Nyerere, J.K. 'President's Inaugural Address', in *Freedom and Unity*, 1962, pp.176–87, p.179.
154. Nyerere, J.K. 'Responsible Self-Government Proposals', in *Freedom and Unity*, pp.75–80, p.127; Locke, *Second Treatise*, p.4.
155. Nyerere, 'Africa's Place', p.150.
156. Nyerere, 'Arusha Declaration', p.231.
157. Nyerere, 'Africa's Place', pp.150–151.
158. Israel, J.I. *Radical Enlightenment: Philosophy and the making of modernity 1650-1750*, Oxford: Oxford University Press, 2002, p.717.
159. Nyerere, 'Africa's Place', p.157. This appears in a slightly different form in Nyerere, J.K. 'Africa's Place in the World', in Mwalimu Nyerere Foundation, ed. *Africa Today and Tomorrow*, Dar es Salaam: Mwalimu Nyerere Foundation, 2000 (1960) pp.4–20, pp.13–14, and is further developed in Nyerere, *Democracy*, pp.22–3.
160. The Rousseau observation is made in Glickman, H. 'Dilemmas of Political Theory in an African Context: The ideology of Julius Nyerere'. In Butler, J, Castagno, AA, ed. *Transition in African Politics*, New York: Praeger, 1967, pp.195–223, p.207, and later in Stöger-Eising, 'Ujamaa', p.135.
161. Green, *Political Obligation*; Bosanquet, *Philosophical*.
162. Rousseau, 'Social Contract', p.80.
163. Nyerere, 'Africa's Place', p.158.
164. Pratt, C.R. 'The Cabinet and Presidential Leadership in Tanzania, 1960–1966', in Cliffe, Saul, *Socialism in Tanzania Volume 1*, Nairobi: East African Publishing House, 1972, pp.226–40, p.237. See also Schneider, 'Freedom', p.367, note 40.
165. Green, *Political Obligation*, p.121.
166. Nyerere, 'The Challenge', p.339.
167. Nyerere, J.K. 'A Long-Term Optimist', in *Freedom and Development*, 1972, p. 337
168. Lindsay, A.D. 'Introduction', in Green, *Lectures*, 1948 (1895), pp.vii–xix, p.xiii; Sweet, 'Bernard Bosanquet'.
169. Costello, *Macmurray*, p.58.
170. Nyerere, 'Introduction to *Freedom and Unity*, p.8. My italics.
171. Nyerere, 'Responsible', p.76.
172. Nyerere, 'The African', p.106.
173. Green, *Political Obligation*, pp.17, 100; also pp.2–27 passim.
174. ibid., p.101.
175. ibid., p.118.
176. See reference to Bunting's interview in Chapter 1, note 132.

Notes for Chapter 6, pp. 132–162

177. Green, *Political Obligation*, p.8.
178. Nyerere, 'Inaugural Address', p.178.
179. On the appeal of *umoja*, see Sanders, 'African Association', pp.173–205.
180. Note the similarity of Nyerere's three titles to those of the triumvirate by Ramsay MacDonald, Britain's first Labour party Prime Minister: *Socialism and Society* (1905), *Socialism* (1907) and *Socialism and Government* (1909).
181. Mill, J.S. 'On Liberty', in *Utilitarianism, Liberty, Representative Government*, 1972 (1859), London: Dent, pp.63–170, p.75.
182. Nyerere, Introduction to *Freedom and Unity*, p.16.
183. Nyerere, Introduction to *Freedom and Socialism*, p.5; Nyerere, 'One Party', p.10.
184. Nyerere, 'Freedom', p.58.
185. Nyerere, Introduction to *Freedom and Unity*, p.7.
186. Mill, J.S. 1972 (1861). 'Representative Government', p.184; Nyerere, 'Rational Choice'.
187. Nyerere, *Democracy*, p.16.
188. ibid., p.1.
189. Nyerere, J.K. 'Opening of the New National Assembly', in *Freedom and Socialism*, pp.86–103, p.88.
190. Nyerere, 'Entrenchment', p.87.
191. Nyerere, 'Guide', p.261.
192. Nyerere, *Democracy*, p.2.
193. Kant, I. *The Philosophy of Law: An exposition of the fundamental principles of jurisprudence as the science of right*, Edinburgh: T.&T. Clark, 1887 (1790), p.210.
194. Nyerere, *Democracy*, passim; Rousseau, 'Social Contract', p.63–4.
195. Nyerere, 'The African', p.103.
196. Nyerere, 'Independence Message', p.140.
197. Nyerere, 'Freedom', p.63. Also Nyerere, Introduction to *Freedom and Unity*, p.14.
198. Mill, 'On Liberty', p.78–113; Mill, 'Representative Government', pp.202–18.
199. Mill, 'On Liberty', pp.124–5.
200. Nyerere, J.K. 'Groping Forward', in *Freedom and Unity*, pp.119–23, p.122.
201. Nyerere, 'The African', p.106.
202. Rousseau, 'Social Contract', pp.78, 87–91; Green, *Political Obligation*, p.90, within pp.89–92.
203. Nyerere, Introduction to *Freedom and Unity*, pp.8, 16.
204. Nyerere, 'Africa's Place', p.156. Also Nyerere, 'The African', p.105.
205. Nyerere, Introduction to *Freedom and Unity*, p.12. The 'noble savage' phrase that Nyerere attributes to Rousseau does not occur in any of the philosopher's writings.
206. Rousseau, 'Social Contract', p.3.
207. ibid., p.4.
208. Nyerere, 'Ujamaa', p.162; Nyerere, Introduction to *Freedom and Socialism*, p.2.
209. Nyerere, 'The African', p.105.
210. Nursey-Bray, 'Consensus', p.101. On the strong influence of Rousseau on African nationalist theory, see Hodgkin, T. 'A Note on the Language of African Nationalism'. In Kirkwood, K, ed. *African Affairs*, London: Chatto and Windus, 1961, pp.22–40, especially pp.39–40.
211. Gaus, G.F., Sweet, W. 'Introduction', in Gaus, G.F., Sweet, W., ed. *The Philosophical Theory of the State and Related Essays by Bernard Bosanquet*, South Bend, Indiana: St Augustine's Press, 2001, pp.vii–xxxvii, p.xviii.
212. Edinburgh University. *1951–1952*, pp.223.
213. Green, *Political Obligation*, p.175.
214. Brink, D.O. *Perfectionism and the Common Good: Themes in the philosophy of T.H. Green*, Oxford: Clarendon, 2003, p.92.
215. For example, Green, *Political Obligation*, p.xiii.
216. Gaus 'Introduction', p.ix.
217. ibid., p.xxxii.
218. Sweet, 'Bernard Bosanquet'.

Notes for Chapter 7, pp. 163–179

219. See, for example, Costello, *Macmurray*, pp.101–2 for excerpts of Macmurray's lecture notes on Bosanquet's *Philosophical Theory of the State*.
220. Edinburgh University, *1951–1952*, pp.223. Nyerere refers to Laski in his introduction to *Freedom and Socialism*, p.17.
221. Kramnick, I., Sheerman, B. *Harold Laski: A life on the left*, London: Hamish Hamilton, 1993, p.362.
222. Laski, H.J. *A Grammar of Politics*, London: George Allen & Unwin, 1950, p.70. This section also draws on Kramnick & Sheerman, *Harold Laski*, pp.227–35.
223. Laski, *Grammar*, pp.94, 273.
224. ibid., p.184.
225. ibid., p.120.
226. ibid., p.280.
227. Kramnick & Sheerman, *Harold Laski*, p.333.
228. Milliband, R. 'Harold Laski's Socialism', *The Socialist Register*, 31, 1995, pp.239–63, p.242.
229. ibid.
230. M.M. Review: 'A Grammar of Politics', *Public Administration*, 4 (1), 1926, pp.63–5, p.63.
231. Kramnick & Sheerman, *Harold Laski*, p.227.
232. Pratt, *Critical*, p.74, see also p.63, 72–7.
233. Kramnick & Sheerman, *Harold Laski*, p.320.
234. Costello, *Macmurray*, p.16.

Chapter 7

1. Nyerere, 'Inaugural Address', p.187.
2. Piddington, *An Introduction*.
3. This section draws on Nyerere's April 1950 copy that is held in his personal library.
4. Piddington, *An Introduction*, p.228.
5. ibid., p.231.
6. ibid., p.238.
7. Nyerere, 'Socialism', p.337–8.
8. ibid., p.338.
9. Piddington, *An Introduction*, p.238.
10. Malinowski, B. 'Introduction', in Hogbin, H.I. *Law and Order in Polynesia*, 1934. London: Christophers, p.xxxiii (also on the course reading list); cited in Piddington, *An Introduction*, p.238.
11. Nyerere, 'Socialism', p.338.
12. Piddington, *An Introduction*, p.269.
13. ibid., p.268; Nyerere, 'Ujamaa', p.165.
14. Nyerere, 'Socialism', pp.348–9.
15. Piddington, *An Introduction*, p.274.
16. Nyerere, 'Ujamaa', p.165.
17. Nyerere, 'Socialism', p.339, 346–7.
18. Piddington, *An Introduction*, pp.314–18.
19. Geoffrey Owens, pers.comm., 10 May 2013.
20. Piddington, *An Introduction*, p.316.
21. JUKANYE, 'African Socialism'.
22. Piddington, *An Introduction*, p.316.
23. Nyerere, 'Socialism', p.339.
24. Nkrumah, K. 'African Socialism Revisited', *African Forum*, 1 (3) 1966, pp.3–9, pp.4–5.
25. Fortes, *African*, p.5; Edinburgh University, *1949–1950*, p.218. Subsequent references to titles listed under 'books recommended' for Piddington's Social Anthropology course are found on this page.
26. Fortes, *African*, pp.6, 9.
27. ibid., p.17.
28. Nyerere, 'Socialism', p.338.

Notes for Chapter 7, pp. 163–179

29. Fortes, *African*, p.23.
30. Graham, *Anthropology*, p.14.
31. ibid., p.16.
32. ibid., p.18.
33. For a critique of this position – the great flaw in British religious humanitarianism from its origins – see the influential Hall, C. *Civilising Subjects: Metropole and colony in the English imagination, 1830–1867*, Oxford: Polity, 2002.
34. Mair, L.P. *Native Policies in Africa*. London: George Routledge & Sons, 1936. Mair dedicates her book to Bronisław Malinowski, whose *Argonauts of the Western Pacific*, *The Sexual Life of Savages*, and *Crime and Custom in Savage Society* also featured on Nyerere's reading list.
35. ibid., p.284.
36. ibid., p.283.
37. The Latin phrase is literally translated as 'Who will guard the guards themselves?', or 'Who watches the watchmen?', and is often, and incorrectly, attributed to Plato's *The Republic* (which Nyerere began to translate; see Legère, 'Marehemu', p.46, note 30). The phrase is also linked to the Roman poet Juvenal's *Satires*, where the context actually deals with the problem of ensuring marital fidelity.
38. Macmillan, *Africa*, p.265. The 'leading African governor' may well have been Tanganyika's Sir Donald Cameron, who was the subject of the text preceding this quote and was certainly a well-respected administrator – and, along with another Tanganyika administrator, was acknowledged by Macmillan in the introduction to his 1938 edition as a major influence in his work. Note especially the reference to 'trusteeship', which furthers the case that the author is writing of Tanganyika.
39. Nyerere's British History notebook (October 1950 to May 1951) is housed in file 29 of the University of York's Marion Lady Chesham Papers, in the Borthwick Institute. Shepperson to Nyerere, 2 March 1989, CLX-A-16/6, Shep.Coln. A facsimile is held in the Shepperson Collection. The dictation style seems not to have been unique to Pares, for the notes given by Nyerere's lecturer in Constitutional Law, Professor Saunders, were similarly 'concise and in good order'. J.M.W. 'Constitutional Lawyer', *The Student*, 1952–53, 49 (5) 1952, pp.220–1, p.221.
40. Nyerere outlines his vision of villagization in 'Socialism', pp.351–66. See also Mwapachu, J.V. 'Operation Planned Villages in Rural Tanzania: A revolutionary strategy for development', *The African Review*, 6 (1) 1976, pp.1–16.
41. Bjerk, 'Establishment', p.135.
42. Edinburgh University, *1951–1952*, p.252.
43. Fei, H.-T. *Peasant Life in China: A field study of country life in the Yangtze Valley*, London: Kegan Paul, Trench, Trubner, 1939.
44. ibid., pp.30 and 101.
45. ibid., p.84.
46. ibid., p.25.
47. ibid., p.26.
48. ibid., p.106.
49. ibid., p.109.
50. Nyerere, 'Ujamaa', p.162.
51. ibid., p.163.
52. ibid., pp.166–8; 'Socialism', pp.346 and 338.
53. Nyerere, 'Socialism', pp.351, 353 and 347.
54. ibid., p.353.
55. Nyerere, 'Ujamaa', p.165; 'Socialism', p.351.
56. ibid., p.358.
57. Fei, *Peasant*, pp.107–108.
58. ibid., p.110.
59. Nyerere, 'Freedom', p.67.
60. Fei, *Peasant*, p.110.
61. Nyerere, 'Socialism', p.353.

Notes for Chapter 7, pp. 163–179

62. See, for example, Proctor, J.H. (ed.) *The Cell System of the Tanganyika African National Union*, University of Dar es Salaam, Studies in Political Science No. 1. Dar es Salaam: Tanzania Publishing House, 1971; O'Barr, J.F. 'Cell Leaders in Tanzania', *African Studies Review*, 15 (3) 1972, pp.437–65.
63. Fei, *Peasant*, pp.111, 116.
64. ibid., p.112.
65. Nyerere, 'Socialism', p.348.
66. Nyerere, 'Freedom', p.60.
67. Hinton, W. *Fanshen: A documentary of revolution in a Chinese village*, New York and London: Monthly Review Press, 1966. A first edition is held in Nyerere's personal library. On similarities between *ujamaa* and the tradition-oriented Narodnik movement in Russia, see Mueller, S.D. 'Retarded Capitalism in Tanzania', *Socialist Register*, 17, 1980, pp.203–26.
68. Nyerere's fascination with China sees that it features more positively than any other country in his collective writings and speeches. See, for example, Nyerere, 'The Party Must Speak for the People', in *Freedom and Development*, pp.30–9, p.38.
69. Shepperson, 'First African', p.23.
70. Shepperson to Kalinjuma, 1 March 1988, CLX-A-16/4, Shep.Coln.
71. Cattanach to Molony, n.d. November 2000, p.2.
72. E. Stables to Shepperson, 18 January 1960, CLX-A-16/4, Shep.Coln.
73. MacKenzie, 'Portraits', p.2.
74. Hatch, *African Statesmen*, p.28.
75. Interview, Keto. Despite Keto's apparent distance from Nyerere in Edinburgh, they did of course co-author the 'Central African Federation' article in *The Student*.
76. Neve, 'Political Life', p.33. Neve relies heavily on Smith, W.E.S., *We Must Run While They Walk*, New York: Random House, 1971, but to which he does little justice. This work of Smith is almost identical in text to his *Nyerere of Tanzania*, which was published in London two years later by Victor Gollancz.
77. Iliffe, *Modern History*, p.508.
78. Interview, Keto.
79. The most definitive examples are Nyerere's 'Ujamaa' and 'Socialism'.
80. Neve, 'Political Life', p.29, note 1.
81. Glickman, 'Dilemmas', p.204.
82. See also Westerlund, *Ujamaa na Dini*, p.79 and Hastings, A. *A History of African Christianity, 1950–1975*, Cambridge: Cambridge University Press, 1979, p.185.
83. Mark 4:25; Nyerere, 'Church', pp.214–15. The same verse is also quoted in Nyerere, 'European Socialists', p.375.
84. Nyerere, 'Church', pp.213–28, 215–16.
85. ibid., p.223. It is probably not a coincidence that on the cover of *Freedom and Development* (in which 'Church and Society' appears) Nyerere is wearing the *kibaragashia* hat that is favoured by many Muslim men.
86. Nyerere, 'Arusha Declaration', pp.244, 246.
87. Nyerere, 'Ujamaa', p.164.
88. Nyerere, 'Socialism', p.358; Nyerere, 'The Purpose', p.316.
89. Nyerere, 'National Property', in *Freedom and Unity*, pp.53–8.
90. Nyerere, 'Introduction', *Freedom and Socialism*, p.13.
91. ibid., pp.12–14. But see also Lacy, C. '"Christian" Socialism in Tanzania: An interview with President Julius Nyerere', *Christian Century*, 89 (9) 1972, pp.245–9.
92. Nyerere, Introduction to *Freedom and Socialism*, p.12.
93. ibid., p.12.
94. Ludwig, F. *Church and State in Tanzania: Aspects of changing relationship, 1961–1994*, Leiden: Brill, 1999, p.39. Also Dar es Salaam University Catholic Students' Association, eds, *The Arusha Declaration and Christian Socialism*, Dar es Salaam: Tanzania Publishing House, 1969.
95. Nyerere, 'Ujamaa', p.163; I Timothy 6:10.
96. Matthew 4:4; Nyerere, 'Principles', p.199. As might be expected, 'Church and Society'

Notes for Chapter 7, pp. 163–179

has a number of passages from the Bible.
97. Butler, J. (Roberts, T.A., ed.) *Butler's Fifteen Sermons*, London: SPCK, 1970 (1726); Edinburgh University, *1951–1952*, p.223.
98. Garrett, A. 'Joseph Butler's Moral Philosophy', in Zalta, *Stanford Encyclopedia of Philosophy*.
99. Matthew 22:39.
100. Mang'enya, *Discipline*, p.285; Bates, *Gust*, p.222.
101. Kilongola, 'Kumbukumbu ya Tano', p.105.
102. Iliffe, *Modern History*, p.546. Wildly contrasting photographs of Collins in Musoma at this time are available at http://digitallibrary.usc.edu/cdm/ref/collection/p15799coll123/id/15002/rec/3, http://digitallibrary.usc.edu/cdm/ref/collection/p15799coll123/id/15039/rec/11 and http://digitallibrary.usc.edu/cdm/ref/collection/p15799coll123/id/15048/rec/3, accessed 24 March 2014.
103. Booker T. Washington on the president of Hampton Institute, General Samuel Armstrong, quoted by Julius Nyerere in undated personal notes for a presentation at Makerere College, pp.6–7. 'Uhuru wa Wanawake' notebook, Mwalimu Nyerere Foundation, Dar es Salaam. The original quote can be found at Washington, *Up from Slavery*, p.55.
104. Banda to Mwase, 4 September 1938; cited in Banda to Matako, 8 October 1938; cited in Morrow, 'Two Previously', pp.348–9.
105. Interview, Keto. Keto 'stayed with Mrs Brown, and an Asian, and a West African fellow from Nigeria or Ghana.'
106. On communal violence between Catholics and Protestants, see Gallagher, T. *Edinburgh Divided: John Cormack and No Popery in the 1930s*, Edinburgh: Polygon, 1987. The enmity between denominations also comes through in Ross, *Root*.
107. Molony, 'Nyerere', p.12; Stern to Shepperson, 21 August 1960, CLX-A-16/4, Shep.Coln.
108. Listowel, *Making*, p.205.
109. Mang'enya, *Discipline*, p.267.
110. Short, *Banda*, p.34.
111. Molony, 'Nyerere', p.12.
112. Hatch, *African Statesmen*, p.28. See Little's preface to the published version of Alex Carey's thesis, *Colonial Students*. Little also shared with students his article on literacy in Sierra Leone: Little, K. 1953. 'Education in a Non-Literate Society'. *The Student*, 1953–54, 50 (10). pp.344–5.
113. Nicholson to Cattanach, 15 February 1952, 7/1, f 123, FCB; cited in Ross, 'European Support', p.310. Also correspondence between Nicholson and Little (at the LSE at the time), 17–23 April 1950, FCB; cited in Smith, *Influence*, p.24.
114. Molony, 'Nyerere', p.12.
115. MacKenzie, 'Portraits', p.1.
116. Hatch, *African Statesmen*, p.236.
117. Stirrat, *Student's Handbook*, p.50.
118. In 1560 the church in Scotland broke with Rome in a process of Protestant reform known as the Scottish Reformation, led by John Knox.
119. This section on Catholic Students' Union and The Chaplaincy is based on Stirrat, *Student's Handbook*, p.60.
120. Augustine of Hippo, *Confessions*, 8:17.
121. For a description of the Catholic chaplaincy, see Ross, *Root*, p.120–3.
122. ibid., p.122.
123. Stirrat, *Student's Handbook*, p.60; *The Student*, 1949–50, 46 (1), p.3.
124. Waugh studied at Oxford's Hertford College from 1922, which coincided with the studies at Balliol of Nyerere's British History lecturer, Richard Pares. Shortly after Pares had graduated and entered All Souls College, Monsignor Knox was Roman Catholic chaplain at Oxford, and both were in the city at the same time for a period of thirteen years. Waugh wrote a biography – some say a hagiography – on Knox, and while at Oxford had a homosexual relationship with Richard Pares. As a biographer of Waugh

Notes for Chapter 8, pp. 180–198

put it, Richard Pares was 'the subject of Evelyn's first love affair.... At Oxford... most of these young men, Pares and Waugh among them, were still emotionally immature. Accustomed to the all-male society of their public schools, they continued to find their friends and sometimes lovers within the confines of that same society, translated unchanging from school to university.' Hastings, S. *Evelyn Waugh: A biography*, London: Minerva, 1995, p.96. Waugh visited Zanzibar in 1931, and Tanganyika in 1959. Knox visited the year after Nyerere returned to Tanganyika from Edinburgh.

125. Iliffe, *Modern History*, p.509; Listowel, *Making*, p.205. Father Walsh confirmed this later to Westerlund. Westerlund, *Ujamaa na Dini*, p.80, note 8.
126. Wille, 'Recollections', p.5.
127. Aylward Shorter, pers.comm., 30 November 2011.
128. *Archives de la Société des Missionnaires d'Afrique (Pères Blancs)*, Rome (hereafter 'ASMA'), Nyerere to Marchant, 22 July 1952, 434516-7.
129. NACO981/16556/Minute Paper entry 105, Stone; see also NACO981/16556/105 and 120.
130. Listowel, *Making*, p.207.
131. ibid., p.427.
132. Bjerk, 'Establishment', p.253.
133. Catholic Church in Tanganyika, 'Africans and the Christian Way of Life: Pastoral Letter of the Archbishops, Bishops and Prefects Apostolic to the Catholic People of Tanganyika', 1953, pp.18–19, partially quoted in Sivalon, J.C. 'Roman Catholicism and the Defining of Tanzanian Socialism: 1955–1985', unpublished Ph.D. thesis, University of St. Michael's College, Toronto, 1990, p.99; cited in Bjerk, 'Establishment', p.253.
134. Edinburgh University. *1951–1952*, p.223; Bjerk, 'Establishment', p.253–254. Bjerk also observes that another of Walsh's publications re-stated, nearly word-for-word, Nyerere's thinking on the need for a one-party state. Sivalon, 'Roman Catholicism', p.113; cited in Bjerk, 'Establishment', p.253.
135. Walsh died in 1979: http://dspace.dial.pipex.com/suttonlink/350ta_fct.html. On an official visit to London Nyerere made a point of visiting Walsh's grave in Dublin www.thepelicans.co.uk/thepriory.htm, at which point he was presented a copy of James Connolly's *Labour in Ireland* (now located in his personal library in Butiama), in which is written 'To President Julius Nyerere, from his comrades in the Labour Party (Dublin, September 1979)', both accessed on 5 February 2014. On the relationship between Nyerere and Walsh in laying the foundations of church-state relations in the country, see also Hastings, *History*, p.100.
136. Nyerere; cited in Smith, *Nyerere*, p.50. Also Listowel, *Making*, p.208.

Chapter 8

1. Gray, A. *The Socialist Tradition: From Moses to Lenin*, London: Longmans, Green and Co., 1946, p.488.
2. Edinburgh University, *University Calendar: 1952–1953*, Edinburgh: James Thin, p.705; Graduates in Arts, 1952, EUA IN1/ADS/STA/5, EUL.
3. Nyerere to Marchant, 22 July 1952, 434516-7, ASMA.
4. Bridgland, F. 15 October 1999. 'Obituary: Julius Nyerere, former President of Tanzania', *Scotsman*, p.19.
5. E. Stables to Shepperson, 18 January 1960, CLX-A-16/4, Shep.Coln.; NACO981/16556/131 and 136; Edinburgh University, *1952–1953*, p.705.
6. NACO981/16556/123a and 123b, 124a and 124b, 126a, 128 and 146. The visits were likely arranged through the Central Bureau for Educational Visits and Exchanges, founded in 1948 and close to the British Council. Lee, 'Commonwealth', p.9.
7. Nyerere to Marchant, 22 July 1952, 434516-7, ASMA.
8. Hill, *Tanganyika*, p.66.
9. May, *Economic*, p.425. Five thousand destroyed or damaged schools had to be replaced or repaired following the war.

Notes for Chapter 8, pp. 180–198

10. Nyerere to Marchant, 22 July 1952, 434516-7, ASMA.
11. NACO981/16556/Minute Paper entry 109.
12. ibid./124, 128, 146 and 148; Nyerere to Marchant, 22 July 1952, 434516-7, ASMA.
13. Carey, *Colonial Students*, p.76. Hans Crescent was only for male students. The Colonial Girls' Club for women was located at 18, Collingham Gardens, London. British Council, *How To Live*, pp.36, 45.
14. A list of talks presented at Hans Crescent in 1952 is given in 'Welfare of Colonial Students 1952', Appendix C, EUA IN1/ADS/SEC/A/34/1, EUL. The talks are not dated, but Kojo Botsio is listed as having spoken on 'Current Affairs in the Gold Coast' and on 'Education in the Gold Coast'.
15. Carey, *Colonial Students*, p.234.
16. ibid., p.238–9.
17. Mang'enya, *Discipline*, pp.269, 278. Note that Mang'enya was anxious to portray himself as a Tanzanian nationalist and staunch anti-colonialist, despite evidence which could suggest he was tribalist and/or a collaborator with the colonial state. Willis, 'Administration of Bonde', p.63. See also Eckert, 'Cultural', p.263. If the meeting ever took place, Kirilo Japhet may also have attended. Iliffe notes (*Modern History*, p.502) that he was in London for some months during this same period.
18. In 1951 there were about 2,300 West African students in Britain. Garigue, 'West African', p.64, note 1.
19. Nyerere; cited in Obe, 'Teacher', p.6.
20. NACO981/16556/126 and 140. For an insight into race relations back home, see Mwakikagile, G. *Life in Tanganyika in the Fifties*, Dar es Salaam: New Africa Press, 2010.
21. ibid. Minute Paper entry 141.
22. ibid.
23. ibid. /130 and 142.
24. Hill, *Tanganyika*, p.170.
25. NACO981/16556/130, 136, 142, 148, 149, 151 and Minute Paper entries 133. Hatch, *African Statesmen*, p.33 completely omits the circumstances that led to the cancellation, merely stating that because 'his August sailing had been cancelled to allow him to accept the British Council invitations, he decided to travel by air'.
26. NACO981/16556/Minute Paper entry 151. The list is more likely to have been a list of CDWS students rather than a list of Africans who the British authorities wanted to keep an eye on.
27. ibid. /148 and 149. Accounts vary as to who was at the airport to greet Nyerere. Cross-referencing of sources, including the Catholic records and the recollections of Maria Nyerere (who was not present because 'In Bantu culture it is only appropriate for a wife to welcome her husband – not a fiancée') suggest that Hatch's account (*African Statesmen*, p.89) is more accurate than that of Wille ('Recollections', p.5). Interview, Maria Nyerere. See also www.tanserve.com/facts/index_files/history.htm, accessed on 5 February 2014. I am unable to find the original text on which this webpage is based.
28. Interview, Maria Nyerere.
29. In support of her point, Maria Nyerere adds, 'When I returned from Uganda my parents did not ask me how my studies had been.' Interview, Maria Nyerere.
30. Enahoro, 'Private', p.107. Nyerere made a similar statement in Bunting, 'Heart'.
31. Kitundu, 'Reflections', p.48.
32. Interview, Adam Marwa.
33. Interview, Nyamwaga.
34. Interview, Adam Marwa.
35. ibid.
36. Marchant, 'The Return from Edinburgh', in *The Nyerere Years*, p.13; *Tanzanian Affairs*, 2000, 'Obituaries: Brian Hodgson, CMG'; *Tanzanian Affairs*, 65, p.31.
37. Mustafa, K. 'The Concept of Authority and the Study of African Colonial History', *Kenya Historical Review: The journal of the Historical Association of Kenya*, 3 (1) 1975, pp.55-83, p.76. James Giblin puts the year of the accusation and deposition of Ihunyo, and

Notes for Chapter 8, pp. 180–198

the inauguration of Edward Wanzagi, as 1951: Giblin, J. 'Some Complexities of Family and State in Colonial Njombe', in Maddox & Giblin, *In Search of a Nation*, p.14. See Smith, *Nyerere*, pp.38–9 for an account of the riot, and Nyerere's disparaging comments on Ihunyo. Bischofberger (*Generation*, p.56) records that Ihunyo died in prison in 1953 (apparently of quaternary neurosyphilis). By 1956 the annual report was commenting that 'particular attention is to be made of the Zanaki Chiefdom Council, which under the leadership of the Chief Edward Wanzagi is on its way to becoming a responsible advisory and consultative body'.

38. Interview, Nyamwaga.
39. Bischofberger, *Generation*, p.18, 47, 98; Listowel, *Making*, p.172–3.
40. Feierman, *Peasant*, p.123. On chiefs' social authority being dependent on their ability to control the rains, see Maddox, G.H. 'Narrating Power in Colonial Ugogo: Mazengo of Mvumi', in Maddox & Giblin, *In Search of a Nation*.
41. The literature on rain as a metaphor for political power in African societies is vast. Relevant contributions include Jedrej, M.C. 'Rain Makers, Women, and Sovereignty in the Sahel and East Africa', in Fradenburg, L.O., ed. *Women and Sovereignty*, Edinburgh: Edinburgh University Press, 1992, pp.290–300; Lan, D. *Guns and Rain: Guerrillas and spirit mediums in Zimbabwe*, London: James Currey, 1985; Packard, R.M. *Chiefship and Cosmology: An historical study of political competition*, Bloomington, IN: University of Indiana Press, 1981. For an excellent summary, see Sheridan, M.J. 'Global Warming and Global War: Tanzanian farmers' discourse on climate and political disorder', *Journal of Eastern African Studies*, 6 (2) 2012, pp.230–45, p.231.
42. Nyerere narrated this event much later to Madaraka, and several others have given his son a similar account of the incident. Madaraka Nyerere, pers.comm., 9 July 2012, Mwanza. See also Nyerere, G.M. 9 February 2006. 'Letter From Butiama: The Rainmakers'. *The Daily News* (available at http://madarakanyerere.blogspot.co.uk/2010/09/letter-from-butiama-rainmakers.html, accessed 14 July 2012).
43. For rainmaking and ritual in Tanzania and neighbouring Kenya, see Sanders, T. 2008. *Beyond Bodies: Rainmaking and sense making in Tanzania*. Toronto, London: University of Toronto Press; Akong'a, J. 'Rain Making Rituals: A comparative study of two Kenyan societies', *African Study Monographs*, 8 (2) 1987, pp.71–85.
44. Iliffe, *Modern History*, pp.536–537.
45. Kitundu, 'Reflections', p.48.
46. Interview, Jackton Nyerere.
47. Interview, Adam Marwa.
48. Feinstein, *African*, p.102.
49. Wille, 'Recollections', p.5. Many miners lived in Edinburgh at the time when Nyerere was in the city, but it is not clear whether the mining family here refers to the Wilsons and their relatives. Equally, it may have been a family who Nyerere stayed with on one of his educational short visits elsewhere in the United Kingdom.
50. Interview, Adam Marwa.
51. *MDB*, Tanganyika Territory East African population census 1948, 'Regional distribution of civil population by districts' ('copy 62'); 'African population of Musoma District' (no page number). For a general description of Tanganyika in the 1950s, see Hill, *Tanganyika*, p.15–25, and p.852 on Musoma.
52. Carey, *Colonial*, p.43. This is expressed, for example, in Mgonja, C.Y. *Johari ya Maisha Yangu*, Dar es Salaam: Dar es Salaam University Press, 2003, p.42–5. I thank Anna Mulungu for bringing this book to my attention.
53. See Katoke and Rwehumbiza, 'The Administrator', p.60–1 for background on the Joint Committee of the British Parliament.
54. Kayamba, M. 'The Story of Martin Kayamba Mdumi, M.B.E., of the Bondei Tribe', in Perham, M, ed. *Ten Africans*, 1936, pp.173–272. London: Faber and Faber.
55. Mang'enya, *Discipline*, p.247. In a subsequent book Kayamba described a future central village that anticipates Nyerere's *ujamaa* vision. Kayamba, M. *African Problems*, London: United Society for Christian Literature, 1948, p.7; cited in Brennan, *Taifa*, p.127.

Notes for Chapter 8, pp. 180–198

56. Obe, 'Teacher', p.6. For a similar sentiment, see Chiume, *Kwacha*, pp.105–12.
57. CORY, 80.
58. Hatch, *African Statesmen*, p.8.
59. No hard and fast rule applied for the bridewealth quantities in Uzanaki, and there was (and still is) much room for negotiation, depending on circumstance. Writing four years before his initial marital agreement, and some eight years before the final exchange, Nyerere stated that for a man to take a wife in his area he must supply twelve cows and twenty-five goats. This tallies with Baxter's approximations from around the same time, which came to 'anything up to 15 or even twenty head of cattle and 20 to 30 goats but the average is about 8 head of cattle and say 20 goats'. Nyerere, *Uhuru wa Wanawake*, p.9–10; *MDB*, Laws, Manner and Customs: Zanaki tribe, Sheet 3, p.1.
60. The family of Magori Watiha may have been slow to return the bridewealth that they received from Burito for the union with his son, probably because they had to raise it again. The elderly Magori states that she had to marry another man so that her parents could receive the bridewealth from her new husband's family, and this was then returned to Chief Burito's family. Interview, Magori Watiha.
61. Interview, Maria Nyerere.
62. Interviews, Maria Nyerere, Adam Marwa.
63. The same date is also given by both Maria Nyerere (interview with author, and in Mwakikagile, *Nyerere*, p.392) and Wille, 'Recollections', p.6. In another text (Mwakikagile, *Nyerere*, p.404) Wille, as Hatch (*African Statesmen*, p.89) put the date at 24 January 1953.
64. Rose Nyerere, pers.comm., 11 July 2012; Wille, 'Recollections', p.6.
65. Nyerere to Marchant, 22 July 1952, 434516-7, ASMA.
66. Bowen, J.P., ed. *The Missionary Letters of Vincent Bowen, 1957–1973*, Eugene, OR: Pickwick, 2011, p.27; Wille, 'Recollections', p.6.
67. Wille, in Mwakikagile, *Nyerere*, p.404.
68. Nyerere; cited in Smith, *Nyerere*, p.50; Listowel, *Making*, p.208.
69. Goldsworthy, *Mboya*, p.8; Kaunda, K. *Zambia Shall Be Free*, London: Heinemann, 1962, pp.13, 23.
70. Feinstein, *African*, p.53.
71. Goldsworthy, *Mboya*, p.62.
72. See pp.93 and 188. Also Iliffe, *Modern History*, pp.503–507; Maguire, *Toward*, pp.81–159.
73. Ethan Sanders, pers.comm., 18 June 2013.
74. Iliffe, *Modern History*, p.509.
75. For a contemporary view on salary scales by race, see Oxford undergraduates in *East African*, p.14.
76. Hatch, *African Statesmen*, p.91. Wille, in Mwakikagile, *Nyerere*, p.404, put the figures at £30 and £45, respectively. It is claimed elsewhere that Barclay Leechman, Member of social services, made the suggestion that Nyerere should be given a European teacher's salary. www.tanserve.com/facts/index_files/history.htm, accessed on 5 February 2014. I am unable to find the original text on which this webpage is based.
77. Mugaya Nyerere; cited in Drum, 'Nyerere Story', pp.30–1.
78. Hamza Mwapachu informed his son that it was he who convinced Dossa Aziz and Abdul Sykes that Nyerere was the right man to lead TAA. Juma Mwapachu, pers.comm., 2 September 2011.
79. Sykes, A.K. 24 May 2013, 'Ally Sykes: Story of my life', Part 3, *The Citizen*, p.7. See also http://www.mohammedsaid.com/2013/12/tracing-footsteps-of-mwalimu-julius.html, accessed on 31 March 2014.
80. Iliffe, *Modern History*, p.508.
81. Sanders, 'African Association', p.226.
82. Mugaya Nyerere; cited in Drum, 'Nyerere Story', pp.30–31.
83. Interviews, Nyamwaga, Adam Marwa. Andrew Nyerere is said to have been named after Andrew Tibandebage.
84. The TAA is said to have included some Kenyan nationalists who were considered Mau Mau suspects. Said, *Abdulwahid*, p.122. Nyerere had to convince people that TANU

Notes for Chapter 8, pp. 180–198

would not commit 'things of the forest'. *Mwangaza*, 7 July 1956; cited in Iliffe, *Modern History*, p.520.
85. Interview, Nyamwaga. The District Commissioner may have been accompanied by the Special Branch rather than the CID. Nyerere did not move permanently to Dar es Salaam until late September or early October 1955. See Maguire, *Toward*, p.55, note 1.
86. Transition, 'The Transition Profile: Julius Nyerere', *Transition* (2) 1961, pp.21–2, p.21. Benjamin Mkapa was an Associate Editor of this issue, and very likely the author of the profile on Nyerere.
87. Lacy, 'Christian', p.247.
88. Wicken to Molony, 14 March 2001, p.5.
89. Neath, R. 'Who was to stay where?' in *The Nyerere Years*, p.15.
90. Brewin, 'Brief', p.16.
91. Wicken to Molony, 14 March 2001, p.5; Nyerere to Shepperson, 8 January 1988, CLX-A-16/4, Shep.Coln.
92. Shepperson to Nyerere, 28 April 1960, CLX-A-16/4, Shep.Coln.
93. Film footage of Nyerere being interviewed by a University of Edinburgh student, 1961, Dar es Salaam, EUL, E93.100. The 1961 date in the catalogue listing for the film is probably correct. Nyerere was Chief Minister of Tanganyika from September 1960 to May 1961, then Prime Minister (until January 1962). The footage shows the Union Flag ('Union Jack') flying high, suggesting that the footage was created before Tanganyika gained independence from Britain in December 1961. The film is available at http://youtu.be/0_-LW7rNiCg, accessed on 9 January 2013.
94. Edinburgh University, *1962–1963*. Edinburgh: James Thin, p.753, which reads: 'Julius Kambarage Nyerere, M.A. (Edin.), formerly Prime Minister of Tanganyika'.
95. Little to Hay, 24 January 1962, CLX-A-16/4, Shep.Coln.
96. Nyerere to Appleton, 31 March 1962, Acceptances of Honorary Degrees, 1962, EUA IN1/ADS/STA/15, EUL.
97. Shepperson to Nyerere, 15 December 1990, CLX-A-16/1, Shep.Coln.
98. The Honorary Degree of LL.D., Laureation Addresses, 5 July 1962, p.4, EUA IN1/ADS/SEC/A/86, EUL.
99. Appleton's Speech at Dinner to Honorary Graduates in the Upper Library, 5 July 1962, pp.5–6, EUA IN1/ADS/SEC/A/86, EUL.
100. 'Vote Nyerere', 1963 Rectorial Election campaign pamphlet, CLX-A-16/1, Shep.Coln.
101. Norman Clark, pers.comm., 21 August 2011.
102. Norman Clark, 1963, 'Nyerere the Man', Umoja! The magazine of the Nyerere Rectorial campaign committee, CLX-A-16/1, Shep.Coln.
103. Shepperson, pers.comm., 20 August 2012. Brockway gave Nyerere a copy of *African Socialism* in December 1963.
104. Wintersgill, *Rectors*, p.144–5.
105. Shepperson to Nyerere, 15 November 1963, CLX-A-16/1, Shep.Coln. During Justice's time as Rector of the University of Edinburgh (1957–1960 and 1963–1966), he featured in *Those Magnificent Men in Their Flying Machines*, a couple of years before his role as Lord Scrumptious in *Chitty Chitty Bang Bang*. Albert John Luthuli (1898–1967) was president of the ANC from 1952 to 1960, the year in which he was awarded the Nobel Peace Prize for his role in the non-violent struggle against apartheid.
106. Pia, S. 17 January 2005. 'Brown's failed bid to depose Duke'. *Scotsman*, p.12.
107. Wicken to Smith, 20 March 1975, CLX-A-16/1, Shep.Coln.
108. Nyerere to Barron, 9 April 1986. Facsimile in author's possession.
109. Owen Dudley Edwards, pers.comm., 31 August 2012, Edinburgh.
110. Nyerere, J.K. 'Reflections on Constitutions and African Experience', in Barron, T., Dudley Edwards, O., Storey, P.J., eds, *Constitutions and National Identity*, Edinburgh: Quadriga, 1993, pp.8–19. The original paper is available at EUL, Ms3218/3 (E88.109). The BBC asked the University for the tapes so that they could broadcast excerpts, but it was soon realised that the audio-visual technician covering the event had failed to press the record button.

111. Dudley Edwards, pers.comm., 31 August 2012, Edinburgh.
112. Nyerere, 'Reflections', p.10.
113. Dudley Edwards, pers.comm., 31 August 2012, Edinburgh.
114. ibid.
115. Edinburgh University, 'A highland gathering for Dr Nyerere', *Bulletin*, 24 (1) 1987, pp.14.
116. Nicholas Flavin, pers.comm., 3 September 2012, Edinburgh.
117. Nyerere, 'Third Liberation'.

Chapter 9
1. Twain, M. *Mark Twain's Autobiography*, New York: Harper & Brothers, 1924, p.220–221.
2. Enahoro, 'Private', p.107.
3. An excellent account of the context of racial politics during the colonial and post-colonial period is provided in Brennan, *Taifa*.
4. Sanders, 'African Association', p.246.
5. This point is developed from discussion with Paul Swanepoel.
6. Mang'enya, *Discipline*, p.246.
7. Saul, J.S. 'Julius Nyerere and the Theory and Practice of (Un)Democratic Socialism in Africa', in McDonald & Sahle, *Legacies of Julius Nyerere*, pp.15–26, p.21.
8. Iliffe, J. 'Introduction', in *Modern Tanzanians*, p.i.

Index

Bold page reference denotes an illustration. Page reference in *italics* denotes an entry in Select Biographies (pp.208–18).

Abhakibhweege clan 12
Abdallah, H. 47
Aberystwyth, University of 134
abhakuru 17
abhanyikura 18, 22, 27–8
abharwazi 28, 32
African Association (Tanganyika) 73, 76–8, 81–2, 87, 89, 93, 109, 112, 129, 133, 135–7, 181, 191–2, 203
African National Congress (Tanganyika) 125, 136
African Socialism *see ujamaa*
Aggrey, J.K. 66, 85, 234 n.133, 243 n.43
*akida*s 28–30, 35
Ali, A. 76
ancestor worship *see* traditional beliefs
Appleton, Sir E. 194
Appiah, J. 103
Arusha Declaration (1967) 127, 147, 150, 162, 172
Asquith Commission (1945) 109
Attitude to Africa 143–6
Aziz, D. 76, 191–2

Baker, E.C. 25, 27, 30, *208*
Baker, G.W. *208*, 257 n.141
Banda, H. 109, 110, 120–1, 123, 139, 141–2, 174, 205
Bankole Bright, H.R. 110
Bantu, J.K. 81, 136, 192, *208*
Baraki, Tarime/North Mara 89–90
Baumann, O. 20
Baxter, H.C. 25
beatification *see* 'canonization'
Bell, M. 113
Besson, W. 121
biography

as method 3–4, 8, 199
of African nationalists 2, 3, 7
of Nyerere 1–2, 4–8, 199–201
of Tanzanians 4, 207
Birnie, A. 112, 162
birth 37–8
Bischofberger, O. 18–22, 26–7, 38
Blumer, J.A.C. 57, 86, 240 n.149
Bomani, P.L. 133, *208*
Bosanquet, B. 132, 150, 155, 159–61
Botsio, K. 122, 135
Boy Scouts 54–6, 58, 206
bridewealth 83–4, 97–8, 120, 188, 257 n.132
British Council 106, 119–20, 122, 134, 181
Brockway, F. 196, 277 n.103
Broome Hall (England) 108
Brown, G. 196
Buchman, F. 103
Bukiri, M. 38, 263 n.50
Buhoro, Chief 32, *208*
Buhoro, K. **14**, 46
Bukoba 24, 64
Burito, Chief Nyerere 12–14, 16–17, 22, 29, 32–6, 41–4, 46, 49, 59–61, 63–4, 82–4, 120, 140, 186, 199, 203–4, *209*
Butiama 4, 11–23, 27, 32–4, 36–9, 43, 45–6, 50, 59–60, 62–4, 79, 82, 84, 93, 97–8, 111, 169, 184, 186–8, 192–3, 199
Butler, J. 173
Buturi 90
Bwiru 98

Cambridge, University of 25, 101
Cameron, Sir D. 25, 30, 35–6, 54, *209*
'canonization' 1–2

279

Index

Cardiff, University College of South Wales 87, 101, 103
Carmichael, D.D. 112, 181, *209*
Cattanach, Rev. Dr. W.D. 103, 137–8, 174–5
Central African Federation 7, 115, 124, 132, 137–42, 184
Chagga tribe 42, 101, 135, 165
Chamshama, S. **195**
chia 169
chieftaincy 39–43, 81–2, 93, 96
childhood 38–43
child marriage 78, 82–4, 199
China, (People's) Republic of 88–9, 94, 127, 163, 168–70
Chirwa, W.M. 140
Chiume, K. 26, 46, 53, 59, 86
Christianity 111, 141, 149, 186, 190–1, 206
　introduction to 48–51
　baptism 62–4
　confirmation 75–6
　vocation 171–9
circumcision and teeth filing 38–9, 52
Clark, N. 195–6
Cohen, A. 96
Colonial Development and Welfare Scheme 94, 96, 134
Colonial Office 25–7, 29–30, 43, 54, 95–6, 98, 102–4, 106–7, 112, 115–18, 120, 127, 129, 178, 180–3, 205
Colonial Paper 191 (1945) 89
Colonial Paper 210 (1947) 87, 135
Collings, R. 6
Collins, S. 143, 175
Collins, Fr. W.J. 93, 171, 173, 188–9
common good 151, 153
Communism 69–71, 94, 100–4, 112, 127, 145, 165, 175
Cory, H. 24–7, 29, 32, 97, 188, *209*
Cosmopolitan Club 137, 143, 175
Crook, Lt.Col. W.V. 117–9, 133–5, 183, *209*

Dar es Salaam 6, 21, 23, 53, 59, 69, 76–8, 81–2, 87–9, 93, 100–1, 116–18, 173, 183, 189–4, 196, 206
debating 7, 56, 58–9, 66–7, 76, 78, 86, 89, 97, 111, 124, 133, 143, 158, 176, 201, 204, 206
democracy 20, 32, 41, 70, 87, 112, 115, 125–6, 137, 142, 148–9, 151, 154–5, 157–60, 162, 197, 204, 206
demystification of British 188, 205
discrimination against 182–3 *see also* race
Durham, University of 101, 107, 134

East African Standard 124, 137
ebhitara 15, 40
Edinburgh, University of
　decision to study at 107–8
　choice of degree 108–9
　degree studies 111–15, 145–70, 173
　financial difficulties 115–121
　Palmerston Road (Colonial House) 104, 105, 122, 143, 176
　contact with Tanganyikans 133–6
　vocation *see under* Christianity
　Honorary Degree, LL.D. 110, 194–5
　Rectorial candidate 195–6
education 70, 85–6, 112–13, 117, 132, 153, 161, 166–7, 173, 181, 202–5 *see also* Mwisenge, Tabora Government, Makerere, St Mary's, Edinburgh, St Francis
ekyaaro 22–3, 27, 36, 93–4
Eliufoo, S. 87, *209*
Engels, F. 151
equality 42–3, 73, 145, 149–50, 153–9, 161, 165, 171–2, 187, 195, 202, 205
eriikura 27–8
eriisaga 20–1, 165
erisaambwa (*amasaambwa*) 16–17, 38, 49
Evans-Pritchard, E. 27, 166
ezinyaangi 27–8

Fabianism 95, 100, 103, 124, 129, 132, 142, 144–6, 160–1, 175, 204
Fairclough, J.L. 25
Fei, H.-T. 127, 168–70
Festival of Britain 135–6
Flavin, N. 197
Fortes, M. 166
freedom 1, 72, 73, 86, 114, 125–6, 138, 143, 150–1, 155–9, 165
Fundikira, A.S. 56, 66, 77, 96, *210*

Gabizuryo 16, 38
Gambia, The 96, 110–11, 130
Gandhi, M. 66
Gangji, A.H. 135
gender relations 34, 73–4, 97–8, 156, 173
Gerrard, C.M. 134
Glasgow 121
Glasgow, University of 108, 110–11, 141, 175, 196
Gogo tribe 186
Gold Coast 66, 72, 103, 122, 125, 127, 131, 135, 143, 151, 175, 184
governance 114, 158, 160, 170
government by discussion 126, 157–8
Graham, J. 166–7

280

Index

Gray, Sir A. 114, 147–8, 180
Green, T.H. 132, 150, 155–7, 159–61
Groundnut Scheme 130

hagiography 1–2, 7
Hamsa u Ishirini club 87–9, 173
hard work 147, 152, 165–6, 169, 172, 187, 204
Hatch, J. 7, 41, 43, 141, 175
Hehe tribe 165–6
Hinchcliffe, C. 118–19
Hinden, R. 95, 103
Hobbes, T. 150, 153, 160
Hodgson, A.B. **45**, 185, *210*
Holy Ghost Fathers 45, 189
Horton, J.A.B. 110
Huggins, Sir G. 138
human dignity 116, 150, 153, 154, 157, 159
human need 164
Hunter, M. (Wilson) 51
Huxley, J. 54

Ihunyo, Chief 32, 44, 185–6
Ihunyo, M. 44, 46, *210*
Ikizu tribe 24, 33, 34, 44, 62, 186
India 156, 161
indirect rule 30, 32, 35, 54, 95, 167
Irenge, J. 46–7, 52–3, 83, 90, 96–7, 191
Ishingoma, I.S. 96

Jaberi 29–30, 33, 35, *210*
Jawara, Sir D. 110–11
Jenga, Chief 83
Jennings, Sir A. 126
Jita tribe 23–4, 33, 62
Jones, A.C. 85–6, 95–6, 103–4, 138, 142, 145, *210*
Junker, Fr. A. 63, *210*

Kaihsienkung (China) 127, 168–70
Kambona, O. 246 n.25
Kampala 64, 67–9, 72–4, 77, 102, 165, 203
Kandoro, S.A. 133, *211*
Kano, A. 7, 53, 103, 187, 189
Kant, I. 145, 149–50, 155–8, 160
Kassum, N. 261 n.11
Katilungu, L.C. 140
Kawawa, R. 86
Kayamba, G. 65, 101, 106–7, 184
Kayamba, H.P. 101
Kayamba, M. 187–8
Keith, J.L. 105, 116–19, *211*
Kenyatta, J. 2, 102, 130, 205
Keto, J.E. 3, 6, 112, 122, 132, 135–9, **140**, 141, 143, 171, 174, *211*

Khama, S. 123
Kiasaga, W. 82
Kibira, E. 56
Kiernan, V. 175
Kiletta, G.J. 134
Kimalando, J. 81
Kimbu tribe 49
King's African Rifles 64, 91
Kirigini, D. 46, 84, 91
Kissula, J. 50
Kitigwa, J.M. 90–1, 98
Kitundu, S. 46–7, 53, 184, 187
Knox, Rev. Msgr. R. 176
Könen, Fr. M. 63, *211*
Kunambi, G.P. 56, *211*
Kyaruzi, V.K. 4, 57, 66–7, 77, 81, 88, 110, 133, 192, *212*

Labour Party (UK) 7, 95, 125, 127, 142, 161
Lake Province 33, 40, 45, 53, 93, 188, 190–1
Lake Victoria 12, 16, 23–4, 28, 32, 40, 62, 82, 133
Lamont, W. 85
Laski, H. 132, 146, 161–2
Lavigerie, Card. C.M.A. 50
Legislative Council 87, 120, 129, 135–6
Legum, C. 145
Lethem, Sir G. 141
Lewis, Sir W.A. 145
Listowel, J. (Judith Hare, Countess of Listowel) 4–5, 7, 44
Little, K. 141, 175, 194
Locke, J. 152–4, 160
Loltgen, W.G.W. 181, 183, *212*
London 2, 72, 100, 101, 102, 103, 105, 107, 115–18, 121–2, 123, 130, 132, 134–6, 139, 141–2, 175, 180–3, 187–8
London, University of 25, 93, 94, 101, 103, 105–6, 130, 134, 145, 161–2
London School of Economics *see* London, University of
Lugusha, H. 56, 248 n.65
Luthuli, Chief 196
Lwamugira, F. 187

McNaughton, Mr 107
MacKenzie, Rev. K. 115, 122, 137–8, 141, 170–1, 174–5
Macmillan, H. 194
Macmillan, W. 40, 168
Macmurray, W. 6, 114, 149–56, 159–62
Magero, Chief 33
Mageta, N. 47

281

Index

Mageye, Chief 33
Magige, G. 89–90, 189
Maillot, P. 23–4, 28–9
Mair, L. 167
Majaliwa, C. 101
Makerere College 1, 2, 34, 43, 55, 61, 62–77, 78, 79, 80, 81, 85–6, 87, 91, 96, 102, 107, 109, 112, 113, 129, 133, 147, 152, 154, 156, 166, 167, 178, 184, 187, 189, 192, 200–2
Makoba, M. 47
Makongoro, Chief 33, 34, 44, **45**, 186
Makwaia, Chief 101, 187
Makwaia, D.K. 56, 66, 77, 87, 95, 101, 135–6, 187, *212*
Malima, W. 32
Malinowski, B. 19, 164
Mama Maria *see* Nyerere, Maria Waningu Gabriel Magige
Mandela, N. 2–3
Mang'enya, E. 71, 74, 80, 82, 137, 142, 174, 181–2, 187–8, *212*
Mang'ombe, Chief M.O.I. 44, 46
Manuwa, Sir S. 110
Manyama, Chief 33
Manyori, Chief 33
Maranta, E. 173, 183, 250 n.99
Marasi, M. 120, 257 n.132
Marchant, Fr. L. 177–8, 180–1
Marealle, Chief P.I. 135
Marealle, T.L. 56, 95, 101, 135, 253 n.24, 262 n.15
Maritain, J. 75
Maruma, J.N. 56
Marwa, A. 56–7, 187
Marwa, B.A.M. 189
Marwa, O.M. **45**, 46, 48, 50, 63, 91, 98, 187, 189, *213*
Marwa, P.M. 63
Marxism 151, 253 n.30
Maryknoll missionaries 44, 93, 171–2, 173, 175
Masai tribe 21, 24, 165
Masubugu, M. 13–14, *213*
Masudi, G. 81
Maswanya, S.A. 133, *213*
Matovu, J.B. 53, 134, *213*
Mau Mau 193, 276 n.84
Mazembe, B. 32, 227 n.25
Mbelwa, J.C.A. 96
Mboya, T. 59, 189
Mchauru, F. 101
Mfinanga, D. 137
Mfundo, F. 120, 134
Mhando, S. 133

Mill, J.S. 73, 114, 126, 132, 146–8, 152, 156–60, 179
Milliband, R. 161
Mills, D. 74
Missionaries of Africa *see* White Fathers
Mkirya, B. 21
Mongi, F.L.N. 134
Mousheng, L. 88–9
Mpwapwa Teacher Training College 46
Msuguri, D. *213*, 239 n.102
Mtemvu, Z. 125
Mtuzu 16, 38, 39
Muhunda 16–19, 227 n.25
Munanka, B.I.M. 133, *213*
Mushi, M.M. 134
Musoma 12, 21, 24, 25, 26, 28, 30, 33, 36, 43–6, 48, 50–1, 53, 62, 64, 67, 82, 90, 97, 116, 118, 133, 173, 187, 189, 205
Mustafa, K. 21, 27
Mustafa, S. **195**, *214*
Mwaisumo, L. 51
Mwanza 12, 18, 24–5, 28, 29, 61, 76, 82, 90, 93, 205
Mwapachu, H.K.B. 75, 76–7, 78, 81, 87–9, 101, 103, 133, 191–2, *214*
Mwinyipembe, P.S. 101, 120, 134
Mwisenge Native Administration School 43–53, 66, 91, 98, 191, 201
Mwitongo 1, 12–19, 23, 37–40, 59, 61

Namugongo (Uganda) 75
Nasibu, H. 101
nationalisation (of industries) 127
Nehru, J. 161
Newspaper Act (1976) 126
New Towns Act (1946) 127
Ngoreme tribe 62, 63
Nicholl, D. 174
Nicholson, M. 95, 124, 144–5
Nigeria(ns) 7, 103, 110, 112, 135, 142–3, 151, 182, 197, 253 n.30, 255 n.88
Nkrumah, K. 2, 59, 72, 102, 103, 111, 120, 131, 135, 166, 184, 205
Nkumbula, H. 80, 139, 263 n.46
Northern Rhodesia 65, 80, 137–42 *see also* Central African Federation
Nsube (Uganda) 98, 116, 118
Nyabambe, A. and N. 90–1
Nyaburi 84
Nyakigi, N. 14, 235 n.6
Nyakyusa tribe 51, 165
Nyambata, Chief 34
Nyambeho, J. 22, 37–9, 46, 52
Nyambura 84
Nyamwaga, J. 18, 22, 59, 63, 79, 91, 185,

192–3, *214*, **221**
Nyamwezi tribe 25, 42, 66, 86–7
Nyangeta, A. 14
Nyang'ombe, M. 13–14, 34, 35, 42, 191–2
Nyang'ombe, W. 29, 34–5
Nyasaland 65, 109, 121, 137, 139–42 *see also* Central African Federation
Nyashiboha, H. 89
Nyauli, R.B. 134
Nyegina 48, 62–3, 90–1
Nyerere, Andrew 192
Nyerere, Burito 64, 69, 91
Nyerere, Chief Burito *see* Burito, Chief Nyerere
Nyerere, Chief Edward Wanzagi 13, 17–18, 20, 24, 33, 34, 36, 43–6, 60–1, 96–8, 115, 178, 185, 188, *214–15*
Nyerere, Jackton Nyamberekera 83, 187, **221**, 239 n.102, 251 n.136
Nyerere, Joseph Kizurira Burito 13, 21, 27, 29, 80, 83–4, *215*
Nyerere, Joseph Muhunda 82, 83–4, 86–7, *215*
Nyerere, Maria Waningu Gabriel Magige 8, 12, 15, 34, 78, 89–91, 97–8, **99**, 115–16, 123, 173–4, 180, 183–4, 188–9, 192, 199
Nyigina 98–9, 192
nyumba kumi 170, 247 n.33

O'Donovan, P. 130–1
Obasanjo, O. 3
Omari, D.A. 56–7, 134, 181–2, *215*
Omoniyi, B. 110
omugabhu (abhagabhu) 17–18, 38
orukobha 22, 234 n.123
Owen, R. 151
Oxford 176, 181
Oxford, University of 25, 101, 112, 123, 129, 135, 136, 144, 150, 160

Padmore, G. 72, 102
Pares, R. 112, 162, 168, 170, 272 n.124
Parker, T. 158
Paton, A. 250 n.102
Perham, M. 145
Piddington, R. 6, 111, 162–8, 175
Plantan, T. 76
Port Bell (Uganda) 64
Pratt, C. 21, 155, 162
Preventative Detention Act (1962) 81, 136
Prewitt, K. 72

race 5, 25, 29, 51, 65, 67–8, 74, 82, 88–9, 94, 96, 104–7, 115, 120–2, 125, 127–9, 130, 132, 134, 136, 140–5, 154, 173–5, 182–4, 195, 202–3
Ramadhani, M.D. 101, 181, *215*
Robert, S. 114
Robert Gordon's Technical College, Aberdeen 107
Robertson Justice, J. 196
da Rocha, M. 110, 121
Rogers, T. 118
Rivers-Smith, S. 54
Rubaga Mission (Uganda) 76
Rousseau, J.-J. 132, 152–6, 158–60
de Rouvroy, C.H. 151
Ruri tribe 24, 62
Rutabanzibwa, G.M. 134, *215*

Samba, Nyanjiga 33, 64
Samkange, T. 49
Saunders, L. 112–13, 126, 196–7, 270 n.39
Sawe, J.A. 56, 134, 181–2, *216*
Schiavoul, Rev. Fr. A. 189
Schlobach, Capt. 32–3
Schnee, H. 29
Scotsman, The 122–4, 127–31, 141, 196
Scottish Council on African Questions 142
Scottish nationalism 128, 176, 204–5
Second World War 40, 69, 73, 91, 114, 151
Senghor, L.S. 60, 68
Senghor, R. 60
Seree, Dr. 133
Shakespeare, W. 111–12
Shangali, Chief 81, 87, 136
Shariff, O. 110–11
Sheffield, University of 101
Shepperson, G. 6–7, 29, 37, 112, 114, 122–3, 133, 137, **195**, 196–7, *216*
Shirati 28, 29, 38
Smith, A. 147–8
Smith, D.J. 3
Smith, D.R. 95
Smith, W.E. 5, 7, 34, 58
socialism *see ujamaa*
South Africa 3, 59, 72, 127–8, 151, 183
Southampton 101–2
Southampton, University of 106
Southern Rhodesia 137, 142, 189 *see also* Central African Federation
Soviet Bloc 94
St Andrews, University of 107–8
St Andrew's College, Minaki 55, 65
St Augustine's College, Canterbury 101
St Francis College, Pugu 9, 189–93
St Mary's school, Tabora 9, 55, 57, 58, 64, 65, 78–81, 86, 88–9, 93–4, 176, 177, 200, 203, 246 n.17

Index

Stanley, Fr. J.S. 94, 178, 200, *216*
Stern, A. 114, 143, 150, 162, 175
Stöger-Eising, V. 20–1, 41
supranatural beings *see* traditional beliefs
Sykes family 76, 133, 191–2, 247 n.34

Tabora 45, 81–8, 90, 93, 98, 102, 116, 118, 165, 190–2, 203, 205 *see also* Tabora Government School *and* St Mary's school, Tabora
Tabora Government School ('Tabora Boys') 43, 53–61, 63–4, 66, 74, 76, 79–80, 83, 86, 133, 173, 200, 201–2, 206
Tanganyika African Association *see* African Association (Tanganyika)
Tanganyika African National Union 2, 4, 5, 7, 12, 20–1, 41, 81, 120, 125–7, 135, 147, 154, 158, 173, 192–5
Tanganyika African Welfare Association 76–7
Tanganyika Committee on Constitutional Reform 136
Tanganyika Standard 68–9, 72–3, 87, 124
Tanganyika Students Association *see* Tanganyika African Welfare Association
Tanganyika Students Welfare Association *see* Tanganyika African Welfare Association
Tarime 18, 22, 89–90
Teilhard de Chardin, P. 250 n.99
Thornton, H.H. 88
Tibandebage, A.K. 59, 64, 66, 75–7, 79–82, 84, 86–7, 99, *216*, 276 n.83
Trevelyan, M. 105
Tumbo, C.K. **195**, *217*
Twining, Sir E.F. 101, 135–6, 144, 205, *217*, 249 n.75

Uche, A.O. **182**, 255 n.88
uhuru see freedom
Uhuru wa Wanawake (J.K. Nyerere) *see* gender relations
ujamaa 19, 20–1, 39, 68, 70–2, 127, 130, 145–53, 155, 157, 159, 160–2, 164–72, 173, 176, 196, 204 *see also eriisaga*
Ukerewe Island 24, 62, 90, 133, 189
umoja see unity
United Nations Trusteeship Council 88–9, 203
United States of America 25, 105, 115, 120, 154, 196–7

United Tanganyika Party 125
unity 22, 81, 150, 157, 159, 173, 187

Victoria Federation of Co-operative Unions 133

Wagi, T. 134
Walsh, Fr. R.M. 79–81, 93–4, 98, 108, 167, 173, 176–9, 183, 189–91, *217*
Waningu *see* Nyerere, Maria Waningu Gabriel Magige
Wanzagi *see* Nyerere, Chief Edward Wanzagi
Wanzagi, M. 14, 36
Warioba 36
Warioba, E.N. 84
Washington, B.T. 54, 68, 78, 85, 173
Watiha, M. 78, 82–5, 90, 188, 199, *217*
Waugh, E. 176
welfare state 127, 130
Wellensky, Sir R. 142
Welsh nationalism 128
West African students (union) 112, 142–3, 182 *see also* Nigerians.
West Indian Students (Association) 142–3, 171, 182
White Fathers 4, 45, 50–1, 62, 100, 108, 175, 178, 204
White Sisters 90
Wicken, J. 4–7, 12, 16, 34, 43, 48, 63, 193, 196, *217*
Wille, Fr. A. 44, 48, 57, 58, 75, 80, 83, 84, 90, 91, 93, 98, 171, 173, 176, 187, 189, *218*
Williams, E.S. **58**, 63
Wilson, J.W. 122–3, 143, 174, 193, 195, 205, *218*
Wilson, W. 122, 195
Wollstonecraft, M. 73

Yankson, J.K. 140
Young, Rev. C. 174

Zanaki tribe 12
    traditional beliefs 16–19, 38
    social structures 13, 19–22
    origins 23–8
    under colonial rule 28–36
    politics 49, 93, 96–7, 188
    rainmaking 24, 185–6
    customs/language and Tanzania xvi, 21–3

284